WITTGENSTEIN ON THOUGHT, LANGUAGE AND PHILOSOPHY

Wittgenstein on Thought, Language and Philosophy
From theory to therapy

CHRISTOFFER GEFWERT
University of Helsinki, Finland

LONDON AND NEW YORK

First published 2000 by Ashgate Publishing

Reissued 2018 by Routledge
2 Park Square, Milton Park, Abingdon, Oxon OX14 4RN
711 Third Avenue, New York, NY 10017, USA

Routledge is an imprint of the Taylor & Francis Group, an informa business

Copyright © Christoffer Gefwert 2000

All rights reserved. No part of this book may be reprinted or reproduced or utilised in any form or by any electronic, mechanical, or other means, now known or hereafter invented, including photocopying and recording, or in any information storage or retrieval system, without permission in writing from the publishers.

Notice:
Product or corporate names may be trademarks or registered trademarks, and are used only for identification and explanation without intent to infringe.

Publisher's Note
The publisher has gone to great lengths to ensure the quality of this reprint but points out that some imperfections in the original copies may be apparent.

Disclaimer
The publisher has made every effort to trace copyright holders and welcomes correspondence from those they have been unable to contact.

A Library of Congress record exists under LC control number: 99085928

ISBN 13: 978-1-138-73885-0 (hbk)
ISBN 13: 978-1-315-18453-1 (ebk)

Contents

Acknowledgements   *vii*
Abbreviations   *viii*

INTRODUCTION   1

I THE UNIVERSAL MEDIUM

I.1 Introduction   22
I.2 Metaphysical Realism   26
I.3 Logical Atomism   29
I.4 The Transcendental Reading   33
I.5 The Limit(s) of Language   36
I.6 Logistical Positivism   39
I.7 Logical Semantics   43
I.8 The Hintikka Interpretation   44
I.9 The Post-1937 Wittgenstein   48

II METHODOLOGICAL ILLUSIONS

II.1 Introduction: Observer to Participator   62
II.2 Philosophy and Science   67
II.3 On Behaviourism   72
II.4 On Causal Relations   76
II.5 The Problem of Verification   86

III THOUGHT AND PRIVACY

III.1 Introduction   101
III.2 Intention: Historical Sources   108

III.3 The Continuation of Wittgenstein's Thought	114
III.4 Correcting the 'Picture-Theory'	117
III.5 Mental Processes	125
III.6 The 'Private Language' Arguments	140
III.7 Conclusion: Thought is Public	149

IV PHILOSOPHY AS GRAMMAR

IV.1 Introduction	160
IV.2 The Problem of Ostensive Definitions	164
IV.3 Language-Games	169
IV.4 Meaning as Practice	186
IV.5 Forms of Life	195
IV.6 The 'Earlier' and the 'Later' Wittgenstein	205

V THE REALIST/ANTI-REALIST ILLUSION

V.1 Introduction	217
V.2 The Anti-Realist Research Programme	218
V.3 The Interpretation of Wittgenstein	230
V.4 The 'Rules-as-Theory' Confusion	238
V.5 Conclusion: Understanding a 'Rule'	246

VI CONCEPTUAL INVESTIGATIONS

VI.1 Introduction	265
VI.2 Is Philosophy Theoretical?	268
VI.3 What is a Philosophical Investigation?	273
VI.4 The Psychoanalytical Analogue	278
VI.5 Calculation and Philosophy	285

CONCLUSION	303

Acknowledgements

I would like to express my deep gratitude to Professor Pertti Saariluoma, Professor Lars Hertzberg, Professor Sören Stenlund, Professor André Maury, Professor G.H. von Wright, Mr. Pauli Salo and Mr. Max Ingman without whose encouragement and help this work would never have been completed. Of course I will take responsibility for any mistakes that may occur in the text.

I would also like to express my gratitude to the Institute of General Psychology, Department of Cognitive Science, University of Helsinki for their kindness and generosity in allowing me to finish the book.

Finally I want to express my gratitude to my wife Marjukka and my son Sebastian and daughter Joanna for their constant support.

Christoffer Gefwert
Helsinki
September 1999

Abbreviations

Below we have the abbreviations for the literature used in this work. As far as Wittgenstein is concerned these abbreviations are for the most part the ones that have over the years been more or less 'standardized' in the literature dealing with his philosophical writings.

Works by Brouwer:

CW	*L.E.J. Brouwer: Collected Works,* Vol. I - II. Edited by A. Heyting, Amsterdam (1975).
BCL	*Brouwer's Cambridge Lectures on Intuitionism.* Edited by D. van Dalen, Cambridge (1981).
LAM	*Life, Art and Mysticism,* Delft (1905). In CW I, pp. 1-10.
OGW	*On the foundations of mathematics,* Thesis, Amsterdam (1907). Reprinted in CW I, pp. 11-101.
IF	'Intuitionism and formalism'. *Bull. Amer. Math. Soc.* **20** (1913), pp. 96. Reprinted in CW I, pp. 123-138.
MWS	'Mathematik, Wissenschaft und Sprache'. *Monatsh. Math.,* **36** (1929), pp. 153-164. Reprinted in CW I, pp. 417-428.
CPM	'Consciousness, Philosophy and Mathematics'. *Proc. 10th International Congress of Philosophy,* Amsterdam (1948), pp. 1235-49. Reprinted in CW I, pp. 480-494.

WVS	'Willen, weten, spreken', *Euclides* **9** (1933), pp. 177-193.
HB	'Historical background, principles and methods of intuitionism'. *South African J. Sci.* **49** (1952), pp. 139-146. Reprinted in CW I, pp. 508-515.

Works by Frege:

B	*Begriffschrift, eine der aritmetischen nachgebildete Formelsprache des reinen Denkens*, Halle (1879). Translated in van Heijenoort, J., (ed.), *A Source Book in Mathematical Logic, 1879-1931*, Cambridge, Mass. and London, England (1976), pp. 1-81.
BLA	*The Basic Laws of Arithmetic*. Berkeley and Los Angeles (1964). Translated and edited with an Introduction by Montgomery Furth.
FA	*The Foundations of Arithmetic*. Translated by J.L. Austin, Oxford (1968). Fifth impression with corrections 1980.
FG	*Gottlob Frege: On the Foundations of Geometry and Formal Theories of Arithmetic*. Translated with an introduction by Eike Henner and W. Kluge, New Haven and London (1971).
G I	*Grundgesetze der Arithmetik, begriffschriftlich abgeleitet, I Band*, Jena (1893).
G II	*Grundgesetze der Arithmetik, begriffschriftlich abgeleitet, II Band*, Jena (1903).

LoI   *Logical Investigations*, Oxford (1977). Edited with a preface by P.T. Geach. Translated by P.T. Geach and R.H. Stoothoff.

PW   *Translations from the Philosophical Writings of Gottlob Frege,* Oxford (1952). Third edition 1980. Edited by Peter Geach and Max Black.

PMC   *Philosophical and Mathematical Correspondence,* Gabriel et.al., (eds.), Oxford (1980).

PoW   *Posthumous Writings,* Hermes et al., (eds.) Translated by P. Long and R. White, Oxford (1979).

Works by Gefwert:

Gefwert (1)   *Wittgenstein on Mathematics, Minds and Mental Machines,* Avebury Series in Philosophy, Ashgate Publishing Limited, Aldershot, Great Britain, Brookfield USA, Singapore, Sydney AUS (1998).

Works by Martin-Löf:

M-L (1)   'An Intuitionistic Theory of Types: Predicative Part', in H.E. Rose and J. Sheperdson, (eds.), *Logic Colloquium 73,* Amsterdam (1975), pp. 73-118.

M-L (2)   'About Models for Intuitionistic Type Theories and The Notion of Definitional Equality', in Kanger, S., (ed.), *Proc. Third. Scand. Logic Symposium,* Amsterdam (1975), pp. 81-109.

M-L (3)   *Intuitionistic Type Theory*, Notes by Giovanni Sambin of a series of lectures given in Padova, June 1980, Bibliopolis, Naples.

M-L (4)   'Constructive mathematics and computer programming', in L.J. Cohen et al., (eds.), *Logic Methodology and Philosophy of Science VI*, Amsterdam (1982), pp. 153-175.

M-L (5)   'On The Meanings of The Logical Constants and The Justification of The Logical Laws', Unpublished. This paper has later been published in *Atti degli incontri di logica mattematica Vol. 2.*, Scuola di Specializazzione in Logica Matematica, Dipartimento di Matematica, Università di Siena (1985), pp. 203-281.

M-L (6)   'Truth of a Proposition, Evidence of a Judgment, Validity of A Proof', Unpublished. This talk was given at the workshop Theories of Meaning organized by the Centro Fiorentino di Storia e Filosofia della Scienza at the Villa di Mondeggi near Florence, 3-7 June 1985. This paper has later been published in *Synthèse* **73** (1987), pp. 407-420.

M-L (7)   'On the distinction between propositions and judgments', *Abstract of the 7th International Congress of Logic, Methodology and Philosophy of Science,* Salzburg, Austria, July 11-16, 1983, Salzburg (1983), p. 24.

M-L (8)   'Analytic and Synthetic Judgments in Type Theory', Unpublished. Talk given at the workshop on Kant and Contemporary Epistemology, Florence, 27-30 May (1992), organized by the Centro Fiorentino di Storia e Filosofia della Scienza.

M-L (9)   'Verificationism Then and Now', Unpublished. Talk given as part of the conference *The Foundational Debate: Complexity and Constructivity in Mathematics and Physics,* Vienna, 15-17 September (1994).

Works by Russell:

PrM   *The Principles of Mathematics*, London (1903), Second edition, 1937, eighth impression (1964).

PM   *Principia Mathematica* (with A.N. Whitehead), Vol. I - II, Second edition (1927), Cambridge.

IMP   *Introduction to Mathematical Philosophy*, London (1919), fourteenth impression (1975).

LK   *Logic and Knowledge*, Essays 1901-1950. Edited by R.C. Marsh, London (1956).

Works by Stenlund:

S (1)   *Language and Philosophical Problems*, Routledge: London and New York (1990).

Works by Waismann:

IMT   *Introduction to Mathematical Thinking*, New York (1951).

PLP   *The Principles of Linguistic Philosophy.* Edited by R. Harré, New York (1965).

LSP	*Logik, Sprache, Philosophie*. Edited by G.P. Baker and B. McGuinness, Stuttgart (1976).
WM	The Nature of Mathematics: Wittgenstein's Standpoint', translated by S.G.Shanker in Shanker, S.G. (ed.), *Ludwig Wittgenstein, Critical Assessments,* Volume Three, London, Sydney, New Hampshire (1987).

Works and Letters of Wittgenstein:

NB	*Notebooks 1914-16*, Blackwell, Oxford (1969). Edited by G.H. von Wright and G.E.M. Anscombe. Translated by G.E.M. Anscombe.
T	*Tractatus Logico-Philosophicus*, Routledge & Kegan Paul, London (1921). Translated by C.K. Ogden, Second edition (1961). With an Introduction by Bertrand Russell, F.R.S. Translated by D.F. Pears and B.F. McGuinness.
PT	*ProtoTractatus - An Early Version of Tractatus Logico-Philosophicus,* (ed.) by B.F. McGuinness, T. Nyberg and G.H. von Wright. Translated by D.F. Pears and B.F. McGuinness, London (1971).
PhR	*Philosophical Remarks*. Edited by R.Rhees. Translated by R. Hargreaves and R. White, Blackwell, Oxford (1975).
PhG	*Philosophical Grammar.* Edited by R. Rhees. Translated by A. Kenny, Blackwell, Oxford (1974).
BB	*The Blue and Brown Books,* Blackwell, Oxford (1969).

PhI	*Philosophical Investigations,* Blackwell, Oxford (1958).
RFM	*Remarks on the Foundations of Mathematics.* Edited by G.H. von Wright, R. Rhees. Translated by G.E.M. Anscombe, Blackwell, Oxford (1968).
Z	*Zettel.* Edited by G.E.M. Anscombe and G.H. von Wright. Translated by G.E.M. Anscombe, Blackwell, Oxford (1967).
OC	*On Certainty.* Edited by G.E.M. Anscombe and G.H. von Wright. Translated by D. Paul and G.E.M. Anscombe, Blackwell, Oxford (1974).
R	*Letters to Russell, Keynes and Moore.* Edited by G.H. von Wright assisted by B.F. McGuinness, Blackwell, Oxford (1974).
RLF	'Some Remarks on Logical Form', *Proceedings of the Aristotelian Society Supplement,* Vol. **9** (1929), pp. 162-171.
O	*Letters to C.K. Ogden.* Edited by G.H. von Wright, Blackwell, Oxford (1973).
CV	*Culture and Value.* Edited by G.H. von Wright in collaboration with Heikki Nyman. Translated by P. Winch, Blackwell, Oxford (1980).
RPP I	*Remarks on the Philosophy of Psychology,* Volume I. Edited by G.E.M. Anscombe and G.H. von Wright, Transl., G.E.M. Anscombe, Blackwell, Oxford (1980).
RPP II	*Remarks on the Philosophy of Psychology,* Volume II. Edited by G.H. von Wright and H. Nyman. Transl. C.G. Luckhardt and M.A.E. Aue, Blackwell, Oxford (1980).

NPL 'Notes for the "Philosophical Lecture"', in J. Klagge and A. Nordmann, (eds.) *Ludwig Wittgenstein, Philosophical Occasions: 1912-1951,* Indianapolis (1993), pp. 447-458.

NSP 'Notes for Lectures on "Sense Data" and "Private Experience"', in J. Klagge, and A. Nordmann, (eds.), *Ludwig Wittgenstein, Philosophical Occasions: 1912-1951,* Indianapolis (1993), pp. 200-288.

LC *Lectures and Conversations on Aesthetics, Psychology and Religious Beliefs,* (ed.) by C. Barrett, Blackwell, Oxford (1970).

LW I *Last Writings on the Philosophy of Psychology,* Volume I. Edited by G.H. von Wright and H. Nyman. Translated by C.G. Luckhardt and M.A.E. Aue, Blackwell, Oxford (1982).

LW II *Last Writings on the Philosophy of Psychology,* Volume II. Edited by G.H. von Wright and H. Nyman. Translated by C.G. Luckhardt and M.A.E. Aue, Blackwell, Oxford (1992).

Lecture and Discussion Notes not made by Wittgenstein:

L (1) 'Wittgenstein's lectures in 1930-33', in G.E. Moore, *Philosophical Papers,* London (1959).

L (2) *Wittgenstein's Lectures, Cambridge 1930-1932,* from the notes of John King and Desmond Lee. Edited by D. Lee, Oxford (1980).

L (3)   *Wittgenstein's Lectures, Cambridge 1932-1935*, from the notes of Alice Ambrose and Margaret Macdonald. Edited by A. Ambrose, Oxford (1979).

WVC   *Ludwig Wittgenstein and the Vienna Circle: Conversations recorded by Friedrich Waismann*. Edited by Brian McGuinness. Translated by Joachim Schulte and Brian McGuinness, Oxford (1979).

LFM   *Wittgenstein's Lectures on the Foundations of Mathematics*, Cambridge 1939, from the notes of R.G. Bosanquet, Norman Malcolm, Rush Rhees, and Yorick Smythies. Edited by Cora Diamond, New York (1976).

WLPP   *Wittgenstein's Lectures on Philosophical Psychology 1946-47,* P. Geach, (ed.), University of Chicago Press, Chicago, and Hemel Hempstead (1989).

A Note on Wittgenstein's *Nachlass:*

The original publication of the study of Wittgenstein's Nachlass, i.e., the work unpublished at Wittgenstein's death, was originally published in the *Philosophical Review* **78** (1969). However, the corrected and expanded version which is used in this work is based on the version written by professor G.H. von Wright in 1981. Unpublished manuscripts by Wittgenstein are referred to by their numbers in von Wright, 'The Wittgenstein Papers', pp. 36-62, in von Wright, G. H., *Wittgenstein,* Oxford (1982), and by pages in the original MSS.

NEDO I   *Philosophische Bemerkungen,* Band 1-4, Wiener Ausgabe, Springer-Verlag (1994), Wien, New York.

NEDO II	*Philosophische Grammatik,* Band 5, Wiener Ausgabe, Springer-Verlag (1995), Wien, New York.
BT	The so-called 'Big Typescript'. Probably 1933, viii + 768 pp.

This manuscript is probably the most complete manuscript in Wittgenstein's Nachlass. The most finished form, concerning the philosophy of mathematics, has been published as *Philosophical Grammar*. It was in connection with the philosophy of mathematics that von Wright writes that '[t]his last third of it, on the philosophy of mathematics, was evidently relatively finished even in the author's opinion' (von Wright, G.H., Philosophical Review **78** (1969) op.cit., p. 502). For an historical account of the relation of *Philosophical Grammar* and the *Big Typescript,* cf. Kenny, Anthony, 'From the Big Typescript to the Philosophical Grammar', *Acta Philosophica Fennica,* Vol. **28**, Nos. 1-3, Amsterdam (1976), pp. 41-53. However, a number of chapters have been excluded from the *Philosophical Grammar,* notably such chapters which deal with 'Expectation and Wishing', 'Philosophy', 'Phenomenology' and 'Idealism', etc. The chapter dealing with philosophy, however, has been published by Heikki Nyman as 'Ludwig Wittgenstein "Philosophie" §§86-93 (S. 405-435) aus dem sogenannten "Big Typescript" (Katalognummer 213)', in *Revue Internationale de Philosophie,* Vol. **43**, No. 169 (1989), pp. 175-203.

Introduction

In this book we are to discuss a problem that one encounters in connection with Wittgenstein's texts concerning philosophy: the problem if philosophy - when understood in the way he understands it - amounts (1) to a systematic and (2) to a theoretical (general) activity.[1] When first encountering such questions they may sound strange to somebody educated, say, in modern academic philosophy. In ordinary analytic philosophy, for example, one finds that the expression 'theory of meaning' is very common, for example, in the writings of Donald Davidson and Michael Dummett.[2] Nevertheless, the aim of this book is to show that such a 'theoretical' (analytical or empirical; mathematical or scientific) view does not correspond to Wittgenstein's conception concerning philosophy. We are therefore not to formulate a general 'theory of meaning' of any kind. What we are to argue instead is that philosophy, as Wittgenstein understands the term in his post-1937 writings, corresponds to something that can be characterised as conceptual therapy. That is, a philosophical investigation is analogous to a freudian psychotherapeutical session in that the aim is to dissolve the conceptual problems occurring in language that haunt us in our everyday life.

In modern philosophical vocabulary it is a very common feature that one in discussions, books and articles by analytically minded philosophers (like, for example, Donald Davidson, Michael Dummett, Jaakko Hintikka, Saul Kripke, Dag Prawitz and Crispin Wright) frequently encounters what is characterised as certain kind of general 'theories' in philosophical discourse. These amount, for example, to semantical 'analytically a priori' kind of theories which are assumed to be distinct from the empirical ones that we are accustomed to meet in the sciences. In Dummett's terminology, these general theories of meaning are, basically, of two kinds: Realist and Anti-Realist. Usually we meet these terms in connection with the task to formulate semantical theories of meaning for natural and formal languages [Infra

V.2]. They are, furthermore, assumed to be 'scientific' (universal) in some form or another. This attitude we find, for example, reflected in an article by Dummett when he says that 'I am maintaining that we have now reached a position where the search for such a theory of meaning can take on a genuinly scientific character'.[3]

Historically speaking a general 'theory of meaning' is not a novel term. On the contrary. The term 'theory of meaning' has a long and interesting history going back at least to Edmund Husserl (1859-1938) and the Phenomenological School as well as to the Logical Empiricists of the Vienna Circle. I shall not pursue this interesting history here.[4] Be it enough to state that the term 'theory of meaning' which amounts to a first philosophy is today regarded as one of the trademarks concerning what is usually called analytical philosophy.

But, now one can ask: Are there any connections between this general and theoretical conception of 'philosophy' and Wittgenstein's post-1937 conception of philosophy? To provide an answer we have to look at Wittgenstein's developing view concerning the role of natural language. It has often been said that he had one, three or more conceptions of (natural) language during his career but that he surely doesn't have two as it is sometimes claimed.[5] We are in this work to investigate the evolution of Wittgenstein's views concerning philosophy and everyday language. In addition, we shall also comment on certain interpretations made by other scholars concerning Wittgenstein's assumed views of philosophy between 1912-1951. By this I mean, for example, the 'observer' based views entertained by philosophical 'schools' like Logical Atomism (Russell, Carnap), Transcendental Philosophy (Stenius, Kannisto, Hintikka, Garver, Apel and Gefwert), Logical Empiricism (Carnap, Feigl, Neurath) and Waismann's general (universal) interpretation of Wittgenstein's discussions which were posthumously published by Baker (IMT; PLP).

As I have argued in *Wittgenstein on Mathematics, Minds and Mental Machines* one can argue that Wittgenstein did not accept any specific general 'theory of meaning' in his pre-1929 writings on mathematics [Gefwert (1) 54-56]. He came to the conclusion that no structure (theory of types) can state the distinctions between the different types: instead such distinctions **show** themselves. One cannot treat distinctions of type as an object of theorizing and at the same time as something that necessarily conditions all theorizing. Wittgenstein ended up with the conclusion that an extensional theory of types (or 'theory of symbolism') cannot be dressed up as a formal and general 'theory' in the first place. Such a 'theory' amounts to an illusion. Therefore the expressions a 'theory of types' and a 'theory of symbolism' are misnomers. The result is that such an *a priori* and general 'theory' of symbolism cannot exist as far as informal and **ordinary** language is concerned [Gefwert (1) 54]. We can therefore ask (since the texts of the pre-1929 Wittgenstein are often mentioned - partly due to a mistake - in connection with the Logical Empiricists (Schlick, Carnap, Feigl and Waismann)): What was Wittgenstein's relation to a general 'theory of meaning' in his final post-1937 thought on philosophy? We are, among other things, to look into this problem from different angles with the intent of providing some answers to this query [Infra V.4].

However, when we attempt to do this we have to be aware that philosophy in Wittgenstein's final post-1937 sense is different to its nature from what we usually are being taught in courses on academic philosophy (say, 'analytical' philosophy). In G.E. Moore's notes (made from Wittgenstein's lectures already in 1930-33), probably from the Michaelmas Term 1930, we read that [L (1) 322; cf. L (1) 21-22],

> I was a good deal surprised by some of the things he said about the difference between 'philosophy' in the sense in which what he was doing might be called 'philosophy' (he called this term 'modern philosophy'), and what has traditionally been called 'philosophy'. He said that what he was doing was a 'new subject', and not merely a stage in a 'continuous development'; that

> there was now, in philosophy, a 'kink' in the 'development of human thought' comparable to that which occurred when Galileo and his contemporaries invented dynamics; that a 'new method' had been discovered, as had happened when 'chemistry was developed out of alchemy'.

From the quotation above one gets the distinct impression that Wittgenstein was developing an entirely 'new method' to be called philosophy. But, when we say this, we have to be cautious. Wittgenstein's 'new subject' cannot, despite what he says, be formulated as a novel method. It cannot be structuralized. One can, perhaps, informally characterize it (but not entirely) as a 'philosophy of "philosophy"'. We use this term to show that Wittgenstein tries to undo philosophy as a theory of any kind.[6] But, we have to be aware. It does not amount to a novel kind of first philosophy. It is not, for example, Kantian in nature. Instead one should, perhaps, talk of numerous grammatical (conceptual) investigations that we perform with everyday language. It is the nature of the different conceptual 'problems' that makes one call Wittgenstein's investigations for **philosophical** investigations. But how did this 'new subject' ('modern philosophy') differ from the old idea of philosophy? What, exactly, did this 'new subject' amount to? To better understand this problem we are to investigate it and attempt to provide an answer to this intriguing question.

***

Having returned to Cambridge in 1929 and taken his PhD examination that same year [Infra I.2] we know that Wittgenstein began lecturing on 'philosophy' in January 1930. We also know that he lectured during all three terms that year [L (2) xvi]. In these lectures we get a glimpse of what his novel philosophical views amounted to. It seems that Wittgenstein regarded philosophy to be an activity of a completely different kind than what we are accustomed to in our foundational studies of mathematics or scientific practices. What we encounter in natural science are practices which amount to factual investigations (for example, we have empirical investigations in physics, astronomy, chemistry, biology, psychology, etc.). But sometimes this is not enough. In addition we require the 'correct' **interpretation** of the scientific fact. Just think of the numerous interpretations of quantum mechanics (e.g., the 'many-worlds' interpretation by Hugh Everett III).[7] We have a similar case when we deal with facts of pure mathematical calculations, although they are not empirical, when we attempt to formulate their foundations according to a 'correct' interpretation (cf. the logistic, formalistic and intuitionistic interpretations).

Genuine philosophical investigations, on the other hand, do not amount to interpretations of any kind. They do not amount to mathematical deductions (proofs) nor to scientific explanations (which are factual in nature)[PhI §126]. Such factual investigations - both in pure mathematics and in science (despite a certain difference between them) - are, according to Wittgenstein, completely different in kind than the ones we encounter when performing philosophical investigations. What we encounter when doing philosophy amounts to problems of meaning, that is, we encounter **conceptual** problems. Therefore we are interested in the forms of language as manifestations of numerous conceptual systems and relationships. Such philosophical problems are not explanatory in kind, that is, they are not to be dealt by explanations (nor deductions) of any kind; they are conceptual and have to be treated by descriptions [PhI §124]. Such investigations cannot be captured by a theoretical and general structure of any kind. They do **not** amount to a general theory that needs to be formulated (say, as Wittgenstein seems to have attempted in the *Brown Book* (1934-1935) or Waismann attempted in the *Principles of Linguistic Philosophy* and *Introduction to Mathematical Thinking*). It was precisely the insight conveyed by these arguments which led to an overall philosophical breakthrough in Wittgenstein's own development - to the anti-mentalism and anti-essentialism characteristic of his post-1937 views. It is this that we mean by the title of this book: from theory to therapy.

However, we find there to be a certain difference between philosophy in Wittgenstein's 'older' (pre-1929) and his 'final' (post-1937) writings. It seems that the non-academic period in his life had certain implications on his conception. We shall therefore briefly recapitulate this period. After the publication of the German version of the *Tractatus,* in 1921 (English version 1922), Wittgenstein abandoned active philosophical work for number of years. The reason for this seems, among other things, to have been that he thought he had solved all the outstanding problems concerning thought, language and philosophy. Consequently, he now wanted to do something else in his life. He chose to become a teacher. He therefore attended the Vienna Teachers' Training College during the academic year 1919-20 (where, incidentally, also Sir Karl Popper (1902-1994) was a student at the same time). After completing his studies Wittgenstein became an elementary school teacher in Lower Austria between 1920 and 1926. Among other places, he taught in the villages of Trattenbach and Puchberg am Schneeberg in Nieder-Österreich. Incidentally, it seems that Wittgenstein was especially good at teaching mathematics.[8] One can, perhaps, say, despite the numerous problems that he had in his relation to the parents of his pupils, that this kind of life suited his desire to live a simple and secluded life very well for the time being.

* * *

When Wittgenstein lived in the village of Puchberg in Lower Austria he was visited, in 1923 and again in 1924, the latter time on several occasions, by the young Cambridge logician Frank Ramsey (1903-1930). The history behind Ramsey's visits seems, in its bare outlines, to be as follows. Ramsey had translated the *Tractatus* into English in 1922 [O 8-9]. Then, some time before September 1923, Wittgenstein '... got word from Ogden that Frank Ramsey would be coming to Austria'[O Appx 77]. We do not know exactly when he received this message. But, we do know that Ramsey arrived from Vienna to Puchberg in September with the intention to stay for a couple of weeks. The aim of his visit was to discuss certain points with

Wittgenstein concerning the *Tractatus* which he found to be especially problematic. As a result of his discussions Ramsey also wrote a review of the book to the philosophical journal *Mind* (which was published in the autumn of 1923).

The discussions themselves were quite intensive. They seem to have taken place from 2 pm until 7 pm each day [O 79]. In a letter to his mother, on 20th September 1923, Ramsey wrote, concerning the first meeting, that [O Appx 78]

> [h]e [Wittgenstein] has already answered my chief difficulty which I have puzzled over for a year and given up in despair myself and decided he had not seen ... He is great. I used to think Moore a great man but beside W[ittgenstein]! ... He is, I can see, a little annoyed that Russell is doing a new edit[ion] of Principia because he thought he had shown R[ussell] that it was so wrong that a new edition would be futile. It must be done altogether afresh. He had a week with Russell 4 y[ea]rs ago.

A year later, in March, 1924, Ramsey repeated his visit to Austria. He came mainly in order to be psychoanalyzed by Dr. Sigmund Freud (1856-1939) and therefore stayed for the most part in Vienna. He seems to have socialized fairly regularly with Wittgenstein's sister, Mrs. Margarethe Stonborough, and her family circle. In fact, he saw Wittgenstein quite seldom. Nevertheless, he went to see him on four occasions, in March, May and September at Puchberg and in October in the village of Otterthal. There exist a couple of letters to his mother originating from the first two visits. One letter is from his first visit to Puchberg in March and the second letter from his second visit in May [O Appx 85]. When reading these letters one gets the distinct impression that Ramsey found Wittgenstein's lack of interest in discussing topics on the foundations of mathematics problematic. For example, as he said in May, in a letter to his mother, the result of these discussions were that ' ... he is no good for my work'[O Appx 85].

There is also a letter from Ramsey to Wittgenstein on February 20, 1924, before his arriwal to Austria, which is interesting because it clearly illuminates his reaction to the attempt by Russell to produce a second edition of the *Principia Mathematica*. We know that Ramsey had been asked by Russell to help him in getting the second edition ready for publication. The details concerning his comments to the request by Russell are unknown. But we know that Ramsey accepted and was, consequently, given certain manuscripts with the intention that he should read and comment upon them. Now, the letter itself is interesting because here we clearly see that Ramsey was aware of Wittgenstein's critical attitude to such an attempt by Russell. Thus, he writes that [O 84]

> I went to see Russell a few weeks ago, and I am reading the manuscript of the new stuff he is putting into the Principia. You are quite right that it is of no importance; all it really amounts to is a clever proof of mathematical induction without using the axiom of reducibility. There are no fundamental changes, identity just as it used to be. I felt he was too old: he seemed to understand and say "yes" to each separate thing, but it made no impression so that 3 minutes afterwards he talked on his old lines. Of all your work he seems now to accept only this: that it is nonsense to put an adjective where a substantive ought to be which helps in his theory of types.

Ramsey also tried to persuade Wittgenstein to visit England to meet his friends. The result was that Wittgenstein did indeed, in August 1925, visit them (W. Eccles, F.P. Ramsey, W.E. Johnson, and J.M. Keynes) in Cambridge, but only to return once again to being a school teacher. The meeting with Ramsey is especially interesting. Ramsey was to give a lecture at the London Mathematical Society later that year on the 'foundations of mathematics'. This aroused a big quarrel between them. The reason seems to have been that Wittgenstein disliked the idea that Ramsey was to give the lecture in a logicistic fashion (and thus, probably, also mention the notion of 'tautology' in 'classical' truth-conditional circumstances which, according to him, were not correct [Gefwert (1) 131-133]). This unfortunate quarrel had the result that it made a temporary break in their contact.

Despite the fact that Wittgenstein and Ramsey, due to this quarrel, did not see each other for a number of years - between 1925 and 1929 - they did not break off contact completely. In 1927 they started to correspond again - with Schlick acting as a mediator - when Wittgenstein criticized the view of identity put forward by Ramsey in *The Foundations of Mathematics* (which was the printed version of his talk in November, 1925)[WVC 189-191]. But this was not the end of all collaboration because we know that '[a]fter his return to Cambridge in 1929 Wittgenstein resumed contact with Ramsey and had with him the "innumerable conversations" for which he acknowledges his great indebtedness in the Preface to the Philosophical Investigations'[O Appx 87].

* * *

In April, 1926, due to certain incidents between Wittgenstein and the parents of some of the schoolchildren, he left his position as teacher for good. After this he worked for a while in the monastery of Hütteldorf in the vicinity of Vienna as a gardener. According to von Wright, it seems that Wittgenstein in this period contemplated entering a monastery and that the same thought occurred to him at other times in his life too.[9] These intentions were never fulfilled, partly at least, because for him the inner conditions of monastic life were not satisfied.[10] Then, in the autumn of 1926, Wittgenstein moved to Vienna in order to work as an architect. He was to design a house for his sister Margarethe. The result was a house, in the Kundmanngasse, Vienna, that Wittgenstein designed in collaboration with his friend, the architecht Paul Engelmann (1891-1967). This work absorbed the next two years until it was completed in the autumn of 1928.

In 1922 Moritz Schlick (1882-1936) was appointed professor of philosophy at the University of Vienna. Some years later, through arrangement by his sister, Margarethe, Wittgenstein became acquainted to Schlick and '[a]pparently Wittgenstein had several conversations with Schlick before he would agree to meet other members of the Circle'[WVC 15]. The result was, finally, that in 1927, Wittgenstein felt that he could meet a selected number of members belonging to the Viennese philosophical community. The result was that he met certain members of the Vienna Circle in 1927 and 1928 [Infra I.1]. During this time he also became acquainted with Friedrich Waismann (1896-1959) - with whom he was to start an intense collaboration for a number of years - and came to meet the philosophers Herbert Feigl, Marie Kaspar (later Mrs Feigl) and Rudolf Carnap. It seems that Wittgenstein during the summer of 1927 regularly met Schlick, Carnap and Waismann. The meetings continued in 1928. Unfortunately no records seem to have been kept during these years [WVC 15]. In addition Wittgenstein had, between December, 1929, and July, 1932, on a number of occasions, when he was already back in Cambridge [Infra I.1], repeated discussions with Schlick and Waismann during his visits to Vienna which have partly been recorded [WVC 15].

In 1927 Schlick, Waismann, Carnap and Wittgenstein seem to have discussed Ramsey's paper from 1925 on a number of occasions. Indeed, we know that Wittgenstein and the members of Schlick's Circle were able to have a number of profitable discussions on philosophical issues, one focus of interest being provided by Frank Ramsey's paper 'The Foundations of Mathematics' delivered as a lecture to the London Mathematical Society in November 1925. It had been published in the Proceedings of the Society.[11] In this paper Ramsey wanted to restore the credibility of the logicist research programme of Frege, Russell and Whitehead by applying what he thought was Wittgenstein's notion of tautology. He wanted to show that the propositions and equations in mathematics are logical propositions and thus amount to tautologies in a 'classical' truth-functional sense.[12]

This was not what Wittgenstein actually had said [Gefwert (1) 131-133]. It seems that Ramsey had misunderstood Wittgenstein's genuine intentions concerning the status of pseudo-propositions in mathematics. One can, in connection with a letter from Wittgenstein to Ramsey, concerning this project, which is dated July 2nd, 1927 [WVC 189-191], clearly notice the deep difference between the two philosophers in that ' ... whereas Wittgenstein's objection attempts to go straight to the heart of the matter, and to demonstrate that Ramsey's whole enterprise of reconstructing Russellian foundations of mathematics was philosophically misguided, Ramsey's reply is concerned only with the logical and mathematical question of whether his function will do the task for which it was designed'.[13]

Interestingly enough, Ramsey did not reply to Wittgenstein directly, probably because of their quarrel in 1925 concerning the content of the lecture at the London Mathematical Society. Instead he wrote an answer to Schlick who sent an extract of it to Wittgenstein in a letter dated 15 August 1927 [WVC 191-192]. As far as Wittgenstein's own philosophical work on mathematics is concerned nothing substantial seems to have happened until the spring of 1928 when he heard the eminent Dutch mathematician L.E.J. Brouwer (1881-1966) lecture in Vienna [Gefwert (1) 159-165]. Wittgenstein was persuaded by Waismann and Feigl to attend the first (and perhaps the second) lecture on intuitionistic mathematics and its philosophy. One can say that the lecture by Brouwer seems to have acted as catalyst when it comes to Wittgenstein's return to active work in philosophy.

This crucial incident contributed, one year later, to Wittgenstein's return, in January 1929, to Cambridge and active work on philosophy. But now, as we shall see, Ramsey seems finally to have accepted Wittgenstein's critique at least in the sense that he now accepted a strict finitist foundation (method) of mathematics instead of a logicistic one. But, it was, nevertheless, still a **foundation**. What Ramsey didn't understand was how intimately coupled the critique of the general 'foundations of mathematics' by Wittgenstein was to the novel characterization of what a specific philosophical investigation amounts to. Indeed, Wittgenstein commented on this very difference between him and Ramsey in the beginning of the decade in his diary. In order to exhibit what this novel characterization concerning **philosophy** amounts to - in contrast to a general (and theoretical) 'foundation' - we are in this work to investigate this problem, as well as different aspects of it, in more detail.

* * *

We are in this work to investigate how the required 'philosophy' of Wittgenstein is to be understood. We are therefore to distinguish his idea of philosophy from the interpretation of philosophy that we encounter in Analytical Philosophy (Logical Positivism) which can be called logical analysis (requiring 'classical' truth-conditional logic). But, we also have another interpretation. For example, we find that Carnap took 'philosophy' - after discussions with Gödel in the 1930's - to be equivalent to his term 'meta-language'. This gives rise to his later writings on 'classical' semantics which has played an important role, for example, in Cognitive Science.

We have provided the interpretation that Wittgenstein required his philosophical investigations in his pre-1929 thought to terminate in 'transcendental' statements of natural (everyday) language which **show** their sense in ordinary practice [Infra I.4]. By the term 'transcendental' he seems to have meant conditions (meaningful statements of language) which are necessary in order for experience to be able to arise in the first place [Gefwert (1) 3-5]. We call this position (interpretation) for an **observer** based view: we basically 'see' different objects [Infra II.1].[14] It can be understood as being applied both in his early pre-1929 writings as well as in some of his post-1929 writings [T §6.13]. This seems to be the case despite the fact that he in the post-1929 writings emphasizes that he now works *within* language (but, what is then 'outside'?)[cf. WVC 186]. For example, one can notice this when he compares philosophical investigations with the therapeutical treatment that we find in Freud's psychoanalysis [BT 410, 417].

But, it is important to understand that Wittgenstein was still influenced by an 'observer' based view of everyday language at this time. His change of paradigm comes piece by piece between 1929-1936. The final change, as far as language-games are concerned, is completed in 1937. He now ends up with a **participator** insight concerning our everyday language-games. He regards meaningful everyday language-games to be a universal medium (in Stenlund's sense). Such a 'participatory' view does **not** amount to an interpretation of any kind. For example, it is impossible to have a transcendental (or a metaphysical Realistic or a rational Idealistic) 'observer' based general interpretation ('theory of meaning') of the Inner and the Outer according to Wittgenstein [Infra II.1].

When we investigate what Wittgenstein writes on philosophy we notice that from a 'methodological' point of view the notion of causality plays **no** role whatsoever in Wittgenstein's texts [Infra II.4]. To perform a philosophical investigation amounts to a descriptive conceptual analysis which cannot be treated causally. Likewise we also note that the notion of 'mental process', which is a key concept in empirical psychology (as well as in Cognitive Science), has no important role to play in Wittgenstein's participatory way of doing philosophy (other than as an example of a mistaken concept)[Infra III.5]. Due to the fact that Wittgenstein in his post-1937 writings also adheres to the impossibility of a 'private language' it follows that thoughts (language) are public practices. Our everyday (primary) language-games are conceptual (but there is no psychological sub-linguistic 'mental language', in the sense of Chomsky and Fodor, to be found)[Infra III.7]. Thus, the impossibility of 'private languages' to occure cannot be isolated from the rest of Wittgenstein's work (including his writings on philosophy). These arguments are like a needle's eye that one must pass through in order to enter into his later thought. The arguments which undermine the idea of privacy should be viewed not as the completion but as its delineation; although they contain the seeds of a positive account, they also raise a vast array of new problems which Wittgenstein's texts are devoted to solve.

For example, as a result of this account we note that ostensive definitions are not the basic means whereby human beings learn to speak their language [Infra V.2]. The case of the private linguist is dependent on the possibility of a private ostensive definition to exist. But, according to Wittgenstein, to assume the existence of such a definition involves a fundamental misunderstanding of the nature of it. He focusses on the example of sensations and considers the idea of a language whose words 'refer to what can only be known to the person speaking; to his immediate private sensations'[PhI §243]. Such a 'private language' would be incomprehensible to anyone else other than its creator, for no one else could know what its words referred to. Interestingly enough, this clashes with the fact that we do talk about our immediate sensations. How is this possible? But, if we leave this point to one side, however, Wittgenstein spells out in more detail what such a private language would have to involve.

The sensation words in a private language would be defined by the individual forging a private link between the name and the sensation. For example, if a person wanted to keep a diary about the recurrence of a certain sensation, it would have to be done by associating the sensation with the sign 'S' and writing the sign down on every occasion on which the sensation occurred. This procedure differs from normal ostensive definitions in that the individual would not be able to point to what she is defining, since the sensation is of course private. Instead the individual is assumed to point as it were mentally, forging the link between sign and its referent by concentrating her attention on the sensation she is trying to name. In this way, the private linguist impresses upon herself the connection between the sign and the sensation; although for everyone else the sign is meaningless, for her it has a meaning.

Wittgenstein's investigation of the concept of a private language shows why our traditional ('observer' based) approach to the Inner won't work. We cannot, by any scientific means (linguistic, psychological or semantical 'theory'), exactly tell (by explanation) how human beings, in the first place, learn to speak their natural language [Infra IV.2]. The primary reason for this is that such factual investigations (when we try to falsify them) would already require the ability to speak a certain (natural) language. Thus the 'subject' is weiled (excluded). The attempt to answer this question (scientifically) would be like standing on one's head. Any attempt to provide an answer that is founded on an 'observer' based scientific investigation is like putting the cart before the horse. In order to be able to perform such investigations we already have to be able to speak. We simply have to accept the competence of speech (when we ask this kind of question [T §6.13]). We are genuinely participating in language-games. When we already speak (some language) the situation is, of course, different. In such a situation, what we can do is to formulate (secondary) structures, or 'spaces of intention', by our primary language-games when we, say, programme computers to perform different tasks, for example, complicated 'expert systems' according to the typed vocabulary of constructive mathematics and constructive linguistics in computing science [Gefwert (1) 337ff.].

The purpose behind all this talk of the impossibility of a 'private language' to occure is to show that, for example, our mathematical and psychological concepts could be seen and treated in a very different way [PhI 232]. My aim in this book has simply been to outline the problem of the Outer and the Inner and sketch Wittgenstein's dissolution to it in order to clearify his position on what philosophy amounts to. It is important that we note that the dissolution does not amount to a rejection of the Inner (nor the Outer), or, indeed, our picture of the Inner (nor the Outer) as such: all it rejects is a confused **interpretation** of that picture. The force of Wittgenstein's claims is to call for a radical rethinking of our approach to the Outer and the Inner without suggesting that talk of them in any way amounts to an illusion or error.

* * *

We are in this work also to look at the difference between Wittgenstein's post-1937 conception of philosophy and the idea of 'philosophy', for example, in Davidson's Realistic or Dummett's Anti-Realistic terminology, that is required in analytical philosophy when attempting to formulate the correct 'theory of meaning'. Such attempts require what can be characterized as 'research programmes' (in the terminology of Lakatos) where the task amounts to formulate the correct 'observer' based semantical theory. As a result of these research programmes we have: (1) the doctrine called logical analysis (which can also be called Realism), and (2) the competing intuitionistic doctrine (which can also be called Anti-Realism). One of the key points in our distinction of these doctrines concerns their rival (and different) type of syntactical and semantical structure. The first 'theory of meaning' is **atomistic** (Realistic) as far as its syntactical and semantical structure is concerned whereas the second is **molecular** (Anti-Realistic).[15] Thus they have a similar kind of structure as far as they both require an 'analytical a priori' external theory of meaning to be formulated (despite the fact that it is different in the respective cases).

In contrast to this view of a first 'philosophy' it is important to emphasize that a philosophical investigation in Wittgenstein's sense is neither Realist nor Anti-Realist in nature. To assume that it is semantical in the first place is to make a crucial mistake. It gives, for example, raise to Kripke's 'Rules-as-Theory' confusion [Infra V.4]. Wittgenstein's insight does not require an explicitly formulated semantical (theoretical) 'observer' based structure because it replaces the two semantical doctrines ('atomistic' (Realistic) vs. 'molecular' (Anti-Realistic)) with numerous informal everyday language-games. For example, he portrays the extremely persistent nomenclaturist view of language as a source of numerous problems (cf. 'ostensive definitions'). Contrary to what one sometimes sees in the literature, written by certain Anti-Realists (e.g., Dummett, Prawitz, Martin-Löf, Wright, etc.), the 'universal medium' is not a theory of meaning (a general 'observer' based structure) in the first place. No, numerous everyday (specific) language-games that we use on a 'participatory' insight constitute our universal medium of communication. Thus it is possible to call this view of everyday language-games, in Stenlund's terminology, for the universal medium of communication without making the mistake of assuming that it is aiming to establish a first philosophy [Infra I.1].

We then arrive at the position that philosophy, in Wittgenstein's sense, does not amount to some kind of a general and 'analytical a priori' theory of meaning nor to any kind of theoretical enterprize in an empirical sense (like, for example, theoretical physics is).[16] Philosophy is not 'scientific' (theoretical) in either way, i.e., it is not concerned with factual investigations (mathematical nor empirical) that needs to be justified (interpreted) by formulating laws. According to Wittgenstein there is nothing like a general and systematic 'theoretical (hypothetical) philosophy' in this specific sense [Infra VI.2].[17] Problems which are of philosophical (conceptual) nature are not solved by factual investigations. On the contrary, philosophical problems amount to pseudo-problems and are to be **dissolved**. Therefore, one could say that philosophical investigations, according to Wittgenstein, are therapeutical in nature (they can be seen as analogues to Freud's psycho-analysis)[Infra VI.4].

A philosophical investigation is conceptual in nature (but, in contrast to the view expressed by adherents of Cognitive Science, the concepts do not occure independently of everyday language ('mentally'); they belong to genuine language-games). Therefore a philosophical investigation can only take place when we have the competence to already orally use ordinary language-games. To perform philosophy in this sense can be called conceptual investigations [Z §458]. We thus note that philosophy is a very different activity, according to the post-1937 Wittgenstein, than was assumed, e.g., by the Logical Positivists of the Vienna Circle. Some of them, like Feigl and Carnap, adherred at various times to the logic-as-language paradigm (earlier) as well as to the language-as-calculus paradigm (later)[Infra I.1]. For Wittgenstein the situation is completely different. A philosophical investigation is a specific kind of (verbal) practice that is reminiscent of a Socratean dialogue (or psychoanalysis in the sense of Freud) that, for example, a mathematician (when acting as a philosopher) performs in order to purify a calculation (proof) from conceptual illusions brought about by the uncritical use of formal and informal language.

I have in this work tried to exhibit what philosophical investigations, according to Wittgenstein in his post-1937 texts, amounts to. What is important to understand is that there is a continuation in his development of philosophy (despite certain important differences concerning everyday language, for example, the difference between an 'observer' based and a full-blooded 'particpatory' view) between the pre-1929 and the post-1937 writings. The result is, as I already said in my earlier book, that '[i]t is less often realized that Wittgenstein's requirement of seeking to change nothing but only the ways by which we understand in fact changes everything'[Gefwert (1) 12].

But, it is also important to understand that Wittgenstein's insights, indeed, have an historical background. When we take this background into account his philosophical texts appear far less original and unique than it does when seen in the light of the standard internal philosophical historiography, at least when it comes to the kind of problems that he takes up. Some of Wittgenstein's ideas would no longer seem as if they simply came unbidden from a solitary, spontaneous act of creation on the part of a dedicated genius. They do indeed have a historical background and this background needs to be documented. Wittgenstein is far from the first to have emphasized how we are lead into philosophical confusion by language (even if Wittgenstein gives this idea a new and radical content).

It is important that we make this point clear to ourselves in order to fully understand the change in Wittgenstein's final post-1937 thought on philosophy. We can say that it is not philosophy in Wittgenstein's sense that should be influenced, for example, (1) by the calculations that we find in pure mathematics, logic, computing science as well as computational linguistics or (2) by the empirical practices (including the sciences, for example, scientific theories in theoretical physics, chemistry, genetics, neurophysiology, cognitive psychology, empirical linguistics, etc.). On the contrary, it is the numerous mathematical practices as well as the numerous empirical practices (including the sciences) that should be influenced by philosophical investigations when they exhibit, in Wittgenstein's terminology, conceptual 'prose' (or 'gas') in the numerous different contexts (language-games) which they constitute.

Notes

[1] Gefwert, Christoffer, *Wittgenstein on Mathematics, Minds and Mental Machines*, Aldershot, UK; Brookfield, U.S.A; Singapore; Sydney, AUS (1998), xx + 349 pp; Gefwert, Christoffer, 'Wittgenstein: Is Philosophy Systematic?', in Pihlström, S., Kuokkanen, M. and Sandu, G., (eds.), *Filosofisia Tienviittoja: Heikki Kanniston 50-vuotispäivän kunniaksi*, Reports from the Department of Philosophy, University of Helsinki, **No. 3** (1995), pp. 129-134.

[2] Wiggins, David, 'Meaning and truth conditions: from Frege's grand design to Davidson's', pp. 3-28; Skorupski, John, 'Meaning, use, verification', pp. 29-59, in Hale, B. and Wright, C., *A Companion to the Philosophy of Language,* Basil Blackwell: Oxford (1997). Both Davidson's view that a 'classical' Tarskian theory of truth, as well as Dummett's view that criticized that meaning should be understood in terms of 'classical' truth conditions, provoked intense debate in North America, Great Britain and Scandinavia. Cf. Davidson, Donald, 'Truth and Meaning', *Synthese* **17** (1967), pp. 304-323; Dummett, Michael, 'The Philosophical Basis of Intuitionistic Logic' (1973), reprinted in Dummett, M., *Truth and Other Enigmas,* Duckworth & Co.: London (1978), pp. 215-247.

[3] Dummett, Michael, 'Can Analytical Philosophy be Systematic, and Ought it to Be?', in Dummett, M., *Truth and Other Enigmas,* Duckworth & Co: London (1978), op.cit., p. 454.

[4] Despite that it is interesting I would say that it is not this kind of history that we at the moment urgently require. What we need is a work which takes philosophical thinking on the nature of language during different epochs as its unifying perspective. Perhaps one could say that the present book amounts to a preliminary of such a more extensive work. According to Stenlund, such a work would ' ... distinguish itself from standard surveys in the history of philosophy with respect to which names would be included as having made the most significant contributions. Kant would receive

relatively little attention, while Locke and Condillac, for example, as well as thinkers who follow in their tracks (such as Saussure) would require close study. The presentation would not retain the traditional classificatory apparatus of the history of philosophy. It is doubtful, for example, that there would be much point in dividing philosophers up into idealists, rationalists and empiricists in the historiography I am imagining here', Stenlund, Sören, 'On the Linguistic Turn in Philosophy', in Gustavsson, M. and Hertzberg, L., (eds.), *The Practice of Language,* (unpublished), p. 52.

[5] Kenny, Anthony, *The Legacy of Wittgenstein,* Oxford: Basil Blackwell (1982), p. viii; But cf. also Hintikka, Merrill B. and Jaakko, *Investigating Wittgenstein,* Oxford: Basil Blackwell (1986), pp. 137-138.

[6] We are here reminded of the writings of Cora Diamond and James Conant [cf. chapter I, n. 17] which stress that Wittgenstein's texts (both earlier and later) aimed at a goal that is quite different from that of convincing a reader of a thesis, where a thesis is something that can be stated and understood, something for which, or against which, there might be arguments. The attempt to convince someone that what he says is nonsense requires a different approach than does the attempt to convince that what he says is false. One can hardly treat what someone who speaks nonsense says as something that fits into the logically articulated structure of an argument.

[7] A good example of this mistaken view concerning philosophy is provided by the otherwise excellent book by Max Jammer concerning *The Philosophy of Quantum Mechanics: The Interpretations of Quantum Mechanics in Historical Perspective,* John Wiley & Sons: New York, London, Sydney, Toronto (1974). Jammer sets out from the mathematical concept of a Hilbert Space which was used by von Neumann when he formulated quantum mechanics as an operator calculus. The view that Jammer then takes is that it is the task of **philosophy** of quantum mechanics to provide the 'correct' interpretation. That is, a physical theory amounts to a partially interpreted formal system. Needless to say we have a number of interpretations of the quantum mechanical formalism, just think, for example, of the Copenhagen interpretation, the Stochastic interpretation, Statistical interpretation and the Many-World interpretation.

[8] Janik, Allan & Toulmin, Stephen, *Wittgenstein's Vienna,* Simon and Schuster: New York (1973), p. 207.

[9] von Wright, Georg H., 'A Biographical Sketch' in Fann, K.T., (ed.), *Ludwig Wittgenstein: The Man and His Philosophy,* New Jersey and Sussex (1967), p. 20.

[10] Ibid., op.cit. p. 20.

[11] Monk, Ray, *Ludwig Wittgenstein: The Duty of Genius,* London (1990), op.cit., p. 244.

[12] Ibid., p. 245.

[13] Ibid., op.cit., p. 246.

[14] When we assume an 'observational' view on philosophy we can distinguish between two kinds of insights that transcendental arguments can support. First, we have 'negative' transcendental insights which are about the limits of knowledge. They are about what we cannot know. The paradigm example is that we cannot, for example, know 'things-in-themselves'. Secondly, we have 'positive' transcendental insights which are derived from proofs which allows us to say that we have infallible or indubitable knowledge of certain things. The paradigm example is, for example, Kant's transcendental deduction of the categories that form the necessary conditions for the possibility of experience.

[15] Dummett, Michael, 'The Justification of Deduction', in Dummett, M., *Truth and Other Enigmas,* [cf.n.2], p. 314.

[16] The contemporary idea of philosophical issues belonging to 'pure' philosophy of language is a relatively recent twentieth-century phenomenon. What is discussed and studied is different theoretical representations of language, although these are discussed as if they were language itself. In connection with this, we can mention that it seems that Wittgenstein still in the *Brown Book* attempts to formulate (a mistaken) general presentation of his philosophy. It is therefore interesting to compare, for example, Waismann's writings with this work (note: they were still collaborating when Wittgenstein wrote the text of *the Brown Book*).

[17] Gefwert, Christoffer, 'Wittgenstein: Is Philosophy Systematic?', in Pihlström, S., Kuokkanen, M. and Sandu, G., (eds.), *Filosofisia Tienviittoja: Heikki Kanniston 50-vuotispäivän kunniaksi,* Reports from the Department of Philosophy, University of Helsinki, No. 3 (1995), pp. 129-134.

I The Universal Medium

I.1 INTRODUCTION

The language studied by the young pre-1929 Wittgenstein amounted to everyday language as we find it. But, this does not mean that we have a language as our primary target. Language in general is not something conceptually similar to particular (natural) languages (like English, French, Swedish, etc.) nor to symbolisms in that it can be regarded as a means to an end. It is important to understand this point. We acquire the **general** notion of 'language' from examples of different particular (natural) languages and linguistic phenomena which are called 'language' on the basis of various common features some of which are characteristic of what we call 'communication'. We have to understand that there exists a no more general notion of communication of experience, thoughts, ideas or information than this. The very idea of communicating thoughts, feelings, etc., is given with 'language' (in the most general sense of the word). It sets limits on what can be communicated in principle. But note that by a 'language' is not meant a formal language. Thus it is important to understand that we do not primarily learn to speak by what we call a 'language' in the universalist (formal) tradition (for example, by a theoretical grammar or some technical language) of a calculus. This version is often confused with the 'universalist tradition' due to the fact that the very paradigm is confused with the universalist calculus paradigm (view) of language.

It is in such a restricted sense that we ('I') can claim to have only one primary 'language' (dependent on the 'language' we ('I') as children learn to speak). But, then one can ask: Who - or what - is this non-empirical we (or 'I')? Can this subject ('I') be empirically investigated (by some kind of Cognitive Science)? These are important questions. We know that Wittgenstein is explicitly talking about a non-empirical ('metaphysical') subject in his pre-1929 texts. But, what does he mean by such a subject? Where is such a subject to be found? In order to be able to answer this question we have to understand that such a non-empirical subject does not belong to the (empirical) world. In Wittgenstein's pre-1929 thought it amounts to a 'limit of the world'[T §5.632]. It is related to the world as the eye is related to the visual field. Thus the world offers itself to the transcendental ('metaphysical') subject in a similar way as something in the visual field offers itself to the eye. The term 'idea', or form, is **visually** based. It comes, actually, from the same root as the Latin term 'video'. Therefore platonic form is form conceived of by analogy with visible form. It is in this way that the world is **my** world, as all the thoughts are **my** thoughts. But, what does this, in turn, mean?

In order to understand this question correctly we have to grasp that by the transcendental non-empirical self (the 'metaphysical' subject) is not meant the human being, or the human soul, with which empirical psychology deals. We do not mean the empirical subject. In contrast to the empirical subject we are here meeting the transcendental ('metaphysical') subject [T §6.13]. It is this subject that amounts to the limits of language. This transcendental subject **can** be characterized as constituting the bounds of our language-games. This is so because provided one wants to say something meaningful then one 'cannot step outside language', that is, the demarcation between sense and nonsense. But note that we are always allowed to express nonsense when speaking or writing (for example, in certain kind of literature). The freedom to transgress the limits of language is the freedom to express nonsense, i.e., nothing. Consequently, there is a crucial difference between the 'empirical' and the 'transcendental' subjects despite the fact that they are both called subjects. We can say that an 'empirical' subject belongs to (is part of) a 'transcendental' subject in this sense. Consequently, if this is the way the metaphysical self of the pre-1929 Wittgenstein is to be understood then we can say that it resembles the transcendental subject of Immanuel Kant (1724-1804) and Arthur Schopenhauer (1788-1860)[Gefwert (1) 27-36; 70-81].

It is important to understand that what we call the transcendental ('metaphysical') subject does not amount to an individual, that is, it cannot be objectified. Therefore, it is characteristic of such a subject that it is impossible to empirically investigate it. Consequently, a transcendental subject cannot be the object of a theoretical (hypothetical) investigation in science. One cannot formulate it as a theory and attempt to falsify it by experiments in the sense that, say, fallibilism requires. Therefore, we have to understand that [T §5.631]

> [t]here is no such thing as the subject that thinks or entertains ideas.

But, if the transcendental subject is no thing that thinks or entertains ideas then what is it? Well, we can characterize it as a kind of a metaphor. We can say that the transcendental ('metaphysical') subject amounts to the limit(s) of everyday language. According to Wittgenstein, '[t]he subject does not belong to the world: rather, it is a limit of the world'[T §5.632]. But, if such a subject amounts to the 'limits of the world' then it can be said to coincide with solipsism and simultaneously also with pure realism. That is, ' ... solipsism, when its implications are followed out strictly, coincide with pure realism'[T §5.64]. Indeed, solipsism and pure realism coincide perfectly in such a case (but note that this does not apply to metaphysical Realism [Infra I.2]).

There really is a sense in which one can talk about the self in a non-psychological way. This 'self' amounts to the 'transcendental' subject which is the 'limits of the world'. Another way of expressing this point is to say that we always 'participate' when the empirical subject **uses** everyday spoken language. Novel signs can be introduced into language, but we are still always starting with everyday (primary) spoken language, ready-made and already understood. We have to distinguish oral from written language. We can say that language presupposes language [PhR 54].

The Greek alphabet was definitely established by 700 BC, but it was not until Plato's days that the Greeks had at long last effectively assimilated writing. It was with written language that solo and silent reading became the general practice. Writing, so to speak, separated the knower from the known, intensified the sense of self and freed the mind for more original, more abstract thought. For example, it was precisely this deeply interiorized experience of writing, of written language, that in a crucial way seems to have shaped the philosophy of Plato (428-384 BC).

Between Homer and Plato the method of storage began to alter, as the information became alphabetised, and correspondingly the eye supplanted the ear as the chief organ employed for this purpose. The complete results of literacy did not supervene in Greece until the arrival of the Hellenistic age, when conceptual thought achieved as it were fluency and its vocabulary become more or less standardised. Plato, living in the midst of this revolution, announced it and became its prophet.[1] Contrary to a widespread predjudice and belief there is nothing mystical with this insight. As an example, we easily slip into the Realistic (scientific) 'picture' [Supra I.2], which, for example, tells us that we as children learn to talk. This is, of course, absolutely correct (how this is done is a fact that needs to be empirically explained by science) but we have to understand that this is not what is important here.

What is important to understand is that the Realistic 'picture' is dependent on us **already** having the capacity to speak in order to even be able to understand (observe and formulate) such an empirical theory of how we, for example, learn to speak or how our sub-conscious mind functions. This becomes clear when we thoughtfully contemplate on the situation. For example, all our analytical and empirical practices are possible to perform (philosophical, mathematical, logical, psychological, physical, astronomical, chemical, neurological and biological, etc.) because we have primary language-games at our disposal that we can apply. As we said already earlier, one, nevertheless, always has the freedom to transgress the limits of language. But we have to understand that this freedom amounts to the liberty of being allowed to express nonsense. What we have here is Stenlunds version of the thesis which Hintikka has called *Language as the Universal Medium*.[2]

I.2 METAPHYSICAL REALISM

In the philosophical literature we are accustomed to meet a basic conception concerning our relation to the 'world'. We call this conception **metaphysical Realism**. The core of the metaphysical conception of philosophy is the notion that it is about the essence, or nature, of things (or words, phenomena, thoughts, reality ...). It can also be understood as telling us how things truly are or what they truly mean. In order to do this the world has to consist of some fixed totality of mind-independent ('separated') objects. According to Realism 'we' ('I') have a direct and external - isomorphic (Stenius) - relation to the world [Gefwert (1) 56ff]. There is exactly one correct and complete description of 'the way the world is'. However, it needs to be formulated. We have an analogous case with the Realistic foundations of mathematics called Platonism. Also here we have a direct relation to the mathematical objects. It also needs to be formulated. In both cases of Realism, i.e., empirical and mathematical, the ultimate aim of a foundation is to clearify what such an external relation between object and language (between object-language and meta-language) amounts to.

Following Stenlund (and Hintikka) we call this conception the language-as-calculus view. The origin of this view is Hilbert (but also Russell [T xxii]) who developed it when he created the formalist foundations of mathematics. Alternatively, we can say that this amounts to an **externalist** perspective because in both cases (the empirical and the mathematical) the favourite point of view amounts to an external God's Eye point of view. It is this that I mean by the metaphor of the 'observer' that is used in this book. According to this view, e.g., modern philosophy (**of** language (Realism and Anti-Realism), mathematics (Platonism and Intuitionism), science, mind

(Idealism), psychology, linguistics, Cognitive Science (Rationalism)) in its present forms are dominated by what one might call the 'observer' based calculus conception. According to this view the subject ('I') is as if it were separated from the universe by a pane of glass, i.e., one takes the general view of language (or mathematics, mind and Cognitive Science) as being an 'observer' based calculus (or formal system) similar to the view that we meet in 'classical' mathematics and formal logic.

To begin with, we have to understand that we ('I') don't exist in a 'linguistic vacuum' (behind a pane of glass) as the calculus conception tells us. We ('I') are not languageless (metaphysical) 'observers'. Why? According to the view of language-as-calculus the basic semantical relations are presupposed in all use of language which in turn is separable from reality (Realism). But these kinds of separable relations cannot themselves be meaningfully discussed in language. For example, what would be the case if the semantical relations between language and the world were different? Such a question is nonsensical because one cannot vary the representative relations between our expressions (concepts) and reality. The question is inexpressible (it exhibits 'prose') according to Wittgenstein's view. Thus, it is important to realize that the external language-as-calculus view presupposes a never ending regress in our way of looking at the problem when we attempt to justify what are the correct rules to apply in such a case [O 69]. What we require is another way of understanding the problem. We have to set out from the fact that we are stuck, logically speaking, with our one and only everyday language. Thus one can characterize the situation by saying that the empirical subject is no external metaphysical 'observer' of natural (and formal) language in the sense epistemological Realism requires.[3]

It is Wittgenstein's belief in **this** aspect of everyday language as a universal medium that is important here, not an independent commitment to finitism or operationalism as such. For example, he is committed to rejecting all attempts to produce consistency proofs in meta-mathematics or, alternatively and a shade more interestingly, he is committed to considering such proofs as merely another mathematical calculus, on a par with the original mathematical system. Another, even more general, consequence of Wittgenstein's belief in the impossibility of semantics in the calculus sense is that he cannot use in mathematics any external semantical conception of truth different from provability in some system. Thus provability of a proposition equals truth of it (in this sense it is reminiscent of Brouwer's position). This is one of the most characteristic features of his discussions of the 'foundations of mathematics' in his post-1937 texts [PhI §136; RFM Appx. §§5-6].

It is because of this that we have **no** use for any meta-language according to the language as the universal medium thesis which would explain (or describe) the logical features of our natural (and mathematical) language as if it were from **outside** of what is investigated. For example, Hilbert, Gödel, Tarski, Carnap, Simon, Davidson, Dummett and Hintikka take such an external view in their syntactical and semantical works. But, according to the pre-1929 Wittgenstein, it cannot be performed externally. This insight was also emphasized (in the context of linguistics) by de Saussure.[4] Language as it really is, i.e., *la langue,* is **only** given to us as speakers or users of language.[5] It is only in retrospect that we then take the connections between the various aspects of language (concept and sound, language and thought, the individual and the social, etc.) for what they are: internal relations.

There is a clear similarity between Saussure's discussion of the indissoluble bonds in language and the discussion by Wittgenstein of the internal relations that can only be shown in language. Both of these discussions rest on the idea of the immanence of thought in the totality of human language. As such, language is only accessible to us from the inside. It is in this sense that we have to understand what is meant by the impossibility of getting 'outside' our primary language. We cannot view its 'logic' (or 'semantics') in the paradigm of language-as-calculus sense, based as it is on representative relations to reality, because ' ... any kind of explanation of a language presupposes a language already'[PhR 54].

The impossibility of varying the interpretation of our language is an important additional reason why, for example, 'classical' semantics and 'classical' model theory is impossible on the view of language as the universal medium (but we have internal versions of both constructive semantics as well as model theory). The possibility of a systematic variation of the representative relations between language (or at least its non-logical vocabulary) and the world is a conceptual cornerstone of all 'observer' based 'classical' logical semantics. We note that the development of 'classical' semantics and its technical twin, 'classical' model theory, has gone hand in hand with a gradual transition from the view of language as the universal medium to the view of language-as-calculus. But, according to Wittgenstein, this transition amounts to a mistake. Now we understand why he stressed in his later (and earlier) thought that there is no genuine meta-mathematics [PhG 296]. It is similar with ordinary 'classical' semantics of natural language when it is being formulated (constructed) according to the language-as-calculus view. In such a case a language is determined (or given) by its vocabulary (its lexicon) and grammar, or - through the influence of meta-mathematics and logical semantics - by its syntax and semantics. This is why Wittgenstein, according to the version advocated by the Hintikkas, can be said (mistakenly) to adhere to a 'semantics without semantics' concerning our primary language.[6]

I.3 LOGICAL ATOMISM

George Edward Moore (1873-1958) and Bertrand Russell (1872-1970) were the founders of the school called Logical Analysis (or Logical Atomism). They were advocating Realism in philosophy in opposition to English hegelianism which in turn advocated Idealism. In addition, we also know that Russell adhered to the paradigmatic view of logic-as-language. We shall therefore concentrate our efforts on Russell who published his version of Logical Atomism in articles between 1905 ('On Denoting') and 1924 ('Logical Atomism'). In addition, he seems to have been the first to talk of the 'logic-analythical method' in philosophy.

We know that Wittgenstein worked in a close relation to Russell between 1912-1914. We therefore need to look at Russell's view of 'language' in more detail if we want to understand the relationship between Russell and Wittgenstein. To begin with, Russell's method was inspired by the new logic that he had, together with Alfred North Whitehead (1861-1947), been developing (after the collapse of Frege's programme) for the logicistic foundations of mathematics.[7] It seems that he was one of the first (in addition to Frege) to have officially acknowledged the value and importance of logic for philosophy when he said that 'I hold that logic is what is fundamental in philosophy, and that schools should be characterized rather by their logic than by their metaphysic'.[8] Note, that Russell (similarly to Wittgenstein) did not accept the view of logic-as-calculus which was initiated by Hilbert (and later by Carnap as language-as-calculus). Today we can regard this 'novel' logic-as-language of Russell and Whitehead (which originated with Frege) to be a 'classical' logic (it is not a 'constructive' one: it does not adhere to the propositions-as-types principle)[Gefwert (1) 104].

But what does logical analysis (logical atomism) amount to? We can say that this notion is connected to the **definitions** of concepts. We distinguish between **nominal** definitions and **real** definitions. The last mentioned, i.e., real definitions, we find to be used in the literature in a number of ways. We don't need to bother with these definitions here. We know that this was not what Russell advocated. As far as he is concerned, he defends a nominal position (logic-as-language). We find this to be the case, for example, when he (together with A.N. Whitehead) says that [9]

> [a] definition is a declaration that a certain newly-introduced symbol or combination of symbols is to mean the same as a certain other combination of symbols of which the meaning is already known ... a definition is concerned wholly with the symbols, not with what they symbolize. Moreover it is not true or false, being the expression of a volition ... .

There are a number of problems with Russell's opinions concerning the use of the logic-analytical method. But, in general, he gave valuable examples of this method (for example, his in articles on 'definite descriptions', 'reducibility to acquaintance' and 'logical constructions').

Russell presented Logical Atomism in course of eight lectures which he delivered during the three first months of 1918. According to him these lectures were ' ... largely concerned with explaining certain ideas which I learnt from my friend and former pupil Ludwig Wittgenstein'.[10] In these lectures Russell claimed that material things cannot be undivided factual parts. The atoms of physics are not atoms in the logical sense. The ultimate part (a logical atom) of a fact is by Russell called a 'simple'. These 'simples' are part of reality and we have direct knowledge of them. This is why they cannot be picturized but only named. The logical atoms form the border of the outermost part of Reality. But how do we come to know them? According to Russell the logical atoms are connected to our way of understanding language. The words we use must be meaningful so that they can constitute meaningful sentences. And the meaning of a word has in the last instance to be something which we know according to aquaintance.[11] It is interesting to note that Russell never says what these logical atoms really amount to. He is, nevertheless, convinced that they exist and refers at this point to the famous philosopher and mathematician Gottfried Wilhelm Leibniz (1646-1716).

But this is not the whole story as far as Logical Atomism is concerned. It was developed further by Rudolf Carnap (1891-1970) in his work *Der logische Aufbau der Welt* which was published in 1928.[12] It has sometimes been said that this work amounts to the fourth part of the *Principia Mathematica*. This is certainly a claim that can be defended. In this work Carnap continues the analytical tradition which Russell between 1905 (On Denoting) and 1924 (Logical Atomism) attempted to extend to the philosophy of nature. Thus we notice the interesting fact that Carnap at this time held the view of logic-as-language (which he was at the beginning of the 1930's to change due to Gödel's influence). Logical Atomism, in the sense of

Russell and the early Carnap, still exists but it has been beside the main currents of analytical philosophy in the last five decades.

Now, it has also been claimed that Wittgenstein in his early thought had some connection to Logical Atomism.[13] This is certainly, to some extent, a correct claim (for example, in the sense that he held the view of language as a universal medium). But, now we can ask: What kind of connection to Logical Atomism does Wittgenstein have and what does such an interpretation amount to? To begin with, such an interpretation of the pre-1929 Wittgenstein makes his elementary propositions into Russell's atomic propositions (or Carnap's protocol sentences). For example, we notice this in the comment that the objects form the substance of the world [T §2.021, 2.024]. But note, that Wittgenstein did not provide any example of an object. This can easily be seen as a mistake. This is, however, made on purpose. The reason is, according to Wittgenstein, that it is impossible to say what the ultimate parts of a factual situation are [Gefwert (1) 76-78]. Another example is given by Wittgenstein's claim that only an idealized sentence can be said to be completely analyzed. Every sentence that claims something about reality can be logically analyzed in a unique way [T §3.25]. A completely analyzed sentence thus corresponds to the conceptual foundations of a fact [T §§3.2, 3.201-3]. This is in accordance with the way of thinking that we find Leibniz and Russell to be doing. This conception is the starting point of the way of doing philosophy by the pre-1929 Wittgenstein according to the tradition of Logical Atomism (as well as the early Carnap).

Thus, we notice that there seems, on this interpretation, to be a certain kind of similarity between the thought of Russell, Carnap and the early Wittgenstein. They all seem to use 'language' in a very 'technical' sense. But, when we look at the situation more carefully we notice that this amounts to a crucial mistake. There is a big difference, on the one hand, between Wittgenstein and, on the other, between Russell and Carnap despite their common adherence to the view of logic-as-language. This is clearly emphasized in their respective view concerning what is to be understood by 'language'. Whereas Wittgenstein took 'language' to mean informal and ordinary (everyday) language we find that Russell and Carnap took it to be formalized (technical) language. As far as Carnap is concerned he never changed his mind on this point. But, there was one big change in his thought. In contrast to Russell we find that Carnap adopted the language-as-calculus paradigm in 1929-1930 (due to his discussions with Gödel) and continued into his semantical stage as a result of this. We shall look at this in more detail later. But I shall now attempt to vizualize some of the points that we find in the writings of the early Wittgenstein in order to provide another reading of his pre-1929 texts which takes this difference between ordinary vs. formalized language into account.

I.4 THE TRANSCENDENTAL READING

It is well known, although not usually taken very seriously, that Wittgenstein says that logic is **transcendental** [T §6.13]. This has given rize to a transcendental reading of his pre-1929 writings. However, this was not a novel view on his part. Already earlier (1913) one finds that he had written that [NB 9]

> logic is interested only in reality. And thus in sentences
> ONLY in so far as they are pictures of reality.

This is very far from the way logic is commonly seen. What is usually understood as being of concern to logic, for example, in ordinary 'classical' truth-conditional first-order Predicate Logic, are only the forms (structures, laws, principles, etc.) of thought, not those of reality. But, from a transcendental viewpoint the distinction itself is spurious.

The forms of thought that transcendental logic is interested in are at the same time the forms of reality. In Wittgenstein's version of this basic transcendentalist 'axiom' (rule) of language we find that it is presupposed to share its form with reality. They have a common **logical form**. It is this common logical form of language and reality which makes the former consist of 'pictures' of the latter [T §2.17].

According to Wittgenstein, this is the reason why it becomes clear [T §6.1224],

> ... why logic was called the theory of forms (**die Lehre von den Formen**) and of inference.

The rules existing in the 'theory of forms' exhibits the transcendental logic of our primary language in contrast to the 'theory of inferential rules' which show the meaning of, say, secondary mathematical language. Therefore, it is important to note that there are two ways of understanding the word 'logic' here. It can be understood as [Gefwert (1) 76-78]:

> (1) referring to the secondary inferential rules of (constructive) mathematics (including formal logic), constructively typed programming 'language' and constructive linguistics which deals with what can be characterized as 'pure possibilities'[cf. T. §2.0121].[14]

> (2) referring to the more general and primary transcendental logic of unstructuralized natural language which shows what can be characterized as 'transcendental possibilities'.

It is transcendental logic which **shows** the possibility of expressing ourselves with sentences in ordinary (primary) language exhibiting 'linguistic immanence' in Stenlund's terminology. As far as natural language is concerned we know how to use signs properly without being able to express **how** and **what** they signify [cf. PT 3.202111]. One can say that '[l]anguage (logic) takes care of itself', as Wittgenstein was fond of putting it [NB 1]. The problem is to understand its way of doing this [cf. NB 43]. We understand that once we have learnt to speak our natural (and formal) language it shows the **possibility** of expressing ourselves in a meaningful way. This gives rise to a transcendental aspect of language which shows the possibility of language to express empirical **facts** (not objects!) in the world [T §1.1]. Therefore language deals with (the possibility of there existing) facts [T §2.0121]. Note, that our language does **not** express pure 'objects' ('things-in-themselves') as such. The transcendental aspect concerns the realisation that there is something - objects - which can configure in a certain way to states of affairs [T §2.0272].

We have to understand that **names** of objects cannot be defined by ordinary verbal means. We can only speak with names, but we cannot put them directly as such into words [T §3.221]. The conception of a pure object ('thing-in-itself') in this sense amounts to a Realistic misconception. The nature of an object, what it is, depends on the context of the activity in which we are engaged. The only available means for us to introduce new signs in a primary sense (by linguistic means) is to use the language we already have. In this sense **language**, being the provider of a **form** (there are a number of forms of language: speech, writing, temporal sequences of electrical impulses on a wire, configurations of holes punched on a tape, or what not), is a necessary medium without which we simply would have, for example, no thoughts and facts (and no science).

The form of an object is its possibilities of combining with other objects. It is with these possibilities that transcendental logic is concerned [T §2.0121]. In order for (transcendental) logic to have facts to deal with, there has to be objects. This makes form a necessity. One can then say that form is the possibility of structure [T §2.033]. That is, one cannot look (search) for the form of an element [WVC 234]. It is not in our power to choose (by a decision procedure) the form by which we think. Because of this it is not in our power to choose to either obey or break the rules of transcendental logic. These 'rules' are not optional (decidable), on the contrary, they are necessary relative to facts.

Perhaps the most important conclusion from the above discussion of natural language is that most of what is usually taken to belong to semantics when we look at it in an external (and separable) way is instead part of transcendental logic, i.e., it belongs to the internal part of our natural language. Particularly, this accounts for the fact that we can state that a name **necessarily** refers (internally) to an object. If the referential relation of a name to an object were of a semantic (external) kind in the language-as-calculus sense one would rather think that this would amount to a contingent relation. We can therefore, for example, say that Wittgenstein adheres to the ineffability of all semantical relations.

This is why we can say that Wittgenstein's 'picture theory' of the proposition on this reading is not ontological (i.e., it is not reflecting externally the logical structure of language), it is transcendental.[15] In other words: there is no external separability present between 'language' and 'world'. We have a transcendental version of language as the universal medium. The 'world' is, like experience in Kant's texts, something which the subject 'encounters' in the sense that 'world' and 'life' coincide [PhR 80-81]. If the 'logic' in Wittgenstein's pre-1929 thought is understood as being transcendental in the Kantian sense then the claim that we cannot think anything illogical [T §3.03] turns out to be a natural consequence of the whole appoach rather than a piece of scholastic subtlety. If there really is an identical order prevailing in our thought as well as in reality, it is not at all surprising that our capacity to think would be restricted to thoughts that represents situations which themselves are possible. This is how it should be if language is to have its logical form in common with reality.

I.5 THE LIMIT(S) OF LANGUAGE

This insight gives rise to the 'limit(s) of language' thesis in Wittgenstein's thought. We know that Wittgenstein adhered both in his early, pre-1929, post-1929 as well as in his later, post-1937 texts, to the 'limit(s) of language' principle [T §5.6;VB 27;PhI §119]. However, we have to understand that he does not mean the same thing even if he uses the same expression in these cases. In his pre-1929 thought this reference is not only one of approval, but one positively in the spirit of Wittgenstein's Kantian enterprize (the 'Critique of Pure Language'). It is largely this task of limiting the realm of the thinkable which makes Wittgenstein's philosophical enterprize not only analogous to but intrinsically similar to Kant's view (it is a 'linguistic' version)[Gefwert (1) 4].

In Wittgenstein's pre-1929 thought the 'limit(s) of language' thesis provides a distinction between what can be **said** and what can only be **shown** [T §4.1212]. The latter aspect amounts to the logical form which exhibits the common form of thinking and reality [T §2.18]. This logical form of the 'world' is known **a priori** [cf. WVC 217] and shows itself [T §4.121]: this is why it is transcendental. To reflect on logical form is a secondary (philosophical) activity (which cannot be said). Even if the results of a philosophical (secondary) activities are incomplete, that does not in any way imperil the basic transcendental 'axiom', i.e., that there is a common form in our 'thoughts' and in 'reality', and that there is, outside this form, nothing which could (meaningfully) be expressed by propositions. The result is then that logic, both as the 'logic of our thoughts' and as the 'logic of the world', is an 'effective logic', that is, it actually shapes 'reality' and our thoughts concerning it.

It is said that Wittgenstein, in his post-1929 writings, gives the impression that he want's to leave the 'limit(s) of language' view entertained in his earlier thought. Instead he says that he now wants to remain 'completely within language'[WVC 186]. But, what does this mean? Has he renounced the pre-1929 version of the 'limit(s) of language' thesis? The correct answer still seems to be shrouded in mystery but it is possible to argue that the answer is negative [Infra I.1]. In his fuzzy 'middle' period we find the following example of this thesis. The Kantian connection is emphasized by Wittgenstein, as late as in 1929, when he says that [VB 27]:

> The limit of language shows itself in the impossibility
> of describing the fact that corresponds to a sentence ...
> without repeating that very sentence.
>
> What we are dealing with here is the Kantian solution
> to the problem of philosophy.

But, in addition, it is important to understand that this can also be counted as a critique against a Kantian solution to the 'problem of philosophy'. The point is that we have to **use** a sentence (or sentences) when we want to describe a fact [PhI §43]. This, as we shall see, is a crucial and very important point in the development of Wittgenstein's thought.

Indeed, one can argue that there still is a 'limit(s) of language' thesis in Wittgenstein's post-1929 thought which is characterized by nonsensical statements the meaning of which cannot be said. The whole Realistic (metaphysical) idea of 'reality' imposing its structure on 'language' from the 'outside' is gone. Wittgenstein saw that the difference between these aspects vanishes when logical form is the common form of reality and language. He does not look for any kind of external 'structure' at all (in the logic-as-calculus sense) because there simply is no structure to be found. Alternatively, one can metaphorically say that the view that he seeks does not amount to a small-scale map - the whole terrain observable from a high altitude (like an 'observer') - but a complete grasp of the various moves made on the ground by people **using** language.

In his final, post-1937 thought, the most important feature of the 'limit(s) of language' was then, not the 'external' (as it were) boundary of language, but the 'internal' limitation of language-games, viz. the inevitable restrictions on what one, being a 'participator', can say, for example, in (secondary) language-games **about** practices being primary language-games. These restrictions amount, for example, to the distinction between sense and nonsense when we express ourselves in philosophical investigations.[16] As Wittgenstein says [PhI §119]

> [t]he results of philosophy are the uncovering of one or another piece of plain nonsense and of bumps that the understanding has got by running its head up against the limits of language.

One can then say that an 'effective logic' is a participatory logic: we are always **already** expressing ourselves by language-games, i.e., our 'universal' medium, when we express ourselves (e.g., in informal discussions, mathematical calculations, elementary particle physics or in cognitive psychology). In order to express ourselves in the first place we have to be able to participate in using language-games. We therefore understand the difference between sense and nonsense (in natural language). The limits of language of our language-games is something we just have to grasp in order for us to understand that the words in a proposition say anything at all. The result is that a proposition of our primary everyday language **cannot** say what its own limits of language is in words. That is, one cannot say that there are certain truths beyond the limits of language, or even that there are not truths beyond the limits of language, we need to understand that the desire one wants to express as a desire for such truths is **no** desire at all.17 Meaning is not constituted by some peculiar mental act from which the logical properties of language flow. This is an important point.

But, then the obvious question becomes (for the empirically minded scientist): Is it somehow possible to causally (by a scientific theory and experiments like Cognitive Science would like to have it) to explain and describe **how** we come to grasp this point? According to Wittgenstein the answer is: No [cf. T xxi]. This is an impossible task (it is 'nonsense') because we cannot take an 'observer' based view and 'step outside' our primary language-games into a linguistic 'vacuum' as this would require. We are truly 'participators' in the practices we perform by our natural language-games.

I.6 LOGISTICAL POSITIVISM

There is yet another interpretation of Wittgenstein's early pre-1929 thought. It is related to Logical Atomism. This is the familiar one provided by the Logical Positivists (e.g., Carnap, Reichenbach, Neurath, Ayer, Kaila, Jörgensen, Naess) of the Vienna Circle. Later the movement became known also as Logical Empircism. Now, it is important to understand that this interpretation only incorporates part of the pre-1929 Wittgenstein's ideas (like Logical Atomism does). For example, it completely ignores his central thesis of **language as picture** [T §4.021]. Therefore, one can say that the interpretation by the Logical Positivists applies certain well-chosen parts of his writings. For example, this makes the point they advocated concerning senselessness statements completely different from Wittgenstein's conception, i.e., that there are certain things that cannot be put into words: the transcendental [T §6.13]. In addition, it is also interesting to note that there has been a deep-rooted reluctance to acknowledge the extent to which Logical Positivism was inspired and guided by ideas derived from Wittgenstein's pre-1929 thinking. This insight was well-known to the members of the Vienna Circle (and resented by some of them). Despite this it is a fact that the interpretation by the Logical Empiricists is built on a couple of principles which have their roots in Wittgenstein's thought. We shall look at them below.

The first thesis concerns the statement which says that '[a] proposition is an expression of agreement and disagreement with truth-possibilities of elementary propositions'[T §4.4]. According to the positivist interpretation of this statement all meaningful sentences are ('classical') truth-functions of such sentences where the truth-value is decided by the immediate truth of the **senses**. If we still assume that every meaningful sentence is the truth-function of a finitary set of elementary sentences then it follows that the sentence is meaningful only if it can be shown to be true or false by assertions. This is the famous statement concerning the notion of **verification**: the meaning of a sentence amounts to its method of verification.[18] However, it is important to understand that this positivistic methodological principle of verification is assumed to presuppose a logically independent - 'detached' - world where the objects are in a Kantian 'an sich' (Realistic) form.

The Logical Positivists understood the texts of the pre-1929 Wittgenstein as incorporating such a Principle of Verification. However, according to them, such a principle had certain restrictions. They restricted it to be valid only for empirical propositions (mathematical and logical ones in a logicistical sense were excluded). According to them the thesis established the view that all statements which cannot be empirically verified are senseless. To this category belongs, for example, all metaphysical statements. It is correct that Wittgenstein nowhere, in his pre-1929 texts, mentions anything about 'verification' but that one, nevertheless, according to this interpretation, can read certain statements in the *Tractatus* so that one can find this principle to be indirectly formulated [T §§4.063, 4.431, 4.41, 4.4, 4.2]. It is also a fact that we do not find the term 'verification' to explicitly occure in this text. Instead we find it in Wittgenstein's conversations with Waismann, Carnap and Schlick from 1928-1929 [VWC 20]. For example, it is explicitly mentioned when Wittgenstein, in his discussions with Waismann, says that '[t]he sense of a proposition is the method of its verification'[WVC 79; cf. 227].

Despite this it comes as a surprise or, indeed, as a shock, to many present-day philosophers to be reminded that the principle of verification is rightly to be called 'Wittgenstein's principle of verification'[Infra II.5]. But note, that this is not enough. In addition it has also been showed that Wittgenstein's concept of verification cannot be the same as the logical positivist's concept of verification.[19] This is due to the fact that whereras the Logical Empiricists wanted verification to be possible only for empirical statements (according to them mathematical and logical statements are 'classical' truth-functional 'tautologies' in accordance with Logicism) we find that Wittgenstein incorporated also mathematical (and logical) statements under the term verification. This is his version of the maxim adopted by the Logical Empiricists as the Principle of Verification, but here, interestingly enough, intended to be applied also to mathematical calculations. But, this does not mean that Wittgenstein took language to be a formal (external) system (language-as-calculus). On the contrary. Thus we notice that his aim was to formulate a completely different kind of philosophy which cannot take 'language' to stand for a technical language (like, for example, Russell's Logical Atomism does despite its adherence to logic-as-language).

This leads us to the second paradigm concerning how the concept of 'language' is to be understood. As we have noticed Wittgenstein used 'language' in the sense of 'ordinary language' during his entire life. But, the Logical Empiricists came little by little to understand 'language' in the technical logic-as-language sense (reminiscent of Russell and the early Carnap). Except Schlick and Waismann part of them also later changed paradigm, i.e., they came (due to the influence by Gödel) to understand 'language' as a 'calculus' (Carnap, Hempel, etc.) in the same sense as it was understood in the formalist context of mathematics and formal logic (according to the paradigm of language-as-calculus).

What is important to grasp is that we on both of these readings have a non-conceptual separability between language and reality (or between 'object-language' and 'meta-language', in the terminology formulated by the later calculus and 'observer' based 'semantical' Carnap). The separability can be characterized as a kind of non-conceptual 'vacuum'. We always provide a suitable **interpretation** between language and reality (by our non-formalized meta-language in the 'classical' logic-as-calculus sense). This gives rize to an extremely conventionalistic view which according to Carnap has been called the Principle of Tolerance and which is closely connected to the view of language-as-calculus.[20]

This is also the perspective according to which Ogden and Richards wanted their interpretations of meaning to be understood.[21] We know that Wittgenstein opposed this view. The reason for his opposition is that when we learn to **use** sentences of a language (when we, e.g., learn to speak) we cannot **begin** by interpreting these sentences. This would mean that we already had a Language of Thought at our disposal (as, e.g., Rationalistic Cognitive Science emphasizes). Therefore any kind of a 'causal theory of meaning' (Ogden & Richards, Russell) is a mistaken view as far as the learning of our primary language is concerned. It was **this** point that Wittgenstein reacted against in his letter to Ogden when he wrote that, 'I ought to confess to you frankly that I believe you have not quite caught the problems which - for instance - I was at in my book (whether or not I have given the correct solution)'[O 69].

This is the same view concerning language that we met when we discussed the Realistic foundations of language which has by Stenlund (and Hintikka) been called language-as-calculus. In Hilbert's formalist foundations of mathematics we find it to occure in Carnap's term 'meta-mathematics' where we have (formalized) mathematical language and (non-formalized) meta-language. According to this view 'philosophy', which amounts to critique of language, is **meta-language** itself. The object for meta-language amounts to the technical languages (of mathematics and natural science) which are assumed to be a kind of calculus. But, note that the object can be 'natural language' as well. We therefore understand that on this reading philosophy amounts to 'the logical syntax of scientific language' as formulated by Carnap in his work the *Logische Syntax der Sprache* (1934).[22]

I.7 LOGICAL SEMANTICS

The adoption of the language-as-calculus view also provides the beginning of the development of the doctrine called 'logical (philosophical) semantics' which has been regarded as being on the borderline between 'philosophy' and 'classical' formal logic.[23] Logical semantics can be seen as enlarging the scope of formal logic (syntax) in the 'classical' observer based sense. Thus semantics in this sense has been regarded as having close ties to 'classical' mathematics. For example, we find Carnap stating that philosophy (i.e., meta-language) amounts to 'semiotic' analysis, that is, ' ... the problems of philosophy does not concern the uttermost principles of existence, but the semiotic structure of scientific and ordinary language'.[24]

By 'ordinary language' Carnap does not mean the same as Wittgenstein did by the very same expression. We also notice this split within the Vienna Circle: Schlick and Waismann, among others, followed Wittgenstein's lead and turned increasingly away from the idea that an ideal structure of some kind lay at the foundation of language and that it was necessary to describe this structure by an artificial language in order to clarify philosophical problems. Carnap, Neurath and others, on the other hand, held firmly to the view that it was possible to dispose of philosophical problems only by drawing up a more perfect language, framed in accordance with the rules of logical syntax (of a formal language). We therefore note that Carnap (and 'analytical' philosophers in general) definitely means something else by the term 'philosophy' (meta-language) than both the pre-/post-1929 Wittgenstein meant by this term. Nevertheless, logical semantics (in a 'classical' sense) has been advocated by a number of philosophers and scientists during the 20th century (e.g., Tarski, Carnap, Simon, Fodor, etc.).

This interpretation by Carnap in accordance with the 'classical' language-as-calculus view of semantics has provided the basis, for example, to such independent scientific enterprizes like the rational theories of Simon and Fodor in Cognitive Science. But here we face a problem because as little as Carnap's 'logical syntax' was a genuine 'language' in Wittgenstein's sense (cf. 'there is no meta-mathematics'[PhG 296-298]) as little does logical semantics in Carnaps sense amount to a genuine ordinary language according to Wittgenstein. Both 'syntax' and 'semantics' in Carnap's sense amount to an observer based 'classical' **calculus** in the logic/language-as-calculus sense. So it does not seem that logical semantics is going to solve the genuine philosophical problems (in Wittgenstein's sense) occurring in ordinary language that Logical Empiricism was facing with its view of the external ('observer' based) language-as-calculus interpretation. Recall, that for Wittgenstein natural language is a medium which is in perfectly good order as it is - we don't start by interpretating it when we learn to use it (because there is, for example, nothing like a language-game semantics in a primary sense) - although that order is concealed by a confusing outward clothing.

I.8 THE HINTIKKA INTERPRETATION

We know that Wittgenstein, in January 1929, returned to Cambridge to work on his dissertation - the *Tractatus* - with Frank Plumpton Ramsey (1903-1930) as his supervisor. After the completion of his thesis he began to write on philosophy. But, we have to be aware that

Wittgenstein as a result of this did not immediately change his mind to his post-1937 'mature' view. To make such an assumption amounts to an illusion. It has given rize to the familiar distinction between the 'earlier' (pre-1929) and the 'later' (post-1929) Wittgenstein. This distinction, however, amounts to a mistake. Instead we can say that the change came piece-by-piece between the years 1929-1936. However, it is correct that we, historically speaking, find evidence for a 'holistic' dictum already in Wittgenstein's earlier pre-1929 writings as well as in his later post-1929 texts that he wrote before 1937 in Cambridge.

This has given rize to an interesting interpretation provided by Merrill and Jaakko Hintikka. It is a generalization of the famous distinction between 'logic-as-language' and 'logic-as-calculus' originally made by van Heijenoort.[25] The interpretations of the distinction is called Language-as-Calculus respectively Language as the Universal Medium (but note that the latter one is not similar to Stenlund's version with the same name)[Infra I.1]. According to this interpretation we **basically** have only one Wittgenstein. It is characterized by the view that language-games are primary to their rules. This view of Language as the Universal Medium has by the two authors been characterized (contrary to Stenlund's version) as a 'semantics without semantics'. It is an attempt to show how language (in addition to its 'horizontal links') is tied to reality in a direct way by 'vertical links'. It therefore presupposes metaphysical (Realistic) separability between Reality and Language. Far from trying to get rid of 'vertical links' between language and reality this interpretation assumes that Wittgenstein emphasized these 'links'. But, it is important to understand that one cannot look at one's language from the 'outside' and describe it (like an 'observer') as one can do to other objects that can be specified, referred to, described, discussed, and theorized about in language. Therefore, according to this interpretation, it is a characteristic feature that ' ... you are a prisoner ... of your language. You cannot step outside it, you cannot re-interpret it in a large scale, and you cannot even express its semantics in the language itself'.[26]

But there is one important difference according to the view advocated by this interpretation. It is the view according to which basic semantics **shows** itself. The 'gist' of this version of Language as the Universal Medium lies in the thesis of the ineffability of semantics. The Hintikkas make it clear that they regard the question of how language and reality are related as the overriding question of semantics.[27] But, one cannot meaningfully and significantly say in language what these meaning relations are, for in any attempt to do so one must already presuppose them. Nevertheless, it allows semantics to exist as rule-like primary language-games. It delegates primary semantics to occure as primary language-games which, according to the Hintikkas, amount to the basic semantical 'links' between language and reality in Wittgenstein's whole mature philosophy.[28] Thus we find that the Hintikkas want to read Wittgenstein as developing the notion of language-games in order to be able to put forward a new and clever 'theory of meaning' while at the same time having deprived himself of the possibility of saying that this is what he is doing. Indeed, the theory is to show itself.

But, there is, at least, one problem. We notice the important point that Wittgenstein is assumed to have emphasized separability according to this interpretation. Far from trying to get rid of 'vertical' links between language and reality Wittgenstein is on this reading assumed to have emphasized them. The foremost function of language-games is precisely to serve as such links. This is the distinction between vertical links ' ... that would relate our words to objects and our sentences to facts' and horizontal links which are defined as the links ' ... between different moves in our language-games'.[29] This amounts to the doctrine (interpretation) of a 'semantics without semantics'. But, then we notice that, by being an interpretation, the language as the universal medium thesis advocated by the Hintikkas in fact amounts to a version of language-as-calculus: it is 'observer' based. The characteristic feature, according to the interpretation by the Hintikkas, is that Wittgenstein is to have accepted **this** kind of 'holistic' dictum (with small changes) during his entire career in philosophy.[30]

However, this amounts to mistake. The Hintikkas argue as if anyone interested in semantics were presented with an initial choice between adopting the language-as-calculus or the language as the universal medium perspective on language and as if this choice would then direct our way in semantics. But that suggests that we somehow can know **before** any study of language what can be meant by the distinctioin (decision) the Hintikkas use. In one of his articles in which Jaakko Hintikka introduced the distinction between language-as-calculus and language as the universal medium he made this presupposition evident. He wrote that ' ... our language ... presupposes in all its uses certain semantical relations (relations of representation) between language and reality. (Otherwise we could not use language in our transactions with reality.)'.[31] It is the presupposition that our language always (in all its uses) presupposes certain semantical relations that provides the basis for the claim by the Hintikkas that we can distinguish between different 'philosophies' (interpretations) of language which state that these presupposed semantical relations can be expressed and those which claim that they cannot be expressed, i.e., the views of language-as-calculus vs. language as the universal medium as they understand these doctrines to occure [Infra V.4].

However, the Hintikkas seem to be correct as far as their reading of Wittgenstein is concerned in that he seems to have had an increasingly diminishing Kantian ('observer' based) perspective between 1929-1936. We should therefore look at this as a transition period (which needs to be investigated more thoroughly). However, it is a fact that by 1937 this Kantian view is definitely abandoned and a 'participator' view is upheld. We cannot find any sources to the effect that the Kantian inspired 'observer' based interpretation is conclusively corroborated anywhere in Wittgenstein's *Nachlass* after 1937.[32] It is therefore important to undestand that the interpretation by the Hintikkas - by being a semantical one - seems to be mistaken as far as Wittgensteins position on language, thought and philosophy in his post-1937 writings is concerned.[33]

I.9 THE POST-1937 WITTGENSTEIN

It is misleading if we believe that the mature, post-1937, Wittgenstein adheres to one of the interpretations exhibited above. In the sense in which he uses the notion of 'logic' (or 'logical grammar'), in his post-1937 writings, it aims to exhibit the point that illogical thought in the first place is impossible.[34] This is to say that when we think we are always subject to the necessities of 'logic': the primary language-games. This is why all justification can only take place by spoken (and written) language-games, i.e., within systems of distinct and partly overlapping rule-like linguistic practices: primary language-games.

One can, perhaps, characterize this situation as a kind of holism: in order to understand a word, one must understand the sentence (the 'Frege Principle'[FA x, §§60-62,106; PoW 15-16,253])[cf. PhI §49], and to understand a sentence one must, in turn, understand a language [PhI §199; BB 5; RFM VI §§41,47], that is, the primary language-games and forms of life in which the words and sentences have their life. But when we read the 'holism' in this way we have to be extremely cautious. Because Wittgenstein does not accept any non-conceptual separability ('linghuistic vacuum') between 'language-games' and 'nature' (reality) we have to understand that by these sentences he cannot mean anything like 'semantics without semantics' in the sense of the Hintikkas (which is assumed to be metaphysically separable in the language-as-calculus sense).[35]

Another way of saying this is that we have no metaphysical separability present in our practices. It is because of these arguments that it is possible for Wittgenstein to deal with a language which satisfies the seemingly incompatible demands of being at the same time both actual and ideal. Thus, it is important to note that one can argue that the 'meaning is use' thesis is **not** to replace the post-1937 'limit(s) of language' thesis (which it is sometimes taken to be). On the contrary, it is to complement this argument. One may say about someone that she is 'imprisoned' in a specific language for empirical or historical reasons, but certainly not for conceptual reasons or the reasons of principle. It is important that we bear this in mind in order to to understand Wittgenstein's position.

In 1931 Wittgenstein said, in a discussion with Waismann, that he believes that understanding is not a particular psychological process at all that is there in addition, supplementary to the perception of a propositional picture [WVC 167]. He said that it is correct that various mental processes are going on inside him when he hears or reads a proposition (as postulated in Cognitive Science). He is not denying this. But this is **not** what Wittgenstein is interested in here. These mental processes amount to empirical problems (e.g., of cognitive psychology) but he is not primarily interested in such problems. What he is interested in is that [WVC 167]

> [o]ne understands a proposition by applying it. Understanding is thus not a particular process; it is operating with a proposition. The point of a proposition is that we should operate with it.

Therefore, Wittgenstein does not any longer explicitly emphasize the importance of the thesis of 'limits of language' in his post-1937 thought. But, it is not completely forgotten either. However, this thesis has now changed from an 'observer' based perspective to a 'participator' insight [PhI §119]. We know that he in his post-1937 texts wants to leave everything as it is and no justification is necessary [PhI §124]. The point is that our (primary) language-games are perfectly adequate for their jobs as they are. It is important to understand that there are no 'interpretations' going on when we use (primary) language-games (for example, no ostensive gestures can function as primary means when we learn to talk in the language-as-calculus sense [Infra IV.2]). Therefore, no reform of language (e.g., from underlying 'mentalism' to ordinary language as Cognitive Science presupposes) is necessary when, for example, we are learning to talk [BB 28; PhI §§131, 133]. To assume this amounts to a conceptual mistake.

We also have Wittgenstein's famous doctrine which has in the literature been called the 'private language' argument [PhI §269]. It has been claimed that '[i]n teaching the philosophy of Wittgenstein there is hardly any part that is more difficult to convey than his discussion about private languages. It is like a needle's eye that one must pass through in order to enter into his later thought'.[36] This is certainly correct. According to Wittgenstein there cannot occur any 'private language' (a 'language' that only I can understand) when we in our practices use (primary) language-games.[37] That is, a language that only one person understands (for example, by which somebody speaks to oneself about one's own conceptions and which cannot be translated to normal language) is, in fact, not a genuine language at all. It does not allow us in a meaningful way to speak of a correct or a mistaken way of using that language (which as a concept requires the contradiction 'mistakenly understood' to be available when doing this). Wittgenstein's argument against the possibility of such a 'private language' is highlighted in his assertion that such a language does not allow enough criteria for the meanings of its words and the lack of such criteria results in that the words do not mean anything or cannot mean anything [PhI §269].

For example, the 'metaphysical connection' (or the conceptual 'vacuum') that is said to exist between Language and Reality (according to epistemological Realism) amounts to such a languageless relation (cf. Hintikkas interpretation). Therefore it seriously violates the impossibility stated by the metaphor of the 'private language' argument.[38] We notice this when we try to apply Realistic and Idealistic statements without taking the dimension of immediate **practice** (use) into consideration.[39] According to the mature, post-1937, Wittgenstein there isn't any non-conceptual separability (or 'linguistic vacuum') between language and reality. Thus one cannot say anything about the correspondence between language and reality, at least not without repeating oneself [CV 27]. The correspondence cannot be pointed out from a Realistic (metaphysical) vantage point, a vantage-point outside (primary) language-games. As Wittgenstein puts it on various occasions: the harmony between thinking/language and reality is to be found in the grammar of language. In other words, one cannot place a statement next to reality, step back (and look at it as an 'observer'), and say, pointing to both: 'that corresponds to that'.

> When one asks someone 'how do you know that the description renders what you see' he could answer for instance 'I mean that by these words'. But what is this 'that', if it is not <u>itself</u> again articulated, that is, language. Consequently, 'I mean that' is no answer at all. The answer is an explanation of the meaning of the word [MS 213, p. 190].

The meaning of words cannot be defined ostensively, either publicly or privately; such definitions in turn presupposes (primary) language-games. The problem of how language can refer to reality can only be approached within the limits of language [Infra I.5]. A metaphysical explanation of this relationship via entities (e.g., by language independent thoughts) 'outside' language-games is circular: these entities in turn need to be thought or talked about and this is only possible by a medium, i.e., our language-games. Within the limits of language-games one should not expect too much of a 'solution' either. For, asking about the correspondence between language and reality, one's answer is again a linguistic formulation, so that in a certain sense one repeats oneself [Cf. CV p.10].

Can 'something non-linguistic' then be understood as language? According to Wittgenstein the answer is: No. 'What is spoken can only be explained in language and so (<u>in this sense</u>) language cannot be explained'[TS 213, p. 2]. One can interpret and translate language, but this still presupposes language: 'I want to say: one cannot interpret the whole language. An interpretation is only one as opposed to another. It attaches itself to the sign and incorporates it into a broader system'[TS 213, p.2]. Not only is language as a whole incapable of being interpreted into something non-linguistic, language is not interpreted in this way at all. If, for instance, one asks somebody 'What do you mean', one gets the answer, 'I mean that you should come home', or something to that effect. In any case one does not say - as a continual interpretation of language would imply - 'I mean what I mean by "coming along"'. Or in Wittgenstein's example: if you ask somebody something, you are satisfied with an answer and you will not complain that this answer is merely a linguistic sign, since its true meaning is supposedly hidden behind this sign and still needs to be interpreted. You expect nothing but an answer: 'It is clear that nothing else could be expected and that the answer presupposes then use of language. Like everything that can be said'[TS 213, p. 3].

This presupposing role of language-games as rules entails that they cannot be justified or explained via empirical statements. Constitutive language-games ('rules') cannot be founded on a simple method of empirical verification: such methods themselves presuppose constitutive rules ad. inf. (language-as-calculus). In other words: grammatical rules cannot be justified by reference to or description of reality, since 'reference to', 'description of', and *a fortiori* 'justification' are themselves certain forms of language which also presupposes agreement in forms of life. Only where certain constitutive concepts and standards are actually being employed can these 'references' and 'descriptions' get off the ground. But this means that the grammatical rules themselves determine what counts as a description or reference to reality. That is why it is meaningless to talk about founding such rules via extra-linguistic facts (like, e.g., mental 'thoughts' in Cognitive Science). We have to understand that (primary) language-games cannot be empirically justified and are in this sense autonomous. It is in this sense that we are 'beyond' the Inner and the Outer (when they are understood in the sense of metaphysical Idealism or metaphysical Realism).

What conclusions can now be drawn from this aspect of the post-1937 Wittgenstein with regard to the kind of 'universal medium' which a practice or form of life is? We can say that human beings are always living their lives in different forms of life [Infra IV.5]. Therefore we cannot let a form of life itself be called founded or unfounded since it is a condition for distinguishing between the founded and the unfounded. The constitutive rule-like practices (the primary language-games) have made it clear that forms of life are not founded by something external to themselves. Therefore, '[y]ou must bear in mind that [a] language-game is so to say something unpredictable. I mean: it is not based on grounds. It is not reasonable (or unreasonable). It is there - like our life'[OC §559].

Forms of life (and grammatical rules) are not foundations in the sense that they supposedly correspond to the 'objective facts' or the 'essence of nature': there is no 'observer' based 'separability' (or conceptual 'vacuum') between language and reality. It is (primary) language-games themselves which determine what is to be regarded as 'objective fact' and as 'the essence of nature'. Forms of life (and grammatical rules) are 'foundations' in the sense that they constitute the meaning of our concepts in the first place and that if we were to change the 'rules', the concepts would have an entirely different meaning or no meaning at all. The 'foundation' which the form of life is, is something which we ourselves **are**, i.e., our way of life as 'participators', but **not** something we **have** (as 'observers') and on which we can **base** ourselves as an independent foundation when we, for example, provide decisions (say, in mathematical calculations or in our scientific practices). Therefore we must understand that '[g]iving grounds, (or) justifying the evidence, comes to an end; - but the end is not certain propositions' striking us immediatedly as true, i.e., it is not a kind of seeing on our part; it is our acting, which lies at the bottom of the language-game'[OC §204].

Notes

[1]   Havelock, Eric, *Preface to Plato,* Cambridge, Mass. (1963), p. vii.

[2]   We are here to distinguish between Hintikka's fundamental conception of Language as the Universal Medium and the aspect of language with the same name provided by Stenlund. We are here following Stenlunds version. According to Stenlund we find that in Hintikka's conception '[t]he relation between a language and its use in real-life situations is taken to be of the same kind as the relation between a calculus or theory (such as the probability calculus) and its application. Language is exhaustively defined as

language through its syntactical and semantical rules. That pragmatic rules, the rules for the use of a language in real situations, are determined on the basis of its syntax and semantics, which are therefore supposed to be conceptually prior to and independent of the pragmatic rules ... This contrast has some features in common with my contrast between the calculus conception as a fundamental way of viewing language as a whole, and as a particular scientific approach to the study of language, but there are also important differences ... [It seems that] Hintikka is taking feature (3) in my list of characteristic features of the calculus conception as *the* characteristic one ... There is a sense in which you "cannot step outside" language, and this idea is an example of something that was misunderstood and given a superficial interpretation in the "universalist tradition" - very much due to the fact that the idea was confused with the universalist calculus view of language', Stenlund, Sören, *Language and Philosophical Problems*, Routledge: London (1990), op. cit., pp. 4, 9.

[3] The term 'observer' has given rize to a **spectator theory of knowledge.** Cf. Dewey, John, *The Quest for Certainty*, New York (1960), p.240. It has been discussed in great detail by Rorty, Richard, *Philosophy and The Mirror of Nature*, Princeton: New Jersey (1979), p.39.

[4] de Saussure, F., *Cours de linguistique générale*, (ed.) Tullio de Mauro, Editions Payot: Paris (1972), p. 155.

[5] This less known side of de Saussure's notion of *la langue*, which stands in stark contrast to the received view of *la langue* as an abstract system, has been pointed out by Michael Gustavsson. In addition, it should be noted that the 'total language' of which de Saussure speaks is the language of linguistics, that is, the language framed in traditional grammar. Similarly the 'total language' described by Wittgenstein in the *Tractatus* is the language of the early analytic philosophy, a language framed by the notions of the new mathematical logic. Note, that this conception is one that Wittgenstein would later describe as a fundamental mistake.

[6] Hintikka, M. and Hintikka, J., *Investigating Wittgenstein*, Basil Blackwell: Oxford (1986), pp. 2-3.

[7] Russell, Bertrand and Whitehead, Alfred North, *Principia Mathematica I-III*, Cambridge: Cambridge University Press (1911-13).

[8]   Russell, Bertrand, 'Logical Atomism', in Marsh, R.C., (ed.), Russell, B., *Logic and Knowledge: Essays 1901-1950,* London: George Allen & Unwin Ltd. (1956) fifth impression (1971), op.cit., p. 323.

[9]   Russell, B. and Whitehead, A.N., *Principia Mathematica I-III,* Vol. I., [cf.n.7], p. 11.

[10] Russell, Bertrand, 'The Philosophy of Logical Atomism', reprinted in March, R.G. (ed.), Russell, B., *Logic and Knowledge: Essays 1901-1950,* [cf.n.8], op.cit., p. 177; cf. also p. 205.

[11] 'It will be maintained that acquaintance is a dual relation between a subject and an object which need not have any community of nature', Russell, B., 'On the Nature of Acquaintance', in March, R.G., ed., [cf.n.8], p. 127.

[12] Carnap, Rudolf, *Der logische Aufbau der Welt,* Berlin (1928).

[13] Griffith, James, *Wittgenstein's Logical Atomism,* Oxford: Oxford University Press (1964), pp. 3-5. According to Griffith, the aim of the book is to provide a novel interpretation of Wittgenstein's atomic propositions in the *Tractatus.*

[14] Ranta, Aarne, *Type-Theoretical Grammar,* Oxford University Press: Oxford (1994), p. v.

[15] Gefwert, Christoffer, *Wittgenstein on Mathematics, Minds and Mental Machines,* Ashgate Publishing Limited: Aldershot, Brookfield USA, Singapore, Sydney (1998), p. 9.

[16] Diamond, Cora, *The Realistic Spirit: Wittgenstein, Philosophy and the Mind,* The MIT Press: Cambridge, Mass. and London (1991), pp. 13-38 and 179-204; Cf. Stenlund, Sören, *Language and Philosophical Problems,* Routledge: London (1990), p. 11; Cf. also Reid, Lynette, 'Wittgenstein's Ladder: The Tractatus and Nonsense', *Philosophical Investigations* **21**, No. 2 (1998), pp. 97-151.

[17] There is an interesting anti-metaphysical interpretation by James Conant concerning Wittgenstein's argument of the limit of language in the *Tractatus.* It has also been argued for by Cora Diamond [cf.n.16] and is in sharp contrast with the standard interpretations. It sets out from Wittgenstein's post-1937 texts. In this reading we look at the *Tractatus* through the 'spectacles' of the mature Wittgenstein [cf. PhI x]. According to

this reading the book takes a strong anti-metaphysical stand; one that is most explicit in Wittgenstein's statement that the apparently metaphysical sentences that compose the book are not false, they amount to **nonsense** (they say **nothing** at all)[cf. T 3; PhI §500]. According to Conant (and Diamond) we have to put the image of the ladder in the centre of their exegesis because we must realize that the ladder must be **completely** thrown away at the end, i.e., that the propositions in question are **completely** nonsensical.

The usual metaphysical reading of the *Tractatus* therefore skips the preface and has little to say in order to make sense of the closing remarks. With its frame removed, the book begins with what appears to be an account of the ultimate constitutents of any possible world; then it moves to what appears to be an account of the logic required by any language that will have the capacity to represent any possible world; it closes with what appears to be a recommendation that one adopt a mystical attitude towards what lies beyond the limits of experience powers of any language. What could this suggest to the reader if not the idea that logic has its foundation in the metaphysical structure of reality, and the idea that the ineffable nature of that metaphysical structure is a consequence of the nature of language?

The fundamental problem with this reading, apart from the fact that it contradicts the *Tractatus* preface and closing assertions that it is **nonsense**, is that, as Conant (and Diamond) argue, it is **unintelligible** on the *Tractatus* view to say that there is something that is true but that is, nonetheless, impossible to state [T 3, §6.54]. There simply is no such thing as deep and important nonsense. It is not 'observer' based. There is only one kind of nonsense, and it is fundamentally uninteresting, since it has no logical structure. So there is no such thing as 'grasping' the propositions of the *Tractatus,* no such thing as saying that they are true, but that they nonetheless cannot be stated. We are not to understand the doctrine expressed by these propositions. Instead we are to understand the point of Wittgenstein's activity as a person who is seeking to free us of 'observer' based illusion: **activity**, not doctrine, and **illusion**, not error.

It is the importance of this point (which, by the way, is **not** a thesis) that has been argued for by Conant (and Diamond). Cf. Conant, James, 'Throwing Away the Top of the Ladder', *Yale Review* **79** (January 1991), pp. 328-364; 'Must We Show What We Cannot Say', in Fleming, R. and Payne, M., (eds.) *The Senses of Stanley Cavell,* Bucknell University Press: Lewisburg (1989), pp. 242-283; 'Kierkegaard, Wittgenstein and Nonsense', in Cohen, T., Gruyer, P. and Putnam, H. (eds.), *Pursuits of Reason,* Texas Tech. University Press: Lubbock (1992), pp. 195-224; 'The Search for Logically Alien Thought: Descartes, Kant, Frege, and the *Tractatus',*

Philosophical Topics **20** (1991), pp. 101-166; 'Putting Two and Two Together: Kierkegaard, Wittgenstein, and the Point of View for Their Work as Authors', in Tessin, T. and von der Ruhr, M., (eds.), *Philosophy and the Grammar of religious Belief,* Macmillan: London and St. Martin's Press: New York (1995), pp. 248-331.

[18] Schlick, Moritz, 'Meaning and Verification', *Philosophical Review* **45** (1936). This article has been reprinted, for example, in Feigl, H. and Sellars, W. (eds.), *Readings in Philosophical Analysis,* New York (1949).

[19] According to Baker, 'Wittgenstein himself attached great importance to this lecture. He gave Waismann an outline of what he was to say [WVC 102ff.) ... This lecture should have been a very important event in the development of the ideas of the Vienna Circle, since some of the members looked to Wittgenstein for a synthesis of logicism and intuitionism that would give a constructivist account of mathematics developed on an acceptable empiricist basis. In fact it seems to have had a very limited influence, partly because of Gödel's simultaneous announcement of his celebrated incompleteness theorem, and partly because Waismann failed to complete the text for publication with the other papers in the symposium. As a result, the members of the Circle seem to have ignored its fundamental message, the application of the principle of verification to mathematical statements', Baker, Gordon, P., 'Verehrung and Verkehrung: Waismann and Wittgenstein', in Luckhardt, C.G., (ed.), *Wittgenstein: Sources and Perspectives,* The Harvester Press: Hassocks, Sussex (1979), p. 252. Also Wrigley has emphasized that there is some indirect evidence that verificationism in the context of mathematics, *as Wittgenstein understood verification,* was always present (in the forms of operations), even in the *Tractatus,* although by no means in such an explicit form as we find it formulated in his post-1929 texts and in his writings by the scholars of the Vienna Circle commenting on this principle. Cf. Wrigley, Michael, 'The Origins of Wittgenstein's Verificationism', *Synthèse* **78** (1989), p. 283.

[20] According to the Principle of Tolerance there is no moral in logic. By this is meant that everyone can build his own logic, i.e., the form of his language, as he best sees. But, provided he wants to discuss with adherents of this principle he must clearly report how he is going to do that. Thus he must, instead of philosophical clearafications, produce syntactical rules. Cf. Carnap, Rudolf, *Logishe Syntax der Sprache,* Verlag von Julius Springer: Wien (1934). We notice clearly the difference in that, for example, Kant was not interested in formulating some kind of abstract philosophical pursuit

apart from science as was the case with adherers of Logical Positivism which Hans Reichenbach (1891-1953) characterizes as a 'specialty' for philosophers which is largely detached from actual scientific practice, in Reichenbach, Hans, *The Rise of Scientific Philosophy,* Berkeley (1951), p. 123.

[21] Ogden, C.K. and Richards, I.A., *The Meaning of Meaning: a Study of the Influence of Language upon Thought,* Keegan Paul,Trench, Trubner & Co., Ltd.: London (1923), tenth edition (eight impression) (1972).

[22] Carnap, Rudolf, *Logishe Syntax der Sprache,* Verlag von Julius Springer: Wien (1934), pp. 1-4. In this work the object for the critique of philosophy (the meta-language) is the language of natural science (the object-language) which is thought of as a calculus. Philosophy is then the logical syntax of the scientific language.

[23] A recent work by Alberto Coffa entitled *The Semantic Tradition from Kant to Carnap,* edited by L. Wessels, Cambridge University Press: Cambridge (1991), gives the impression that the way of approaching language that has come to be designated 'semantics' and the sorts of problems taken up in that approach existed already before the latter half of the nineteenth century, when the term first came into use. This amounts to a mistake because the meaning of statements and expressions which we call 'semantic' were just the sorts of questions that one began to pose when the linguistic turn is supposed to have taken place.

[24] Carnap, Rudolf, *Introduction to Semantics,* Harvard University Press: Cambridge, Mass. (1942), pp. 8-11. By *semiotics* Carnap means the general structure of language and signs. He divides semiotics according to the american philosopher Morris into three parts: *pragmatics, semantics* and *syntax.* By pragmatics Carnap is investigating the way humans are using linguistic expressions. By semantics he is investigating the signs of the language and their relation of meaning (disregarding the person who is using the language). By syntax Carnap means the investigation of the common relations of the linguistic signs (disregarding the speaking person and the meaning of the signs).

[25] For Frege, language (the logically complete and perfect language) is universal; it is the universal medium for all that can be meaningfully said or thought. This feature of Frege's philosophy is most clearly in evidence in his critique of attempts to define the concept of truth. In particular, he is critical of definitions of truth formulated in terms of correspondence, in which at

least one side of the correspondence is thought to be something 'non-liguistic', i.e., something that would be given in some other way than in language, the universal medium of truth-telling. This aspect of Frege's thought has been discussed by van Heijenoort, Jean, 'Logic as language and logic as calculus', *Synthèse,* Vol. **17** (1967), pp. 324-330. For additional insight on this element in Frege's critique of language, cf. Gundersen, O., 'Frege, semantikens umulighet og skriftens privilegium', *Norsk Filosofisk tidskrift,* **33** (1998).

[26] Hintikka, Merrill .B. & Jaakko, *Investigating Wittgenstein,* Basil Blackwell: Oxford (1986), chapter I. Cf. also Hintikka, Jaakko, 'On the development of the model-theoretic viewpoint in logical theory', Synthèse **77** (1988), pp. 1-36.

[27] Hintikka, Merrill B. and Jaakko, [cf. n. 26], op.cit., p. 2.

[28] Ibid., pp. 212-213. There are varietes in the wording used by the Hintikkas. For example, 'language and reality', 'words and things' and 'language and world' are all used interchaingably, although they claim that Wittgenstein's ineffability view prevents him from saying so.

[29] Ibid., p. 213.

[30] Ibid., pp. 20f.

[31] Hintikka, Jaakko, 'Frege's hidden semantics', *Revue internationale de philosophie,* vol. **33** (1979), op.cit., p. 716.

[32] Curiously enough the Hintikkas give as the sole argument §120 of the Investigations for the thesis of the ineffability of semantics. They provide only a brief comment concerning their interpretation of this paragraph when they say that '[t]his is as explicit a statement of the view of language as the universal medium as one can hope to find. The first three paragraphs affirm the thesis of the universality of language. At the end of the second paragraph (and again in the fifth) Wittgenstein subscribes once again to the "formalistic" consequences of the ineffability of semantics. (only the 'exterior facts about language' can be expressed in it.) The last paragraph is particularly interesting in that it shows how Wittgenstein's doctrine of meaning as use was based on his belief in language as the universal medium', Hintikka & Hintikka (1986) [cf.n.26], op.cit., pp. 20f.

[33] According to the reading that I emphasize here it may milden our enthusiasm for the prospect of a theory of the 'general form of a proposition' or a general theory of 'the world-language relation'. Hintikka and many other 20th century analytic philosophers are enthusiased by notions such as 'the general theory of the world-language relation', 'universal semantic theory', and 'basic semantical relations'. Due to this enthusiasm they want to explain away Wittgenstein's sceptical attitude towards the idea of a systematic (and external) semantic theory. But, then, it may be quite difficult to understand the post-1929 Wittgenstein if you are not prepared to read him as a philosopher who may lead you to give up your old loves.

[34] Wittgenstein writes: '"So you are saying that human agreement decides what is true and what is false?" - It is what human beings say that is true and false; and they agree in the language they use. That is not agreement in opinions but in form of life'[PhI §241]. 'If language is to be a means of communication there must be agreement not only in definitions but also (queer as it may sound) in judgments. This seems to abolish logic, but does not do so. - It is one thing to describe methods of measurement, and another to obtain and state results of measurement. But what we call "measuring" is partly determined by a certain constancy in results of measurement' [PhI §242].

[35] According to Stenlund '[t]he main difference between Frege, Russell, and the early Wittgenstein and later philosophers in the same tradition, is that the former were much more concerned with and conscious about the philosophical and conceptual presuppositions of their own theorizing about language. This conceptual self-consciousness reached such a height in the *Tractatus* that Wittgenstein was subsequently forced to realize the incoherence of the calculus conception' as the fundamental conception of language. It was seen to be a confusion of different kinds of problems - philosophical-conceptual problems and technical-scientific ones', Stenlund, Sören, *Language and Philosophical Problems,* Routledge: London (1990), p. 10.

[36] Hertzberg, Lars, 'Wittgenstein and the Sharing of Language', in Hertzberg, L., *The Limits of Experience,* Helsinki: Acta Philosophica Fennica, Vol. **56** (1994), p. 16. In this article Hertzberg is arguing for a novel third position of Wittgenstein's 'private language' argument(s) concerning the importance of a community. According to this view ' ... although questions of linguistic meaning can be raised only in connection with a community of speakers, it is misleading to say that meaning is *determined by community agreement',* op.cit. p. 17. This view is compared to the debate between Kripke, Saul,

Wittgenstein on Rules and Private Language, Cambridge, Mass.: Harvard University Press (1983); Baker, G.P. and Hacker, P.M.S., *Wittgenstein: Rules, Grammar and Necessity,* Oxford: Basil Blackwell (1985), pp. 169ff., who reject the importance of the community; and Malcolm, Norman, *Nothing is Hidden,* Oxford: Basil Blackwell (1986), chap. 9, who, on the other hand, supports it.

[37] There cannot be any genuine 'argument' against the possibility of a private language to occure. It would require that we take the 'private language argument' as a discussion of the essence, core, limits of language or meaning. Such an attempt would require that we could somehow transcend our primary language-games. Perhaps one could say that the impossibility of a private language to occure 'shows' itself in the sense of being used as a metaphor in our (secondary) language-games.

[38] Rhees, Rush, 'Can there be a Private Language?', in Rhees, R., *Discussions of Wittgenstein,* London: Routledge & Kegan Paul (1970), p. 55; Diamond, Cora, 'Rules: Looking in the Right Place', in Phillips, D.Z. and Winch, P., (eds.), *Wittgenstein: Attention to Particulars,* Macmillan: Basinstroke and London (1989).

[39] In order to avoid misconception I have to stress that the notion of 'rule' (which we follow in language) and 'use' (of words) as introduced into contemporary philosophy by Wittgenstein are not technical terms designed to inform us about how the performance of philosophical investigations can be made mechanical and results reliable and easy to achieve. It is difficult to 'look' at the 'use' of a concept. No calculation to that effect is available. Wittgenstein's 'meaning is use' -idea is neither a philosophical doctrine, nor a methodological device. It is a grammatical observation concerning the concepts meaning and use and their relation. - Cf. Diamond, Cora, 'Rules: Looking in the Right Place', in Phillips, D.Z. and Winch, P. (eds.), *Wittgenstein: Attention to Particulars,* Macmillan: Basingstroke and London (1989), pp. 12-34. Cf. also Diamond, C., 'Introduction II: Wittgenstein and Metaphysics', and 'Throwing Away the Ladder: How to read the *Tractatus*' in *The Realistic Spirit: Wittgenstein, Philosophy and the Mind,* The MIT Press: Cambridge, Mass. and London (1991), pp. 13-38 and 179-204.

II Methodological Illusions

II.1 INTRODUCTION: OBSERVER TO PARTICIPATOR

We find that Wittgenstein, in his lectures during 1930-1933, elaborated his novel view of philosophy a bit further and stated, according to Moore's notes, that ' ... it required a "sort of thinking" to which we are not accustomed and to which we have not been trained - a sort of thinking very different from what is required in the sciences'[L (1) 322]. From this comment we notice that Wittgenstein does not seem to have understood this novel 'sort of thinking' as being subordinated to the accepted methods occurring in the context of empirical science. By this I mean, for example, the paradigmatic research programmes that we find in natural science, for example, Sir Isaac Newton's (1642-1727) classical mechanics, where we, in principle, formulate a scientific theory and attempt to falsify it by experiments and observations, as advocated by Sir Karl Popper (1902-1994). The entities which we conjecture to be real should be able to exert a causal effect upon the *prima facie* real things. What we can explain changes in the ordinary material world of things by the causal effects of entities conjectured to be real. According to the fallibilist view the result is, then, that ' ... scientific theories are either falsified or forever remain hypotheses or conjectures'.[1]

According to this view the theories formulated in science are mathematical because it is assumed that the 'correct' nature of reality can somehow be 'captured' by mathematical methods. But the question **how** they explicitly are captured is nevertheless shrouded in mystery. To understand this point, one has to recognize the crucial shift that the philosopher René Descartes (1596-1650) institutes in the famous line in the second *Meditation* in which he sets out to explain the nature of the human mind:[2]

> I am, then, in the strict sense only a thing that thinks, that is, I am a mind, or intelligence, or intellect, or reason.

Descartes is here telling us that, for the remainder of the work, the first-person pronoun will refer conjointly to the person René Descartes or to his 'mind'. There are serious problems with both readings of the first-person pronoun, but our concern with the philosophy of psychology limits us to consideration of the latter: to the fact that, when Descartes asks 'But what then am I?', he sees this as a question about the nature of that mind. His answer can thus be read as stating: the mind is a thing (a faculty) that thinks, that doubts, understands, affirms, denies, is willing, unwilling, imagines and has sensory perceptions. Missing in this preliminary list but predominant throughout the rest of the Meditation is the further attribute that the mind is that which judges: e.g., it is Descartes' mind which infers that certain figures on a painting are men and not automatons.

It is no wonder, then, that this Meditation should have given birth to a science (not to mention three centuries of philosophical polemics); for whether it was his mind or his brain, some element of the organism 'René Descartes' was occupied in enough activities to keep several generations of technicians happily engaged in analysing its operations. In historical terms, Descartes was formulating the Renaissance view of science: the quest for truth, constant doubt, the need for trained observation, inference and revision. We therefore note, according to this view, that there is a yawning gulf between appearance and reality, for example, between 'the world' as it appears to us (and the scientists) and 'the universe' (consisting of, for example, fields, elementary particles, planets, stars, black holes, hydrogen, organic molecules, DNA-accid, fossils, animals ...) as it is independently of our observations. According to this Realist picture the appearance of 'the world' and 'the universe' are separate. The 'world' consists of all objects and they are beheld by what can be characterized as the 'glue' (the Cognitive Structure) which constitutes our 'black box', 'consciousness', 'subject' or the 'ego'. As long as we haven't added the cognitive structure the world-view isn't complete.

Something like this occurs, for example, when we deal with perceptual psychology or neurophysiology. There one ordinarily analyzes the process of perception in terms of light waves, pressures and so on, that act upon the sense organs of the percipient and excite certain electrical and chemical phenomena within his nervous system. Interpreted in this way, this view is perfectly alright. The gulf between appearance and reality can (inherently so) only be partially understood and in order to fulfil that condition it requires explanation and justification by the natural sciences (for example, by causal explanations in physics, chemistry, astronomy and biology). Such a fallibilistic hypothetico-deductive model of science gives rise to a number of different theories - well motivated conjectures - within the scientific community which the scientist, in principle, attempts to falsify (verify) by crucial experiments. This is generally regarded to be the case in the natural sciences, for example, in physics, chemistry, astronomy, biology as well as in empirical psychology. But, in order to be made complete the theories have to be formulated by an additional Cognitive Science which is assumed to be required by the different scientific theories.

But, we also have the 'philosophical' (e,g., syntactical and semantical) way of looking at the problem. In the 'philosophical' (Realistic) interpretation of the picture the subject receives sense impressions from the objects in reality (Ogden & Richards, Russell), which are organized and sorted according to the categories of pure reason, paradigms, canons of induction, or what not, into iterative complexes through which we have knowledge of reality. On the other hand, as far as mathematical objects are concerned, these are in general either in a region of reality, called mathematical reality (Platonism), perceived by mathematical intuition, or they are part of the conceptual (mental) apparatus by which empirical sense impressions are organized (Idealism).

Apart from the paralyzing influence these 'philosophical' pictures have, we find that they, in addition, have some rather unsatisfactory features, among them the following ones:

> (1) The picture gives rise to an uneasy oscillation between Realism and Idealism. What I have tried to describe above is the realist version of the picture. In the idealist version the 'arrows' between reality and the subject point the other way. Reality is not so much beheld by the subject as constructed by him/her so that it is a product of of his/her consciousness and depends on him/her (Brouwer).
>
> (2) The picture is silent about how the two sides of it are connected, how, if one has access to reality only through one's impressions the connection is set up between those impressions and the objects they are impressions of or what principles regulate the construction of those objects and out of what.
>
> (3) In this picture the subject is separated from reality as it were by a pane of glass. The subject is a 'spectator' ('observer'), watching, perhaps, shadows on a wall, or an internal theatre. So, we can ask, is the subject unreal? And why is the picture incommensurable with regards to different subjects? Isn't the subject part of the world?

The whole picture gives an impression of ill health whatever way one looks at it. And it isn't clear that it is adequate even for physics after the advent of quantum theory with its promotion of the 'observer' to 'participator' as Wheeler has put it.[3]

But, the picture we have been discussing can be further elaborated in order to modify its subjective aspects. When we do this, we, for example, replace the subjective aspects by an intersubjectivity (a 'collective') sustained between different subjects through their use of language. The problem with this picture is that it still leaves the subjects outside the universe (reality) whereas they ought to be a part of it. In addition the connection between language and the universe (reality) remains obscure. Remember that language and universe (reality) are still separate systems. Thus we still have the following 'observer' based picture in this Realist elaboration. To begin with, there is the reality which is independent of and prior to language. Next, we set up the language in order to communicate among ourselves and record facts we have discovered about it. Then, we assign nonlinguistic items to linguistic ones as their denotations (i.e., 'classical' semantics), thereby showing their meaning and setting up the interpretation.

There is something fundamentally wrong with this second ('collective') 'philosophical' picture which was also presented in another form in the first one we considered. In either form the Realist semantics has the following problems: The sharp separation of the whole system into a linguistic third, a nonlinguistic third and an obscure third which connects them (by interpretation). It is wrong because it makes any account of this last third obscure. According to this picture we could not have access to anything real which we wished to make the denotation of in the language. For any means employed to identify that real thing would have an ineradicably linguistic aspect. The result is then only that another linguistic system would interpose itself between the first and its field of denotation for which the same problems of interpretation would then arise. In this sense such a view gives rise to a never-ending regress. We have an infinite number of (semantical) interpretations. For example, the familiar distinction between object-language and meta-language that we meet in 'classical' atomic semantics is of this kind.

As we shall see, Wittgenstein is of the opinion that it is not new empirical (nor 'formal' or 'philosophical') facts concerning 'thinking' that will dispel the mystery that seems to surround thought. For example, recourse to experiments (empiricism) at this point, according to him, merely compounds confusion because [RPP I §1093]:

> "[t]hinking is an enigmatic process, and we are a long way off from complete understanding of it". And now one starts experimenting. Evidently without realizing *what* it is that makes thinking enigmatic to us.

> The experimental method does *something;* its failure to solve the problem is blamed on its still being in its beginnings. It is as if one were to try to determine what matter and spirit are by chemical experiments.

II.2 PHILOSOPHY AND SCIENCE

It was this Renaissance view of science (and philosophy): the quest for truth, constant doubt, the need for trained observation, inference and revision which taken from Newton's 'classical' physics, notably classical mechanics (excluding the problematic 'interpretation problem' of quantum mechanics), which set the methodological standard for natural science. Now, this fallibilistic model has also been applied when the question concerning **how** we can speak a natural language has been the target of scientific investigations, that is, in the context of the science called psycholinguistics. We notice this, for example, in the well known statement of John Locke (1632-1704) when he says,[4]

> The Comfort and Advantage of Society, not being to be had without Communication of Thoughts, it was necessary that Man should find out some external sensible Signs, whereof those invisible Ideas which his thoughts are made up of, might be known to others.

One can still find that this is the standard way the science of psycholinguistics is being introduced and portrayed in many textbooks. This attitude is still dominant in modern characterizations of this subject. Even in more recently published texts we find that this attitude is still being upheld when one finds that theoretical linguistics is being characterized, for example, by Lyons, as a scientific discipline aiming ' ... to give a scientific answer to the question "What is language?" [which is to be] systematically [carried out] on the basis of objectively verifiable observations ... within the framework of some general theory ... '.[5]

According to this view the explicit goal of the science of linguistics (and 'cognitive linguistics') is to provide a scientifically acceptable answer to the question:

What is language?

In order to attempt to solve this problem there has been different strategies at our disposal. During the twentieth century we have (mainly) witnessed three positions concernig the question what a 'mind' determining 'what a language is' amounts to:

- (1) The doctrine of 'structuralism' (which by many is also called 'introspectionism') is influential roughly from 1880 to 1920.

- (2) The doctrine of 'behaviourism' which is influential from about 1920 to 1960.

- (3) The doctrine of '(philosophical) functionalism' which is influential from 1960 to the present.

For example, the doctrine of functionalism is to study 'the cognitive foundations of language', i.e., to identify those processes in our mental sphere which determine our linguistic behaviour. According to this view the task of cognitive linguistics to attempt to locate the reality of grammar outside language is none other than the elderly notion of language as the 'dress' of separately existing thought: first you have your thought then you search for the *motes justes* (found in the best dictionaries) to clothe it in. This is still the ultimate aim for an 'observer' based Cognitive Science or science of language ('cognitive linguistics'), for example, in the sense of Chomsky's rational theory of 'generative grammar' where the rules of the theory are assumed to be internalized in the mind (or, alternatively, encoded in the brain) but inaccessible to introspection or to current neurological investigation.

When representatives for Cognitive Science ('philosophical functionalism') present themselves they usually make a distinction between different niveaus of analysis or niveaus of explanations concerning human behaviour:

> (1) The niveau of commonsense, i.e., our common way of explaining actions by reference to feelings, will, interest, determinations, etc.
>
> (2) The physiological niveau, e.g., as an aspect of human behaviour based on the method of natural science when, say, a certain behaviour is being described as effects of neurophysiological processes in the brain.
>
> (3) The niveau of mental representations. Among these 'mental representations' we have schemata, mental pictures, rules, mental states, cognitive processes, conceptualisations and systems of knowledge. Here we attempt to define a 'niveau' which actually amounts to a more or less technical vocabulary where human behaviour is described and explained in terms of these 'mental representations'. That a person has acquired some kind of language understanding is being explained in terms of mental representations like pictures, rules or cognitive processes.

Thus, this is the first task to be performed in order to answer the question 'What is language?' according to the 'observer' based view the science 'cognitive linguistics' is assumed to be (note, that in the beginning Linguistics was not Cognitive at all).[6] It is somehow to show that this question is a genuine scientific - and empirical - question about the way in which our natural language makes infinite use of finite means. We are to provide an answer to this question by formulating an empirical theory (hypothesis) of some kind regarding our pictures, rules or cognitive processes assumed to function in this context. It is in this sense that language is thought to be structuralized in a scientific (empirical) sense. This scientific position is clearly reflected, for example, by Dineen when he characterizes the crucial claims of theoretical linguists as being ' ... that their study of language is scientific ... Thus a scientific study should be **empirical, exact,** and, therefore, **objective**'.[7]

Now, it is, today, a well known fact that Wittgenstein put an extraordinary emphasis on language during his whole career when it came to questions dealing with philosophical (conceptual) problems. But here, however, before we continue, we need a word of caution. It is important to understand that Wittgenstein is **not** aiming for a scientific theory (of any kind) when it comes to problems concerning our use of language. Contrary to the scientific aim of a theoretical linguist, or a generative grammarian, which we superficially portrayed above, it is important to understand that Wittgenstein by his investigations into problems that occure when we use language does not mean the exact, empirical and objective science of language called linguistics as, for example, characterized by the linguists Ferdinand de Saussure (1857-1913) or Noam Chomsky (b. 1928).[8]

Linguistics and Cognitive Science (or any other science for that matter) are of no importance when it comes to dissolve philosophical (conceptual) problems. We have to understand that philosophy, in Wittgenstein's sense, deals with conceptual problems which occures when we **use** language. However, such problems are **not** mental ones. That is, the aim of a philosophical investigation is not to produce any (empirical) linguistic nor a mental 'cognitive' (neither empirical nor analytical *a priori* [Infra V.2]) and reductionistic 'super-theory' of language. To do a philosophical investigation is not to engage oneself in a scientific (methodological) programme of any kind. That is, a philosophical investigation, in Wittgenstein's sense, is definitely not equivalent, for example, to some kind of 'cognitive linguistics' amounting to a 'super-linguistics' (whatever that may be), the aim of which, in the words of Chomsky, would be to exhibit a ' ... "superlanguage" in terms of which each individual's understanding of his own language must be explained'.[9]

A philosophical investigation in Wittgenstein's sense does not aim to answer a question like 'What is language?' in a scientific (e.g., a causal) way by attempting to determine the existence of some assumed hidden structure of language (like Chomsky) since ' ... in philosophy "we know at the start all the facts we need to know'"[L (1) 323]. However, within certain philosophical traditions (for example, in analytical philosophy) it is not too uncommon that philosophers confuse the scientific (methodological) aim with the philosophical one. Wittgenstein characterized this confusion, in one of his lectures (Lecture B I) in 1930, when he said that ' ... philosophers ask "Why?" and "What?" without knowing clearly what their questions are. They are expressing a feeling of mental uneasiness'[L (2) 22].

Due to his emphasis of ordinary language, one of the crucial points that Wittgenstein seems to have kept intact from his pre-1929 period is that a question like 'What is language?' when understood as a philosophical (conceptual) question concerning our everyday language is meaningless [Gefwert (1) 1-24]. One simply cannot in a philosophical investigation ask 'What is language?' and genuinely expect a serious sounding answer, contrary to what is the case in the science of linguistics, biology or Cognitive Science, which either follows the Galilean tradition (emphasizing causal explanations) or, alternatively, the Aristotelian tradition (emphasizing teleological explanations).[10] The reason is that unstructuralized eveyday language (speach) is itself the very 'space' which provides sense to scientific questions (formulated by language) and thus cannot be 'founded' on something logically more fundamental (for example, on some kind of mental 'cognitive process' in the brain) which could somehow be unearthed [Infra II.3].

On the other hand, there does indeed occur genuine philosophical (conceptual) problems in connection with the languages of different (scientific) practices. But note: such problems take place and are dissolved in natural language [L (2) 62]. It is in connection with attempts to philosophically tidy up conceptual confusions within different practices that one, according to Wittgenstein, can say that we ' ... can speak of *skillful* philosophers'[L (2) 21]. If, for example, we discuss the possibility of investigating ordinary language with a certain scientific linguistic method (structure) adhering to, say, 'cognitive linguistics', and notice certain conceptual problems when we do this, then this would be the target for a philosophical investigation of the linguistic theory (method) in question. However, such an activity is to be clearly distinguished from the assumption that to perform 'philosophy of linguistics' (in Wittgenstein's sense) amounts to the same as to engage in a 'research programme' (in Lakatos terminology) concerning the development of the correct scientific method of cognitive linguistics. We have to understand that we have a clear distinction between, on the one hand, an empirical (or, alternatively, an analytic *a priori*) research programme and, on the other, a conceptual (philosophical) investigation [Gefwert (1) 14-15].

II.3 ON BEHAVIOURISM

The technical way of using vocabulary, in the third niveau of explanation that we gave above: the mental representations [Infra II.2], is characterized by a certain way of using terms like 'mental images', 'rules', 'processes', 'systems' in our descriptions and explanations of human activities. It is in this sense that it amounts to a technical vocabulary. What one wants to claim by the thesis of the necessity of 'cognitive processes' in the postulation of mental representations is that this vocabulary is not only a linguistic instrument; it is, indeed, in addition mirroring and reflecting existing psychical realities. It is this 'scientific realism' referring to mental representations that distinguishes Cognitive Science from behaviourism (which was the dominating trend in American psychology around the middle of the the 20th century). The break with the behaviourists that this realism referring to mental representations implies is what the predecessors of Cognitive Science want to see as the occurrence which initiates their novel scientific direction for the study of human behaviour.

Wittgenstein had been dead for nine years before Cognitive Science became established as a science. Therefore, it is no wonder that he did not take Cognitive Science into account but only the doctrine of behaviourism. This new science concerning 'cognition' is not only a cross-disciplinary research programme of an empirical and experimental nature. In addition to these empirical and experimental practices one also has certain philosophical conceptions concerning psychology, human performance and language. To be able to reach a basic view concerning what is 'soulful' in cognitivism and how one is thinking about human language and performance it is imperative to look at what cognitivism and behaviourism have in *common* and not what distinguishes them.[11] For example, one of the crucial questions concerns how the concept of 'intention' is to be understood when it is connected to the doctrine of behaviourism. It is therefore on the concept of 'intention' that I am now focussing my attention. Note, however, that it will also have certain implications on how we are to understand Cognitive Science.

How has the concept of 'intention' been connected to the doctrine of behaviourism in Wittgenstein's texts? To begin with, the problem posed by the concept of 'intention' has by certain commentators sometimes been attempted - quite independently of Wittgenstein - to be answered by denying any importance of it whatsoever. Thus, there has on numerous occasions been attempts to provide answers to the problem of 'intention' in accordance with the doctrine of behaviourism. However, it is a typical feature of these attempts that the commentators do not completely agree about how this 'behaviourism' should be interpreted. Despite this problem, many of them, nevertheless, tells us that Wittgenstein adhered to this doctrine. For example, we have (1) Hallett, who suggest's that Wittgenstein is a 'methodological behaviourist' and not a substantive one, (2) Chichara and Fodor who are convinced that Wittgenstein is strikingly similar to Hull's 'logical behaviourism' and we have (3) Day and Waller, as a third example, who both argue that there are many similarities between Wittgenstein and the well known behaviourist psychologist B. F. Skinner of Harvard University.[12]

These are just some of the commentaries concerning the alledged 'behaviourism' of Wittgenstein. But, we also find there to exist a number of other interpretations as well. Just because Wittgenstein had a background as an engineer and, admittedly, was interested in behaviouristic mechanisms and stimulus-response models, as expressed in his writings, it does not make him a behaviourist in the sense which involves 'physicalism', 'reductionism', 'atomism' or 'external relations'. It is true that Wittgenstein sometimes uses the expression 'behaviourism' in a somewhat uncritical way [PhG 99-100; BT 49] but this does not mean that he accepts the doctrine of behaviourism as we commonly understand it, say, in psychology. We find this clearly indicated when, for example, Wittgenstein writes that '[i]f behaviourism is correct, then it would be intelligible to say that a camera perceives'[BT 462; cf. Z §§487, 526]. We can then without any doubt be sure of his renounce of behaviourism and establish that Wittgenstein was not a behaviourist of any kind (but, note, that he would not have accepted the 'philosophical' view - Rationalism - of modern Cognitive Science either).

In the history of philosophy this 'behaviourist' problem (characterized by the question 'What is "intention"?') has exhibited influence on the 'philosophy of psychology' which is quite similar to the way we find that the Platonist conception of number (characterized by the question 'What is a "number"?') has influenced the 'philosophy of mathematics'[Gefwert (1) 195-201]. When faced with questions about the nature of thought, we are as lost as when faced with parallel questions, for example, about the nature of the number 1 [PhG 108]. Wittgenstein said that '[t]hought anticipates its fulfilment in the same sense that a calculation anticipates its fulfilment'[L (2) 62; WVC 178ff, PhR 178, PhG 63,67,70]. That accounts for Wittgenstein's consequential claim that meaning is set up in language and it is given by explanation [L (2) 62; cf. PhG 60,66,94-95]. The result is that those distinct themes which can be incorporated beneath the general term 'the problem of intention' concerns both conceptual investigations of psychology (including Cognitive Science) as well as conceptual investigations of mathematical calculations (including genuine 'artificial/machine intelligence')[Gefwert (1) 195-252, 295-336]. But note that Wittgenstein did not understand these investigations as exhibiting factual and contingent problems; they are of a completely different kind. According to him philosophical problems amount to conceptual problems [Z §458]. It is conceptual problems, within both of these areas, that are to be understood through his novel 'method' of doing philosophy [PhI 226; Infra VI.1].

According to Wittgenstein the notions of 'thought' and 'intention' concern living human beings because only they exhibit thought (in this sense) and thus '[i]t comes to this: only of a living human being and what resembles (behaves like) a living human being can one say: it has sensations; it sees; is blind; hears; is deaf; is conscious or unconscious'[PhI §281]. We can thus establish that for Wittgenstein applications of the theme of 'thought' and 'intention' only occur in connection with selfconscious living human beings who use a language (including, perhaps, beings on an intellectual level near to humans). We notice this 'vitalization', for example, in Wittgenstein's interesting claim that ' ... in every case what is meant by "thought" is the living element in the sentence, without which it is dead, a mere succession of sounds or series of written shapes'[PhG 107].

Now, if we focus our attention on one theme, 'intention', and simply skip the minor differences that one can pinpoint in connection with the different, but related, themes like, for example, 'the relation between the sign and the world', 'how a thought can be directed towards something existing outside itself', 'how thinking is possible in the first place', 'how meaning something is possible' and 'what kind of substance is the mind of which thinking is said to be the attribute', we notice that these themes become almost identical with the theme of 'intention'. The reason why I have chosen not to explicitly investigate these other themes here but instead decided to focus my attention entirely on the problem of 'intention' is that in my opinion it seems to be possible to capture the essence of these other themes - not, as we shall see, in the form of explicit answers - but by acknowledging the fact that our investigation will, at a later stage, make it possible to ask certain pertinent questions in connection with these particular themes. For example, we can ask more pertinent questions in connection with the problems if there can occur a genuine and independent 'artificial/machine intelligence' or a genuine Cognitive Science which investigates some inherent 'mental process' which is somehow neurologically 'realized'. The result of this is that '[w]e interpret the enigma created by our misunderstanding as the enigma of an incomprehensible process'[PhG 155].

II.4 ON CAUSAL RELATIONS

The significance of Descartes' shift in the second Meditation goes further. The essence of the mechanist view of science promoted by Descartes is the search for causal regularities. This is also the case with the mind: whether it be *vis-à-vis* the movements of external objects or the actions of men. Just like the scientist who dissects the body of an animal in order to ascertain whether, as is demanded by his theory of heat, its heart is warmer than the other organs, so too the mind assumes that the figures it observes are men, but it must nonetheless test the reliability of such inferences about humans (and for that matter, automata). All I (my mind) can see are 'mere movements'; what the causes of these might be I (my mind) can only infer from my own experiences. Judgments about thoughts, motives, intentions, desires, beliefs, attitudes, personally traits: all must be inferences formed by past experience about the presence of those causal antecedents with which I am acquainted.

What Wittgenstein is primarily doing in his reading of Cartesianism is placing all the emphasis on the above shift from man to mind in order to bring us to see that it is a shift in the first place. As such, it is perilous for both philosophy and psychology. This elicits from Wittgenstein a poweful reverse shift from mind to man [PhI §§281,360; Z §§129-130]. More specifically, we have a shift from an epistemological to a logico-grammatical asymmetry. It is a shift which frees logic from the trammels of psychology, and no less significant, frees psychology from the shackles of epistemology. But it would be a mistake to see this as an attack on Descartes *per se*. To speak of Wittgenstein's reading of Cartesianism is merely to draw attention to his overriding concern with psychological attempts to bridge the epistemological 'gap' between thought and reality.

Wittgenstein already distinguishes between internal and external relations in his earlier writings. Ever since the dictation and writing of the notebooks between 1914 and 1917 - which Wittgenstein compiled prior to the publication of the *Tractatus* - we find that he demanded there to be an **internal** relation between Language and the World [NB 42]. Without going too much into the details concerning what he meant by internal relations and properties (which I have done elsewhere [Gefwert (1) 50-56]) we can establish that he characterized an internal property (relation) by saying that '[a] property is internal if it is unthinkable that its object should not possess it'[T §4.123]. One can therefore characterize an internal relation of an object as determining what kind (what type) of an object it is. Another way of formulating this insight is to say that when an internal relation changes then the object itself becomes a **categorically different** object.

In the *Tractatus* we find that the characteristing feature of an internal relation is that the occurrence of it cannot be said - it can only be **shown** [T §3.262; WVC 54-55; Gefwert (1) 46-56]. For example, the relation that one finds between knowing and what is known amounts, in a logical sense, to such a necessary kind of relation. In contrast to an internal relation we have, the notion of an **external** relation of which the contingent and causal relation, familiar from analytical philosophy and the natural sciences, is an example.[13] It is also important to note, that we, in a causal relation, lack the internal necessity. When an object is being influenced by an external relation it is quite feasible to imagine it to remain unaltered (in contrast to what is the case with an internal relation) even if it should be influenced by different causal relations.

We know that Wittgenstein did not (similarly to Brouwer, but for different reasons) accept any kind of 'causal (and external) theory of meaning'[Gefwert (1) 165-174]. According to the lecture notes written by Moore, he characterized such a theory by saying that, ' ... the meaning of a word [is] some image which it calls up by association'[L (1) 260]. Thus 'meaning' does not stand for any kind of 'process' which could in principle be exhibited by a successful falsifiable (empirical) scientific 'causal (and external) theory of meaning'. We know that

Wittgenstein had previously encountered such a 'causal theory of meaning' in (1) the book *The Analysis of Mind*, by Russell, published in 1921, but also (2) in the book *The Meaning of Meaning*, by C.K. Ogden and I.A. Richards, which was published in 1923.[14] That Wittgenstein was acquainted with both of these books is shown by the fact that he during Lent Term 1930 (lecture A IV) explicitly referred to them when he said that 'Ogden & Richards and Russell consider that the relation of proposition to fact is an external relation; this is not correct. It is an internal relation'[L (2) 9].

The difference between, on the one hand, the 'causal' view and, on the other, the 'intentionalistic' analyses, is clearly revealed when one, for example, investigates mental 'acts' as being directed into the future. Thus we find Russell writing that [15]

> [a] mental occurrence of any kind - sensation, image, belief, or emotion - may be the cause of a series of actions, continuing, unless interrupted, until some more or less definite state of affairs is realized. Such a series of actions we call a 'behaviour cycle' ... The property of causing such a cycle of occurrences is called 'discomfort' ... The cycle ends in a condition of quiescence, or of such actions as tends only to preserve the *status quo*. The state of affairs in which this is a condition of quiescence is called the 'purpose' of the cycle, and the initial mental occurrence involving discomfort is called a 'desire' for the state of affairs that brings quiescence.

For example, a hungry animal is restless until it finds food and only when it has satisfied its hunger will it become quiescent. The situation which will bring such a restless expectation to a halt is said to be the fulfilment of that which is desired. Similarly with humans when we deal with a verbally expressed conscious intention.[16]

According to Russell the expression by which we express a desire to achieve a certain intention amounts to a hypothesis where the truth or falsity will become definitely clear when fulfilled.[17] Wittgenstein who had read this passage by Russell seems to have regarded it as leading to absurdities. We find this indicated in his comment that 'I believe [that] Russell's theory amounts to the following: if I give someone an order and I am happy with what he then does, then he has carried out my order. (If I wanted to eat an apple, and someone punched me in the stomach, taking away my appetite, then it was this punch that I originally wanted.)'[PhR 64].

A similar position to the one stated by Russell had been offered by Ogden and Richards. According to them the target of the intention is *decided* from an unfulfilled desire (expectation) but we know it only as the result of a fulfilled desire.[18] Now, if we call these Russellian 'desires' and the 'expectations' of Ogden and Richards for 'mental processes' and place them besides the characterizations of 'mental processes' that we find in the texts of Wittgenstein we can clearly exhibit the reason for the dissatisfaction of the latter. To begin with, for Wittgenstein, *'mental processes' amounted to interpretations of signs*, the result being that if there really were to be any genuine 'meaning relations' at all then these had to exist within the 'mental processes' where 'intention' was said to exist. It was within these 'mental processes' that some 'primary signs' were to be included and thus the meaning relation had to be an internal relation. By such an internal relation Wittgenstein meant a relation which was to 'point towards itself', that is, it could not be stated but only showed [cf. WVC 55-56].

In contrast to this view, the meaning of the 'mental processes', as stated by Russell and others, where connected to these meaning relations in a contingent (external) way. The problem was that the 'mental process' and the state of affairs corresponding to the causal 'relation of fulfilment' could not be seen from these two factors alone. One needed, in addition, a third factor, the *interpretation*, through which one could conclude that it was precisely *this* state of affairs that satisfied *that* mental phenomenon. According to Russell, the interpretation (verification) of 'this' state of affairs took place by the help of ' ... a sensation with the feeling of expectedness related to memory of the expectation'.[19] As far as Ogden and Richards is concerned, this interpretation (verification) happened ' ... by means of certain external contexts to which it belongs...'.[20] But, according to Wittgenstein, it was precisely the internal relation occurring between the mental process and the fulfilment of its corresponding state of affairs which excluded any need for any additional third component (which, as we saw above, was required by both Russell as well as Ogden & Richards as an interpretation) in order to satisfy the assertion of a 'mental process'.

Thus Wittgenstein writes that [PhR 63; WA (2) 197; Cf. also PhG 157],

> ... for me, there are only two things involved in the fact that a thought is true, i.e., the thought and the fact; whereas for Russell, there are three, i.e., thought, fact and a third event which, if it occurs, is just recognition. This third event, a sort of satisfaction of hunger (the other two being hunger and [the eating of] a particular kind of food), could, for example, be a feeling of pleasure. It's a matter of complete indifference here how we describe this third event; that is irrelevant to the essence of the theory. The causal connection between speech and action is an external relation, whereas we need an internal one.

It is important to understand that such an account, like, for example, the one entertained by Russell, if contemplated upon carefully enough, can easily be shown to lead into absurdities. It is this postulated causal, and external, connection, said to exist between desire and fulfilment, as formulated by Russell (as well as Ogden & Richards), that produces incoherences and absurdities. Indeed, according to Wittgenstein, the result is that '[i]n philosophy we are always in danger of giving a mythology of the symbolism, or of psychology: instead of simply saying what everyone knows and must admit'[PhR 65].

Despite Wittgenstein's critique against a causal view, he did somewhat later, indeed, acknowledge the existence of such a phenomenon like an 'unfulfilled wish', that is, a subconcious wish whose existence or target is only known when the wish is being fulfilled, which one encounters, for example, in psychoanalysis [LC 23; PhG 106; BB 23,57f.]. However, this kind of a 'mental process' is not what interests Wittgenstein in connection with 'intention' because it cannot itself become the provider of meaning for language and which is the task he specifically set for it. In addition, Russell had in his investigation - which primarily was to be concerned only with the relation between primary signs and what they designated - incorporated the psychophysical state of the organism. Thus he seems to have freely mixed the satisfaction of the wish (the mental process) and the wisher (the 'owner' of the mental process). In response to such a view we find that Wittgenstein, much later, stated that '[s]aying "I should like an apple" does not mean: I believe an apple will quell my feeling of nonsatisfaction. *This* proposition is not an expression of a wish but of nonsatisfaction'[PhI §440].

For Russell the relation between the sign and what it designated was a contingent 'associative-causal' relation - and I want to emphasize this point - a relation which could *only* be said. It was, similarly to the propositions of the natural sciences, to be expressed as an hypothesis concerning what kind of associations each image makes in the hearer, i.e., what meaning it has for each individual person. According to Russell images were the real bearers of meaning.[21] Because an image can only depict singular objects it follows that such a 'look alike' between image and object depicted cannot create meaning, for example, in the case of universal concepts (universals). In addition, one needs causally produced emotional influences and, above all, associations. As Russell said, '[i]f we find, in a given case, that our vague image, say, of a nondescript dog, has those associative effects which all dogs would have, but not those belonging to any special dog or kind of dog, we may say that our image means "dog" in general ... The meaning of an image, according to this analysis, is constituted by a combination of likeness and associations'.[22]

After Wittgenstein had read part of the book by Ogden and Richards one finds his dissatisfaction concerning the 'causal view of meaning' to be condensed in the letter he wrote to Ogden, in March, 1923 (in connection with the publication of the English version of the *Tractatus*). In this letter he dismisses their approach and says - despite the fact that he has not yet been able to read the book thoroughly - that he has ' ... however, read in it and I think I ought to confess to you frankly that I believe you have not quite caught the problems which - for instance - I was at in my book (whether or not I have given the correct solution)'[O 69].

Let us therefore attempt in somewhat more detail to illuminate how Wittgenstein goes about to criticize the causal (scientific) way of explaining language. As I have exhibited this, as far as the *Tractatus* is concerned, in *Wittgenstein on Mathematics, Minds and Mental Machines*, I shall only recapitulate it here [Gefwert (1) 56-78]. In order to understand his critique of the causal view correctly we have to set out from the central feature of the *Tractatus* which states that one can ' ... draw a limit to thought, or rather - not to thought, but to the expression of thoughts'[T 3]. Wittgenstein aims to dissolve the problem of interpretation that we met in the writings of Russell as well as in the book by Ogden & Richards. In order to do this he presupposes that the proposition (the picture) has a **common form** with what is depicted: the **logical form** [T §2.17]. Now, this logical form **cannot** by itself be depicted by the picture: it displays it [T §2.172]. That is, the form cannot be expressed in words, it can only be 'reflected' from the propositions: it shows itself [Cf. T §4.121]. Everything else is - by being pictures of what was depicted (or, say, propositions of what was asserted) - of secondary relevance as far as understanding is concerned.

In his later writings those mental (psychological) processes which are found by 'experience' to accompany sentences of our language are not of any concern to Wittgenstein in that '[w]hat does interest [me] is the understanding that is embodied in an explanation of the sense of the sentence'[PhG 45]. What Wittgenstein is interested in, as he states in the *Philosophical Grammar,* is language when regarded as a 'calculus' (in an 'observer' sense) which he characterizes by the metaphor of acting ' ... according to (explicit) rules ... '[PhG 68]. What we have to understand is that the causal explanation of the operation of language as being a 'psychophysical mechanism' is '... itself a linguistic act and stands ouside the calculus'[PhG 70]. For example, if we take a human being to function like a mechanical 'computer' which 'reads' the notes from a punched tape then we can say that Wittgenstein would be interested in those *rules* by which the holes of the tape transform into computations and *not* in the actual physical function of the tape-mechanism of the 'computer'. Wittgenstein is not interested in the factual and causal influence exhibited by the dependency of numerous contingent facts in the world like, for example, the state of the mechanism when producing one calculation here and another calculation there [Cf. PhG 69-70].

In addition, Wittgenstein - with his critique of the view of 'intention' as exhibiting a causal and external relation - was not only adressing himself to philosophers like, for example, Russell, and linguists, like Ogden & Richards, but, in addition, also to adherers of behaviourist psychology stating their claims, for example, on the work of the Russian physiologist Ivan Pavlov (1849-1916). But, in addition, there are also many other famous behaviourists in psychology. As an example one can provide the works of B.F. Skinner (1904-1990). Wittgenstein thought that the behaviourists altogether missed the point that he himself was making (that expectation contained a 'picture' of what was expected). This point seems to be reflected when he writes that '[t]he expectation, thought, wish, etc., that p will be the case, for processes having the multiplicity that finds expression in p, and thus only if they are *articulated* ... I only call an *articulated* process a thought; you could therefore say "only what has an articulated expression". (Salivation - no matter how precisely measured - is *not* what I call expectation)'[PhR 70].

But, we also have to be aware that Wittgenstein is not only repudiating behaviourism as a doctrine but is simultaneously disregarding the doctrine of rationalism. As an example of this latter view we can mention the hypothetical doctrines of Chomsky in the sense of a Generative Grammar.[23] He offers a series of empirical 'models' of linguistics in which meaning is found somewhere else than in sound or syntax - in psychology - so that meaning is an internal 'component' of language (which is somehow to be shown to exist by scientific means). However, what this 'component' amounts to has never so far been causally explained in a satisfactory way. In fact, if we follow Wittgenstein, it **cannot** be causally explained in the first place because this 'component' amounts to an illusion.[24] What is important to understand is that *Wittgenstein never regarded his writings as being a contribution of any kind to the empirical science of linguistics or empirical Cognitive Science.*

We can now establish that by regarding 'intention' as central, in order to exhibit the phenomenon of language, Wittgenstein, simultaneously, sets himself in opposition to any 'causal' (scientific) conception of (primary) language. As far as problems related to causality as a way of explaining language is concerned, Wittgenstein never had any reason to change his position, i.e., to emphasize the point that to explain language in a causal way does not amount to explain it *as* language. A causal (scientific) explanation of language amounts to explain language as something else (say, as some kind of 'cognitive process'). We find this point echoed when Wittgenstein later writes that ' ... if it were shewn how the words "Come to me" act on the person addressed, so that finally, given certain conditions, the muscles of his legs are innervated, and so on - should we feel that that sentence lost the character of a *sentence?*'[PhI §493]. Note, that, according to Wittgenstein, the same point applies to formal languages as well. When we perform a proof we do not exhibit any causal connection between the calculation (the activity of proof) and the calculated theorem (or result). That is, a calculation (a proof) is no empirical experiment in that '[t]here are no causal connections in a calculation, only the connection of the pattern. And it makes no difference to this that we work over the proof in order to accept it. That we are therefore tempted to say that it arose as the result of a psychological experiment. For the psychical course of events is not psychologically investigated when we calculate'[RFM VII §18].

In a similar way, like a causal analysis, which freely mixes a 'mental process' and the 'owner' of that 'process', a causal process also freely mixes the effect of a sign and its meaning. For example, a senseless command like 'Wine to me log!' in the appropriate context (for example, when adressing a log in a shed when suffering from a state of *delirium tremens*) is not necessarily without effect. It might have the effect of getting a possible hearer to gape. However, the point with this 'command' was not to get the hearer to gape, not even if the giver of the order had wished and awaited such a reaction [Cf. PhI §498; PhG 189].25 The important point is that even if one can, as an answer to the question 'Why ... ?', provide an answer by giving the cause *(Ursache)* as well as the reason *(Grund)*[Cf. PhG 101], it is only the latter which is *philosophically* relevant. In philosophical discussions one often finds that there is confusion between 'reason' and 'cause'. The *reason* that a picture means something is to be found - even if not necessarily in the picture itself, because a 'picture can always be meant in different ways' - in some factor which is relevant to the picture at the moment when it is used. As Wittgenstein says, even if a picture can be understood in different ways '... that doesn't mean that the way the picture is meant only emerges when it elicits a certain reaction, for the intention is already expressed in the way I *now* compare the picture with reality'[PhR 65].

It is precisely intention which makes the picture a picture of reality and '[o]nly the intended picture reaches up to reality like a yardstick'[PhG 146; cf. Z §233].26 Russell's causal picture (like the behaviourist picture) doesn't 'reach' anywhere and there really doesn't occur any comparison to reality in connection with it. One just has to wait for reactions for different state of affairs to occur so that one can make it clear, one step at a time, what picture we are dealing with. Russell's picture (like the behaviourist one) is passive, it simply 'happens', whereas the picture for Wittgenstein is *active,* it is ' ... something that we do, otherwise it would be just dead'[PhG 156]. *It is this 'active element' which amounts to the 'intention'.* But we are still left with the question: If 'intention' cannot be properly (scientifically) explained through a causal relation then what does this mysterious 'intention' amount to? That is, with the words of Wittgenstein, we are forced to ask: What is this ' ... uncheckable, ... so-to-speak metaphysical element ... '[PhR 63] that we encounter but which is not a causal relation [Infra III.5]?

II.5 THE PROBLEM OF VERIFICATION

When it comes to Wittgenstein's post-1929 texts in philosophy we have to investigate his writings on the topic of 'verification' in connection with mathematics. Among Waismann's papers, presented at the Königsberg symposium, we find the verification principle formulated, in McGuinness' translation, as follows: 'The meaning of a mathematical concept is the mode of its use and the sense *(Sinn)* of a mathematical proposition is the method of its verification *(Die Bedeutung eines mathematischen Begriffes ist die Art seines Gebrauches, der Sinn eines mathematischen Satzes die Methode seiner Verification)*' [WVC 20]. This is Wittgenstein's version of the maxim adopted by the Logical Empiricists as the *Principle of Verification*, but here, interestingly enough, intended to be applied to mathematics. Thus any interpretation of Wittgenstein's philosophy of mathematics claiming to be correct must provide an account of how the two basic points advocated by Wittgenstein are to be understood.

We shall, below, compare Wittgenstein's idea of verification with the one endorsed by the logical empiricist school in somewhat more detail. At this stage, however, in connection with Waismann's talk at the Königsberg conference, it is enough to state that it seems highly probable that Wittgenstein did not get his verificationist ideas from the Vienna Circle, despite a brief flirtation with their version around 1929, but from his earlier philosophy. Indeed, as pointed out by Wrigley,[27] there is some indirect evidence that verificationism in the context of mathematics, *as Wittgenstein understood verification*, was always present even in the *Tractatus*, (in the form of operations [Gefwert (1) 94-101]) although by no means in such an explicit form as we find it formulated in his post-1929 texts and in the writings by the scholars of the Vienna Circle commenting on this principle.

The philosophers of the Vienna Circle, in their *Manifesto*, stated that they had been influenced, for example, in logic and mathematics, by Leibniz, Peano, Frege, Schröder, Hilbert, Russell and Whitehead and in science by Helmholtz, Riemann, Mach, Poincaré, Duhem,

Boltzmann and Einstein.28 But, perhaps more than anyone else, they were influenced by Schlick's *Allgemeine Erkenntnislehre* and Wittgenstein's *Tractatus Logico-Philosophicus.*29 Appearing in 1921, the *Tractatus* was the object of Hahn's seminar in 1922; it was read and discussed by members of the circle for the first time in 1924, and for the second time in 1926. Now, the following question emerges: Did all the members of the circle mean the same thing by the notion of verification as Wittgenstein? We shall, briefly, attempt to answer this question here. In order to understand Wittgenstein's conception of verification in connection with mathematics it is necessary to understand it within his novel philosophical context in general. This context sets out from the insight that when dealing with philosophical problems an attitude towards the target of investigation inspired by the scientific method of theory and experiment is mistaken [Supra II.2].

This insight Wittgenstein carried over to his post-1929 conception of verification. According to him the verificationist principle needed to be dislodged from 'theoretical' overtones. It does not have its conceptual home within any theoretical activity called 'philosophy' modelled after the way theoretical sciences are performed [Infra VI.3]. That is, by 'verification' is not to be understood the task of constructing, for example, some explicit 'theory of meaning' in the sense of Dummett [Infra V.1]. This is indirectly seen, in Wittgenstein's comment in one of his lectures on philosophy in 1932-1933, when he says that '[i]f you want to know the meaning of a sentence, ask for its verification. I stress the point that the meaning of a symbol is its place in the calculus, the way it is used. ... Attending to the way the meaning of a sentence is explained makes clear the connection between meaning and verification' [L (3) 29]. When we explain to a person how to perform a proof (to perform a calculation) this explanation shows how to verify the theorem proved. *By proving correctly we verify the mathematical statement.* Basically, it was this that enabled Wittgenstein to equate provability and verification in mathematics, i.e., as he said in 1929-30, '[a]s the immediate datum is to a proposition which it verifies, so is the arithmetical relation we see in the structure to the equation which it verifies'[PhR 200].

We find that Wittgenstein during his later years denied that he had ever accepted the Verification Principle.[30] This seems strange since there is a large amount of indirect evidence which is easily interpreted as corroborating that Wittgenstein for a short period of time, around 1929-1930, had a 'positivist interlude'.[31] Admittedly, we find that Wittgenstein writes and states in his discussions immediatedly after his return to philosophy in 1929 a number of statements which could be interpreted in this way. For example, one finds that he writes statements like 'Every proposition is a signpost for a verification'[PhR 174], 'The verification is not one token of the truth, it is the sense of the proposition'[PhR 200], 'In order to determine the sense of a proposition, I should have to know a very specific procedure for when to count the proposition as verified'[WVC 47], 'Where there are different verifications there are also different meanings'[WVC 53], 'The sense of a proposition is the method of its verification'[WVC 79] and 'I should like to say: for any question there is always a corresponding *method* of finding. Or you might say, a question denotes a method of searching ... To understand the sense of a proposition means knowing how the issue of its truth or falsity is to be decided ... You cannot compare a picture with reality unless you can set it against it as a yardstick. One must be able to lay the proposition alongside reality'[PhR 77]. These remarks ought to convince even the most sceptical reader that during this brief period in the beginning of the turn of the decade 1929-1930 Wittgenstein can easily be interpreted as being committed to some kind of verificationism in a sense required by the logical empiricists. Nevertheless, to assume this amounts to a mistake.

As far as the empirical sciences are concerned the members of the Logical Empiricist movement (e.g., Rudolf Carnap (1891-1970), Carl Hempel (b. 1905)) applied the principle of verification in their quest for a systematic 'theory of meaning' or a verificationist formal semantics. Thus the principle of verification within this foundational school is to be understood as being a methodological principle which is part of a certain research programme the aim of which is to produce a certain 'theory of empirical meaning' (as, for example, in the structure by Simon when investigating Cognitive Science). It seems to be a fact that the logical empiricists (for example, Carnap, Feigl, Neurath, etc.) understood the *Tractatus* as incorporating a principle of verification, but only for empirical propositions. Especially they read the remark that ' ... in order to be able to say that a point is black or white, I must first know when a point is called black, and then white: in order to be able to say, "'p' is true (or false)", I must have determined in what circumstances I call "p" true, and in so doing I determine the sense of the proposition'[T §4.063] in this way.

This paragraph was by the logical empiricists interpreted as providing evidence that Wittgenstein was committed to some kind of (theoretical) verificationism. Such a reading of the *Tractatus* by the logical empiricists would have constituted an interpretation based on a viewpoint of radical verificationism. Thus, for example, Carnap, for one, consistently credited Wittgenstein with originating this principle. 'The requirement of verifiability [for meaningfulness]', he wrote, in his article *Testability and Meaning,* in 1936, ' ... was first stated by Wittgenstein'.[32] Now, Wittgenstein was not someone to take a misinterpretation of his views lightly, and if verificationism were as remote from the views of the *Tractatus* as is commonly assumed, then we can be sure that Wittgenstein would have had no interest in taking part in any further discussions with these people who had so radically misunderstood his ideas. Yet the texts that we find in Wittgenstein's *Nachlass* gives the impression that he accepted the Vienna Circle's interpretation. And this can only mean that despite its apparent absence from the *Tractatus* some form of radical verificationism had always been implicit in it, and that the only change after 1929 was that it became fully explicit.

However, interestingly enough, already at the time of writing the *Philosophical Remarks* we find indications that Wittgenstein seems to have distanced himself from the position taken by the Logical Empiricists. According to him it is not important to formulate any novel 'philosophical theories of meaning'. What is important is to properly understand conceptual problems occurring in our everyday (and formal) language. Thus we find him writing that '[a]ll that is possible and necessary is to separate what is essential from what is inessential in *our* language'[PhR 51-52; cf. 84]. But the question is: If this remark (and similar ones) in the *Philosophical Remarks* do not indicate adherence to positivism on Wittgenstein's part, then, what does this assumed verificationism amount to? Monk (admittedly in connection with Wittgenstein's 'phenomenology') has characterized the situation by saying that Wittgenstein ' ... uses the tools adopted by the Vienna Circle for a task diametrically opposed to their own'.[33] But what does such a claim mean as far as verification and, say, mathematics is concerned?

As far as the foundations of mathematics is concerned we know (1) that the Logical Empiricists adhered to the logicist school and (2) that within this foundational research programme verification plays no explicit role whatsoever. This is testified, for example, in their *Manifesto* where the members of the Circle explicitly declared that '[t]he conception of mathematics [is] tautological in character, which is based on the investigations of Russell and Wittgenstein, is also held by the Vienna Circle'.[34] The situation, however, is not as simple as this. Why? To begin with, according to the logical empiricists, any attempt to connect a mathematical investigation with verification is not correct as we said above. For them mathematical propositions were (in principle) reducible to logical propositions. Thus they were analytical truths: 'classical' truth-functional tautologies. This position amounted - as far as Wittgenstein is concerned - to the mistaken position they assumed that he had taken in the *Tractatus* [Gefwert (1) 94-101]. For example, according to Hahn, '[t]he propositions of mathematics are of exactly the same kind as the propositions of logic: they are tautologous [and] we have no doubt that the belief in the tautological character of mathematics is essentially correct'.[35] But more important than this is the fact that certain logical empiricists wanted to formulate a verificationist 'theory of meaning', or a 'verificationst semantics', in order to deal with 'philosophical' - in fact foundational - problems concerning the empirical sciences [Supra II.2]. We are thus faced with the problem that when Wittgenstein talks of 'verification' he - when connecting it with mathematics - must mean by this expression something completely different than the members of the Vienna Circle meant by it. This requires some clarification in order to be correctly understood.

To begin with, the famous 'verification principle of meaning' does not occur in the manifesto of the Logical Empiricist's pamphlet *Die wissenschaftliche Weltauffassung: Der Wiener Kreis* which was compiled in 1929 through a combined effort by Feigl, Neurath and Carnap.36 It was only at a later stage that the principle of verification was explicitly adopted and this as a result of the direct (but misunderstood) influence of Wittgenstein. The principle is for the first time explicitly stated in Waismann's *Logische Analyse des Wahrscheinlichkeitsbegriffs* in 1930.37 It is also a fact that the members of the Vienna Circle never connected the 'verification principle of meaning' with mathematics. On the contrary, verification was reserved for directly verifiable (observational) sentences, for example, factual sentences that are uttered in connection with empirical investigations as the results of experiments in physics. Thus the basic feature in the principle of verification is that a (synthetic) sentence which seems to be concerned with some feature of reality is meaningful only if it can be corroborated by observations.

However, one finds that for the members of the Vienna Circle *mathematical* propositions, in contrast to empirical propositions, were characterized as being 'classical' truth-functional tautologies in accordance with Logicism. This, however, was not the case with Wittgenstein [Gefwert (1) 118-125] who understood mathematical propositions (mathematical equations) as exhibiting their truths in themselves and thus being reminiscent of Kant's synthetic a priori, i.e., as he explicitly said, '[w]hat I said earlier about the nature of arithmetical equations and about an equation's not being replaceable by a tautology explains - I believe - what Kant means when he insists that $7 + 5 = 12$ is not an analytic proposition, but synthetic *a priori*'[PhR 129]. With this comment Wittgenstein wanted to state that what Kant and the kantian followers had attempted to *say* concerning the truth of the equations of mathematics, he, on the other hand, regarded as being *shown* by mathematical equations. The relation between a mathematical proof and theorem proved is internal [Gefwert (1) 56-69].

But, we are also left with a confusing situation as far as the interpretation by the Vienna Circle of mathematical statements as being 'classical' truth-functional tautologies and the explicit claim of adherence to the *Tractatus* as a guiding influence is concerned. It seems that *the logical empiricists all along completely misunderstood the way mathematical propositions are to be understood according to the Tractatus* [Gefwert (1) 70-77]. Thus it seems mistaken to state, for example, as Haller does, that '[i]t is not my intention here to impose on anyone the belief that Wittgenstein should have been a conventionalist, in spite of the fact that I cannot see how one can put some of the main ideas of his philosophy of mathematics on the opposite (non conventionalist) side'.[38]

The difference between the foundational schools and Wittgenstein's novel philosophical 'method' is that Logicism, Formalism and Intuitionism, respectively, advocated certain mathematical methods in order to solve the foundations crisis which was generally acknowledged to exist in mathematics. These foundational research programmes exhibited different (conventionalist) mathematical methods which were part of mathematics and formal logic proper in order to cope with the 'foundational crisis'. Wittgenstein's comments (and questions), on the other hand, are philosophical and not mathematical (nor scientific) in nature [Infra VI.2]. *Wittgenstein regarded verificationism primarily as a means of clarifying how the meaning of a proposition is determined by its relation to other propositions.* Here verification is not connected with any 'foundational' investigations of mathematics of any kind. It is not part of any foundational research programme the aim of which is to produce some kind of 'theory of meaning' for mathematics [T §5.132].

As Wittgenstein understands the term 'verification' it belongs to the sphere of mathematical calculation (as well as empirical practices) whereas the aim of philosophy, in mathematics, is to purge the method of proof (method of verification) from unnecessary and redundant expressions (concepts)[Gefwert (1) 195-201]. *Thus it belongs to the philosophical activity to resolve conceptual problems occurring in proofs (and calculations)*. While this philosophical 'method', in connection with mathematics, stresses the importance of conceptual investigations of calculations (proofs) as the target for philosophy, it does not employ any foundational 'machinery' in these investigations. It does not require any kind of formal language in order to succeed in clarifying philosophical (conceptual) problems occurring in proofs and calculations. As far as Wittgenstein is concerned, the emphasis on verification in mathematics is solely inspired by his calculus conception of mathematics [Gefwert (1) 94-101].

Mathematics consists of a multitude of different calculations and to perform a proof (calculation) means to verify (to judge) a mathematical proposition to be correct. When encountering conceptual problems we investigate such proofs (and calculations) by clarifying the 'logical syntax' of mathematical (pseudo) propositions [Gefwert (1) 195-200]. We do it, for example, when performing analytical calculations because they exhibit the structure (the inference-rules) of the 'logical syntax' applied in the informal (synthetical) proofs (and, thus, they simultaneously clarify any conceptual problems occurring in them)[Gefwert (1) 201-209]. We find indirect evidence for this view in Waismann's lecture at Königsberg where he said that '[t]he significance of a mathematical proposition is the method of its verification. (From this it follows that mathematical propositions and their proofs cannot be separated)'[WM 61]. Needless to say, this last point was never appreciated and properly understood by the philosophers, logicians and mathematicians of the Vienna Circle.

Wittgenstein's philosophical method was not motivated by the requirement of a novel foundational research programme as were the three other foundational schools of Logicism, Formalism and Intuitionism. What Wittgenstein stressed was the need for a philosophical investigation, the explicit aim of which was to clarify the conceptual problems occurring within different mathematical calculations [Gefwert (1) 195-200]. The aim of his philosophical method was to dissolve any philosophical, i.e., conceptual, problems that we find within different calculations of mathematics in order to get rid of these problems once and for all. The expectations for this 'method' seem to have been high because, as Waismann said, '[n]othing serves to remove more quickly and thoroughly the confusions and errors which the use of ordinary word-language (with its grammatical categories) brings about'[WM 61]. By the expression 'word-language' Waismann seems to refer to what was by Wittgenstein called 'prose'[Gefwert (1) 195-200]. In a footnote to the quotation above Waismann specified Wittgenstein's point concerning the interdependence of a mathematical proposition and its proof, i.e., that '[t]his yields in particular the following important point of view: a proposition and a proof must be regarded and treated as one and the same thing in mathematics. One must not believe that mathematical propositions possess a meaning of their own. Only a proof gives sense to a mathematical proposition, however, and as long as one does not have a proof one does not know what the expression means'[WM 67, n. 4].

It is this closed whole - the calculation providing meaning for a mathematical proposition - which has to be purged of unnecessary **interpretations** (Logicism, Intuitionism, Formalism) by performing philosophical investigations (conceptual analysis) which clarifies how the proposition is verified (calculated, proved). Thus the term 'verification' shows what we do when we perform a mathematical calculation, or proof, whereas a philosophical investigation purifies the calculation from 'prose' by conceptual analysis [Gefwert (1) 195-200]. The latter characterizes what concepts we apply in a calculation when it is being performed as an (analytical) investigation of, say, an informal (synthetical) proof (cf., for example, the distinction made by Martin-Löf in a proof regarding a proof-act/process, proof-object/construction as well as proof-trace/track).[39] We find this insight to be reflected in a remark that Wittgenstein, much later, made: 'Asking whether and how a proposition can be verified is only a particular way of asking "How d'you mean?". The answer is a contribution to the grammar of the proposition'[PhI §353]. One can thus say that it is a fact that '[t]he distinction between Wittgenstein's version of the verificationist principle and that propounded by the Logical Positivists is thus subtle but extremely important'.[40]

Notes

[1] Popper, Karl, 'Autobiography of Karl Popper', in Schilpp, P.A.,(ed.), *The Philosophy of Karl Popper,* LaSalle, Illinois (1974), op.cit., p. 62; Popper, Karl R. and Eccles, John C., *The Self and Its Brain,* Berlin, Heidelberg, London, New York (1977). Here Popper writes that '[t]o sum up, I share with old-fashioned materialists the view that material things are real, and even the view that, for us, solid material bodies are the paradigms of reality. And I also share with the modern materialists or physicalists the view that forces and fields of forces, charges, and so on - that is, theoretical physical entities other than matter - are also real' op.cit., p.10.

[2] Descartes, René, 'Meditations on first philosophy', in Cottingham, J., Stoothoff, R. and Murdoch, D., transl., *The Philosophical Writings of Descartes,* Vol. II, Cambridge University Press: Cambridge (1986), p. 18.

[3] According to Patton and Wheeler this view ' ... demolishes the view we once held that the universe sits safely "out there", that we can observe what goes on in it from behind a foot-thick slab of plate glass without ourselves being involved in what goes on ... We have to cross out that old word "observer" and replace it by the new word "participator". In some strange sense the quantum principle tells us that we are dealing with a participatory universe'. Cf. Patton, C.M. and Wheeler, J.A., 'Is Physics Legislated by Cosmogony', in C.J. Isham, R. Penrose and D.W. Sciama (eds), *Quantum Gravity: An Oxford Symposium,* Oxford University Press: Oxford (1975), pp. 560-562, 564-568; Cf. also Wheeler, J.A., 'Genesis and Observership', in Butts, R.E. & Hintika, J. (eds), *Foundational Problems in the Special Sciences,* D. Reidel Publishing Company: Dordrecht, Holland/Boston, U.S.A. (1975), pp. 3-33.

[4] Locke, John, *An Essay Concerning Human Understanding,* Book III, chap. II, sec. I.

[5] Lyons, John, *Chomsky,* Modern Masters Series (1970), op.cit., pp. 11,16.

[6] Chomsky, Noam, *Syntactic Structures,* Mouton: The Hague (1976).

[7] Dineen, Francis P., *An Introduction to General Linguistics,* New York (1967), op.cit., p. 4.

[8] For the scientific view of cognitive linguistics cf. De Saussure, Ferdinand, *Course in General Linguistics,* translated by Baskin, W., (1960). We can now ask: Was Saussure a linguist or a philosopher? He had a background in philology, but when one looks at the questions that he wanted to answer with his innovative ideas ('la language', the concept od structure, the synchronic aspect of language, etc.), one is inclined to say that Saussure was no less of a philosopher of language than Frege - who, by the way, was a professor of mathematics. One can say that both Frege and Saussure were philosophers of language to a far greater degree than many contemporaneous professors of philosophy were; Chomsky's view of linguistics was originally published in Chomsky, Noam, *Syntactic Structures,* The Hague (1957). Chomsky is, of course, deeply influenced by Saussure and derives his competence/performance distinction from Saussure's equally dangerous *language/parole.* Baskin's Introduction shows that de Saussure's career is a remarkable prefiguring of Chomsky's leap from the atomistic frying pan into the universal fire; For a critique of Chomkys generative grammar, from a Wittgensteinian position, cf. Robinson, Ian, *The New Grammarians' Funeral: A critique of Noam Chomsky's linguistics,* Cambridge University Press: Cambridge (1975).

[9] Chomsky, Noam, *Rules and Representations,* Oxford University Press: Oxford (1980), op.cit., p. 118.

[10] As to their respective views of scientific explanation, the contrast between the two traditions is ususaly characterized as **causal** versus **teleological** explanation. For an introduction to the these two terms, cf. von Wright, G.H., *Explanation and understaning,* Routledge & Kegan Paul: London (1971), pp. 1-33. For a teleological (and scientific) explanation cf. also Granit, Ragnar, *The Purposive Brain,* The MIT Press: Cambridge, Massachusetts and London, England (1977).

[11] Stenlund, Sören, 'Language, Action and Mind' in Johnson, D.E. and Erneling, C.E. (eds.), *The Future of the Cognitive Revolution,* Oxford University Press: Oxford (1977), p. 304.

[12] Hallett, Garth, *A Companion to Wittgenstein's "Philosophical Investigations"*, Ithaca and London (1977), p. 625; C.W.K. Mundell, '"Private Language" and Wittgenstein's Kind of Behaviourism', *Philosophical Quarterly* **16** (1966), p. 35; C.S. Chichara and J.A. Fodor, 'Operationalism and Ordinary Language: A Critique of Wittgenstein', *American Philosophical Quarterly* **2** (1965), p. 282fn.; Day, W.F., 'On Certain Similarities between the Philosophical Investigations and the Operationism of B.F. Skinner', *Journal of Experimental Analysis of Behaviour* **12** (1969), pp. 489-506; Waller, B., 'Chomsky, Wittgenstein, and the Behaviourist Perspective', *Behaviorism* **5** (1977), p. 49fn. Waller is definitely mistaken when he implies that Wittgenstein is a materialist [p. 45].

[13] For a contrast between an internal relation and a causal relation, cf., Kenny, A., *Wittgenstein*, London (1973), p. 66; The first analysis of causes is, of course, to be found in the writings of Aristotle. In modern times the most famous individual schema for the logic of a causal explanation was developed by Carl Hempel (b. 1905) in his *Aspects of Scientific Explanation*, Free Press: New York (1965). This schema is called the 'nomological-deductive' model and is also known as the 'subsumption theory' of explanation. For a good exposition of this idealistic model, cf. Saariluoma, Pertti, *Foundational Analysis, Presuppositions in experimental psychology*, Routledge: London (1997), pp. 96-99. But, note that we also have different explanations of what causality amounts to. In general, one can say that the popularity of causal explanations make it understandable why they have become the explanatory ideal for psychology. For a good introduction, cf. for example, von Wright, G.H., *Explanation and understanding*, Routledge and Kegan Paul: London (1971), pp. 34-82.

[14] Russell, Bertrand, *The Analysis of Mind*, London (1921), tenth impression 1971; Ogden, C.K., and Richards, I.A., *The Meaning of Meaning: a Study of the Influence of Language upon Thought*, The International Library of Psychology, Philosophy and Scientific Method. Kegan Paul, Trench, Trubner & Co., Ltd. London (1923), tenth edition (eight impression) 1972; We know that Wittgenstein had read parts of Ogden's and Richard's book because he wrote in a letter to Ogden that he had not been quite well and '[t]his is the reason why I have not yet been able to read your book thoroughly. I have however read in it and I think I ought to confess to you frankly that I believe you have not quite caught the problems which - for instance - I was at in my book (whether or not I have given the correct

solution)', Wittgenstein, Ludwig, *Letters to C.K. Ogden with Comments on the English Translation of the Tractatus Logico-Philosophicus.* Edited with an Introduction by G.H. von Wright, Basil Blackwell: Oxford and Routledge & Kegan Paul: London and Boston (1973), p. 69.

[15] Russell, B., *The Analysis of Mind,* [cf.n.14] op.cit., p. 75.

[16] Ibid., p. 82.

[17] Ibid., p. 67.

[18] Ogden, C.K. & Richards, I.A., *The Meaning of Meaning,* [cf.n.14] p. 62.

[19] Russell, B., *The Analysis of Mind,* [cf.n.14] op.cit., p. 270.

[20] Ogden, C.K. & Richards, I.A., *The Meaning of Meaning,* [cf.n.14] op.cit., p. 62.

[21] As Hacker has pointed out, it has the effect that ' ... the consequences of Russell's account are the following absurdities: (a) that we often do not find out what we wanted until our desire is satisfied, i.e., until the behaviour cycle has terminated in a state quiescence; (b) that we are often mistaken about what we wanted (e.g., it would make sense to say "I thought I wanted to go to London, but I actually wanted a piece of cake"); (c) that if we do not know what we want, our knowledge must rest on induction from past experience (e.g., "This feeling of dissatisfaction has, in the past, been alleviated by an apple, so I must want an apple"); (d) that if one wants something one has never had before, one cannot know what one wants', Hacker, P.M.S., *Wittgenstein: Meaning and Mind, An analytical commentary on the Philosophical Investigations,* Volume **3**, Oxford (1990), op.cit., p. 236.

[22] Russell, B., *The Analysis of Mind,* [cf.n.14] op.cit., p. 209.

[23] According to Chomsky he conceived the 'grammar of a language' as the set of rules that every competent speaker internalizes. Cf. Chomsky, Noam, *Aspects of the Theory of Syntax,* Cambridge: MIT Press (1965).

[24] For a critique of Chomsky's ideas concerning the possibility of a Generative Grammar from a Wittgensteinian point of view, cf. Robinson, Ian, *The New Grammarians' Funeral: A Critique of Noam Chomsky's linguistics,* Cambridge University Press: Cambridge (1975). According to Robinson,

'[Chomsky's] 'science' is a framework of would-be perspicuous presentation brought ready-made to the facts and procedures of the study of language. Chomsky is better than his predecessors in seeing the need to put the facts together in a real order; but his failure to see what Wittgenstein is driving at is the final evidence that linguistics for Chomsky cannot be a discipline, i.e., a form of thought with its own self-validating procedures. It does not follow that linguistics, as Chomsky wishes, could be successfully subsumed under psychology', op.cit., p. 155.

[25] Cf. the critique of the causally based *reductio ad absurdum* investigation of art that we find in *Lectures and Conversations* [LC 34].

[26] The sentence in question occurs within brackets in the *Philosophical Grammar* as well as in *Zettel*. Thus it sets the problem and does not provide the answer within this context. It seems, however, probable that the origin of this sentence is to be found somewhere in Wittgenstein's earlier notes or that it, at least, contains his thought which he at some point regarded as correct.

[27] Wrigley, Michael, 'The Origins of Wittgenstein's Verificationism', *Synthèse* 78 (1989), p. 283.

[28] Carnap, Rudolf, Neurath, Otto, Hahn, Hans., 'Wissenschaftliche Weltauffassung: Der Wiener Kreis', Wien (1929). Translated into English in Neurath, O., *Empiricism and Sociology*, Dordrecht (1973).

[29] Schlick, Moritz, *Allgemeine Erkenntnislehre*, translated by Blumberg, A.E., as *General Theory of Knowledge*, New York (1974).

[30] Gasking, D.A.T. and Jackson, A.C., 'Wittgenstein as a Teacher', in Fann, K.T., (ed.), *Ludwig Wittgenstein: The Man and His Philosophy*, New Jersey and Sussex (1967), p. 54.

[31] Hacker, P.M.S., *Insight and Illusion*, Oxford (1972), pp. 104-111.

[32] Carnap, Rudolf, 'Testability and Meaning', *Philosophy of Science*, Vol. **3**, No. 4, (October 1936), op.cit., p. 422; Cf. also his statements in 'Remarks by Author' from 1957 added to the reprint of 'The Old and the New Logic', in Ayer, A. J., (ed.), *Logical Positivism*, London (1959), p. 146.

[33] Monk, Ray, *Ludwig Wittgenstein: The Duty of Genius*, London (1990), op.cit., p. 292.

[34] Neurath, Otto, *Empiricism and Sociology,* Neurath, M. & Cohen, R.S., (eds.), Dordrecht (1973), op.cit., p. 311.

[35] Hahn, Hans, 'Logic, Mathematics and Knowledge of Nature', in Ayer, A.J., (ed.), *Logical Positivism,* London (1959), p. 159.

[36] 'Wissenschaftliche Weltauffassung: Der Wiener Kreis', Wien (1929). Translated into English in Neurath, O., *Empiricsm and Sociology,* Dordrecht (1973). For an account of the history behind this pamphlet, cf. Haller, Rudolf, 'Was Wittgenstein a Neopositivist?', in Haller, R., *Questions on Wittgenstein,* London (1988), pp. 31-32.

[37] Waismann, F., 'Logische Analyse des Wahrscheinlichkeitsbegriffs', *Erkenntnis* (1930).

[38] Haller, Rudolf, 'Was Wittgenstein A Relativist', in Egidi, Rosario, (ed.), *Wittgenstein: Mind and Language,* Dordrecht, Boston, London (1995), op.cit., p. 225.

[39] Sundholm, Göran, 'Questions of Proof', *Manuscrito,* Campinas, **XVI** (2): 47-70, outubro (1993).

[40] Shanker, Stuart, *Wittgenstein and the Turning-Point in the Philosophy of Mathematics,* London (1987), op.cit., p. 42.

III Thought and Privacy

III.1 INTRODUCTION

In an unpublished manuscript, written in 1913, Russell states that 'I think it may be shown that acquaintance with logical form is involved before explicit thought about logic begins, in fact as soon as we can understand a sentence'.[1] Wittgenstein had seen the manuscript and was well acquainted with it. We also know from the available literary sources that Wittgenstein was hostile towards this view - that logical form is somehow distinguished (logically independent) from language (which we, for example, meet in certain interpretations in the modern topic of Cognitive Science) - and that he therefore did reject Russell's thesis. He maintained the insight that logic cannot depend on the experiencing of a fact, whether logical or empirical [NB 3]. Furthermore, in 1914, Wittgenstein explicitly criticized Russell's theory which asserted the existence of an abstract formal structure [NB 2-3] where the logical experience of the structure would precede understanding of any proposition whatsoever. Russell assigned the conditions of the meanings to the elements inherent in the very constituents of the propositions. Therefore, according to Wittgenstein, it is a fact that Russell in his text was ' ... trying to express something that cannot be expressed'[NB 31].

It seems that Wittgenstein entertained the position that a proposition achieves its meaning ' ... as if it were off its own bat'[NB 26]. We know that he retained this position in the *Tractatus* which was published in 1921 (the English version in 1922)[Gefwert (1) 56-69]. For example, he wrote that ' ... the precedent to which we are constantly inclined to appeal must reside in the symbol itself'[T §5.525]. This clearly shows the continuation of his thought during the turn of the decade concerning the question of how a proposition achieves its meaning. We can therefore conclude that this was the situation, as far as the problem of thought (and 'intention') is concerned, when Wittgenstein, in 1920, left active work in philosophy.

But, we also know that he, at the end of the decade, returned to this problem when he began to preoccupy himself with philosophical problems again [Supra I.1]. It is therefore of crucial interest to investigate the situation in somewhat more detail as it occures at this time.

Wittgenstein took up the problem of 'thought' and 'intention' in 1929 when he had returned to Cambridge. In his later texts we encounter two themes which, indeed, could be characterized as the 'problem of thought' and the 'problem of intention'. 'Thinking is the use of symbols', he puts down in his notebook on June 29, 1930, adding, some pages later, that '[t]hought, insofar as one can speak of it at all, must be something quite pedestrian'[MS 108]. We also know that Wittgenstein was occupied with, for example, the problem of 'intention' from 1929 to 1950 because, in his later years, as late as in October 1948, he wrote that [RPP II §178]

> Intent, intention, is neither an emotion, a mood, nor yet a sensation or image. It is not a state of consciousness. It does not have a genuine duration. Intention can be called a mental disposition. This term is misleading inasmuch as one does not perceive such a disposition within himself as a matter of experience.

From this quotation one can notice that the 'problem of intention' was still an important topic for him at this late stage of his life. But what, exactly, did Wittgenstein mean by 'thought' and 'intention'? How is one to understand the 'problem of thought' and the 'problem of intention' (for example, when we perform a calculation in mathematics or program a task in computing science with the explicit intention of achieving a certain result)? It is these problems that we shall investigate here and try to provide an answer to.

We shall focus the attention on the theme of 'thought' and 'intention', as we find that they are being investigated by Wittgenstein in the beginning of the 1930's, in the texts which he came to call *Philosophische Bemerkungen* [WA I-IV]. It is in these manuscripts that we find, for example, the whole complex of problems concerning the topic of 'intention' to reach their peak. In connection with this topic one finds that Wittgenstein is weaving what can be characterized as a kind of thematic fabric concerning different aspects around the topic of 'intention'. These aspects amount to the examples he provides in conjunction with his thoughts concerning such additional themes as 'thinking', 'meaning', 'waiting', 'understanding', 'reading', etc. Thus, one can say, like Wittgenstein, that this 'concrete' and apparently mental problem, in its most general form, ' ... gets its light, that is to say its purpose, from the philosophical problems'[PhI §109].

I do not assume the problems of 'thought' and 'intention' to occur everywhere in his texts as an explicit and major theme within those of his numerous writings in which we find him specifically discussing aspects of it. To make such an assumption would, indeed, in reality be to simplify matters far too much. Neither do I assume 'thought' and 'intention' to occure as an explicit topic everywhere in Wittgenstein's texts during the different periods in his philosophical production. Perhaps one can characterize the situation by saying that, on the one hand, 'thought' and 'intention', as themes, are 'implicitly' in a dominating position as far as his whole production is concerned, but, on the other hand, that this is not the case as far as each distinguishable part of his philosophical production is concerned.

Secondly, we are not dealing with what can be characterized as a single monolithic and sharply demarcated problem (that we, e.g., find in science between universals and particulars) but, rather, with what we can characterize, in Wittgensteinian terminology, as a 'family' of problems [PhI §67]. This 'family' of problems exhibits the characteristic features of both overlapping and partial similarity - 'family resemblance' properties - as far as the common thematic resemblance is concerned [Infra IV.4]. Indeed, this is indicated, for example, when Wittgenstein says that '[t]he expression of the intention can't contain the intention, for language can't explain itself'[L (2) 112]. But it is nevertheless connected with that constructive impulse which is asserted by Wittgenstein to bridge the gap holding between a sign and its application. This is an unavoidable gap which cannot be saved by any explanation, nor negotiated by any reason, since, as Wittgenstein emphasized, '[n]o reason compels us to learn language'[L (2) 67].

Another point which it is important to be aware of is that when reading Wittgenstein's texts one notices that the word 'intention' occurs relatively seldom in his vocabulary. We encounter this expression most frequently in those texts which he wrote during a brief period in the beginning of the 1930's. Thus we find, for example, in the *Philosophische Bemerkungen* [WA I-IV], where the first part was written around the turn of the decade 1929-1930, a quite remarkable discussion by Wittgenstein concerning 'internal relations' as well as 'intentionality'[PhR 63-74]. Here we find that he, in one of his manuscripts, writes the interesting comment that [WA II 196]:

> Wenn man das Element der Intention aus der Sprache
> entfernt so bricht damit ihre ganze Funktion zusammen.

This crucial comment, i.e., that if one excludes the element of intention from language then its whole function collapses, is especially interesting [PhR 63]. For those members of the school of Logical Empiricism, i.e., the majority (cf., for example, Carnap), who only knew of Wittgenstein's philosophical thought through their specific (and mistaken) interpretation of the *Tractatus* [Supra II.5], these writings concerning 'intentionality' would have been extremely disturbing [cf. PhR 63-74]. But, it is important to remember that Wittgenstein did not, despite, for example, his contacts with Schlick and Waismann, regard himself as being a member of the philosophical school of Logical Empiricism [Supra I.2].

It seems to be a fact that after the brief - but intense - period, in the beginning of the 1930's, we find the theme of 'intention' to occur less frequently in his texts. Nevertheless, it does not entirely disappear because one can still find this theme explicitly mentioned in a few places in those texts which Wittgenstein wrote after 1937. For example, in a paragraph written between 1938 and 1939, we encounter the following remark connected to this theme when Wittgenstein asks ' ... what kind of super-strong connexion exists between the act of intending and the thing intended?'[RFM I §130]. In the same manuscript one also finds that he emphasizes the important insight that such an 'intentional connection' does not amount to an empirical one [RFM I §128]. Thus, his position is that 'intention' cannot be treated, for example, by an ordinary scientific (and empirical) 'behaviourist' Outer view, or, alternatively, a rational cognitive Inner view of some kind. But, he also later, say, in the *Philosophical Investigations,* explicitly acknowledges the importance of 'intention'. But here, in this text - in contrast to his earlier texts - he seems to treat this problem in more or less a random fashion [PhI §197]. Thus one is given the impression that the notion of 'intention' in these later post-1937 texts seems to have lost the key feature that we find them still to inhabit in his earlier writings.[2]

This feature is connected to Wittgenstein's overall path of intellectual evolution; an evolution which one could, perhaps, characterize as being reminiscent of what could be called a continuous evolvment 'towards the concrete'. This tendency of evolvment 'towards the concrete' (for example, in connection with calculations) must be seen as one of the most central efforts through the whole of Wittgenstein's philosophical span of evolution. As a result of this it does, when superficially viewed, indeed look as if Wittgenstein during his most 'mature' period completely dismantles the theme of 'intention'. *However, it is important to understand that such an account amounts to an illusion and is therefore not correct.* In this chapter I will attempt to show that even if we cannot identify 'intention' as an explicit theme in these latter texts one can, nevertheless, still find it to be a genuine ingredient 'surfacing' now and then. Thus we can always read and understand his later texts within the scope of this theme. That is, regardless of the fact that the theme of 'intention' is not everywhere explicitly mentioned in Wittgenstein's texts we find it - due to the illusions that one encounters again and again in 'philosophical' discourse - to be constantly at work in the background.

We shall attempt to show how Wittgenstein wanted to understand the problems of 'thought' and 'intention' by focusing our attention on certain specific aspects of these problems. To begin with it is a fact that when studying Wittgenstein's texts we do not, for example, find a single explicit chapter named 'Intention' in his *Nachlass*. Thus we cannot by 'intention' mean something occurring in his texts as an explicit theme or as a theory of some sort. However, what we can do is to attempt to exhibit those 'implicit' aspects of Wittgenstein's view of 'intention' which one cannot find to be explicitly mentioned in his published texts. These aspects show themselves when one is able to correctly understand them. This does not mean that our aim is to primarily extract any particular 'philosophical theses' (as in 'analytical philosophy') which one may assume to be, say, subconsciously (or, in an Anti-Realist vocabulary, 'implicitly') existing 'below the surface' of these texts. That is, our aim is not, for example, to formulate any kind of 'theory of meaning' (a semantical structure), so even in that respect we are not interested in anything that can be characterized - in a psychoanalytical terminology - as being some kind of 'repressed intentions'. What we are to do is simply to rearrange (but not distort) Wittgenstein's written material in accordance with our own limited philosophical needs (in Wittgenstein's sense). If we express our task with his own words, then, what we aim to do here is to make an attempt to investigate the notion of 'intention' as something ' ... which we see when we look into the thing, and which an analysis digs out'[PhI §92].

What we shall do is to make an attempt to reconstruct the main outlines of Wittgenstein's thought as far the problems of 'thought' and 'intention' are concerned. This we shall do by scetching the assumed evolution of the problem for Wittgenstein (1) as it seems to occur in his 'earlier' writings, notably the *Tractatus* [Gefwert (1) 46-70], (2) by drawing the outlines of the 'problem of intention' as we find it in his texts during the beginning of the 1930's and (3) by characterizing the problem when it culminates in his so called 'mature philosophy' in his post-1937 writings [Infra IV.3-5].

When reading Wittgenstein's texts the typical feature that one frequently encounters is the strong impression that there is something which the writer attempts to *show*, or indicate, with his comments

[Gefwert (1) 27-35]. This is connected to two main points in Wittgenstein's writings:

(1) Structuralist (introspectionist) psychology can never explain meaning.

(2) Contrary to the ideas of the Realists/Anti-Realists the primary creation of meaning is indescribable (as a 'theory of meaning').

According to Kenny, the result is that ' ... common to both [points] are the tasks and method of philosophy of mind: to clarify psychological statements by separating out the logical and intentional from the contingent and empirical'.[3] These aspects of his writings are extremely important and need to be taken into account.

When one views Wittgenstein from such an angle one can notice an interesting and quite remarkable reminiscence to one of the famous oracles of Greece. Similarly to the oracle of Delphi, as we, for example, find it to be depicted by the Greek philosopher Heraclitus of Ephesos (ca. 540-480 BC), one can characterize what Wittgenstein is attempting to achieve by saying that he, like the ' ... oracle [of] Delphi neither utters nor hides [the] meaning, but shows it by a sign'.[4] By emphasizing also this side of Wittgenstein one finds that his investigations become an act of balancing between, on the one hand, the requirement of not to say what, according to him, cannot be said, and, on the other hand, the requirement to avoid the danger of shortcutting and trivialising relevant thoughts.

We are then faced, when we look at the problem from an historical and chronological point of view, with the necessity to recognize the fact that, despite Wittgenstein's continuous development of his thoughts after the composition of the documents called the *Philosophische Bemerkungen,* it becomes, after the writings of these texts, virtually impossible to find any major changes in his views as far as the problem of 'intention' is concerned. For example, already in the *Big Typescript* [BT], compiled around 1931-1933, we encounter certain remarks concerning 'intention' which we also find, in essence, to be repeated almost *verbatim* in the *Philosophical Investigations*. The upshot of the previous discussion is then to make it clear to the reader that what we are to do below is to investigate Wittgenstein's notion of 'intention' in the spirit of his own philosophical investigations.

III.2 INTENTION: HISTORICAL SOURCES

We shall now attempt to historically trace the most important literary sources from which Wittgenstein may have received his views concerning the theme of 'intention'. This is not an easy task because it has never been solved in a satisfactory way from where he, suddenly, around the turn of the decade 1929-1930, acquired the concept of 'intention'. There are, nevertheless, a few likely texts which could have acted as literary sources for his novel insights. Thus it seems highly plausible that the concept of 'intention' that we find Wittgenstein to apply in his texts in the beginning of the decade can be traced back to at least two - perhaps three - possible sources. We can mention (1) the article *Der Gedanke* [LoI 1-30], from 1918, by Gottlob Frege, (2) the book *Allgemeine Erkenntnislehre,* from 1923, by Moritz Schlick[5] and (3) certain writings by Edmund Husserl (1859-1938) and Martin Heidegger (1889-1976) concerning the phenomenological school of philosophy, as being possible sources for Wittgenstein's texts on 'intention'.

If we begin our investigation in chronological order the first likely source for the concept of 'intention' may have been the article *Der Gedanke* published, in 1918, by Frege in the periodical *Beiträge zur Philosophie des deutschen Idealismus*. This article was intended to be a part of a book called *Logische Untersuchungen* which Frege was never able to finish. We do not know *when* Wittgenstein read this article but we know that Wittgenstein *had* read this article [LoI Preface]. This is testified, for example, by Geach who tells us that ' ... readers may be interested in the remarks Wittgenstein made to me about this work in the last months of his life. He took a good deal of interest in the plan Max Black and I had for a little book of Frege translations; and it was through him that I was able to locate some rare works of Frege - the review [in 1894] of Husserl's *Philosophie der Arithmetik* and the essays "Was ist eine Funktion?" and "Die Verneinung" - in the Cambridge University Library'[LoI vii; Cf. PMC 60]. According to Geach it is the case that despite Wittgenstein's unfavourable view of *Der Gedanke* it is quite plausible that his own later thought ' ... may have been influenced by it. It would not be the only time that Frege's criticism had a delayed action in modifying Wittgenstein's views after he had initially rejected the criticism'[LoI viii]. It seems to be a historical fact that Wittgenstein remained conscious of his great debt to Frege until the end of his life. We find this intellectual debt to be reflected, for example, in a paragraph in *Zettel*, written sometimes in 1945-1948, where Wittgenstein says that '[t]he style of my sentences is extraordinarily strongly influenced by Frege. And if I wanted to I could establish this influence where at first sight no one would see it'[Z §712].

But, what was it that Frege had written in *Der Gedanke* and which drew the attention of Wittgenstein? In this article we find that Frege criticized the 'correspondence theory of truth' by saying that [LoI 4]

> ... the attempted explanation of truth as correspondence breaks down. And any other attempt to define truth also breaks down. For in a definition certain characteristics would have to be specified. And in application to any particular case the question would always arise whether it were *true* that the characteristics were present. So it seems likely that the content of the word 'true' is *sui generis* and indefinable.

One can speculate if this quotation (when stressing the 'breakdown' of the 'attempts' to 'explain' truth by an external relation [Gefwert (1) 255-262]) was by Wittgenstein taken to refer to Frege's later view concerning the problem of 'intention' (concerning how one is to understand the point of a truth-predicate ' ... is true' as exhibiting an internal relation) because, much later, he writes that ' ... what does a proposition "being true" mean? *"p"* is true = *p*. (That is the answer). So we want to ask something like: under what circumstances do we assert a proposition? Or: how is the assertion of the proposition used in the language-game'[RFM Appx. III §6; Cf. PhI §136].

A second important source can, perhaps, be found in the book *Allgemeine Erkenntnislehre* by Schlick. Here, we find that he writes, in connection with the topic of 'intention', that Husserl, the founder of the phenomenological school of philosophy,

> ... points out that every content of consciousness, as Brentano had already asserted, bears an 'intentional' character, that is, it is 'directed to an object' ... In perceiving, something is perceived; in imagining, something is imagined; in judging, something is judged. We cannot love without our love being addressed to a loved object; we cannot think without an object being there of which we are thinking. The objects to which our acts of consciousness are directed are not in our sense of the word experienced: the object that is perceived, judged, loved, is not really present in consciousness. But the being-directed-toward-an-object, the 'intention', is indeed directly experienced. And this is how it is with concepts too. When I think of a triangle, although the triangle itself is not in my consciousness, the intention toward it is.[6]

We know that Wittgenstein had read Schlick's book. From this one can conclude, interestingly enough, that it is very likely that he had read the paragraph in which Schlick refers to Brentano (as well as Husserl). On the other hand, to what extent he was actually influenced by this book (and Brentano) we do not know, but it is interesting to note, according to Feigl and Blumberg, that ' ... we must ... take special note that Schlick, characteristically self-effacing, attributed to Wittgenstein certain highly significant insights that he (Schlick) had *already* arrived at long before he knew even of Wittgenstein's existence. Indeed, some of the most crucial tenets of the *Tractatus* were anticipated in Schlick's epistemology'.[7]

Within the phenomenological movement the concept of 'intention' plays a very central role and thus Wittgenstein might also have been, perhaps through Schlick and Waismann, indirectly influenced by the writings of Husserl [Cf. WVC 67-68]. However, it is not an exaggeration to say that the whole reintroduction of the philosophical problem concerning 'intention' in modern times, in turn, can be traced back to the Austrian philosopher Frantz Brentano (1838-1917). It is not too farfetched to claim that Brentano - who was Husserl's teacher - can be regarded as the first phenomenologist. Despite the fact that Brentano - originally a Catholic priest - in 1873 abandoned the Church, he is, perhaps, the most important modern intellectual descendant of the scholastic tradition of the middle ages. This concerns also what can be characterized as the 'problem of intention'. It is therefore at least plausible that some of Wittgenstein's thoughts on intention, in addition to Frege and Schlick, have some of their intellectual roots in Brentano's writings as mediated by Husserl's texts. Let us therefore take a brief look at how Brentano - and the Scholastics - understood the 'problem of intention'.

Many states of mind are characterized by *aboutness,* or what Brentano called the *intentional in-existence of objects,* that is, what we have earlier called 'intention'. Setting out from the Scholastic tradition we can establish that by the term 'intention' was meant a kind of 'picture' which, being a kind of Aristotelian form, mediated knowledge from the outside world to the soul of the enquirer. According to Spiegelberg '... the term "intentio", as used in scholastic philosophy, signifies the peculiar image or likeness formed in the soul in the process of acquiring knowledge, thus representing, as it were a kind of distillate from the world outside'.[8]

Within medieval scholastic tradition the problem of 'intention' can be characterized as what it is that makes a picture of A a picture *of* A, what makes an image of B an image *of* B or, say, what makes a thought about C be *about* C. The problem sets out from the distinction between what the scholastics called *esse naturale* (existence in nature) and *esse intentionale* (existence in the mind). This dichotomy concerns many different pictures, images or thoughts. The result is that one finds, within scholastic philosophy, that the term 'intention' had many different applications. Phenomenology teaches us that intentionality is 'directedness' *(Richtung)* towards an object. From our point of view, what is interesting is that besides being some kind of an 'intelligible species' (i.e., the 'form' of the object) we find that by 'intention' was also meant a directed mental act of the will. In the form of *intentio intellecta* it amounted to a kind of 'internal word' *(verbum interius)*, that is, the object when it is understood. It was through this 'internal word' which, by being the sign, an external word could refer to an object.[9]

As far as we know Brentano did not use the term 'intention' as such but only the adjectival form 'intentional'.[10] For him intentionality primarily functioned as the factor which divided mental phenomena (the Inner) from the physical ones (the Outer). He held the thesis that aboutness is exclusively a feature of mental phenomena. No physical phenomenon possesses anything similar. This irreducible division ('separability') according to which every intentional phenomenon

> ... is characterized by what the mediaeval Scholastics of the Middle Ages called the intentional (or simply mental) inexistence *(Inexistenz)* of an object *(Gegenstand)*, and what we could call, though not quite unambiguously, reference to a content, direction towards an object *(Objekt)* (by which is not to be understood here something of the character of a thing *(eine Realität)*, or immanent objectivity) has later been called 'Brentano's Thesis'.[11]

One could say that 'intention' amounts to that factor of directness which by its very presence makes some phenomenon an intentional one. If we, like Brentano, characterize intentionality as directed, then we can say that it is precisely this intention which gives and determines that direction. The etymological roots of the latin verb *intendere* is in a real sense to be found precisely in the notion of 'reaching out'. In a metaphorical sense we could say that an intentional phenomenon 'reaches out' until it reaches its target and that the 'active nucleus' of this phenomenon is precisely the intention. The result is that 'intentionality' is not primarily to be regarded as a quality but instead as a two-place relation. The phenomenon of intentionality always require a target and between the subject (provider of thought) and the target (object of thought) in question we always say that there is to be an 'intentional bond' in which we separate the active member (which includes the intention) and the passive member (the target/object) similarly to the way in which we in a causal relation can separate cause and effect.[12]

Another philosopher who follows Brentano (and Husserl) as far as 'intentionality' is concerned is Heidegger. Like many thinkers, both Heidegger and Wittgenstein are better in criticism than in explicit constructivism, but in comparison to Heidegger it seems to be a fact that Wittgenstein does remarkably little constructive investigations when he performs his philosophical investigations. The analysis by Heidegger is not introspective because he, like Wittgenstein, has rejected the post-Cartesian distinction between the Inner and the Outer. Both thinkers begin their analysis in the form of life where there is no subject-object split. These are assumptions that are a product of philosophical reflection, not anything given in our experience. This is the reason why the problems of scepticism, of the external world, and other minds, do not bother Wittgenstein nor Heidegger. For Heidegger being-in-the-world means that one is always and already 'outside' of what could be called the classic ego-centric predicament.[13] We can therefore quite safely claim that both Heidegger's phenomenology and Wittgenstein's philosophical texts have passed beyond the problem of realism vs. idealism.

Heidegger follows Brentano and Husserl when he takes intentionality as the mark of the mental *sine qua non*. Whatever he has to say which is relevant to questions concerning thought (as well as, for example, the possibility of genuine 'strong Artificial Intelligence' to occur) is also going to be relevant to issues concerning intentionality. Therefore Heidegger is relevant when we want to understand Wittgenstein's arguments on intentionality. For example, since the possible intentionality of a state is centrally tied to the possible semantics of that state his thought will be most directly relevant to the possibility semantics of mental events to occur [Infra V.2]. One can say that if Heidegger is right then there is no way in which the mind can be a programme in the sense that the program defines what it is to have a mind: what it is to have intentions can't be captured in any set of formally defined rules (secondary language-games). This is very close to Wittgenstein's later position. We shall return to this question in connection with the 'rules-as-theory' confusion due to Kripke [Infra V.4].

It is highly probable that these were the primary sources that, either directly or indirectly, had influenced Wittgenstein as far as the problem of 'intention' is concerned. But we do not know for sure. Perhaps there are also other sources. There is simply not enough evidence available. Thus, all we can say for the moment is that it is still virtually unknown from which sources Wittgenstein actually did acquire the inspiration for the notion of 'intention' which was to play such an important part in his post-1929 writings. However, what we can say, according to Kenny, is that '[t]he term [intention] appears to have [by Wittgenstein been] taken from Husserl, who in turn took it from Brentano, and scholastic tradition'.[14] As a result of this it is, perhaps, correct to claim that, at least, these three sources seem to have played a very important role in Wittgenstein's intellectual development.

III.3 THE CONTINUATION OF WITTGENSTEIN'S THOUGHT

We have already established that Wittgenstein did not embrace any kind of causal 'theory of meaning'[Supra II.4]. The next step, then, is to exhibit how he wanted the problems of 'thought' and 'intention' to be understood in his post-1929 writings. The background for Wittgenstein's views on these themes are to be found in the *Tractatus* [Gefwert (1) 46-78]. According to a quite generally accepted view the breakdown of the thoughts occurring in the *Tractatus* set out from a contradiction between the assumed qualities of the elementary propositions and the true qualities of the most elementary propositions that we know.15 We shall look at this problem in order to make this point clear.

According to the *Tractatus* elementary propositions where to be logically independent of each other [T §4.211] because an elementary proposition which, for example, connects a certain colour existing at a certain moment to a certain point in the visual field also excludes a number of other propositions which simultaneously connect certain other colours to that specific point. Thus Wittgenstein says that ' ... the simultaneous presence of two colours at the same place in the visual field is impossible, since it is ruled out by the logical structure of colour'[T §6.3751]. We can therefore conclude that it seems that he was by no means unaware of this specific problem but that he chose in the *Tractatus* to draw the conclusion that the colour concepts are not 'simple' ones [cf. T §6.3751].

This, however, was not the end of the story. In Wittgenstein's article *Some Remarks on Logical Form* [RLF], written in 1930, after his return to philosophical work, one finds that he had changed his mind as far as the position formulated in the *Tractatus* is concerned. He now allows elementary propositioins (which occur in this article as 'atomic propositions') to exclude each other even though they cannot contradict one another. As an example of such an 'atomic proposition' he takes assertions concerning the occurrence of a colour at a certain place at a certain moment [RLF 35].

This view was not to last. Almost immediately, when this position was barely formulated, he changed his position again. Later that same year, in the first of the manuscripts called *Philosophische Bemerkungen,* the foreword of which is dated in November, 1930, we find that Wittgenstein already allows the elementary propositions to contradict *(widersprechen)* each other. By assigning a certain quality to some elementary proposition it follows, as Wittgenstein now puts it, that this proposition cannot have any other qualities belonging to the same 'graduation mark' because '[a] co-ordinate of reality may only be determined *once* [in that] *two* determinations of the same kind (co-ordinate) are impossible'[PhR 111-112]. We now also encounter the noteworthy feature that the elementary propositions that we find in our everyday language - in contrast to the assumed elementary propositions that we find characterized in the *Tractatus* - turns out to be primary in relation to the latter ones and thus '[t]he concept of an 'elementary proposition' now loses all of its earlier significance'[PhR 111].

In all other respects the relation between a thought and a sentence seems to be the same as the one we find in the *Tractatus*: thought is the 'bearer' of meaning. That is, when uttering something seemingly nonsensical a person thinks or *means* something which cannot be thought. Wittgenstein seems to indicate this when he writes that [PhR 55-56]

> ... In this sense, if we say it's nonsense to say that one thing is as identical as another, this needs qualification, since if anyone says this with conviction, then at that moment *(meint in diesem Augenblick)* he means something by the word "identical" (perhaps "large"), but isn't aware that he is using the word here with a different meaning from that in $2 + 2 = 4$.

But how does this 'meaning something at that moment' work? Like an antipode to the very subtle 'picture-theory' that we find in the *Tractatus* [Gefwert (1) 56-69] we find that Wittgenstein here refers to what he characterizes as ' ... the naive theory of *forming-an-image (die naive Theorie des Sich-eine-Vorstellung-Machens)*'[PhR 58]. According to this view a word gets its meaning from the 'image' of the speaker/listener when we speak and hear. Even if Wittgenstein does not adhere to this naive 'picture-theory' he gives credit to it to the extent that he says that it ' ... can't be utterly wrong'[PhR 58]. Later, however, we find that he, when discussing the picture and its image, is dissatisfied with the way the 'picture-theory' is depicted. This is, for example, indicated when he says that '[w]e have just used a metaphor and now the metaphor tyrannizes us'[PhR 82]. Thus it seems that the 'picture-theory', regardless of whether the version we deal with is a subtil or a naive version, always creates a number of difficult problems.

III.4 CORRECTING THE 'PICTURE-THEORY'

In order to correct the shortcomings of the pure 'picture-theory'[Gefwert (1) 56-69], be it naive or subtle, we now, around 1929-1930, find that Wittgenstein starts to apply the metaphor of a 'measure rod' (*Maßstab*)[PhR 85]. He emphasises that it is the application which makes the measure rod to what it is. Similarly with language: it is the application which makes it what it is. Thus, according to Wittgenstein, '[b]y application I understand what makes the combination of sounds or marks into a language at all. In the sense that it is the application which makes the rod with marks on it into a *measuring rod: putting* language *up against* reality'[PhR 85].

However, the belief in the objects of the *Tractatus* have - due to the changes made in the ('atomic') elementary propositions - by now completely disappeared and as a result of this one of the crucial features guaranteeing the meaningfulness of thoughts, the 'homogenic' space of logic, has also disappeared (and thus we cannot have any genuine 'semantics' in a Language-as-Calculus sense). The objects of the *Tractatus* contained ' ... all its possible occurrences in state of affairs'[T §2.0123] which was the very reason why one could say that '[i]f all objects are given, then at the same time all *possible* states of affairs are also given'[T §2.0124]. Here the possible facts, when taken as a whole, amounted to the logical space of which an elementary proposition determines one place [T §3.4]. Each proposition is always accompanied with the whole of logical space due to the fact that a genuine proposition (in contrast to a mathematical pseudo-proposition) always contains the possibility of negation and a proposition together with its negation fills the whole of logical space [T §§3.42, 4.463].

But now, that the world has lost its 'substance' (which had its origin in the mistaken ontological 'metaphysical distinction' - or logical separability - between 'mind' and 'world'[Gefwert (1) 76]) the whole conception of how a measure rod is being connected to reality becomes more difficult to understand. Nevertheless, the measure rod has somehow to attach itself to reality in order for its meaningfulness to be guaranteed. It is easy to understand that the real measure rod must be in the 'same space' as the object measured. The metaphorical space of logic that we find in the *Tractatus* was based on the symmetrical (isomorphical) construction between the objects and the names [Gefwert (1) 56-58]. Now, when this symmetry has collapsed, it became more difficult to understand how the words and the objects could occur within the 'same space', the result being, as Wittgenstein characterized the situation, that '[i]t sounds absurd *(Es klingt absurd)*'[PhR 79].

The 'universal' space of logic that we find in the *Tractatus* is now, in the turn of the decade 1929-1930, replaced by a view stressing the 'locality' or 'regionality' of logical space. We no longer set a single proposition against any 'reality'. Instead the unit to be so contrasted is what Wittgenstein characterized as a 'propositional system' *(Satzsysteme)* [Infra IV.4]. Whereas the logical space of the *Tractatus* was a universal and bi-polarical 'yes-no space'[16] we now find this 'two-valued' conception replaced with something which we, perhaps, can characterize as a 'many-valued' space. A single proposition corresponds to a possible value of a logical place and the propositional system - or calculus - to the whole scale of a measure-rod [Cf. WVC 63-64]. Corresponding to propositional systems (calculations) we now find that Wittgenstein talks about parts of space. Thus, for example, the possibility of there occurring a proposition negating (denying) stomach-ache presupposes the possibility of the *concept* of 'stomach-ache' to exist which determines the place within the 'space of stomach-ache' analogously to the way that zero degree centigrade characterizes the zero degree of 'temperature-space'[WVC 85-86; PhR 110-111].

The most important novel feature of the measure-rod metaphor, however, is its ability to bring to the forefront novel problems which have previously been transparent. The ability to (1) make the measure-rod reach out all the way to reality and (2) to the possibility of reality to show the correctness of the measure-rod presupposes that the measure-rod and reality meet in the present. Our propositions are being verified only at instants (at present) and thus the measure-rod has to be what Wittgenstein characterized as 'commensurable' with the present [PhR 81]. However, as is well known, our everyday language is not bound to statements set in the present tense. It allows other tenses as well. Thus, for example, a statement in future (or past) tense, despite the fact that it is set against reality in the present, must point beyond it towards what Wittgenstein characterized as the ' ... direction of the expectation'[PhR 72]. An image (a sentence in past tense) is a 'picture' of the past, but, how is it possible to know it to be just that [PhR 82]? Now, the important thing with questions like these is that they exhibit the difficulties that one encounters with the 'picture-theory' when Wittgenstein began to stress the importance of every-day language in all its variety.[17]

It is these kinds of problems which set the background in order to understand those remarks which Wittgenstein in 1929 presents by applying the novel concept of 'intention'. The novelty here is that Wittgenstein *from now on regards 'intention' as an essential ingredient of language.* This is clearly revealed in his statement that '[i]f you exclude the element of intention from language, its whole function collapses'[PhR 63]. Furthermore, as has been emphasized by Stenius, Kenny as well as Hintikka, it seems that he did not - at least not completely - reject the 'picture-theory'.[18] We have to understand that the 'meaning as use' principle is a *complement* rather than a rival to the 'picture-theory'. It creates a 'bridge', as it were, between language-user(s) and the hidden logical structure of the proposition. The point is that the signs themselves are 'dead' and need use to give them life [PhG 132; BB 4; PhI §§430-433].

It is because of these arguments that it is possible for Wittgenstein to deal with a language which satisfies the seemingly incompatible demands of being at the same time both actual and ideal. This explains why Wittgenstein, on the 5 January 1930, told Waismann that '[t]he essential thing in a proposition is that ... it is a picture'[WVC 90; cf. also PhG 163; PhI §291; Z §244]. But this is not enough. In addition, Wittgenstein regards *intention* to be in an inexorable way connected to a picture. This point is clearly revealed when he says that '[w]hat is essential to intention is the picture: the picture of what is intended'[PhR 63]. Thus, one can argue that the 'meaning is use' thesis is not to replace the 'picture theory' thesis which it is usually taken to be.

In the lecture notes taken by Moore between the years 1930-1933 [L (1) 252-324] (the year they are actually compiled is unknown), we find that Wittgenstein speaks (1) of a picture in relation to some specific system of projection and then (2) about changing from one picture into another by replacing the symbol with another one by something which he characterizes as 'following the rule'. Such a rule, despite the fact that it is not contained in either of the 'pictures', is contained in the 'intention' of the translator. According to Moore, ' ... he [Wittgenstein] said, that though the rule is "contained" in the intention, the intention obviously does not "contain" any expression of the rule, any more than, when I read aloud, I am conscious of the rules I follow in translating the printed signs into sounds'[L (1) 264]. Our next task thus becomes to exhibit how Wittgenstein combined these novel insights of 'meaning as use' and 'intention' to the earlier 'picture theory'.

In the *Big Typescript* (1930-1933) we find that Wittgenstein exhibits the meaning of the concept of 'intention' by saying that '[b]y "intention" I mean here what uses a sign in a thought. The intention seems to interpret, to give the final interpretation; which is not a further sign or picture, but something else, the thing that cannot be further interpreted. But what we have reached is a psychological, not a logical terminus'[PhG 145; Cf. also Z §231]. He also displays the problem of representation that he is concerned with as follows, '[t]hat's *him* (this picture represents *him*) - that contains the whole problem of representation. What is the criterion, how is it to be verified, that this picture is the portrait of that object, i.e., that it is *meant* to represent it? It is not similarity that makes the picture a portrait (it might be a striking resemblance of one person, and yet be a portrait of someone else it resembles less) ... When I remember my friend and see him "in my mind's eye", what is the connection between the memory image and its subject? The likeness between them? ... Here we have the old problem ... the problem of the harmony between world and thought'[PhG 102].

Interestingly enough, the task of 'intention' seems to be precisely the same as the one provided, in the terminology of Stenius, by what he characterized as the 'key of interpretation'.[19] It is 'intention' which ought to provide the sign with a meaning, i.e., make it mean (connotate) something outside itself. In order for 'intention' to achieve this it ought to differ in an essential way from signs, pictures and other such 'phenomena'. The phenomena are 'self-sufficed', that is, too much 'wrapped up' in themselves, in order to function as intentions. The important thing is that intention must incorporate the intended, that is, it must have ' ... a direction given to it'[PhG 143]. The dilemma that Wittgenstein was facing was that '[i]f we consider them [the thoughts and intentions] "from outside" we have to understand thoughts as thoughts, intentions as intentions and so on, without getting any information about something's meaning. For it is with the phenomenon of thinking that meaning belongs'[PhG 144]. When we investigate a thought ' ... there can be no further question of an understanding; for if the thought is seen it must be recognized as a thought with a certain content; it doesn't need to be interpreted! - That really is how it is; when we are thinking, there isn't any interpretation going on'[PhG 144]. As far as thinking is concerned there cannot be any interpretational infinite regress. However, so far we have only reached the psychological end-point, a well-known medium, where we do not have (for, perhaps, subjective reasons) to employ further interpretions anymore. But, it is crucially important to understand that we have not yet reached (unstructuralized) everyday *language* - the logical end-point - which, when metaphorically seen from 'outside', *cannot* be interpreted any further.

Thus we are faced with the insight that it, according to Wittgenstein, is in ordinary *language* that we have to seek the clue in order to reach the logical end-point concerning this 'metaphysical element' of intention'. One easily gets the impression that it seems to be a characteristic feature of the critical comments in the post-1929 writings of Wittgenstein that the metaphor of the 'logical picture' (the 'picture-theory') is now being dropped from the central explanatory place it had occupied in his earlier writings [Gefwert (1) 56-69]. As we have already pointed out it was to survive in a modified form.[20] This insight one can find to be exhibited in numerous places in his texts [WVC 67, 88, 97; PhG 129, BB 54; PhI §251]. As a result of this Wittgenstein now begins to emphasize the aspect of relativity concerning the concept of 'intention'. The upshot of this is that a 'picture' is only a 'picture' in relation to various things, say, a 'key of interpretation', a 'method of projection', a 'rule of projection', etc. It seems that Wittgenstein does not set any logical boundaries concerning what is to be counted as a 'picture' and thus seems to emphasize that anything can be taken to be the picture of anything.

In his early thought it seems that Wittgenstein did not yet regard the 'method of projection' as problematic. He just states that thought provides the projection of the world into language by applying its 'natural' method [Cf. T §4.002]. However, this simplistic view was not to last. After his return to philosophical work in 1929 this view was soon to change. Already in his article *Some Remarks of Logical Form* we find that Wittgenstein talks of the many facetted features that we have as far as the methods of projection is concerned without clarifying the resulting problem concening the 'key of interpretation'[RLF 33]. But the possible plurality of the methods of projection cannot but lead to a certain arbitrariness on their part.

For Wittgenstein, however, this arbitrariness is from the beginning only 'logical'. That is, as he says, ' ... if I showed someone the way by pointing my finger not in the direction in which he was to go, but in the opposite direction, in the absense of a special arrangement I should cause a misunderstanding. It is part of human nature to understand pointing with the finger in the way we do'[PhG 94]. From a logical point of view it would be perfectly alright that the finger could point in any direction, for anything can, indeed, be a 'picture' of anything, because every projection has something in common with what is being projected according to some method of projection [Cf. PhG 163]. Thus, for example, when I ask someone how to find a certain place and that person, as an answer to my request, points out the right way to proceed then this ostensive gesture *might* stand in need of a novel interpretation because the pointing gesture might very well be applied in *another* way than we usually expect [Infra IV.2].

Now, we have to ask: Is this a genuine possibility? The answer is: No! It seems that ultimately it is not possible. The reason for this is that by allowing the possibility of always providing novel re-interpretations at an 'ever increasing deeper level' we can extend interpretations *ad infinitum* which leads to a never ending regress [Cf. BB 33-34]. This leads us into a sceptical dilemma. It is precisely this feature that Kripke wants us to believe that Wittgenstein's intention had been and thus he introduced his 'sceptical paradox'[Infra VI.3].

Now, the same goes for every 'picture'. In order for the meaning of a 'picture' to be made clear to us we must know how it is a projection of reality. In addition to the 'picture' we should also keep in mind the method of projection [Cf. PhI §141] but as far as it is like a 'picture' the projection can itself be interpreted in different ways. We need ever novel interpretations. Wittgenstein exemplifies this by comparing the situation with the reading of a chart. We can, for example, produce a 'colour-chart' where we on the left side of the chart have the names of the colours and on the right side the patches that we use as examples. A natural way of reading such a chart is to move from left to right, that is, from the written name of the colour to the colour patch itself. In order to make this as clear as possible one could even draw arrows from left to right indicating how the chart is to be read. However, from a logical point of view, such a drawing cannot 'force' us to follow the arrows any more than a chart which lacks such arrows can do. It is always possible to read the arrows in some alternative way. By doing this we again apply a novel method of projection [Cf. BB 123-124].

One gets the impression that when left by itself the chart seems to be completely unable to determine its own interpretation. We would encounter an additional difficulty with those 'pictures' which we would like to be generic and thus provide an interpretation concerning our universals [Cf. PhI §73]. Thus 'pictures' are completely unable to function in the capacity as providers of a 'key of interpretation' in Stenius vocabulary [Gefwert (1) 57-70]. They cannot constitute 'intention', i.e., the ultimate interpretation in a logical sense (not in a psychological one). The 'pictures' cannot amount to those 'shadows' which Wittgenstein talks about in the *Blue Book* where he identifies them with the content of sense or the proposition expressed by a sentence [BB 32, 36-37]. Such a 'shadow' ought to function as the previous picture metaphor was assumed to function: accompanying the sentence and determining its meaning by being the 'shadow' of the intended state of affairs. But if the 'picture' cannot by itself interpret what 'picture' it is then how can we determine what 'shadow' each 'shadow' is? Consequently we need the intention at his point. As Wittgenstein says, '[t]he shadow would be some sort of portrait; and therefore I can restate our problem by asking: "What makes a portrait a portrait of Mr. N?" ... An obvious, and correct, answer to the question "What makes a portrait the portrait of so-and-so?" is that it is the *intention*'[BB 32].

However, we have to be aware that such an answer does not tell us yet anything; it only means that anything can be regarded as being a picture of anything. This is why the internal and necessary intentional relation which should exist between a 'picture' and its prototype cannot be explained by the features of the 'picture' itself. It has to be explained by the help of intention, i.e., *how* the 'picture' is meant. Now, because this is the case for all 'pictures' we notice that a mental 'picture' when used as a metaphorical 'picture' does not offer any advantages over the alternative physical 'picture' despite the fact that it offers a seducing temptation concerning the mental substratum. If such an interpretation of 'pictures' can go on *ad infinitum* we better cut it off from the very start. This is why it is the case that ' ... if we wanted a picture of reality the sentence itself is such a picture (though not a picture by similarity)'[BB 41].

If we would be successful in our attempt to exhibit the triviality of the 'picture' metaphor it might help us to become free from the 'mental prison' of separability concerning the Inner vs. the Outer which has captivated us. Thus, we find, some years after the writing of the *Blue Book,* that Wittgenstein is characterizing the situation by saying that '[a] *picture* held us captive. And we could not get outside it, for it lay in our language and language seemed to repeat it to us inexorably'[PhI §115]. But, now we must ask: What does this mysterious 'picture' of the internal really amount to? Is it genuine?

III.5 MENTAL PROCESSES

Today we have become accustomed in our everyday discussions to hear people characterize thought as some kind of pure 'mental process'. It is part of the 'picture' and is a very common feature today. Such a characterization is for the most part connected to (empirical) investigations, for example, in psychology, empirical Cognitive Science as well as in neurophysiology. But, we also find it, for example, in Brouwer's intuitionistic doctrine of mathematics in connection with his famous claim that a 'mental process' (in mathematical calculations) amounts to pure 'uninfected languageless thought'[Gefwert (1) 146-151]. Now, it is in connection with such phenomena that 'intentions' ought to show themselves. We assume, for example, that the self-conscious 'mind' has some kind of relationship with neural events in the liason brain. Thus it is only natural that we want to examine somewhat more closely what is usually meant by our talk of thought as being such a 'mental process'.

When listening to everyday discussions it seems to be a truism that people - following in the footsteps of Descartes - commonly assume thinking to take place 'in the head' (the Inner). Modern developments in neurology, physiology, computing science, etc., seem to make this approach unassailable; indeed, its influence is so pervasive that the identification of the physical brain with the mind has entered into common parlance. We often encounter the popular belief that it is here 'within the head' that what, by most people, is characterized as the 'mind' is assumed to exist. It is here, in the brain, that we have to seek the scientific solution to 'thought'. For example, according to Fodor, it is here in the 'internal' part of ourselves with its 'innately specified system of language' (which is a 'private language' [Infra III.6]) that we have to look for what he call's the 'language of thought'.21

In analytical philosophy as well as in psychology (and also in empirical 'cognitive science') we find that people talk of thought-processes ('what goes on inside someone's head') as a little known and perhaps a mysterious, certainly a complicated, process of the mind. It is a very common way of talking (for example, according to 'cognitivistic' thought) and we find there to be many examples of this view in the history of philosophy and psychology. We find, for example, that Frege notoriously conceived of thinking as a mysterious 'inner' process - ' ... perhaps the most mysterious of all'[PW 145] - of grasping immaterial objects that are like physical objects, only non-spatial and timeless. We are then prone to conceive of thinking as a process of an athereal inner 'mind-stuff' as the psychologist William James (1842-1910) called it .22

Interestingly enough, this picture of the Inner is reinforced by our everyday way of talking. For example, when we utter statements like 'When I was talking to him, I did not know what was going on in his head', 'A thought crossed my mind' and other similar kinds of statements we clearly notice this. One often encounters the position, particularly of those who study the mechanism of perception (neuroscientists), that the brain receives information from the senses, that this information is duly encoded in the brain and interpreted by the brain. By interpreting this information, the brain builds up a representation of the external world and then issues instructions which will, for example, ensure the survival of the organism. Of course, if information is received, encoded, decoded, interpreted and provides grounds for making plans, then there must be a language, or system of representation, in which all of this is done. The trick is to be able to somehow show the existence of such a 'language' - the 'language of thought' (Fodor). In addition the mystery connected to such assumed inner 'thought-processes' is also exacerbated by connecting the phenomena of calculating prodigies of which it is impossible to tell how their feats are accomplished [Supra II.6].

The result of such a view is that although inner experience is taken to be the very essence of human life it seems impossible, at least so far, to describe or define it. Nevertheless, there are some philosophers (and scientists), however, who belive that the 'language of thought' can be described as well as defined (and, indeed, explained). The problem, according to this view, is that ' ... we do not yet have a specific science of consciousness, so we cannot turn to "conscientologists" ... [s]o we must seek help in the field that is called cognitive science: the joint effort of philosophers, psychologists, neuroscientists, and artificial intelligence'.[23] This is, for example, the view entertained in the writings of 'cognitive scientists' and speculative neurophysiologists. They conceive the 'internal' to be an inner mental process which is somehow neurologically realized. The general conception at work involves the supposition that the brain has a 'language' of its own ('mentalese'), which consists of symbols that represent things. It uses the vocabulary of this language to encode information and it produces descriptions of what is seen (or, more generally, perceived). What this internal 'language/mechanism of thought' amounts to will, according to them, one day be unveiled. According to Cognitive Science the problem of the 'internal' is a genuine scientific mystery which given enough time and resources will be duly resolved by good theory and pertinent experiment. The result is the following bold (but note: scientific and empirical) conjecture: We assume there to exist hidden - Inner - mental mechanisms at work here, mechanisms which it becomes the task of empirical psychology, Cognitive Science and neurophysiology to investigate and unveil. The difficulty, however, is that there is no universal agreement in the scientific community concerning what it is that we are actually studying when we do empirical research on the topic called 'consciousness' (the 'internal').

At this stage I want immediatedly to emphasize the following: This was not how Wittgenstein understood the problem.[24] In 1933 we find that Wittgenstein told his students that [BB 6]

> It is misleading ... to talk of thinking as of a 'mental activity'. We may say that thinking is essentially the activity of oprating with signs. This activity is performed by the hand, when we think by writing; ... I would only draw your attention to the fact that you are using a metaphor ... .

Wittgenstein's claim that there is no single agent of thought and that talk of the mind as such an agent being unilluminately and misleadingly metaphorical has been widely discussed.[25] It becomes clear when he, for example, writes that [Z §608]

> [n]o supposition seems to me more natural than that there is no process in the brain correlated with associating or with thinking; so that it would be impossible to read off thought-processes from brain-processes. I mean this: if I talk or write, there is, I assume, a system of impulses going out from my brain and correlated with my spoken or written thoughts. But why should the system continue further in the direction of the centre? Why should this order not proceed, so to speak, out of chaos.

Thus Wittgenstein emphasized that there is no necessary connection between a thought-process and a brain-process. In fact, he emphasizes that there are no processes present in the brain that are necessary when we deal with thinking and natural language.

I also want to issue a warning concerning our use of the 'internal' when understood as part of a dualistic Mind-Body theory of some kind. This term contains a danger, for it fastens the temptation to see various elements of the 'internal' as essentially alike, i.e., as different components of a homogenous whole. In fact, *our psychological concepts fall into various categories* and, within these groups, there are differences as well as similarities. In order to understand these differences we have to explore the 'grammar' (in Wittgenstein's sense) of the words (concepts) in question [Gefwert (1) 236-253]. The complexity of the 'internal' reflects not differences of degree, but differences of concept [cf. RPP I §108].

According to Wittgenstein, there is nothing that can be characterized as a universal (general) feature of 'intention'. The Inner cannot be treated by any kind of scientific (empirical) investigation (in the sense of Cognitive Science). Thus we don't, e.g., have any distinction between 'universals' and 'particulars' at this primary stage. To assume this to be the case is to fall victim to a conceptual illusion. As he, much later, says, '[i]f I now say that the experience of remembering and the experience of pain are different in kind that is misleading: for "experiences of different kinds" makes one think perhaps of a difference like that between a pain, a tickle, and a feeling of familiarity. Whereas the difference of which we are speaking is comparable, rather, to that between the number 1 and $\sqrt{-1}$'[RPP I §108].

We can thus establish that there seems to be a strong temptation to understand the complexity of the 'internal' as an inclination to treat all differences as simply experiental (as some empirical psychologists do). But, according to Wittgenstein, this is not the case. Thus we find that he, in the later part of his life, is writing the interesting comment that '[t]he expression "Who knows what is going on inside him!". The interpretation of outer events as consequences of unknown, or merely surmised, inner ones. The interest that is focused on the Inner, as if on the chemical structure from which behaviour issues. For one needs only to ask "What do I care about inner events, whatever they are?!" to see that a different attitude is conceivable. - "But surely everyone will always be interested in his *own* inner life!" Nonsense. Would I know that pain, etc., etc., was something Inner if I weren't told so?'[RPP II §643]. Thus the postulation of a general and mysterious Inner (like 'mentalese' according to Chomsky and Fodor) does not seem to be the only option we have. But, is there any alternative? We shall look at this important question next.

To begin with, as Wittgenstein noted in his final lecture series at Cambridge, the most striking of the problems that someone like the psychologist (as well as the modern 'cognitivist') encounters is that they cannot directly observe the Inner phenomena they are supposedly studying: all that can be investigated are the manifestations of the

Inner, not the Inner itself (through introspection). Furthermore, to assume that one can investigate the Inner by introspection involves a circularity in that to be able to observe 'thinking' presupposes that one should already have to know what 'thinking' is. *One cannot observe what one cannot identify in the first place.* We easily overlook this problem. But, we have additional problems: If we assume that we somehow had achieved the competence to observe 'thinking' then why should one person's conclusions hold for everyone? What makes the result applicable to me applicable to you as well? Here we easily emphasize the intersubjective 'collective' interpretation [Supra II.1]. Note, that we also have to be able to separate the act of observing the experience from the act of having it. As Wittgenstein said, '[i]f you go about to observe your own mental happenings, you may alter them and create new ones, and the whole point of observing is that you should not do this'[WLPP 235].

The position is - in a loose way - analogous to Heisenberg's uncertainty principle which we encounter in quantum mechanics: one cannot, due to the limit of the wavelength of light, simultaneously measure (observe) the momentum as well as the position of a single electron without altering either variable. But, in connection with the Inner, according to Wittgenstein, the result is that it seems impossible to study the Inner either from the 'outside' or from the 'inside' because ' ... the science of mental phenomena has this puzzle: I can't observe the mental phenomena of others, and I can't observe my own in the proper sense of "observe"'[WLPP 235]. There is no unique object called the Inner that can be identified and studied. Indeed, one can, like Dennett, say that '[t]here is no single, definite "stream of consciousness", because there is no central Headquarters, no Cartesian Theater where "it all comes together" for the perusal of a Central Meaner'.[26] As this suggests, *the Inner is not a brute given, but something structured by the particular concepts we adopt.* One could, perhaps, call it a 'bundle-structure'. But, we have to be aware. We easily simplify the problem because there is a strong temptation to underestimate the complexity of the Inner, and this is reinforced by the inclination to treat all differences as simply experiential. In most cases, however, this amounts to grammatical differences in disguise [Gefwert (1) 195ff].

But this, for many (even today) novel view, was not a novel insight as far as Wittgenstein is concerned. Already in the *Big Typescript* (1931-1933) we find him writing that '[i]n the consideration of our problems one of the most dangerous ideas is the idea that we think with, or in, our heads. The idea of a process in the head, in a completely enclosed space, makes thinking something occult ... It is a travesty of the truth to say "Thinking is an activity of our mind, as writing is of the hand"'[PhG 106]. This quotation tells us clearly that Wittgenstein would not have accepted the universal 'cognitivist' (scientific) claim of there, perhaps, existing some kind of a 'hidden mental mechanism/language' ('mentalese') in the brain which can be discovered (by empirical measurement/observation) to be responsible for thought. This view is further strenghtened by Wittgenstein's claim, written a few years later, that ' ... [i]n the sense, in which there are processes (including mental processes) which are chararcetristic of understanding, understanding is not a mental process'[PhI §154]. The result is therefore that there seems to be ' ... an unbridgeable gulf between consciousness and brain-process'[PhI §412].

This concerns also the mystical notion of 'intention': it is not a 'process' of any kind. It is here, in connection with the assumed Inner, i.e., the 'mental processes' said to take place in the head, that one also encounters the assumption - or *superstition* as Wittgenstein later characterized it [PhI §110] - that there occurs some extremely complex and mysterious 'processes' of the assumed Inner called 'intentions'. Thus we find that Wittgenstein, in the *Philosophical Remarks,* writes that '[a]nother mental process belonging to this group [like, for example, the fulfilment of an expectation], and which ties in with all these things, is *intention*. You could say that language is like a control room operated with a particular *intention* or built for a particular purpose'[PhR 69]. It is interesting to find that Wittgenstein, in this context, calls such 'mental processes' for 'interpretations' or 'uses' without explicitly delimiting their scope. He just talks in general terms about expectations, thoughts, wishes, etc. [cf. PhR 69-70]. A characteristic feature of these phenomena was that they were to be articulated and they were in some sense to incorporate the picture of what could be characterized as the expected, the thought, etc. In one of his lectures Wittgenstein stated that '[w]e are not intersted in ... processes themselves. For us explanation and understanding are the same, understanding being the correlate of explanation, which produces it (though not causally) ... '[L (1) 51]. But how is one to understand Wittgenstein's point as far as these mysterious 'processes' of the Inner are concerned?

To begin with, Wittgenstein seems to be of the same opinion as Brentano that in the end there is always some kind of presentation *(vorstellung)* present. In the *Tractatus* that presentation was always the frame for a judgement [T §4.0311]. However, now, in his later texts, he acknowledges that it can also be connected to other 'mental processes'. But we can now ask: What is a *mental* process like in the first place? What is this immaterial substance called 'thought' which ' ... is liable to be imagined as gaseous, or rather, aethereal' [BB 47]. Despite the fact that it is not right, like René Descartes (1596-1650), to say that the essence of this immaterial substance of 'the mental' is thinking, due to the fact, for example, as pointed out by Kenny,[27] that the Cartesian concept of thinking is not coherent, we can, nevertheless, for the sake of the argument, at this preliminary point in our investigation quite safely set out from the Cartesian *res cogitans*. As did Wittgenstein in the *Tractatus* so did also Descartes in his philosophical writings apply 'thought' as a central concept. One finds that for him even understanding, willing, imagining, not to mention knowing, exhibited aspects of thinking.[28] Thus it was the case for Descartes, as it also was for Baruch Spinoza (1632-1677), that all modifications of the mind amounted to thinking.[29] In contrast to substance the Cartesian spirit (mind) did not have any spatial extension: one was necessarily and immediatedly aware, as far as such an activity - thinking - was concerned. It seems highly probable that Wittgenstein might have had some kind of a Cartesian model of the Outer versus the Inner in mind when he set out to investigate the nature of mental acts.[30]

The factual nature of the 'empirical subject', as it was portrayed by Wittgenstein in the *Tractatus,* gave the impression that 'thought' seemed to have a meaning somehow detached from ourselves as thinking subjects. In the beginning of the 1930's we find that this view changes. In the *Big Typescript* it seems that Wittgenstein was of the opinion that we give 'meaning' by our own activities. Thus he says that ' ... we don't want to say that meaning is a special experience ... but something that we do, otherwise it [meaning] would be just dead'[PhG 156]. He specifies this point by saying that '[y]es, meaning something is like going up to someone'[PhG 157; cf. PhI §§455, 457, 689]. Thus 'to mean' amounts to *do* something ('meaning is use'). In this case the mental processes of meaning and understanding which highlight our interpretational activities becomes especially interesting. When we say something we mean something by the assertion made and, in a similar way, when we read something we understand it. But how does this 'meaning' come about and where does this 'understanding' take place? Now, Wittgenstein formulates the problem like this: 'Must one see an image of the colour blue in one's mind whenever one reads the word "blue" with understanding?'[PhG 74]. Something seems to be necessary in order to be able to separate the understanding from the non-understanding, for example, when reading something or, alternatively, when meaningful (intended) speech is being distinguished from such speech that one does not understand. There seems to be some kind of mental process present which accompanies our activities in the examples that we mentioned, i.e., when reading something as well as in the case of meaningful speech.

If Wittgenstein did, indeed, sometimes understand these mental processes according to the Cartesian model, then one notices that at least in the *Big Typescript* there occurs certain explicit cracks in this model. The first doubt concerns the genuine modality of the mental processes. By being the 'movements' of the Cartesian thinking subject, one should expect these 'mental processes' to be limited as far as the duration in time is concerned in a similar way as we find occurrences to be in connection with material substance. But, as Wittgenstein asks, when does, for example, our understanding begin when we interpret an unknown language, that is, '[a]t what moment of translating into English does understanding begin?'[PhG 43-44]. 'Understanding' (or 'meaning') cannot be understood as something that " ... happens [in] an act of instantaneous, as it were non-discursive, grasp of grammar. As if it could all be swallowed down in a single gulp"[PhG 49]. According to Wittgenstein, we should, in order to get clearer about the grammar of the word 'understanding', ask, for example, questions like ' ... *when do we understand a sentence?*' or, alternatively, '[h]ow long does it take to understand a sentence'[PhG 50].

According to Gilbert Ryle (1900-1976) it is highly misleading to suggest that one thinks 'in anything' (the Inner or the 'Ghost in the Machine')[31] although it is both true and important that whatever one thinks must be *expressible* in words, images or whatever (the Outer). According to Ryle the background to the myth of the 'Ghost in the Machine' (the Inner) is that [32]

> ... mental happenings occur in insulated fields, known as 'minds', and there is, apart maybe from telepathy, no direct causal connexion between what happens in one mind and what happens in another. Only through the medium of the public physical world can the mind of one person make a difference to the mind of another. The mind is its own place and in his inner life each of us lives the life of a ghostly Robinson Crusoe. People can see, hear and jolt one another's bodies, but they are irremediably blind and deaf to the workings of one another's minds and inoperative upon them.

We can thus ask: Provided one speaks and reads in language, does one then also 'think' (intend) in language? Is the parallelism between thought and speech really that simple? That is, when I speak in Swedish do I simultaneously apply a 'mental process' (a version of 'mentalese') in *addition* to the activity of speaking? The scientists adhering to Cognitive Science which is neurophysiologically directed assumes this to be the case.

As we said above, according to Wittgenstein, to assume this amounts to a conceptual illusion. It is not a person's mind that independently thinks for him/her and nor does he/she think with it. To what extent mental activities can be correlated with brain activity is an empirical (scientific) matter and not one which can be decided on purely conceptual grounds. *However, once one drops the assumption that what we call the 'mind' must be reducible to the brain (and neurophysiological processes) then the whole idea of combining them suddenly seems extremely implausible.* The claim that the 'mind' must be empirically explicable in terms of the brain is misguided. The empirical sciences investigating the brain (e.g., neuropsychology, neurophysiology, Cognitive Science, etc.) are of course quite right to assume that there is more to be discovered concerning it (and there certainly will be). However, whatever scientific (empirical) explanation of the function of the brain will one day be achieved is a different and empirical matter. But, we have to realize that it has nothing to do with the philosophical (conceptual) problem of the Inner vs. the Outer.

Wittgenstein denied the meaningfulness of a Cartesian inspired dual Inner vs. Outer account of mental processes. For example, if we ask 'What does ones thinking (intending) consists in?' there is no answer to this question (the sentence is philosophically misleading) because 'thinking' cannot be separated from the activity due to the fact that there is nothing which accompanies and runs concurrently with our thought (intention)[RPP II §184]. We can thus set out to investigate this denial of the modality (possibility) concerning the occurrence of mental processes, say, when we read a newspaper. A good place to begin is that long part which deals with problems connected to reading and which one finds outlined in §§156-171 in the *Philosophical Investigations*. The example of reading (say, a newspaper) is connected to our problem as follows.

As we have seen, according to the 'picture-theory' in the *Tractatus,* a picture is the projection of reality [Gefwert (1) 56-69]. However, later, in the *Blue Book*, we find Wittgenstein saying that ' ... it is easy to describe what we should call processes of deriving a picture from an object (roughly speaking, processes of projection)'[BB 33]. As the result of such a derivation or projection Wittgenstein had hoped to achieve an 'intentional representation' but now he is forced to admit that every projection or process of derivation is inadequate when it comes to characterize 'intention'. The reason for this is, of course, to be found in the fact that it is always possible (in a logical sense) that these 'processes of derivation' can be understood in different ways. We are here specifically concerned with the identification of intention through an 'act of derivation' because in connection with reading where Wittgenstein's problem is to identify that which separates reading from non-reading 'derivation' plays a crucial role. That is: To read amounts - somehow - to *derive* from a text and when such a 'derivation' does not occur we are simply not concerned with the activity of reading. But, to be able to read in such a way does not necessarily imply that one has to understand what one is reading. The reader does not have to understand what he reads (for example, one can quite easily 'read' an Italian text aloud without being able to understand a single sentence) but what is important is that the words that the person utters (we assume that he reads aloud) can be derived from the text.

The result is that if we set out from the condition that the difference between, for example, that of reading and not reading occurs in our consciousness - in the uttering of words in connection with an accompanying mental process - we, in fact, face an ideal case of a Wittgensteinian interpretation of signs as a mental process, i.e., the translation of a 'picture' by what he characterized by the expression of 'to follow a rule'. If the presence of such a 'mental process' was to be counted as a criterion of reading in contrast to, for example, the random utterance of words in a correct order by applying memory, guessing, etc., then the ability to read could in a precise way be distinguished from these other cases of 'non-reading'. In such a case we could talk in a completely meaningful sense, for example, about the *first word* that was read by a child who is learning to speak. But, if learning to speak amounts to a series of events where the criterion for being able to speak amounts to the relative number of decreasing mistakenly 'derived' or 'non-drived' utterances, then how can we talk of anything like the 'first red word' in the first place?

In fact, according to Wittgenstein, we cannot [PhI §157]. The criterion for being able to read cannot amount to any kind of 'conscious or unconscious experience', 'process' or 'occurrence of the mind' which accompanies every word and sentence that we read but which, in contrast, is lacking in any word or expression that has been simply repeated (say, by a parrot), guessed or remembered. Such 'occurrences' would be *hypothetical,* which is why they cannot amount to the criteria for being able to read because ' ... in the case of the living reading-machine [a child] "reading" meant reacting to written signs in such-and-such ways. This concept was therefore quite independent of that of a mental or other mechanism. - Nor can the teacher here say of the pupil: "Perhaps he was already reading when he said that word". For there is no doubt about what he did. - The change when the pupil began to read was a change in his behaviour; and it makes no sense here to speak of "a first word in his new state"'[PhI §157].

The result, according to Wittgenstein, is that 'thought' and 'intention' (which we exhibit in various contexts) amounts to widely ramified concepts having a variety of applications. We usually treat these as being somehow related (or even united). We say that someone who is talking is expressing thoughts, but we also say that someone is thinking if that person is working in a purposeful way, for example, with the intention of making something. We also speak of thinking when a person is sitting silently and apparently is doing nothing but is, for example, later able to give the answer to a problem. In the face of this variety Wittgenstein points out that it would be possible to have different words for the various things we call thinking (intending), '... one for "thinking out aloud"; one for thinking as one talks in the imagination; one for a pause during which something or other floats before the mind (or doesn't) after which, however, we are able to give a confident answer'[RPP II §215]. To 'think' and to 'intend' does not amount to universal 'abstract entities' (as they are regarded, for example, in '*a priori* semantical theories of meaning'). In the end these expressions do not amount to 'universal terms' at all and are, therefore, not referential (or structuralized) in kind. Such terms are not, ultimately, part of any scientific (empirical or analytical *a priori*) theory. To believe that this is the case is to adhere to a mistaken 'picture'. Consequently, we are for the most part being cheated by expressions like 'to think' and 'to intend' (and other expressions as well).

What holds the concept together is the extremely simplified 'picture' of an assumed 'inner process'. This, however, is not a correct view. In all of these widely separated cases the concepts of 'thinking' and 'intending' actually stand for a number of different ramified activities ' ... like a ramified traffic network which connects many out-of-the-way places with each other'[RPP II §216]. In Wittgenstein's terminology: 'thinking' (and 'intending') amounts to 'family-resemblance' expressions [cf. PhI §67]. They do not amount to 'theoretical entities', i.e., universal terms (like 'set' or 'number', etc.), which somehow is said to explicitly refer to 'individuals' (the individual sets or numbers). Such an assumption is mistaken. The success of science (physics, chemistry, biology, etc.) encourages us to assume that there is an explanation for everything, i.e., that the world (the universe) is a pattern of causes which we shall one day track down. This amounts to a conceptual illusion.

Once we have abandoned the idea that a non-reducible 'mind' would be some form of ghostly metaphysical entity, there is no reason for supposing that everything we want to say about the 'mind' and the Inner will one day be rewritable in terms, for example, of the brain. The concepts concerning the Inner do not refer to a brute reality, they are neither a set of private experiences nor a set of brain states: rather they are the concepts which lies at the heart of all our mutual interaction and understanding. That is why we are for the most part cheated by these expressions. What holds the concepts together is the extremely simplified picture of an assumed 'inner process', for '[i]n all of these cases, we say that the mind is not idle, that something is going on inside it; and we thereby distinguish these cases from a state of stupor, from mechanical actions'[RPP II §217].

But, what then is 'thinking' and 'intending'? The answer we arrive at seems to be twofold. On the one hand, *there simply is no unique answer to this question*. 'Thinking' and 'intending' are not, basically, universal terms. On the contrary, they are widely ramified concepts which comprises many manifestations of life [RPP II §220]. Nothing a scientist might discover (by empirical means) could play the role intentions currently play in our lives. According to Wittgenstein 'intention' will always remain as 'mysterious' as life itself due to the fact that the phenomena of it are widely scattered [RPP II §220]. On the other hand, *the answer is that it is a fundamental characteristic of human activity and human life.* The idea that the individual thinks, has intentions, etc., lies at the heart of the notion of a 'person' (individual) and in that sense underlies all our interaction with each other. This is aptly shown in an example provided by Wittgenstein when he says that '[i]f somebody tells me of some incident, or asks me an everyday question (e.g. what time it is), I'm not going to ask him whether he was thinking while he was telling me or asking me. Or again: it would not be immediately clear in what circumstances one might have said that he did this without thinking - even though one can imagine such circumstances'[RPP II §222].

According to Wittgenstein it thus seems as if the concept of 'thinking' (as well as 'intention') does not refer to a single process or to anything that happens. Indeed, '[t]he use of a word such as "thinking" is simply far more erratic than it appears at first sight'[RPP II §234]. That is, there is no single and unique process (which can be scientifically explained) which makes us 'think' and 'intend'. Instead we have an enormous amont of concepts which shows us what 'thinking' and 'intending' amounts to in different contexts. These concepts lie at the heart of the notion of the 'inner' and as such belongs to the special network of concepts which provide the framework for our understanding of human life: what I have called the 'bundle-structure'. For example, in our scientific and mathematical practices (say, the 'measurement problem' in quantum physics or in the investigations of the possibility of there existing a genuine 'machine/artificial intelligence', etc.) we seem to use the concept of thought to pick out one particular aspect of our lives (the 'problem of the detached observer'/the 'thinking machine') and express this in terms of the metaphor of thought and intention as an invisible and unique 'inner mental process'. In order that this claim of the contextual dependance of 'thought' and 'intention' should not sound like an unfounded thesis -

like the Museum Myth of Meaning - but instead as a genuine argument, we have to understand that it is closely connected to what has become customary to call Wittgenstein's argument against the possibility of a 'private language argument(s)'.

III.6 THE 'PRIVATE LANGUAGE' ARGUMENTS

Already as early as in 1932 we find that Wittgenstein had discussed the impossibility of what he calls a 'private language'. Between 1934 and 1936 Wittgenstein compiled a set of lecture notes concerning 'private experience' which have been published by the name 'Notes for Lectures on "Sense Data" and "Private Experience"'[NSP].33 These lecture notes were concerned with a topic which has later been known as the - admittedly controversial - argument against the possibility of a 'private language'. In fact, the characterization of the name 'the private language argument' is slightly misleading because there are actually, not one, but many such arguments to be found in Wittgenstein's texts.

We find that he, in his post-1937 texts, introduces the 'private language' argument by saying that [PhI §269],

> ... there are certain criteria in a man's behaviour for the fact that he does not understand a word: that it means nothing to him, that he can do nothing with it. And criteria for his 'thinking he understands', attaching some meaning to the word, but not the right one. And, lastly, criteria for his understanding the word right. In the second case one might speak of a subjective understanding. And sounds which no one else understands but which I *'appear to understand'* might be called a 'private language'.

This argument amount to the *locus classicus* for Wittgenstein's attack on the traditional conception of the Inner. We also find that he later returned to this topic, notably in the manuscript that has become known as 'Notes for the "Philosophical Lecture"'[NPL; MS 166], which he compiled as a response to an invitation by the British

Academy to give the annual 'Philosophical Lecture' in 1942. Despite the fact that Wittgenstein did talk about ' ... the discussion of a private language'[MS 165, 101] the very name of a 'private language argument' that we find in the literature is not due to him.[34]

But, how should one formulate this argument? In the literature we find some good characterizations of it. One of the best has been provided by Rhees who states that the problem of a 'private language' amounts to[35]

> ... the problem of how words mean. When we talk about something, our language does not point to it, nor mirror it. Pointing or mirroring could refer to things only within a convention, anyway: only when there is a way in which pointing is understood and a way in which mirroring is understood. I point for the sake of someone who understands it. Apart from that it were an idle ceremony; as idle as making sounds in front of things. Our words refer to things by the way they enter in discourse; by their connexions with what people are saying and doing, for instance, and by the way they affect what is said and done. What we say makes a difference. What expressions we use makes a difference ... If it made no difference what sound you made or when, you could not be understood and you would have said nothing. If you have said something your utterance will be taken in one way and not in another.

The importance of this argument is hard to exaggerate because it undermines our natural 'picture' of the Inner. It calls for a general rethinking of our approach to psychological concepts. The argument challenges our most basic presuppositions about how we should understand the Inner and, if these are overthrown, it is by no means clear what we should put in their place. We might be tempted to switch to behaviourism but one has to understand that rather than solving the problem this only suppresses it. Despite the mysteries and uncertainties surrounding it, the Inner plays a crucial part in our lives and, from a Wittgensteinian perspective, the point is to understand that role and not attempt to deny it.

But what is the history behind this argument(s)? When we attempt to trace the historical development of this argument(s) we notice that Wittgenstein, as early as in the *Big Typescript,* was looking for a novel way to understand a 'mental process'. Here 'to understand' means to know something (since, e.g., to understand a word is to know how it is used) which, in turn, is said to amount to a *skill* [PhG 47; 50]. Such a skill, or ability, Wittgenstein calls a 'state' *(Zustand),* but, as such, it is closer to the unconscious rather than the conscious state of the 'mind-model'[PhG 48]. For example, we might have a headache without interruption the whole day, or we might think of something specific for an hour or two, but, what is one to make of a claim stating that one is able to drive a bicycle without interruption (for, say, a month) or that one knows that $2 + 2 = 4$ (for a certain amount of time)? At most it can be taken to mean that we during this time have not suffered any severe psychichal or physical injury. The grammar of the ' ... word "know" isn't a "state of consciousness", but something different. And there is only one way to learn it: to watch how the word is used in practice'[PhG 71]. But this requires that a momentary understanding, the understanding of a sentence, has to be connected to a larger concept of understanding: the understanding of language. When we connect the understanding of a sentence to the understanding of a language we notice that what we deal with here is not a 'state of consciousness' which 'accompanies' the sentence; what we deal with here is what can be characterized as the ' ... understanding or mastery of a calculus, something like the *ability* to multiply'[PhG 50].

 A language that only a single person understands (for example, by which somebody speaks to oneself about one's own conceptions and which cannot be translated to normal language) is, in fact, not a genuine language at all. *We have to understand that there are no concepts determining what such a 'language' amounts to.* Such a 'language' does not allow us in a meaningful way to speak of a correct (or a mistaken) way of using the 'language' and thus not to speak in a meaningful way about understanding it (which as a concept requires the contradiction 'mistakenly understood' to be available).

Wittgenstein's argument against the possibility of such a 'private language' is - in his later texts - highlighted in his assertion that such a language does not allow enough *criteria* for the meanings of its words and the lack of such criteria results in that the words do not mean anything or can mean anything [PhI §269]. But, the question now becomes: how are we to understand this statement? I shall now attempt to explain this point.

If the owner of a 'private language' creates a dictionary referring to his own sensations then the only criterion for the continuing and actual existence of the sign and the corresponding object (sensation) continuously being on par with each other can only amount to something which we can characterize as the 'rational feeling' of the speaker. The recognition of a sensation is then left solely as being the responsibility of an impression. The owner of a 'private language' cannot find support for his memory from any 'official' instance, say, an encyclopaedia. If the owner feels this impression, when he again encounters it, he cannot test and find support for the correctness of this sensation by any other means than by producing ever new images which support the old ones. According to Wittgenstein the situation can be said to remind one of a case where ' ... someone were to buy several copies of the morning paper to assure himself that what it said was true'[PhI §265]. We thus end up in a situation that in a language which itself is founded on images amounting to criteria (sensations, experiences, etc.) everything which feels correct *is* correct which, in turn, means that the word 'correct' in such a language is meaningless [cf. PhI §258]. Such a 'private language' amounts to a conceptual illusion and, consequently, can only in a parasitic way be characterized as a *language* in the first place. This, in turn, is simply, by the fact that the argument itself is due to this illusion, easily taken to point to the possibility of there existing such a genuine 'private' language. The important thing here is to be able to recognize the conceptual illusion of such a 'private language' as being a genuine language.

We shall exhibit the outlines of this argument in order to give the reader the necessary insight into the very point with it. To begin with, we find the 'cornerstone' of this argument outlined in the *Philosophical*

Investigations [cf. PhI §§243-315] where Wittgenstein writes that a 'private language' is a language whose words are to ' ... refer to what can only be known to the person speaking; to his immediate private sensations'[PhI §243]. Other examples of the argument are to be found in the conclusion of Wittgenstein's discussion concerning the possibility of giving oneself a private definition of a sign. Here, he says that ' ... in the present case I have no criterion of correctness. One would like to say: whatever is going to seem right to me is right. And that only means that here we can't talk about the right'[PhI §258] and, at last, when he gives us the advice to '[a]lways get rid of the idea of the private object in this way: assume that it constantly changes, but that you do not notice the change because your memory constantly deceives you'[PhI 207].

The argument itself can be characterized as referring to the possibility of there existing a language which, unlike ordinary language, only the speaker - 'logically' - can understand. That is, the essential characteristic of privacy seems to be that '[n]obody but I can see it, hear it; nobody except myself knows what it's like. Nobody except I can get at it'[NPL 447] and in such a case '[p]rivacy of feelings can mean: nobody can know them unless I show them, or: I can't really show them. Or: if I don't want to, I needn't give any sign of my feeling, but even if I want to I can only show a sign and not the feeling' [NPL 447]. According to Wittgenstein, to entertain a belief in the possibility of there existing such a 'private language' creates a dilemma for the defender of the notion of 'private experience' as well as to the associated conception of 'inner ostension'. *We can therefore conclude that the assumption of there existing such a 'private language' is mistaken and amounts to a conceptual illusion.*

This insight, if correct, has great consequences for many empirically inclined philosophers (and scientists) who think that the only matters of fact that we really know are our own experiences: what we claim to know about the world or about other people is based on our knowledge of our own mental states and processes. We can, following Hacker, dubb this picture of the mind to ' ... the inner/outer conception of the mental'.[36] Analytical philosophers (and scientists) who subscribe to the Cartesian distinction between the Inner and the Outer also, usually, take for granted that our knowledge of our experiences can be expressed in language - at least to ourselves in the sense that its words have acquired their meaning for each of us by an essentially private process: an internal ostensive definition [Infra IV.3] - and that the possibility of such an expression does not presuppose any acquaintance with the external world or other minds. Anyone who accepts this view must believe in the possibility of a 'private language' whose words acquire meaning simply by being linked to private experiences. This kind of 'private empiricism' carries with it a version of scepticism which expresses itself, for example, in a statement like '[f]or all we know, what I call "red" you call "green" and vice versa'[cf. BB 60; PhI §272]. It is against the possibility of such a sceptically inspired view to be correct that Wittgenstein now turns in his characterization of what a philosophical investigation amounts to [Infra V.3].

The debate concerning the 'private language argument(s)' has during the years since its first publication become quite extensive. As a result of this there consequently exits a quite large amount of relevant literature to be found.[37] If we set out from the terminology of the *Tractatus* we can say that a 'private language' would amount to a referential language constituted by the logical names of the language where the function of a word is to *refer* to some object or to *represent* some object. In such a case the basic relation occurring between the 'world' and the units of language (words, sentences) could be expressed by a sentence-schema like, for example, 'the word ... signifies ... '.[38] Now, a language constituted by private sensations of names would be a language which *only* the owner of the sensations *could* understand because the meaning of the words (or sentences) of such a language would uniquely be constituted by their representational or referential relations on the senses which, in turn, would amount to modifications of the Cartesian mind (awareness). Such a language would only be available for that specific mind.

A typical example, and one which Wittgenstein frequently applied, is the various uses of pain words. How do we learn to use these? According to Wittgenstein, we learn them against the background of certain instinctive types of behaviour. For example, such words ' ... are connected with the primitive, the natural, expression of the sensation and used in their place. A child has hurt himself and he cries; and then the adults talk to him and teach him exclamations and, later, sentences. They teach the child new pain-behaviour'[PhI §244]. In this example it is crucial to understand that there is, from the beginning, a *connection* between the Inner experience and its Outer expression. If such a connection did not exist there would be no way to bring language and experience into relation with one another. If this would not be the case, then the mind (awareness) would in an essential way amount to some kind of a 'private object'. But this argument cannot be correct since we do not, for example, learn the use of pain words simply by guessing which specific 'inner processes' are connected with, say, injuring oneself when falling from a ladder, since, ' ... in that case this problem might arise as well: on account of *which* of my sensations do I cry out when I damage myself'[RPP I §305].

The point is that a child behaves in a particular way when it injures oneself and when it, on the basis of this behaviour, is taught to say that it is in pain. Thus a verbal component is added to the behaviour and setting out from this primary verbal utterance (say, 'It hurts') other more sophisticated utterances (like 'My foot hurts', etc.) are added later on in life. The concept of pain can, later in life (for example, when the child has learnt a more sophisticated vocabulary), be described in such a 'richer' vocabulary by saying something like 'she feels as if she had lost all that was most precious to her'. But now it is important to understand that what, according to Wittgenstein, is involved in learning a certain language-game *is not equivalent to embracing crude behaviourism*. This becomes evident when he says that '"[s]o, you are saying that the word 'pain' really means crying" - On the contrary: the verbal expression of pain replaces crying and does not describe it'[PhI §244]. This clear example brings out the special role language plays in relation to the Inner. This shows us - *pace* Kripke - that use of words do not presuppose the learning of explicit rules (the 'rules-as-theory' confusion [Infra V.3]): it builds on natural reaction when a person is being taught to use them in appropriate circumstances.

This example shows us two things. It shows (1) the importance of utterances and (2) their difference from statements based on observation. The result is interesting: we notice that while there are criteria for saying of someone (a third person) that he/she is in pain, there are no such criteria in one's own case. If a person says of someone that he/she is in pain it is a typical requirement that one can support such a statement by pointing to aspects of the other person's behaviour which amount to accepted criteria for pain. In one's own case, however, one cannot observe something which would lead one to say that one is in pain nor can one justify this statement by pointing to some evidence for it. Instead one simply repeats an expression that one has been taught to apply in such circumstances or, alternatively, formulates (at a later stage) another synonymous expression. From this we notice the interesting as well as important insight (contrary to the position forced on us by the 'rules-as-theory' confusion) that an individual's use of an expression is not the end of a language-game but its beginning [PhI §290; Infra V.3]. The result is that whereas pain-behaviour, initially, consists simply of crying, etc., it is the case that verbal components are gradually added as well. These become the basis for ever more sophisticated language-games. What is also striking here is that the individual's use of ordinary language (speech) is not rule-governed in a 'structuralized' (theoretical) sense [Gefwert (1) 88-93]. The individual learns a word and then combines it with others in a new - apparently arbitary - way, but, nevertheless, people are still somehow able 'to understand what he/she means' despite this 'problem'. We shall return to this puzzle below [Infra IV.4].

What we have said so far makes us aware of certain important points that has to be made clear: (1) Our use of language to express aspects of the Inner presupposes certain natural reactions which we as humans share and (2) language extends the individual's possibilities of expression and hence the possibilities of experience. Such experiences requires the ability to speak (for example, a dog cannot hope that its dinner will be served punctually at nine o'clock). It is through the acquisition of language that individuals acquires more complex possibilities of expression and hence the possibility of a more complex inner life. Only as 'behaviour' develops do certain concepts (and certain experiences) become accessible. Thus, while an adult can experience the tragedy of, say, a play like Macbeth by Shakespeare, it is impossible for a child. *Such an approach to the Inner amounts to a novel way of understanding psychological concepts.* It also amounts to rejection of the confusing picture which treats the Inner as if it were some kind of substance whose changes, states and motions the individual observes and reports on (introspection). In conrast to this view, Wittgenstein's approach emphasizes that what interests us is the attitudes and behaviour of human beings. Thus, for example, pain-behaviour of others do indeed matter to us and it is on this basis that the language-game, for example, concerning 'pain' is built up. The individual reacts in a certain way and we teach him/her to use a linguistic expression instead. Such words that we teach the individual to apply are called 'sensation words' ('pain', 'tooth-ache', 'tickle', etc.) because of their role in the language-game. Thus one can say that '[p]rimitive pain-behaviour is a sensation-behaviour; it gets replaced by a linguistic expression. "The word 'pain' is the name of a sensation" is equivalent to "I've got a pain" is an expression (*Aeusserung*) of sensation'[RPP I §313].

But now we have have to be extremely cautious. At this stage we have to be careful so that we do not to misunderstand the insight gained. It concerns the doctrine which John B. Watson (1878-1958) called 'behaviourism' and which states that 'consciousness' does not exist in the first place.[39] *Now, it is important to understand that Wittgenstein's emphasis on the importance of behaviour should not be taken as a form of behaviourism.* One sometimes sees this mistake being made [Supra II.3]. We have also to be aware that this is not to state that we by the Inner are adopting some kind of rational Mentalism (the opposite of Behaviourism).[40] As Wittgenstein said, we want ' ... to see the absurdities of both what the behaviourists say and what their opponents say'[LFM 111]. By the concept of the Inner (in contrast to Mentalists) we express the distinctive nature of our interest in human behaviour. The whole point is that we do treat each other as conscious individulals who act and not simply as walking bodies (like some kind of zombie or machine) which just happens to behave in particular ways. The notion of the Inner does not refer to some distinctly existing 'mental reality' but expresses our relation to other persons. Thus it expresses a particular public way of understanding human action. Our interest in others is usually expressed as an interest in 'what is going on inside them'. In analytical philosophy (as well as in psychology and Cognitive Science), however, this insight gets twisted. In this context we usually misinterpret this picture (due to the 'rules-as-theory' confusion [Infra V.3]).

The result is that we are left with a confused idea of what is essential, say, to pain, when portrayed within science (empirical psychology, neurophysiology and reductive Cognitive Science) as a mysterious and private 'inner event'. The upshot of Wittgenstein's point is to emphasize that the usefulness of psychological concepts is not dependent of some kind of 'inner reality'. But note, that it neither involves the rejection of the Inner (as crude Materialism does), nor, indeed, our picture of the Inner. All this argument rejects is a confused and muddled interpretation of that picture. The force of Wittgenstein's claims is to call for a radical rethinking of our approach to the Inner without suggesting that talk of the Inner as such amounts to an illusion or error.

III.7 CONCLUSION: THOUGHT IS PUBLIC

As the former chapter suggests, understanding the Inner and in particular its relation to language is not as straightforward as it might first appear. We have arrived in the position that we understand that 'mental' expressions are not 'private' ones. We can now understand why, for example, the activity of 'reading' cannot simply be taken to mean any event 'occurring' in the 'consciousness' of a person (and even less so in the 'unconscious'). This is the case because the very *concept* of reading is by necessity independent of such 'private' events. To read cannot be something of which only the reader himself (and, as a matter of fact, not even he) knows whether this capacity is present or not [Cf. PhI §156].

Wittgenstein exemplifies this point, in the *Philosophical Investigations,* with the famous parable of the 'beetle in the box'. The example amounts to the following. We assume that everyone has [PhI §293]

> ... a box with something in it: we call it a 'beetle'. No one can look into anyone else's box, and everyone says he knows what a beetle is only by looking at *his* beetle. - Here it would be quite possible for everyone to have something different in his box. One might even imagine such a thing constantly changing. - But suppose the word 'beetle' had a use in these people's language? - If so it would not be used as the name of a thing. The thing in the box has no place in [language] at all; not even as *something;* for the box might even be empty. - No, one can 'divide through' by the thing in the box; it cancels out, whatever it is.

If the practice of reading amounted to something like the 'beetle' (a 'mental event') in Wittgenstein's example and thus could only be known from its own 'private practice', then it could amount to anything, in fact, it could even amount to nothing. *Ex hypothesi* such a language - 'mentalese' - would be incomprehensible to anyone other than its creator, for no one else could know what its words referred to. Such a language could not be checked by any means at all. This means, for example, that if I am the only one who knows what 'read' means then, clearly, the way of using the expression cannot be a public one. For, by hypothesis, only I could tell when the conditions were satisfied; only I could know whether the conditions for the expression to 'read' where satisfied. But, this is not enough. On Wittgenstein's view we find that I wouldn't know either when the conditions were satisfied because there is no translation in existence. There are no public criteria (constituting a translation) for when the conditions are satisfied. In the search for correctness the individual never reaches firmer ground. Surprisingly enough, each of the statements made is only backed up by her belief that it is correct, so that intrinsically all are on the same level. The result is that I or anyone else simply could not provide any satisfying conditions for when the conditions for 'reading' were satisfied. In fact, *we have to understand that there are no such conditions.*

We can then conclude that because the expression 'to read' indeed *does* have a use (amounting to a rule-like practice) it cannot be the name of a private process. It is a public practice which provides a context for where 'seeming right' and 'being right' are distinguished. Within the practice, there are rules of translations and procedures for checking whether or not these rules have been correctly applied. It is the existence of these rules and procedures which allows a distinction between accurate and inaccurate translation and so justifies our claim to be translating as opposed to simply setting down whatever feels right at the time. The trust of this argument is to refute the idea that the individual's expression of her thoughts amounts to the translation or representation of a 'private process' inside her (like adherents to Cognitive Science claims). It also undermines the very notion of 'private inner events'. The reason for this is that if the individual's statement cannot be seen as reports the only possible means of access to the assumed inner events has been ruled out. Since neither I nor any other person can distinguish between believing that a certain event took place and that event actually taking place, the notion of these events as independently existing occurrences (thought processes) is undermined. *The idea of an independently existing thought process on which the report is made can now be dropped.*

It is also important to understand that what we have said above concerning 'reading' can easily be extended to concern other mental processes as well. We begin to understand that as far as words like 'thinking', 'understanding', 'intending', 'judging', 'waiting', 'wishing', 'hoping', 'being afraid', etc., is concerned, we use them in public language-games [Infra IV.3]. They do not refer to mysterious movements of the Cartesian mind, i.e., to 'beetles' (in Wittgenstein's example) being forever inaccessible to other persons within an hermetically closed box of consciousness - the Cartesian Theatre. To have the correct insight we are to understand that expressions like 'to understand', 'to mean', 'to intend', etc., are not used as *names* for such 'processes' within linguistic practice. Thus, contrary to the claims by Fodor, there cannot exist any 'private mental language of thought' - what we have called 'mentalese' (analogous to a 'machine language' within a computer processor) - acting as a 'foundation' on which the processes of cognitive psychology (as well as Cognitive Science and strong Artificial Intelligence) is founded.[41]

Provided the argument against the possibility of there existing such a genuine 'private language' can be shown (but, of course, not by any kind of empirical experiment!) to be correct - or just simply accepted (similarly to the way epistemological realists, say, within physics, which by something reminiscent of 'an act of God' accepts the dichotomy, or separability, between 'mind' and 'world') - it would have great consequences for epistemology and philosophy of mind (as well as natural sciences. Just think of the problem concerning the 'detached observer' encountered in quantum physics). For example, it would have great consequences to such different schools of thought as central state materialism, functionalism (in all its forms) and to the so-called empirical Cognitive Science which all are beset with the conceptual confusions concerning the assumed division between the Outer and the Inner which Wittgenstein set out to combat. The problems connected to the argument(s) concerning the 'impossibility of a private language' amounts to one of the crucial cornerstones if one is to be able to correctly understand Wittgenstein's insights concerning the nonseparability of thought, language and forms of life [Gefwert (1) 76]. The private language remarks are not part of a restricted argument about the possibility of a certain kind of language, on the contrary, they form the basis for a radical new approach to the whole topic of the Inner.[42]

From what we have established above we notice that Wittgenstein regards what we call 'mental processes' as being something essentially different to what we are - according to the dualistic Cartesian model of science - usually led to believe and assume. It is hard to imagine how any brain state could, for example, capture or correspond to 'intention'. There is no explicit (empirical) process in the brain which is correlated with associating or with thinking. It is impossible to read off a thought from a brain process [Z §608]. The problem is the mismatch between the grammar of any physical event or process and that of mental concepts such as intentionality. If a scientist discovered a connection between brain activity and how people act, this might enable us to predict how someone will act or even cause her to act in a certain way. However, it would neither introduce an alternative to our language-games [Infra IV.3] of, say, 'intention', nor would it give an insight into its 'real foundation'. Whatever the value of the future empirical discoveries of science (like, say, in neurophysiology or Cognitive Science) amount to they cannot reveal (in a metaphysical sense) what 'intention' really is.

Our psychological concepts can be grouped in rough families (sensations, emotions, dispositions, etc.), but even then there are often considerable differences within families or analogies which hold between some members of one group and some of another. The Inner is neither a homogenous series of private experiences nor a conglomerate of ineffable states; rather it comprises of a variety of concepts, each of which relates the Outer and Inner in a slightly different way. Two central features of Wittgenstein's view are, on the one hand, the emphasis of the 'diffuse' existence of the mental processes in time, and, on the other hand, the argument against their privacy. We are here interested in 'mental processes' and, especially, in their role as the assumed 'home' of the family resemblance concepts of 'thought' and 'intention'. Thus the change of view which concerns 'mental processes' must now be extended to concern 'thought' and 'intention' as well. Having established what a 'mental process' cannot be (i.e., a 'private process' of any kind), we can now go on to establish that anything being characterized as specific 'mental processes', like the notions of 'thought' or 'intention', in fact cannot be of such a kind. There is no reduction. We find that Wittgenstein explicitly states this insight - reminiscent of a thesis - when he says that '[i]ntention (*Absicht*) is neither an emotion, a mood, nor yet a sensation or image.

It is not a state of consciousness. It does not have genuine duration'[Z §45].

Notes

[1] Russell, Bertrand, *Theory of Knowledge,* MS in the Russell Archives at McMaster University, op.cit., p. 185. The first six chapters of the book appeared as articles in *The Monist,* January 1914 - April 1915. The work as a whole (all that was ever written) has now been published under the title mentioned above as volume 7 of the *Collected Papers* of Bertrand Russell.

[2] Kenny has investigated the term 'intention' as it appears in Wittgenstein's *Philosophical Remarks,* cf. Kenny, A., *Wittgenstein,* London (1973), pp. 120-158.

[3] Kenny, Anthony, 'Wittgenstein's Early Philosophy of Mind', in Block, I., (ed.), *Perspectives on the Philosophy of Wittgenstein,* Oxford (1981), p. 147.

[4] Copleston, Frederick, A History of Philosophy, Vol. I., New York (1962), op.cit., p. 55.

[5] Schlick, Moritz, *General Theory of Knowledge,* translated by A.E. Blumberg, with an Introduction by A.E. Blumberg and H. Feigl, Springer Verlag: Wien and New York (1974).

[6] Ibid., op.cit., p. 138.

[7] Ibid, op.cit., p. xx.

[8] Spiegelberg, Herbert, *The Phenomenological Movement, A Historical Introduction,* Third Revised and Enlarged Edition, The Hague (1982), op.cit., pp. 47-48, n.19.

[9] For the way the scholastics and especially the different ways St. Thomas Aquinas applied the concept of 'intention', cf. Schmidt, R.W., *The Domain of Logic According to Saint Thomas Aquinas,* The Hague (1966), pp. 94-129.

[10] Spiegelberg, H., *The Phenomenological Movement,* [cf.n.8] p. 48, n.19.

[11] Brentano, Franz, *Psychologie vom empirischen Standpunkt,* Leipzig (1874), Vol. I, Book 2, Chapter 1, sec. v., p. 85; translated in Chisholm, R.M., (ed.), *Realism and the Background of Phenomenology,* Glencoe, Illinois (1960), p. 50. Concerning Brentano's Thesis Chisholm makes a distinction between the psychological aspect (according to which all mental phenomena but no physical phenomena are characteristic of intentionality) and the ontological aspect which deals with the status of the objects which are the targets of our awareness. As far as the latter aspect is concerned Brentano was at least doubtful of its validity. Cf. Roderick Chisholm, 'Intentionality' in P. Edwards, (ed.), *Encyclopedia of Philosophy,* Vol. IV, New York (1967), p. 201.

[12] Also the 'intention' of the scholastics was usually a relation rather than a quality. Cf. R.W. Schmidt, *The Domain of Logic According to Saint Thomas Aquinas,* [cf.n.9] pp. 109-110, 124.

[13] Heidegger, Martin, *Sein und Zeit,* Max Niemeyer Verlag: Tübingen (1979), originally published in 1927, pp. 162, 205.

[14] Kenny, Anthony, *Wittgenstein,* London (1973), op.cit., p. 124.

[15] Allaire, E.B., 'Tractatus 6.3751', in I. Copi and R. Beard, (eds.), *Essays on Wittgenstein's 'Tractatus',* London (1966), pp. 189-193.

[16] For the nature of the 'yes-no' space, cf. Stenius, Erik, *Wittgenstein's Tractatus: An Exposition of the Main Line of Thoughts,* second edition, Oxford (1964), pp. 42-50.

[17] The fact that these problems occur at precisely this stage of Wittgenstein's intellectual development when the elementary propositions have lost their primary function of depicting the world seems to indicate that they had been the target for pictures of immediate (present) experience.

[18] Kenny, Anthony, *Wittgenstein,* Hammondsworth: London (1973), pp. 224-232; Erik Stenius, 'The Picture Theory and Wittgenstein's Later Attitude to it' in I. Block, (ed.), *Perspectives on the Philosophy of Wittgenstein,* Oxford (1981), pp. 110-139; Hintikka, Jaakko, 'Language-Games' in Hintikka, J., (ed.), *Essays on Wittgenstein in Honour of G.H. von Wright,* Acta Philosophical Fennica, Vol. **28**, Nr. 1-3, Amsterdam (1976), pp. 111-112.

[19] Stenius, Erik, *Wittgenstein's Tractatus: An Exposition of the Main Line of Thoughts,* [cf.n.16], p. 98.

[20] According to Kenny '[m]any of the logical features of the [picture] theory ... survived with more or less modification the abandonment of the atomist of the Tractatus. [Especially] one feature of the picture theory ... remained influential throughout Wittgenstein's life: the bipolarity of the proposition. Any proposition which *can* be true, Wittgenstein insisted from 1913 onwards, *can* be false'. Cf. Kenny, Anthony, 'The Ghost of the *Tractatus*', in Kenny, A., *The Legacy of Wittgenstein,* Oxford (1984), op.cit., p. 22.

[21] Cf. for example, Fodor, Jerry A., *The Language of Thought,* Hassocks: Sussex (1975), pp. 2-9, 68-97. According to Fodor it is the case that '[m]any philosophers, and some scientists, seem to hold that the sorts of theories now widely endorsed by cognitive psychologists could not conceivably illuminate the character of mental process ... The line, to put it crudely, is that Ryle and Wittgenstein killed this sort of psychology some time about 1945, and there is no point to speculating on the prospects of the deceased ... The best I can do here is to sketch a preliminary defense of the methodological commitments implicit in the kind of psychological theorizing with which I shall be mainly concerned', op.cit., pp. 2-3.

[22] James, William, *Principles of Psychology,* Vol. I., London (1910).

[23] Revonsuo, Antti, Kamppinen, Matti, & Sajamaa, Seppo, 'General Introduction: The Riddle of Consciousness', op.cit., p. 4, in Revonsuo, A. & Kamppinen, M., (eds.), *Consciousness in Philosophy and Cognitive Neuroscience,* New Jersey (1994), p. 4.

[24] There is an interesting discussion concerning the conceptual confusions occurring in the discussions of psychologists and speculative neurologists concerning the 'process' of thought occurring in the brain. Cf. Hacker, Peter, 'Languages, Minds and Brains' in Blakemore, C. and Greenfield, S., (eds.), *Mindwaves: Thoughts on Intelligence, Identity and Conciousness,* Basil Blackwell, Oxford (1987), pp. 485-505; Cf. also P.M.S. Hacker, *Wittgenstein: Meaning and Mind,* Vol. 3 of a Analytical Commentary on the Philosophical Investigations, Basil Blackwell, Oxford (1990), pp. 295ff.

[25] Cf., for example, Sluga, Hans, 'Wittgenstein's Blaues Buch', *Proceedings of the Xth International Wittgenstein Symposium,* Hölder-Picher-Tempsky: Vienna (1986) and '"Das Ich muss aufgegeben werden". Zur Metaphysik in

der analytischen Philosophie", *Proceedings of the Fifth International Hegel-Congress,* Stuttgart (1987).

[26] Dennett, Daniel C., *Consciousness Explained,* Boston, Toronto, London (1991), op.cit., p. 253. We have, nevertheless, to be aware that what Dennett is attempting to formulate in his research programme is a scientific (empirical) 'theory of consciousness'. But a conceptual investgation does not amount to such an empirical enterprize. We see this mistake being done, for example, in Dennett's book *Brainstorms,* Hassocks (1979), where he writes that ' ... a philosophical theory of the mind is supposed to be a consistent set of answers to the most general questions one can ask about minds, "are there any?", "are they physical?", "what happens in them?" and "how do we know anything about them?" ... Philosophy of mind is unavoidable. As soon as one asserts anything substantive about anything mental, one ipso facto answers at least by implication one or more of the traditional questions and thus places one self in the camp of an ism', op.cit., pp. xii, xiv. In this case Dennet is badly mistaken and, fortunately, this is not correct at all. We do not decide what is the 'correct theory of philosophy'.

[27] Kenny, Anthony, Descartes, New York (1967), pp. 68-78.

[28] Copleston, Frederick, *A History of Philosophy,* Vol. 4., New York (1963), p. 102.

[29] Ibid., p. 224.

[30] It is interesting that the illuminating picture which Descartes creates concerning the notion of spirit, i.e., ' ... something extending thin and subtle, like ... the wind, a candle of light or as very pure air ... ', very much seems to resemble the picture which Wittgenstein later applies in order to illuminate the view he criticizes when he writes of '[t]he conception of thought as a gaseous medium'[PhI §109; cf. also Z §§605-611].

[31] Ryle, Gilbert, *The Concept of Mind,* Published by Hutchinson in 1949. Reprinted by Hammondsworth: London (1973), op.cit., p. 15. According to Popper, he gave a lecture shortly after Ryle's book was published ' ... in which I criticized Ryle's book and tried to give an alternative outline of the body-mind problem. The students were apparently very much impressed by Ryle, but they said all the time, about what I was saying, that it was exactly what Ryle would say. So, in despair, I said: all right, I'll make a confession, I believe in the ghost in the machine. You cannot say that is exactly what

Ryle has said', Karl R. Popper and John C. Eccles, <u>The Self and Its Brain</u>, New York, London, Heidelberg, Berlin (1977), op.cit., p. 464.

[32] Ryle, G., [cf. n. 31], ibid., p. 15.

[33] Wittgenstein, Ludwig, 'Private Experience', edited by Rush Rhees, *Philosophical Review*, LXXVII (1968).

[34] Hacker, P.M.S., *Wittgenstein: Meaning and Mind*, [cf.n.24], p. 15.

[35] Rhees, Rush, 'Can There Be a Private Language?', in R. Rhees, *Discussions of Wittgenstein*, London (1970), op.cit., p. 55; Cf. also Hacker, P.M.S., 'The Private Language Arguments', in P.M.S. Hacker, *Wittgenstein: Meaning and Mind*, [cf.n.24], pp. 15-30.

[36] Hacker, P.M.S., *Wittgenstein: Meaning and Mind*, [cf.n.24], op.cit., p. 16.

[37] Cf. the articles in Jones, O.R., (ed.), *The Private Language Argument*, Bristol (1971); cf. also Morick, Harold, (ed.), *Wittgenstein and the Problem of Other Minds*, McGraw-Hill, Inc.: New York, Toronto, London, Sydney (1967).

[38] Specht, Ernst Konrad, *The Foundations of Wittgenstein's Late Philosophy*, Köln (1969), op.cit., p. 63. Note that Specht takes a Kantian approach to the 'foundational' problem of Wittgenstein's 'later' approach to philosophy, for example, when he says that ' ... we have to accept it [a 'form of life'] as an irreducible ultimate'[op.cit., p. 49]. But, this is an 'observational' (Kantian) position. Therefore, one can ask: What is this (metaphysical) 'irreducible ultimate' which is the foundational basis of all inguistic communication?

[39] For a less ad hominem picture of the beginnings of behaviourism, see Burnham, John C., 'On the origins of behaviourism', *Journal of the History of the Behavioural Sciences*, Vol. 4. (1968), pp. 143-151; For a good discussion cf. Herrnstein, Richard, 'Introduction to John B. Watson's Comparative Psychology', in Henle, M., Jaynes, J., and Sullivan, J.J., (eds.), Historical Conceptions of Psychology, New York (1974), pp. 98-115.

[40] As a clear example of a modern idealistic view in analytic philosophy (as well as in science) we can take the 'memetic' view of consciousness by Dawkins, which get its definition by the words 'mimesis' and 'memory' (as well as, of course, the rime on the word 'gene') and which amounts to ' ... a

unit of cultural transmission, or a unit of imitation. "Mimeme" comes from a suitable Greek root, but I want to monosyllable that sounds a bit like "gene" ... it could alternatively be thought of as being related to "memory" or to the french word même ... If a scientist hears, or reads about, a good idea, he passes it on to his colleagues and students. He mentions it in articles and his lectures. If the idea catches on, it can be said to propagate itself, spreading from brain to brain', Dawkins, Richard, *The Selfish Gene,* Oxford University Press: Oxford (1976), op.cit., p. 206.

[41] Fodor, Jerry A., *The Language of Thought,* Hassocks, Sussex (1975). According to Fodor it is the case that the 'private language' argument(s) by Wittgenstein cannot be upheld because one ' ... can't learn a language unless you already know one. It isn't that you can't learn a language unless you've already learned one. The latter claim leads to infinite regress, but the former doesn't; not, at least by the route currently being explored', op. cit., p. 65; But, this argument has not gone without challenge. For example, Massimo Dell'Utri, when commenting on an article by Diego Marconi, concludes his comments by saying that '[f]ar from constituting an autonomous and complete representational system which precedes and makes possible the learning of any historical language, far from possessing a meaning and a reference per se, mentalese - if there really is such a thing - inherits meaning and reference from spoken language, and therefore all the problems connected with them. Mentalese does not solve any problems: it only duplicates them', Dell'Utri, M., 'Mentalesians and Wittgenstein's Private Language', in Egidi, R., (ed.), *Wittgrenstein: Mind and Language,* Kluwer Academic Publishers: Dordrecht/Boston/London (1995), p. 122.

[42] An interesting beginning in this direction has been made by Johnston, Paul, *Wittgenstein: Rethinking the Inner,* Routledge: London (1993). There are, indeed, therapeuts who take a similar view concerning their work. Cf., for example, de Shazer, S. & Berg, I.K., 'Doing therapy: A post-structural revision', *Journal of Marital and Mental Therapy,* Vol. **18**, No. 1 (1982), pp. 78-88.

IV Philosophy as Grammar

IV.1 INTRODUCTION

What we are to provide in this chapter are introductions to certain topics which shed additional light on the context in which Wittgenstein, after 1930 and again after 1937, wanted his view concerning 'thought' and 'intention' as far as language, psychology and mathematics (including our current positions on Cognitive Science and Artificial Intelligence), to be understood. A novel ingredient in Wittgenstein's writings is that he, in comparison with the conception that he entertained between 1929-1934 [Gefwert (1) 201-210], later, from 1937 onwards, seems to view the remarks in a broader perspective, i.e., as a kind of ' ... natural history of man ... as observations on facts which no one has doubted and which have only gone unremarked because they are always before our eyes' and which show themselves simply as a 'phenomenon of human life'[RFM VI §47; PhI §415].

This historical periodization of his later period seems justified by the fact that Wittgenstein wrote, for example, on mathematics mainly during two distinguishable periods. The first occurs between 1929 and 1934 and the second between 1937 and 1944 [RFM 29]. During the earlier times of his 'later' period, i.e., after his return to active philosophical work in 1929, one finds that Wittgenstein, as far as mathematics is concerned, concentrated his investigations on illuminating what he called 'prose' which was said to occur as conceptual 'diseases' within actual mathematical calculations [Gefwert (1) 236-252]. It was this 'prose' which was to be removed by philosophical investigations. A characteristic feature of this period, when he explicitly dealt with mathematics (1937-1944), is that he now widens the philosophical investigations to incorporate the view of mathematical (and psychological) language in a larger perspective (in a 'form of life').

One might therefore characterize Wittgenstein's overall approach as consisting of four different (but slightly connected) parts:

(1) The pre-1929 'early' emphasis on the transcendental aspect of language.

(2) The formulation of his novel post-1929 'method' of philosophy [Infra VI.1].

(3) The final position in 1937 concerning language-games as making up numerous 'spaces of intention' in our forms of life.

(4) His attempts to apply this novel philosophical 'method' in his post-1937 thought within different contexts, for example, in mathematical and psychological ones [PhI 226].

The transcendental aspect in Wittgenstein's pre-1929 conception of language has been emphasized by Erik Stenius (1911-1990).[1] By the 'transcendental aspect' - in the Kantian sense - we mean ' ... the conditions for the possibility of experience' *(die Bedingungen der Möglichkeit der Erfahrung)* standing for what Kant called the 'Copernican Revolution'.[2] By this Kant emphasized the existence of two components in human experience *qua* human experience. The first of the components emanates from our sensations. It is empirical and *a posteriori*, whereas the second emanates from our *a priori* 'theoretical reason'. According to Kant's Copernican Revolution 'reality' must conform to the forms of thought (i.e., language in the case of Wittgenstein).

There seems to be a wide consensus today that Wittgenstein was influenced by this transcendental view in his pre-1929 writings. Despite its controversial nature there are certain indications that he also later, in his post-1929 philosophical texts (partly, at least), accepts that language exhibits some kind of a transcendental feature. But, the decisive change away from this seems to be documented from 1937 and onwards. Now it seems that Wittgenstein does not anymore assume that our language is 'transcendental' in the original pre-1929 sense. To assume that this is the case requires that one adheres to an 'observer' based view of language. Instead Wittgenstein regards language to exhibit a 'participator' insight [Infra II.1]. This amounts to a big change in outlook. For example, one can - as an often quoted example from his later texts - provide the statement that ' ... grammar tells what kind of object anything is'[PhI §373] as an example of this novel 'participator' insight. We shall return to this question at a later stage.

But, in addition to the change from an 'observer' based view of language to a 'participator' insight we also have the enigma concerning the expression of 'phenomenology' in Wittgenstein's texts. The term 'phenomenology' is often used as an umbrella term to cover all kinds of items - the fauna and flora, one might say - that inhabit our conscious experience: thoughts, smells, itches, pains, etc. Since there is now little disagreement among scholars that phenomenology represents a significant continuation of the Kantian revolution it is only proper to make a short historical comment on Wittgenstein's assumed relation to phenomenology. In the manuscript called the *Big Typescript* we find an entire chapter entitled 'Phänomenologie ist Grammatik'[BT 437]. It has not gone unnoticed. This explicit identification of 'phenomenology' with 'grammar' is the source for the thesis by Spiegelberg that Wittgenstein was a phenomenologist and that his phenomenology continued throughout his later works as 'grammar'.[3]

This is, admittedly, a controversial position. Nevertheless, this is, perhaps, the right place to quote from a letter by von Wright to Spiegelberg where he writes that [4]

> [p]erhaps it is of some interest to mention here that Wittgenstein in the last year of his life did much work on a problem-complex which had always greatly interested him, viz. colour-concepts. He was at the time reading Goethe's *Farbenlehre*, and we had discussions on it and on his own problems and views. He then often used to say that what he was doing was of a kind some philosophers call 'phenomenology'. But he did not himself want to call it by that

name - and I think I can partly see why. His attitude is connected, I believe, with the stress he wanted to lay on language in his philosophical inquiries. For this reason, incidentally, Wittgenstein's use of the term 'grammar' (or 'logical grammar') should be of great interest to phenomenologists.

It is a fact that Wittgenstein on numerous occasions in his writings uses the expression 'phenomenology'. One finds, for example, that he in his post-1929 writings uses the noun 'phenomenology' seven times [PhR 51, 53, 88, 273] and employs this expression on numerous occasions in his discussions with Schlick and Waismann [WVC 63, 65, 101]. In a conversation on the 25th of December, 1929, at Schlick's house, Wittgenstein already (and probably for the first time) claimed 'phenomenology' to be a 'better description of the structure of states of affairs' than physics, because it deals with 'possibility, that is to say, meaning, and not only truth and falsity'[WVC 63]. But, in contrast to this positive use, in the course of a later conversation on the same day, we find that he also criticizes Husserl's conception of phenomenological statements as being synthetic *a priori* judgements [WVC 67].

Later, in his post-1937 writings, we find that he employs the expression 'phenomenon' which is reminiscent of the phenomenological term 'phenomenology'[RFM VII §33]. These important expressions - 'phenomenological' and 'phenomenology' - remind one of the terminology employed by the members of the phenomenological movement. Because of this there has been certain emphasis on the possible historical connection between, on the one hand, Wittgenstein and, on the other, Husserl and Heidegger. These possible conections have, consequently, not passed unnoticed.[5] It is also interesting to note that Wittgenstein continued to use the expression 'phenomenological' in his last writings [Man 105, 122].

I want to emphasize that the comments provided below are not intended to give a complete and precise account of Wittgenstein's thoughts on the nature of 'phenomenology'. What I wish is simply to highlight certain important aspects which seem important to emphasize in connection with this term in order to begin to understand Wittgenstein's conception concerning the internal relation between (mathematical and psychological) language, nature and philosophy. The aim of my comments is solely directed towards the aim of encouraging the reader to undertake more penetrating investigations by herself.

IV.2 THE PROBLEM OF OSTENSIVE DEFINITIONS

For a long time it has been a paradigmatic view that children learn to speak by being trained by the mediation of ostensive gestures, that is, by learning to speak through the example of pointing with a finger at the object which the word to be learned designates. For example, the object in question could be, say, a stone and in order to convey the meaning of this word the teacher consequently utters the word 'stone' and simultaneously points towards a stone. This was, for example, how Aurelius Augustinus (AD 354-430) characterized the learning of speech, when he wrote that [6]

> [w]hen they [my elders] named some object, and accordingly moved towards something, I saw this and I grasped that the thing was called by the sound they uttered when they meant to point it out. Their intention was shewn by their bodily movements, as it were the natural language of all peoples: the expressions of the face, the play of the eyes, the movement of other parts of the body, and the tone of voice which expresses our state of mind in seeking, having, rejecting, or avoiding something. Thus, as I heard words repeatedly used in their proper places in various sentences, I gradually learnt to understand what objects they signified; and after I had trained my mouth to form these signs, I used them to express my own desires.

Wittgenstein took this piece of text, concerning the way 'ostensive definitions' *(hinweisende Erklärungen)* are characterized by

Augustinus, as a paradigmatic example of a mistaken view how children learn to speak. This text constitutes paragraph one of the post-1937 text which is known as the *Philosophical Investigations* [PhI §1].[7]

But, this way of defining the way language can be learnt had, indeed, occurred to Wittgenstein already at an earlier stage. Already in the *Philosophische Grammatik,* written between 1931 and 1933, which is a selective part of the *Big Typescript* [BT], we find that Wittgenstein investigates if ostensive gestures could be the primary marks which are applied when learning to speak. Thus, for example, he asks '[d]oes our language consist of primary signs (ostensive gestures) and secondary signs (words)? One is inclined to ask, whether it isn't the case that our language has to have primary signs while it could get by without the secondary ones'[PhG 88]. For Wittgenstein to search for primary signs is precisely to search for such marks which cannot be reinterpreted, which have a necessary - internal - relation to what is depicted. Having searched for such primary signs in the interior of our 'box' (mind) [Supra III.6-7] Wittgenstein then for a moment turns in another direction in order to draw our attention to activities connected to public language, i.e., to the practice of ostensive gestures. As Hintikka emphasizes, these, however, turn out to be of secondary importance.[8]

Let us investigate this point more closely. To begin with, one can say that ostensive gestures are secondary as far as ordinary language is concerned. An ostensive gesture *(hinweisende Erklärung)* can be described as a rule for teaching gesture-language into word-language, i.e., to connect an uttered word with the help of an ostensive gesture to the object being depicted [cf. BB 90]. However, this rule-like activity turns out to be ambiguous. For example, if we want to define a word, say, 'blue' by an ostensive gesture we have somehow to be able to discern the form of the colour depicted. Usually this is done simply just by saying that 'This colour is blue'. However, if this is the case, then we have to be aware of the fact that the ostensive gesture has lost its character as the primitive gesture that we were looking for as the provider of meaning. At the background we already have to see language and the 'place' of the word in this language (or the 'place' of the ostensive gesture within this language). When reading the *Blue Book* one finds that it begins by such a critique of ostensive definitions. For example, if we in an ostensive gesture refer to a pencil and utter an unknown word it might be the case that we here deal with an ostensive definition for such varying definitions as 'this is a pencil', 'this is round', 'this is wood', 'this is one', 'this is hard', etc. [cf. BB 1-2].

Later Wittgenstein states the rhetoric counter-argument that in order to understand an ostensive definition it is not necessary to understand language in that '[a]ll you need - of course! - is to know or guess what the person giving the explanation is pointing to. That is, whether for example to the shape of the object, or to its colour, or to its number, and so on'[PhI §33]. However, this would presuppose that the person making the ostensive gesture *could* by himself refer in different ways to the shape, the colour, etc. But when asked how this is done, then the only thing we can come up with is to say that the provider of the ostensive definitions *focuses his attention* sometimes on the form, sometimes on the colour, etc. And now we notice that we have come back to the metaphor of the 'beetle in the box'[Supra III.7]. Such a 'mental baptism' - the 'process' of naming - where the relation between the word and the world seems to be established by mental ostension, forces us, in the last instance, back to the problem of linguistic (mental) privacy.

Now, Wittgenstein assures us that ' ... an ostensive gesture can be variously interpreted in *every* case'[PhI §29]. On closer inspection we thus, surprisingly enough, face the fact that there, according to him, *simply does not exist any such unique and primitive naming relation.* As Wittgenstein put it, ' ... in order to establish a name relation we have to establish a technique of use. And we are misled if we think that it is a peculiar process of christening an object which makes a word the word for an object. This is a kind of superstition'[NPL 448]. The problem here is that a 'private linguist' would have no way of knowing if he or she was using a privately defined term correctly or not on a subsequent occasion. Therefore ' ... its no use saying that we have a private object before the mind and give it a name. There is a name only where there is a technique of using it and that technique can be private;

but this only means that nobody but I know about it, in the sense in which I can have a private sewing machine. But in order to be a private sewing machine, it must be an object which deserves the name "sewing machine", not in virtue of its privacy but in virtue of its similarity to sewing machines, private or otherwise'[NPL 448].

But this problem of 'privacy' applies also 'externally' in that the supposed private act of ostension likewise fails to introduce a term in the first place. If an external definition in order to determine the meaning must be equipped with a more specified interpretation - the mental ostensive definition - in order for the mind to be able to 'make' the connection of the word to the object designated, then this genuinely primary sign (definition) amounts precisely to that 'movement of the mind' which is assumed to somehow 'make' the connection. Furthermore, if the interpretation of the sign by the receiver must solely be based on guesses - as it must in such a case - then it has the same value, when viewed from the language point of view, as the 'beetle in the box' has in the 'private language(s) argument'[Supra III.6]. That is, there opens up an infinite possibility of various guesses [NPL 450].

In order to show that this is, indeed, the case we just have to turn the argument around. If a language - in which a public sign (i.e., the word that the owner of a private sensory language writes in his diary) receives its meaning from the private object (the private sense-data) that it depicts - is senseless (i.e., if it is impossible as *a language*) then we can conclude that this is also the case with a language which is constituted by correct public names for public objects but which connects the relations between these names and objects by some 'primary marks' (signs) which, in turn, can only be understood by the person providing these names This 'primary language' would then amount to a 'private language' where the criteria for the identity of the *signs* would be lacking [Cf. NPL 450]. If we now regard language as essentially being constituted by correlations of objects and signs then this lack of identity of signs is as devastating as the lack of criteria for the identity of objects [cf. PhI §181]. The upshot of this argument is then that a 'private object' is one, about which, regardless of whether one has 'got it' or not, one cannot say anything concerning it to others (or to oneself).

However, here it is vital that we do not misunderstand the critique of ostensive definitions that Wittgenstein is providing. He is not denying the obvious fact that we apply ostensive gestures when we talk. We do, indeed, use ostensive definitions - and quite legitimately so - in everyday speech. Ostensive definitions *are* a characteristic feature of our everyday language. The point with his critique, however, is that such ostensive definitions *cannot* stand for primary language-games. We do indeed understand and apply ostensive gestures but we do *not* understand or apply them in the capacity of such primary language-games. For such primary rule-like language-games it is - precisely - what we find Wittgenstein to be emphasizing when he refers to the case concerning reference *(beziehen)* to an object, i.e., to the insight that '[o]ne can refer to an object when speaking by pointing to it [and here] pointing is part of the language-game'[PhI §669].

We can thus establish that, according to Wittgenstein, the ostensive gestures cannot by themselves account for language learning. But if ostensive gestures cannot amount to these required 'primary signs' then how is language learning to be accounted for? It is here that the novel insight gained by the introduction of 'language-games' becomes important [Infra IV.3]. To begin with, according to Wittgenstein, there are certain reactions which are common to children (human beings) and which set the appropriate background for socialization. Wittgenstein states this point when he emphasizes that ' ... the phenomenon of language is based on regularity, on agreement in action'[RFM VI §39]. Thus the child learns to speak, i.e., to apply a language, by learning to do what other human beings do. However, this learning is not accomplished by repeated ostensive gestures (i.e., by the activity of pointing towards objects and stating their names) as, for example, Augustinus mistakenly had assumed [cf. PhI §1]. As we said above, such ostensive definitions are quite legitimately used later in life (when the linguistic 'apparatus' is more developed, that is, when we can already speak) but they *cannot* convey the primary rule-like practices of speech [cf. PhI §669].

The reason is that if ostensive gestures were indeed the 'primary rules', then the pupil would each time have to know (guess), for example, when a name was given to a colour, when given to a form, etc. It is when we already master certain language-games that ostensive definitions can play an important role, say, when learning novel language-games (as a translation) in that '[s]omeone coming into a strange country will sometimes learn the language of the inhabitants from ostensive definitions that they give him; and he will often have to guess the meaning of these definitions; and will guess sometimes right, sometimes wrong'[PhI §32]. Furthermore, if the learning of expressions were to take place through such ostensive gestures then it would require that the pupil would already be familiar with the functionality of the naming process (by applying an already pre-existing 'mental language' as adherers of Cognitive Science would say). This, according to Wittgenstein, is what makes it possible to say that 'Augustine describes the learning of human language as if the child came into a strange country and did not understand the language of the country; that is, as if it already had a language, only not this one. Or again: as if the child could already think, only not yet speak. And "think" would here mean something like "talk to itself"'[PhI §32].

IV.3 LANGUAGE-GAMES

According to the 'earlier' (pre-1929) Wittgenstein the meaning of a name was the object named [Gefwert (1) 56-69]. This position can, as we have seen, be understood in two ways. In Moore's lecture-notes one finds that Wittgenstein puts this (Realistic) view as the target of his critique [L (1) 260-261]. When it is understood in a metaphysical ('observer' based) sense then it is one of the 'mental pictures' which has chained our thought. Then it is the source of much philosophical confusion. It is illuminated by the fact that when we have a noun we think that its meaning ought to be the object represented by that noun

[BB 1]. For example, provided we have a noun for which we do not have an 'outer' object (the Outer) as the meaning then we usually postulate, as an alternative, some 'inner' mental object (the Inner) as the meaning [PhI §36]. Provided the first, the external Cartesian substance, is deficient in providing meaning to our words then we still have a second, an internal substance, at our disposal. This second substance is assumed to consist of mental, 'gaseous', things [BB 47; cf. also PhG 100].

Alternatively, it can also consist of 'chains' of objects, i.e., what we usually call 'processes'. The occult and mystical features of this assumed mental substance makes it easier to deal with such things. In such a substance we can put almost anything [BB 5]. For example, we can put imaginary pictures and other 'shadows' of reality as the meaning where the capacity to provide the meaning of words and sentences is not restricted by the conditions of the real existence. Such a 'shadow' which always accompanies a sentence, i.e., a thought, is the one which we assume that provides the sentence with its 'life'[BB 4]. The sentence, as such, feels dead. As a pure physical mark the only relations outside it could only be causal ones and such relations Wittgenstein does not acknowledge as meaning-carrying ones [Supra II.4]. Therefore the sentence must have some feature which one could characterize as its 'provider of life'. This 'provider of life', whatever it is, we could, in turn, call for a 'mental substance'. But what is such a substance? In order to answer this question Wittgenstein turns in another direction: he turns to our everyday language-games.

Wittgenstein looked for a language that does not require any kind of interpretation (e.g., a 'mental' interpretation). Regardless what kind such a language is it is a fact that this is precisely the kind of language that Wittgenstein was looking for. And he had reasons for his search. The most important one was the postulated ('atomistic') singular reference that was (mistakenly) said to occur in the *Tractatus* [Gefwert (1) 46-55]. According to this view our actual speech is 'crude' and allows the construction of senseless expressions whereas 'meaning' could not be the victim of such deficiency. It is supposed to be clear as crystal. Thus, we are supposed to provide the meaning by the designation of something. This could be done, for example, by thinking or contemplating on what we mean by the 'something' we are to apply. We have to perform something in what Wittgenstein characterizes as the 'area of thought'[PhI §358]. Because this occurrence of meaning 'within' our minds is usually said to be beyond public observation (the Inner) and in the case of ourselves is passing too quickly to even be left for the analytical reflection of our investigating mind, we are certainly facing problems. As Wittgenstein said, '"[t]his queer thing, thought" - but it does not strike us queer when we are thinking. Thought does not strike us as mysterious while we are thinking, but only when we say, as it were retrospectively: "How is that possible?". How was it possible for thought to deal with the very object *itself?* We feel as if by means of it we had caught reality in our net'[PhI §428].

In order to to deal with these questions - with the intention of 'bypassing' them - Wittgenstein needed a view of language learning which does not presuppose how we think (like Cognitive Science presupposes). That is, to 'understand' (and to 'mean') is not a singular occurrence (it is not a 'chain of objects': i.e., a 'process'). This is why to understand a sentence is not something which we can characterize as a unique 'point-like' ('atomic') occurrence. For example, we find that Wittgenstein, already in the *Big Typescript* (1930-1933), when he contemplated on the nature of understanding had come to the conclusion that rather than being of any kind, or state, of our 'consciousness' (as presupposed in Cognitive Science), we have to realize that understanding amounts to ' ... *knowing* how it [language] is used; *being able to* apply it'[PhG 47]. That is: We have to be able to **use** (apply) sentences of a language. To understand a sentence amounts to understand it as a part of a whole: as an entire language (i.e., as a 'form of life')[PhG 50].

According to Wittgenstein understanding (and meaning) is not something that happens only once; to understand a single sentence is not something like a unique and single occurrence. To understand a sentence is part of understanding a 'public' language. By language Wittgenstein at this time understands a calculus (a 'game') which is determined by explicit 'rules' [PhG 68] and the interpretation of the signs is like 'a step in a calculus' (a 'game')[PhG 51]. It is interesting to note that Wittgenstein, at this time (1929-1933), thought that our everyday language has **fixed** rules. This view was, however, to change. He was not satisfied with this way of characterizing the 'game' of ordinary language, i.e., as being determined by strictly determinate rules. Wittgenstein called such fixed rules for criteria [BB 24]. One could easily assume his position to be that he is also advocating this view in his post-1937 writings. But, this amounts to a mistake. Instead explicit rules become primary **rule-like** practices. We have to be aware that there is a gradual transition in his position in the middle 1929-1936 writings towards the view that he finally acknowledges in his more mature post-1937 texts. The view that when we engage in the activity of speaking a language we do it as a kind of 'games' (practices) is left untouched also in the more mature writings of Wittgenstein.

But, contrary to what we usually assume, the post-1929 development is by no means completely cut off from Wittgenstein's previous thought, for example, on questions concerning language (and 'intention') in general. On the contrary. We find this continuation reflected in the change of the terminology applied. The novel view which emerges in his post-1929 thought amounts to the insight that every meaningful sentence in our language belongs to a *Satzsystem*, that is, to numerous calculus-like language contexts, which, in turn, are autonomous grammatical constructions defined by their own internal rules. At this time Wittgenstein called these (grammatical) rules by the name of 'logical syntax' (reminiscent of Carnaps terminological expression)[Cf. WVC 66-67].

The formulation of the concepts used in the contexts of language-games in certain investigations (secondary language-games) are for Wittgenstein a genuinely novel (derivative) kind of activity. That is, when formulated, the learner of the concepts used in the contexts of language has achieved the ability to apply the rules in order to use, say, words correctly, i.e., to perform 'linguistic activities'[PhG 193]. But, we have also to be aware that Wittgenstein was not interested in how the learning of language (in a scientific sense) happens in all its details because he was **not** looking for a theory (of whatever kind) for the learning of language [Supra II.2; Infra V.2]. It is important to understand that we are not to confuse the grammatical with a factual (scientific) investigation. One can say that a scientific (empirical) theory concerning how we learn to speak (in a partial sense) provides a (causal) 'foundation' in Cognitive Science. When formulated and corroborated it provides the uttermost scientific ground [BB 5].

In contrast to this, according to the post-1929 Wittgenstein, the result is that '[f]or us language is a calculus; it is characterized by *linguistic activities*'[PhG 193]. We notice that language, at this time, according to him consists of numerous interlocking 'calculi' (or 'games'). We can then establish that there are multitudes of different calculi and that the general concept of 'language' (in this sense) slowly evaporates into thin air [cf. PhG 115]. There is not any 'language' when it is understood in a metaphysical (external) sense. In addition, Wittgenstein is not satisfied with the 'calculus' conception, especially, as far as it is concerned with the characterization of the necessity of (fixed) rule-dependence [BB 24-25]. But, this was to change (in addition to the change from an external 'observer' based view of language to a 'participator' insight of everyday language-games). Historically one can say that the transition out of the monolithic pre-1929 view goes hand in hand with the transition towards what Wittgenstein came to characterize as ('participatory') 'language-games' *(Sprachspiele)* out of the pre-1937 'calculus' *(Satzsysteme)* conception of language.[9]

In his later, post-1937 writings, the (primary and secondary) 'language-game' conception supersedes his earlier 'calculus' view. Wittgenstein has now realized that a change from a metaphysical 'observer' ('calculus') based to a 'pariticipator' ('language-game') conception concerning our involvement in everyday language is necessary. *Consequently, the mature view, in his post-1937 writings, is that it amounts to an illusion to assume that there is a general account for the whole of language in this external sense.* This means that there is no single and unique **universal** concept of everyday 'language' (the 'universal medium' which we can 'observe' in the language-as-calculus sense). We cannot meaningfully, in a Realistic and metaphysical 'observer' based sense, talk about a 'whole language' (e.g., English, Swedish, French, etc.). To do such a thing amounts to a conceptual mistake. But the view of language as 'competence', that is, as a 'game' requiring a certain skill, was kept intact through the whole of Wittgenstein's later writings.

It is now, during the latter part of his interim period in 1934-35, that he in a mature way begins to apply this novel insight. For example, the notion of 'language-game', when applied to mathematical contexts, is exhibited in connection with the series of the natural numbers and here the practice, or language-game, is involved in characterizing the continuation of this series [BB 93-95]. The general result is that by 'natural language' in his post-1937 thought is to be understood a multitude of (unstructuralized) primary language-games which can be described as being **rule-like** but which are *not* governed by any explicitly formulated rules.[10] We always have primary rule-like language-games before we can have explicitly formulated rules (in technical languages) constituting technical language-games. If 'language' is made up of such primary and secondary language-games then the use of concepts can (when described in philosophical investigations) be characterized, in Wittgenstein's terminology, by logical grammar because '[g]rammar describes the use of words in the language'[PhG 60].

This conception of ordinary language results in Wittgenstein 'founding' all his reflections, in his post-1937 thought, on the central concept of a (primary) language-game. We find that this concept gradually developed in the 1930's to the form in which it appears in his post-1937 work. For example, in the *Blue Book,* dictated in 1933-1934, we find that Wittgenstein applies the notion of 'language-game' and states that [BB 17],

> I shall in the future again and again draw your attention to what I shall call language-games. These are ways of using signs simpler than those in which we use signs of our highly complicated everyday language.

> Language-games are the forms of language with which a child begins to make use of words. The study of language games is the study of primitive forms of language or primitive languages.

This, however, was not the final position. A more mature exposition of the notion of 'language-game' was introduced a year later (1935) in the *Brown Book* [BB 108, 172-73]. Here we find that the term is for the first time used in a fullfledged way. It is again further developed in 1936 when Wittgenstein began a revision of this manuscript called *Philosophische Untersuchungen, Versuch einer Umarbeitung*. This revision was, eventually, to become the manuscript that has been posthumously published (1953) by the title *Philosophische Untersuchungen*.[11] As an example of this latter revision we can provide the following two examples. Here, in the latter manuscript, we find Wittgenstein stating that [PhI §7]

> [w]e can also think of the whole process of using words ... as one of those games by means of which children learn their native language. I will call these games 'language-games' *(Sprachspiele)* and will sometimes speak of a primitive language as a language-game ... I shall also call the whole, consisting of language and the actions into which it is woven, the 'language-game'.

We find that two new meanings of the word 'language-game' has been added in this work which we only found to be hinted at in his earlier writings. Wittgenstein calls the whole of language and all the activities woven into it *the* language-game (but note: this expression is not to be understood in a Realistic (metaphysical 'observer' based) sense)[PhI §7]. In addition, he also calls certain partial systems, or individual ways of using fully developed everyday language, explicitly for language-games [cf. PhI §23].

But, what do such primary language-games amount to? To begin with, we can say that when gradually learning to speak a child exhibits the competence to speak and write by engaging in what Wittgenstein characterized by the metaphoric expression of a language-game [PhI

§7]. He characterizes language-games as being like the orthography of an old town, i.e., as ' ... a maze of little streets and squares, of old and new houses, and of houses with additions from various periods; and this surrounded by a multitude of new boroughs with straight regular streets and uniform houses'[PhI §18]. Our primary language-games are not constructions drawn up according to a uniform plan. Just as no uniform building plan forms the basis of an old town, so neither does our primary language-games erected on the outline of a uniform logic or grammar. The stock of words and grammatical forms, transmitted down the centuries, is like 'the maze of little streets and squares' of the old town. This comparison of our language-games with a town that has gradually come into existence illustrates one of the most important aspects of a primary language-game.

Note, that by a primary language-game is not to be understood a theoretical (structuralized) term in the 'Rules-as-Theory' sense [Infra V.1]. It is a concept belonging to ordinary speech and is not an explanatory (mathematical or scientific) one (i.e., a secondary language-game). The primary language-games of ordinary speech amount (say) to dialogues (discussions) where one applies public expressions and sentences of natural language. When one exhibits the competence to speak - thus conforming to the rule-like behaviour characteristic of primary language-games - one is not doing this by having performed some kind of implicit (or explicit) theoretical decision. It is important to understand the distinction between a primary rule-like language-game vs. the rule-based (theoretical) practice of an artificial language-game. The latter ones are like new annexes and street systems. The secondary artificial (formal) language-games of mathematical and logical calculations can be compared with the modern parts of the town, built on a uniform plan, sometimes still closely connected, at other times only quite loosely connected to the centre of the town. Nevertheless, it is important to undestand that (secondary) artificial and formal language-games always are connected to (primary) informal and everyday language-games [LFM 111].

Primary language-games cannot be taught by explanations in a scientific sense (as secondary language-games can). They can only be taught by learning to *do* the same as people do and thus ' ... the teaching of language is not explanation, but training'[PhI §5]. For example, as a result of such a training a child either learns to talk or it does not. Such a child is in no position to *decide* that it wants to learn to speak. There is no interpretation ('decision procedure') present here (which would require that the child could already talk). Consequently, if it learns to speak then it learns this practice as a *tabula rasa* by mimicking its parents (and other adults). By doing this it conforms to the rule-like sentences occurring in the primary language-games. Thus we can characterize the ability of learning to speak as a gradual (unexplainable) 'process of socialization' whereby one is taught to express thought (meaning). Indeed, as Wittgenstein said, '[t]he understanding of language, as of a game, seems like a background against which a particular sentence acquires meaning'[PhG 50].

We find that Wittgenstein characterized primary language-games as ' ... the forms of language with which a child begins to make use of words. The study of language games is the study of primitive forms of language or primitive languages ... When we look at such simple forms of language the mental mist which seems to enshroud our ordinary use of language disappears'[BB 17; cf. PhI §5]. In such game-contexts it is easy to note what it means to say that understanding is the same as to 'know how' something is done. A move in the language-game is analogous to a move in chess, like an inferential step in a calculation. To understand a word is the skill to use it similarly as the knowledge of a piece of chess amounts to knowledge concerning how to use it, that is, to perform allowed movements in the game with it. To know the game means in both cases to be master of a technique. As Wittgenstein says, '[t]o understand a sentence means to understand a language. To understand a language means to be master of a technique'[PhI §199].

This is to be understood so that it is the primary competence to speak a language (of whatever kind) that makes us humans to what we are. A characteristic feature of human beings is that during a large part of our life we engage in a variety of practices (speaking, writing, thinking, calculating ...). When participating in these practices in everyday circumstances we usually do not explicitly doubt our ability to successfully perform them, for example, when we engage in ordinary everyday discussions (i.e., we master the technique of speaking). That is, in ordinary circumstances we may be uncertain about what to say on a certain occasion (what is the correct answer) but usually we do not for a moment doubt, for example, that we can speak the language by which the answer is formulated. In order to speak we do not contemplate (in ordinary circumstances) each time if an expression or sentence is well-formed before we utter the expression, or sentencs, of ordinary language. In fact, most people would not even have the competence to do this (and still they engage perfectly in discussions). No, we simply think, speak, and write: we behave as humans are 'supposed to do'. To assume otherwise (i.e., to adopt the 'rules-as-theory' illusion) would be like Kripke with his sceptical 'paradox' to put the cart before the horse [Infra V.3]. Not to mention that this would put a child completely at odds with certain social institutions, for example, with the elementary school curriculum.[12]

A consequence of the previous discussion is that the question how we come to learn our first natural language (by training; not explanation!) may be an intriguing (scientific) question, say, in Cognitive Science, but, according to Wittgenstein, this is not the right kind of question [Cf. PhI §5; BB 77]. Thus, as Wittgenstein said, if we ask '[h]ow do I know that this colour is red? - It would be an answer to say: "I have learnt English"'[PhI §381]. Our ability to play primary language-games, i.e., the ability to speak, is the bedrock of all justification be it of whatever kind, mathematical, scientific, etc. [cf. PhI §217]. These basic rule-like activities exhibited in ordinary speech (a practice!) can be compared (but not identified), in a Kantian terminology, with the rules of transcendental logic.[13] These rule-like activities that we exhibit in language-games do not amount to conventions, for example, they do not function like 'theories of rules' (secondary language-games) do in constructive mathematics and linguistics (being applications of Kripke's 'rules-as-theory' idea [Infra V.3]).[14] The primary language-games are themselves instances of rule-like activities (practices) and are learnt by mimicking, that is, by doing the same as everybody else does. Here we do not perform any kind of interpretation (e.g., in some pre-existing 'mental' language) of these rule-like activities. What we learn is speech: a linguistic practice (which is not to be mistaken with the science of linguistics). When we understand this point correctly we can understand what Wittgenstein is saying when he says that [PhI §201]

> ... there is a way of grasping a rule which is *not* an *interpretation,* but which is exhibited in what we call "obeying the rule" and "going against it" in actual cases.

When we learn to speak (and later to write), that is, when we learn to engage in basic primary language-games and customs, we learn to *think* and when we learn to think, we learn to justify (to explain) by secondary language-games. To justify (explain) is possible only by the means of certain primary linguistic contexts (primary language-games). But, it is important to understand that a proposition can be a move only in the context of the 'whole game of language' ('form of life'). That is, '[t]o understand a sentence means to understand a language'[PhI §199; PhG 172; BB 5; LW I §913]. It means that one cannot credit someone with understanding just one sentence of one's language. For a proposition is a sign in a system, one possible combination of words among, and in contrast, with others. Thus, understanding a proposition is part of the 'mastery of a technique'[PhI §199; PhG 63, 152-153]. It involves the ability to employ a word in some other contexts as well as knowledge of some of the 'logical' links between the given sentence and others. Then, we can, indeed, like Wittgenstein, say that '[l]ight dawns gradually over the whole'[OC §§141-142]. Note, that this possibility naturally concerns mathematical calculations (secondary language-games) in addition to primary ones [cf. OC §47].

All justification and calculation can only take place by spoken (and written) primary language-games, i.e., by distinct and partly overlapping rule-like linguistic practices: primary language-games. These primary language-games cannot themselves be (causally) explained: by being part of our human 'form of life' they just have to be 'blindly' accepted (in fact, causal (secondary) explanations presuppose the ability to use these primary language-games). One can say that the primary language-games amounts to the organic element in which arguments (explanations) have their life [OC §105]. Consequently, as Wittgenstein said in 1933, '[w]hat is spoken can only be explained in language, and so in this sense language itself cannot be explained'[PhG 40; Cf. 172; BT 1].

By being an essentially linguistic practice it is impossible, in the last instance, to explain **how** one primarily learns, for example, to calculate. It is outside the scope of explanation (and thus to ask 'How does one learn to calculate?' if meant as a theoretical question of some kind amounts to 'prose'[Gefwert (1) 236-252]). However, this does not mean that learning to calculate as such is a mystery of some kind. It only becomes a 'mystery' when understood along the lines of the distorting 'observer' based Inner/Outer picture concernnig how one learns to calculate [Supra III.5]. As Wittgenstein says, '[a]nd that is why we learn to count as we do: with endless practice, with merciless exactitude; that is why it is inexorably insisted that we shall all say "two" after "one", "three" after "two" and so on'[RFM I §4]. We simply learn to perform certain practices (and in addition to ask certain redundant questions which, in Wittgenstein's terminology, amount to 'prose').

For example, the only thing that counts when teaching mathematics at school is that we somehow achieve the practical skill to perform calculations. Note, that it is not in this case a question of us formulating an 'a priori mathematical theory' (artificial language-game), for example, in the sense of the Intuitionistic Theory of Types (Sets)[Gefwert (1) 102-112]. It is precisely the requirement of such practical skills when calculating which underlies the point of mathematical examinations and tests in schools: to be able to independently perform ordinary calculations. Such practical skills are the basic starting points for everything else that we come to do later in life with mathematics (regardless of whether it is 'pure' or 'applied' mathematics). This is, for example, why Wittgenstein emphasizes the insight that the activities of language-games (e.g., mathematical calculations) must be ' ... still more inexorable than the laws of nature'[RFM I §118]. Such activities exhibits, for example, the rule-like practice to write down the idempotent canonical series of the natural numbers in arithmetic.

However, there are innumerable other such artificial language-games. For example, every single assertion (as well as calculations) exhibits such a rule-like activity. These rule-like practices, being reminiscent of (but not identical with!) Kant's transcendental logic, are what can be characterized and described as 'the primary rules of the language-games' which show themselves in calculations. Such rule-like practices are necessary and compelling if, for example, mathematical thought is to be possible in the first place. They make calculations what they are: mathematical practices. Indeed, one can perfectly well occasionally express (read and write) senseless combinations of words. However, one must (like Alice in Wonderland) come to understand that it is impossble to **think** the pseudosense expressed in such expressions.[15] A single odd expression is no custom (the impossibility of a 'private language'). Only an established rule-like custom amounts to a practice. And only practices are language-**games**. Thus we come to understand that mathematical calculations have their home in our form of life as (artificial) language-games because ' ... to imagine a language means to imagine a form of life'[PhI §19].

We now understand why '[t]he primitive language-game which children are taught needs no justification; attempts at justification need to be rejected'[PhI 200]. We thus seem to have arrived at an analogous position to the one that we find in Wittgenstein's pre-1929 writings concerning the transcendentality of ordinary language: *the rule-like activities of the primary language-games we play show the 'limits of language' and a form of life is described.* Here, it is important to understand that what is 'outside' language-games amount to meaningless expressions (i.e., nonsense) within our forms of life. Therefore we can say, as Cavell has emphasized, that '[h]uman speech and activity, sanity and community, rest upon nothing more, but nothing less, than this [form of life]'.[16]

Provided we now understand the way such rule-like practices function we also understand that one cannot but think in accordance with them. There are no options present here. Such rule-like activities can be described, in a Kantian terminology, as being categorical in the sense that '[t]he propositions of ['transcendental'] logic are "laws of thought", "because they bring out the essence of human thinking" - to put it more correctly: because they bring out, or shew, the essence, the technique, of thinking. They shew what thinking is and also shew kinds of thinking"[RFM I §133]. It is this feature of these (primary) rule-like activities which can be described as exhibiting the 'laws of thought' (as long as we understand what is meant by this expression), i.e., we can describe them as rule-like activities, when occurring, for example, as mathematical calculations (and ordinary speech), which allows one to characterize mathematical propositions as functioning as a kind of 'measure' or 'channel' which regulates, for example, our scientific practices within a form of life [Infra IV.5].

According to Wittgenstein ordinary mathematics consists of a network of different calculations (secondary language-games) where the meaning of each, say, mathematical proposition is in the end given by its internal calculus-specific way of calculation. Perhaps one can characterize this by saying that each artificial language-game (mathematical as well as 'virtual' natural language ones) is an 'island' surrounded by other 'linguistic islands' in the 'sea of everyday language'. For example, in one of his lectures Wittgenstein characterized this view by saying that '[o]ne could say "proof" has as many different meanings as there are proofs. All the proofs form a family, and the word "proof" does not refer to any one characteristic of those processes called proofs'[L (3) 116; cf. L (3) 117; PhG 374]. We have in a loose way to understand that these 'islands' are to be called 'proofs'. We have to understand that they have a **family-resemblance** property [BB 17; PhI §§67-69]. But, in order to be able to show that this is the case we really have to master the primary and secondary language-games that are required. Then one can say, in Wittgenstein's terminology, that a mathematical expression is meaningful when it conforms to the 'logical syntax', or 'logical grammar', of a calculation and, conversely, meaningless when there are no such rules of grammar by which one can exhibit its use [Supra III.4].

The background to the gradual change in terminology from calculi to language-games in 1929-1937 seems to be a result of Wittgenstein's increasing emphasis on the importance of understanding everyday language (exhibiting 'intention' [Supra III.3]) essentially as rule-like practices. Nevertheless, it seems that the language-game idea - in the way Wittgenstein applies it - is born ready-made (out of the 'calculus' view despite the change from rules to rule-like) in a similar way as Pallas Athene is born out of the head of Zeus. The language-games of the *Philosophische Untersuchungen* are developed from the calculi of the *Big Typescript* where we have 'language as a procedure according to explicit rules'[PhG 68] and to which the meaning of a word - its role in the calculus of language - was connected similarly as to the later primary language-games [cf. PhG 67]. Wittgenstein introduced the notion of 'game' in his terminology when he says that '[n]o one will deny that studying the nature of the rules of games must be useful for the study of grammatical rules, since it is beyond doubt that there is some sort of similarity between them'[PhG 187]. He also applies the notion of game in connection with arithmetic when he says that '[c]alling arithmetic a game is no more and no less wrong than calling moving chessmen according to chess-rules a game; for that might be calculation too'[PhG 292]. This 'language-as-calculus' view (with fixed rules but not to be mistaken, for example, with 'classical' logical semantics and model-theoretic practices in Hintikkas sense) was for Wittgenstein the only view of language; at this time it was the only adequate view in a clarification of language [cf. PhG 77, 193].

This was to change. In the *Blue Book* this view seems to be questioned as the instigator of novel philosophical problems. It produces a view by which the genuine ordinary language use somehow seems deficient as if it actually were part of an exact calculus. However, such a view is not correct. A genuine (primary) language is not used according to strict (fixed) rules in that ' ... it hasn't been taught us by means of strict rules ... '[BB 25]. This discrepancy between the exact rules occurring in (secondary) language-games and the way we actually use the primary rule-like expressions in everyday language are to be understood as the 'family resemblance view'[BB 17]. By the notion of a (primary) 'rule' is here to be understood a rule-like sentence. *A 'rule' in this sense does not amount to anything over and above a sentence.* The view requiring us to 'strictly do the same' (as in a calculation with 'fixed' rules) is replaced by the view of doing something in an 'enough similar way' in the context of (primary) language-games. In such (primary) language-games the rule-like practices are as time goes by sometimes tighter and sometimes more loose (they are not 'fixed'). As Wittgenstein says, '"[b]ut then the use of the word is unregulated, the 'game' we play with it is unregulated" - It is not everywhere circumscribed by rules; but no more are there any rules for how high one throws the ball in tennis, or how hard; yet tennis is a game for all that and has rules too'[PhI §68].

The post-1929 'calculations' (later: the primary language-games) could also - mistakenly - be seen as a continuation of attempts to specify what we have called 'transcendental possibilities' in Wittgenstein's pre-1929 thought [Gefwert (1) 70-77]. In his pre-1929 thought the space of ('transcendental') logic had limited the possible area of the state of affairs. Now, the sub-spaces (the different 'calculi' of language and mathematics) functioned in a similar way in the texts of the 1930's [Gefwert (1) 210-219]. A 'calculation' is not a game we play *in* language but one which gives us rules of activities that we carry out *with* language in our practices. Thus the 'Picture-Theory' [Gefwert (1) 56-69] in a natural way develops into his later post-1929 view. One can say that the measure and what is measured were in the same space and this guaranteed their commensurability. This is what makes it possible to perform the things we do with our language-games. Thus the special situation is of course connected to the problem of a false sentence. A false sentence cannot get its meaning from its state of affairs which functions as its 'reference'. In such a case it is enough that we acknowledge the possibility of meaning. In order for us to draw a line between false statements (but meaningful ones), on the one hand, and meaningless sentences, on the other, the possibilities have to be provided somehow before the question of 'truth' or 'falsity' is determined. The objects ('atomism') were an attempt to answer this problem. However, according to Wittgenstein, this amounts to a mistaken assumption. In post-1937 thought the 'grammatical rules' of the language-game draw a line between the possible and the impossible (meaningful and meaningless). In chess the wooden piece becomes a piece of the game when it is being applied in the game of chess. When the rules of the game of chess have been given (an artificial language-game) we have simultaneously provided all the possible moves and situations of the game - not like any 'occult' shadowlike beings but as the genuine possible movements and, as a result of this, the configurations of the pieces of chess.

The difficulty for those who attempt to move this picture into language (e.g., adherers of the language-as-calculus view) is due to the complexity of language and of the 'implicitness' (in Dummett's Anti-Realist terminology) of the 'rules' regulating language. Of course, one can attempt to change that what is possible (and meaningful), but, one cannot make these changes when one likes. They remind us of ordinary games, say, of chess. The changes do require a social acknowledgement in order to be genuine changes. Only changes which are somehow institutionalised may change the rule-like activities of language-games from one position to another, that is, to change the area of the possible meanings. One could say that these are remarks on the grammar of the words 'way of doing' and 'technique'. Except for the changing perifery we are completely within the possibilities of our language-games and even here a single discrepancy does not make any change. We may then say ' ... that we use the command in contrast with other sentences because *our language* contains the possibility of those other sentences'[PhI §20]. We can become a user of those possibilities only if we master the technique of a certain language. For Wittgenstein a human being may only want to say something if he knows how to speak (or master a language)[PhI §338].

In the background we can see a picture which is reminiscent of a sort of rule-like customs, or networks of institutions, where one requires a certain skill. Usually people control the techniques - like the pieces of chess on the board - but '[i]f the technique of the game of chess did not exist, I could not intend to play a game of chess'[PhI §337]. It seems that the reason why Wittgenstein introduced this novel terminology of the language-game in the first place was that he had begun to realize the importance of broadening his investigations to include, besides (everyday) language, thought and mathematical calculations, also conceptual problems arising from these topics in relation to what he called 'the natural history of man' or 'form of life'[cf. PhI §§18,23]. He also wanted to apply the same terminology (language-games) in his investigations connected to psychological contexts as he did in the ones concerning mathematical calculations and everyday language-games. But, the problem of, say, perceptual psychology (as well as, e.g., Cognitive Science, neurophysiology and other scientific practices) in scientific contexts is that there are experimental methods as well as conceptual confusions occurring here [cf. PhI 232]. We have to understand that such problems belong to the tasks of philosophical investigations to investigate.

IV.4 MEANING AS PRACTICE

We have thus established that Wittgenstein came to the insight that ostensive defintions cannot amount to the 'primary rules' whereby, for example, a child talks [Supra IV.2]. Since speech is necessary in order to convey a certain point we thus realize that ostensive gestures (when being 'grounded' in a mentalistic 'observer' based scientific picture of thought) cannot be the ultimate providers for what is to be understood by 'thought' and 'intention'. But, according to Wittgenstein, we are then forced to ask: If 'thought' and 'intention' are not the outcome of the Inner then what do they consist in and how does it come about? Indeed, according to Wittgenstein [LW (II) 61-62],

> [t]he characteristic of the mental seems to be that one has to guess at it according to the Outer in others and knows it only in one's own case. But when, through more careful thought, this opinion goes up in smoke, what turns out to be the case is not that the Inner is something Outer, but that "inner" and "outer" no longer qualify as types of evidence. "Inner

evidence" means nothing and therefore neither does "outer evidence".

How is such a claim to be understood? How do we mean? We shall investigate this next.

As we have seen the Inner/Outer picture is neither an expession of metaphysical truth nor a depiction of the facts of the matter [Supra II.4]. So, where does this leave this picture? To begin with, within traditional (dualistic) philosophy this picture expresses certain conceptual relations which together form our concept of the human subject (the 'mind-brain' relationship).[17] As we have noted, according to Wittgenstein, thinking cannot be accurately represented either as an activity in itself or as an accompaniment of other activities. Rather, the word 'thinkingly' - as opposed to the word 'mechanically' - characterizes the way an activity is carried out. In addition to expressing certain conceptual relations the Inner/Outer picture captures fundamental aspects of our relation to other persons. Indeed, to the extent that the Inner seems irredeemably mysterious, this picture seems to reflect our sense of the mystery of life itself. For example, the absense of predicability and mechanical regularity is paradigmatic and central to our response to something as being alive and more particularly as being human. But this is not a characterization built on empirical evidence: it is conceptual in nature. Thus the Inner ('thought', 'intention') is not a brute 'reality', it is neither a set of private experiences nor a set of brain states: it is this concept which lies at the heart of all mutual interaction and understanding. In fact, thought for Wittgenstein, due to his 'fear for privacy', cannot be anything else than 'talk to oneself' which can be performed because one can speak, that is, 'think publicly'. Indeed, as he said, '[w]hen I think in language, there aren't meanings going through my mind in addition to the verbal expressions; the language is itself the vehicle of thought'[PhG 161].

Wittgenstein needed a way of characterising 'thought', for example, when a child learns to speak, which is not based on the paradigm of ostensive gestures, i.e., which does not require any assumption of thought (as a 'process') previous to the learning of speech [Supra II.2]. But, how is this enigma to be dissolved? To begin with, we find the solution to the Inner/Outer enigma to be embedded in Wittgenstein's emphasis on the 'holistic' view of language and thought which, as we have already noticed, he characterizes by the term 'language-game' [Supra IV.3]. It is the language-games which connect, for example, sentences with reality. It is here, within the language-games, that we find the solution to the enigma of 'thought' and 'intention' to be embedded. It is in connection with 'language-games' that we are to look for an explanation concerning the nature of the Inner as well as the Outer and thus of mysterious 'thought' and 'intention'. Wittgenstein states this insight concerning the crucial (holistic) role played by language-games when it comes to 'intention' when he says that '[a]n intention (*Absicht*) is embedded (*eingebettet*) in its situation, in human customs and institutions'[PhI §337].

Within the Cartesian model it is easy to understand how a mental process is to be understood when setting out from itself. If God had been interested in the thoughts of the 'empirical subject' in the *Tractatus* he could have read them as from an open book (because we cannot assume that the 'key of interpretation' is unknown to Him [Gefwert (1) 56-69]). However, according to Wittgenstein, '[i]f God had looked into our minds he would not have been able to see there whom we were speaking of'[PhI 217]. This leads us to the insight that the mental phenomenon is not anymore - even together with the 'key of interpretation' - what we could call 'self-sufficient' but rather something 'relational' to its surroundings. That is, '[a]n expectation is imbedded in a situation, from which it arises'[PhI §581]. The things to which words like 'expectation', 'wish', 'meaning', etc. refer to are not momentary or other kinds of temporally delimited occurrences in the Cartesian 'thinking substance' but actual phenomena in the human life. A mental phenomenon belongs, as Wittgenstein says, not to the soul but, for example, to Mr. N.N. [cf. PhI §573]. To mean, understand, hope, wish, wait, intend, etc. do not amount to singular movements of the mind but what one could describe as features of human behaviour.

Such a conclusion immediately brings the question of behaviourism to the forefront. For the behaviourist expressions like these were to be removed from the psychological vocabulary altogether. For Wittgenstein, on the other hand, words like these did not disappear. But, as he seems to have felt acquisitions of behaviourism to be coming he delimits his own view as far as it is concerned. He does not deny the existence of mental processes [PhI §306] and does not admit that he is a 'shameful' behaviourist. As he says, '"[a]ren't you at bottom saying that everything except human behaviour is a fiction?" - If I do speak of a fiction, then it is of a *grammatical* fiction'[PhI §307]. What Wittgenstein *wants* to deny is the 'picture' which we have created for ourselves for the processes of the naming of the words we use, i.e., that they should refer to something outside the empirical investigation in a still unidentified 'ether'[PhI §308]. He does not deny that these words have a certain use but he emphasizes that they are not meaningful in this way. Those primary language-games by which the child learns to use these words cannot be founded on any hidden 'mentalese' (as Cognitive Science assumes) - there is nothing occult or mysterious present. The crucial thing which is present in these language-games - and without it ' ... we could not sketch any picture of the world'[T §2.0212] - is a stable enough, rule-like human behaviour.

The view we achieve is, according to Wittgenstein, that the holistic aspect of thought by primary language-games shows itself in the fact that our thoughts always mean something. That is, what could be characterized as dead signs are always symbols, i.e., they are always alive and occur within our ordinary language or form of life. We do not even understand (our language does not contain this possibility) what our thoughts would mean if they were stripped off from our language. In the *Tractatus* it was the transcendental ('metaphysical') subject which were the provider of the logical form of the world [Gefwert (1) 78-87]. Thus we come to an important insight which Wittgenstein emphasized both in his pre-1929 writings as well as in his post-1937 texts: *Our thoughts always mean something and the limits of language (pre-1929) - the calculi and primary language-games (post-1937) - exhibit the various forms of the forms of life by providing the concepts by which aspects of a form of life is described.* In this sense we are always already 'participating' in meaningful language (we cannot, as it were, observe natural and formal language in a metaphysical Realistic sense). This is the case, for example, when we perform mathematical calculations and physical measurements. Thus one could say that we live, or, as one could also characterize this point, we participate with language in an immediate way in the practices we are performing. We are constantly within language (speach), thought and nature (our forms of life) (the transcendental logic in the *Tractatus* [T §6.13]) and thus '... the language-game is so to say something unpredictable. I mean: it is not based on grounds. It is not reasonable (or unreasonable). It is there - like our life'[OC §599].

Such basic rule-like practices that we follow in a blind way (for example, when we speak) when engaging in different everyday practices do **not** amount to conventions (decisions) of any kind. These rule-like activities (Wittgenstein's 'logic' and 'rules') amount to ordinary linguistic practices. For example, an ordinary discussion (say, the language-game of a dialogue) exhibits this feature. Language-games can also be characterized, as they were by Wittgenstein, by saying that they exhibit 'laws of thought'[RFM I §133]. These 'laws of thought' could, perhaps, in turn, be characterized, in philosophical terminology, as exhibiting the 'necessary' conditions of thought. If so, this would show us a couple of extremely important insights:

(1) Our ways of thinking do not amount to some kind of conventions without which thought would be impossible (like, for example, eating a meal which it is perfectly possible to do even in the absense of any - conventional - rules regulating table manners).

(2) One cannot free oneself (in the sense, for example, in which an unprejudiced person might do, say, from the conventional rules of the current fashion) from the rule-like activities of thought; any attempt to free oneself from these rule-like activities is an attempt to free oneself from thinking (and speaking) altogether; it is not to move to a more liberal way of thought (speech), say, by some kind of a Carnapian 'principle of tolerance'.

Now, this gives us the correct background and perspective in order to be able to understand Wittgenstein's point concerning 'thought' and 'intention'. On January 21, 1931, we find that Wittgenstein and Waismann discussed the difficult problems surrounding the topics of 'intention' and 'intentional relation'. In this discussion Wittgenstein said that '[w]hat does it mean to understand a proposition? This is connected with the general question of what it is what people call intention, to mean, meaning. Nowadays the ordinary view is, isn't it, that understanding is a psychological process that accompanies a proposition - i.e., a spoken or written proposition? What structure, then, does this process have?'[WVC 167]. Now, if we take a calculation, like the ordinary practice of solving the equation $x^2 + 2x + 2 = 0$, this constitutes an intentional 'game' in the sense that the moves we do in the game in order to correctly solve the equation are uniquely determined by the internal rules (practice) of second order algebra set by the example. Through this paradigmatic example we clearly see what the relation amounts to in comparison with a causal (and external) relation [Supra II.4]. Now, we can ask: (1) How do we separate such an (internal) rule based relation from a causal relation? and (2) How do we know that the equation above is such an internal rule-based equality?

Interestingly enough, it seems that Wittgenstein does not even attempt to exhibit these assumed 'causal' views as mistaken. Instead, what he does is an attempt to show that any assumption concerning causality stating that it plays any part in this context is simply absurd. This is, for example, indicated when Wittgenstein says that '[i]t is true that various processes are going on inside me when I hear or read a proposition. An image emerges, say, there are associations and so forth. But all these processes are not what I am interested in here. I understand a proposition by applying it. Understanding is thus not a particular process; it is operating with a proposition. The point of a proposition is that we should operate with it'[WVC 167]. It is a fact that in actual life we exhibit the practice ('internal rules') that we have learnt and do not refer to some causal relation (or 'process'), say, in conncection with a mistake, when calculating an equation. Thus we arrive at the important insight that, according to Wittgenstein, we are *always* living within a 'space of intention'.

What does this mean? Well, it means that we always see meaningful activities as practices (say, when performing arithmetical calculations) and dead signs as symbols (say, in an algebraic equation). Thus when I say, for example, '3 + 3' I simultaneously say '6', perhaps not in an explicit way aloud nor just thinking for myself, but in what Wittgenstein characterized as ' ... a state of a disposition'[WVC 167]. However, here we have to be careful so that we do not misunderstand just what Wittgenstein meant by a 'disposition'. By this expression he did not mean some kind of 'implicit' condition of the (empirical) mind, for example, in the way adherents of Cognitive Science or Anti-Realists do. He is not asking if the disposition exists when ' ... all the rules [are] contained in my act of intending? [or when a] superstrong connexion exists between the act of intending and the thing intended'[RFM I §130]. Far from it. What Wittgenstein meant to emphasize was that the very technique of calculating - the practice itself - exhibits this 'intention'. It is the practice of calculation which determines the result of the operation when, say, calculating 3 + 3 to be 6. It is no external rule which accomplishes this result.

That Wittgenstein held this position is indicated when Waismann, summarizing Wittgenstein's position, says that '[t]he meaning of a word is the way it is used. If I give a name to a thing, I by no means establish an association between the thing and the word; I indicate a rule for the use of the word. The so-called 'intentional-relation' dissolves into such rules. In reality there is no relation here at all, and if people talk about such a relation, this is just an unfortunate mode of expression'[WVC 169]. *We thus arrive to the insight that on Wittgenstein's account the notion of 'intention' (and thought) in connection with mathematical calculation (and other practices as well) dissolves into rule-like practices.* This is so because a rule-like practice exhibits how the practice is meant [Supra II.2]. For example, he states that the connection between the sense of the expression 'let's play a game of chess' and the internal rules of chess (the practice) consists ' ... in the list of rules of the game, in the teaching of it, in the day-to-day practice of playing'[RFM I §130]. Likewise, to calculate is only possible when we have the competence to actually perform calculations: to engage in mathematical calculi which we have learnt through ' ... endless practice, with merciless exactitude; that is why it is inexorably insisted that we shall all say "two" after "one", "three" after "two" and so on'[RFM I §4].

We thus come to the conclusion that, according to Wittgenstein, the result of the previous discussion ought to be the realization that there are no 'logically detached' mysterious mental entities called, for example, 'thoughts', 'meanings' or 'intentions' (allowing themselves, in principle, to be the target of empirical investigations of some kind). There are no such objects ('things-in-hemselves') ' ... going through my mind in addition to the verbal explanations; the language is itself the vehicle of thought'[PhG 161]. For example, 'intention' is not some mysterious 'process' or ' ... state inside [us]'[WVC 167]. We can never in the end explain 'thought', 'intention' and 'meaning' in a scientific sense (i.e., as 'captured' by a generalization in a scientific theory of any kind as required by Cognitive Science). To assume that such an approach amounts to a genuine scientific possibility is to make a grammatical mistake. On the contrary, according to Wittgenstein, we live within what we metaphorically can characterize as the 'space of intention': the limit(s) of our experience (which includes thoughts and aspects of our world). One can say that we live in what we can characterize as a multitude of forms of life [Infra IV.5].

In his texts Wittgenstein exemplifies the function of this 'space of intention' by an analogy of the situation we encounter when we sit in a cinema. Thus he says that [Z §233; PhG 146],

> "[o]nly the intended picture reaches up to reality like a yardstick. Looked at from outside, there it is, lifeless and isolated". - It is as if at first we looked at a picture so as to enter into it and the objects in it surrounded us like the real ones; and then we stepped back, and were now outside it; we saw the frame, and the picture was a painted surface. In this way, when we intend, we are

> surrounded by our intention's *pictures,* and we are inside them. But when we step outside intention, they are mere patches on a canvas, without life and of no interest to us. When we intend, we exist in the space of intention, among the pictures (shadows) of intention, as well as with real things. Let us imagine we are sitting in a darkened cinema and entering into the film. Now the lights are turned on, though the film continues on the screen. But suddenly we are outside it and see it as movements of light and dark patches on a screen.

We notice that Wittgenstein wants to draw our attention to the insight that we are always (in 'normal' situations) within the 'space of intention'. Thus, paradoxically enough, we can say that intention - contrary to the view of Cognitive Science (if taken as an empirical scientific enterprize) - is not something existing inside us (on sub-linguistic level in our brains), on the contrary, it is rather the other way around: *it is we who constantly live within the spaces of 'intention'.* This is to say: signs always mean something and arrows always point.

When we attempt to say the same of our thoughts that we said of signs and arrows we notice our complete subordination to our language: our thoughts are always 'alive' for us. Perhaps, by making a really big effort, we could momentarily be able to get a glimpse of what it would amount to be able to 'see', in the sense of 'seeing-as', for example, symbols as signs, practices as movements, computers as intelligent or humans as machines. However, in the end we don't even understand what it would be like to really 'see' these examples, including our own thoughts (standing for the Inner), when cut off from their 'home' or form of life. If we apply the analogy provided by Wittgenstein, we can say that there is nothing corresponding to the light when it is being turned on in the cinema after the film. Even if our form of life allows the conceptual disintegration of the world (just think of the story of armagheddon in the Bible) such a conceptual bracketing (in Husserl's terminology) cannot be 'done' to us as living beings.

But, it is important that we do not misunderstand this point. It does not amount to say that we (as human beings) are what could, in anthropological vocabulary, be characterized as animists. The point is rather that even if our forms of life allows us, in phenomenological terminology, in certain instances to 'bracket' the world, it does not allow this possibility concerning ourselves as far as thinking beings are concerned: there simply is no technique for doing this. We are thus led to the insight that the limits of language (including thoughts and aspects of the world) - in an irreversable way - amounts to what Wittgenstein characterized as forms of life which simply cannot but be accepted [PhI 226].

These forms of life makes up a hopeless tangle (of the Inner and the Outer) and it is against this background that Wittgenstein now asks how ' ... human behaviour [could] be described?' and answers that this is possible ' ... only by showing the actions of a variety of humans, as they are all mixed up together. Not what one man is doing now, but the whole hurly-burly, is the background against which we see an action, and it determines our judgment, our concepts, and our reactions'[RPP II §629]. The point is that we should not attempt to scientifically explain this hurly-burly. In fact we cannot causally explain it. The primary expression of the Inner and the Outer is based on spontaneous, unstructuralized use of (primary) language-games. However, it is not the privacy of experience which seems to be a puzzle. No, it is the fact that aspects of the Inner is expressible in the first place which makes it look mysterious to us. Thus the crucial insight amounts to the realization that we are, for example, '[n]ot to explain, but to accept the psychological phenomenon [and] that is what is difficult'[RPP I §509]. But, in addition to this acceptance, we must also understand that our forms of life ultimately - and, furthermore, in an irreducible way - always amounts to forms of LIFE.

IV.5 FORMS OF LIFE

We said that our life ultimately amounts to aspects of our forms of life. This leads us to Wittgenstein's expression 'form of life'. Now, we discussed above the view advocated by Stenius that logical form as

Wittgenstein understands it in the *Tractatus* is transcendental [Supra III.3]. Kant's trancendental boundary conditions where fixed and Wittgenstein seems to have regarded them in a similar way in the *Tractatus*. In both cases this is without any doubt related to our understanding of the transcendental subject as an ahistorical construction of human consciousness. Today this seems to be a quite commonly accepted view by many scholars. But, if the interpretation of the pre-1929 writngs as incorporating Kantian themes is established by the investigations of Stenius, then what can we say about Wittgenstein's later, post-1929, texts? Do they also show some kind of Kantian influences? This is still a controversial issue.[18]

However, there are certain features in Wittgenstein's writing which nevertheless makes an investigation of this question worth while. One could, perhaps, say that the transcendental aspect of language slowly fades away in his post-1929 writings. But it is interesting to ask if the transcendental aspect completely disappears. When reading texts of Wittgenstein - published as well as unpublished - one now and then encounter comments which might be interpreted as indicating that, as far as this Kantian inspired connection is concerned, the break between his earlier and his post-1929 writings was not as complete as one is sometimes led to believe. This fact has prompted, for example, Monk to write, admittedly in connection with Wittgenstein's verificationism [Supra II.5], that '[w]e can, it seems, talk of a "Verificationist Phase" of Wittgenstein's thought. But only if we distance the verification principle from the logical empiricism of Schlick, Ayer etc., and place it within the more Kantian framework of Wittgenstein's "phenomenological", or "grammatical", investigations'.[19] We are, nevertheless, claiming that there is a crucial distinction between Wittgenstein's pre-1929 'observer' based vs. his later post-1937 'participator' insight concernnig our involvement in natural (everyday) language.

When we set out to investigate the problem to what extent Wittgenstein still adhered to some view reminiscent of Kant's position concerning the 'transcendentality' of language we find that the general background for such an assumption is being provided by Wittgenstein himself. In the preface to the *Philosophical Investigations*, which he wrote in January 1945, he says that [PhI x],

> [f]our years ago I had occasion to re-read my first book (the *Tractatus Logico-Philosophicus*) and to explain its ideas to someone. It suddenly seemed to me that I should publish those old thoughts and the new ones together: that the latter could be seen in the right light only by contrast with and against the background of my old way of thinking ... For since beginning to occupy myself with philosophy again, sixteen years ago, I have been forced to recognize grave mistakes in what I wrote in that first book. I was helped to realize these mistakes - to a degree which I myself am hardly able to estimate - by the criticism which my ideas encountered from Frank Ramsey, with whom I discussed them in innumerable conversations during the last two years of his life.

How is one to understand this quotation? Is it to be understood as saying that Wittgenstein here completely rejects what he, much earlier, said in the *Tractatus* concerning transcendentality of language and mathematics (logic) [Gefwert (1) 70-78]? Or, are we to interpret him, in view of what he writes in these texts, as saying that his earlier thoughts on language, although not completely mistaken, nevertheless, are still incomplete, i.e., they require additional and complementary investigations 'within language' in order to correctly convey the nature of such different topics as, say, the nature of philosophy, mathematics and psychology [Gefwert (1) 236-252]. This is the view taken by some commentators. A well-known example is the one provided by **Kenny**. According to him there grew up the popular - but mistaken - idea that Wittgenstein ' ... had fathered two wholly dissimilar and disconnected philosophies. [However,] the posthumous publication of the works of the thirties shows that this view is too simple. There are many connections between the earlier and the later work, and many assumptions common to both'.[20]

What could these connections and common assumptions amount to? There has been a number of advocates for the interpretation that these 'later' (post-1929) texts also exhibits both influence as well as explicitly incorporates Kantian themes, notably the insight that language is transcendental. Thus we find, for example, Harries writing the suggestion that '[w]hile some of Wittgenstein's remarks suggests what we call a *realistic* interpretation of language, others support a *transcendental* interpretation. ... By a transcendental interpretation of language (or thought) I mean one which takes language to be constitutive of the world; the limits of language are the limits of reality'.[21] But, note, that we have to be cautious here. Despite the fact that Harries formulates himself in an extremely bad way (in that for Wittgenstein there could never have been anything like an 'idealistic transcendental interpretation'[Supra II.2.]) the point concerning a Kantian inspired view of language is explicitly acknowledged by Wittgenstein. We shall investigate this in more detail below.

Additional examples of similar commentaries are provided, for example, by Shwayder, who writes that 'Wittgenstein's philosophy was Kantian from beginning to end ... Logic and mathematics are methods for the "transcendental" demonstration of the logical, essential properties of our "civil" (nonmathematical) ways of thinking and talking about the world' and Mandel who maintains the highly interesting thesis that both Wittgenstein as well as Martin Heidegger (1889-1976) were involved in nothing less than a second Copernican Revolution, i.e., in an extension of the critical philosophy to a fourth Critique where the pre-1929 writings are concerned with a Critique of Pure Language and the post-1937 writings are concerned with a Critique of Practical Language.[22] Indeed, there is a certain similarity in outlook between Heidegger and Wittgenstein consisting of (1) their mutual emphasis on the importance of the social context as the foundation of intelligibility and (2) in their common view that most philosophical problems can be dissolved by a description of everyday practice.[23]

In the remaining primary and secondary literature one finds that Wittgenstein's direct references to Kant are few. However, there are some notable quotations to be found in the texts. In one of his lectures in 1931-1932, when commenting on the Cambridge philosopher C.D. Broad (1887-1971), we find Wittgenstein stating that Kant's critical method if read without the peculiar applications Kant made of it ' ... is the right kind of approach'[L (2) 73]. One also finds that Wittgenstein explicitly referred to Kant on a couple of other occasions, both concerning mathematical propositions as being synthetic *a priori* [PhR 129; PhG 404].

Despite the fact that one finds Wittgenstein sometimes explicitly referring to Kant I think it is important to understand that one is not to misunderstand these comments. They are by no means meant to indicate that Wittgenstein accepts a position *identical* to the one exposed by Kant. For example, he does not accept mathematical (pseudo) propositions as being synthetic *a priori* [Gefwert (1) 128-129]. On the contrary, he regards fully analyzed pure mathematical propositions to be analytic. What we have to realize is that this, with all plausibility, means that Wittgenstein indeed accepts certain carefully contemplated Kantian influenced insights but that these comments get an interesting twist and formulation which is uniquely of his own design and which were written with this specific purpose in mind.

The most important category of Wittgenstein's comments of this kind concerns those involving the Tractarian doctrine of the limit(s) of language [Gefwert (1) 56-69]. In 1931 we find Wittgenstein writing that '[t]he limit of language shows itself in the impossibility of describing the fact which correspond's to a proposition ... without just repeating that proposition. (We have to do here with the Kantian solution to the problem)'[CV 27]. This quotation can be interpreted - although it need not necessarily be so - as indicating that Wittgenstein continued to cling to a version of the old Cartesian conviction that there is some 'ground' on which to stand (when doing science) although this 'ground' is no longer sought in clear and distinct ideas but in language. Thus it is extremely important to grasp that by a 'ground' is not meant any kind of 'foundation of language' (structuralization) that we find in an external sense the science of linguistics or in analytic philosophy [Supra II.2].

The expression 'ground' that we find here is explicitly to be understood in a metaphoric sense. One can characterize the situation by saying that Wittgenstein accepts that we have language as a universal medium.[24] Here it is important to understand that we do not mean by a 'universal medium' that the general notion of language is *a* language (a calulus, a system of notation) which being general must be thought of as universal. By language (the 'ground') is instead to be understood the numerous 'spaces' of everyday and public language by which we communicate. By 'language' is therefore not meant some kind of linguistic (or semantical) theory being the outcome of any scientific (theoretical) reflection of whatever kind. Thus one must note that language can furnish such a 'ground' only as long as it is not understood as standing for a realistic (or any other 'foundationalist' Realistic or Anti-Realistic) interpretation in accordance with the 'rules-as-theory' illusion [Infra V.3].

Only on an 'observer' based 'transcendental' interpretation can language function as such a 'ground'. Thus the quotation above [CV 27] can be read as expressing a 'transcendental' view of language which tells us that the limit(s) of language (now taken to show itself in the numerous distinct calculi/language-games) are also the limit(s) of nature. On this view Language and the World are not to be conceptually separated. Our factual enterprises (in virtue of which, in Ryle's terminology, we come to 'know that' something is the case) are - from a 'transcendental' point - to be understood as showing themselves in all their variety within our 'form(s) of life'. This point seems to be echoed when Wittgenstein in 1933-1934 writes that '[a]gain and again there is the attempt to define the world in language and to display it - but that doesn't work. The self-evidence of the world is expressed in the very fact that language means only it, and can only mean it. As language gets its way of meaning from what it means, from the world, no language is thinkable which doesn't represent this world'[BT 429].

In the phenomenological vocabulary of Husserl we can say that a language exhibiting a form of life amounts to a genuine Life-World. But, in contrast to Husserl, who declared that the *a priori* Life-World can never be thought of as plural, there is, according to the post-1929

Wittgenstein, not one single Life-World, but many, because there are numerous different language-games (for example, mathematical, scientific and philosophical) and thus also numerous ordinary and stratified forms of life. This point with the 'stratification' (but not in a Realistic object/meta-language sense) of the forms of life into (primary and secondary) language-games seem to be echoed in an unpublished manuscript where Wittgenstein writes that there are ' ... those forms of life which are primitive and those which rise out of them'[MS 119].

When Wittgenstein works his way to clarify language-games as constituting, for example, the name-object relationships and language teaching as consisting in training the learner in the appropriate language-games (rule-like practices) rather than in ostensive definitions, then explicit rules - criteria (belonging to secondary forms of life) - are relegated to a secondary role by him. As he says, '[t]o use a word without justification does not mean to use it without right. What I do is not, of course, to identify my sensations by criteria: but to repeat an expression'[PhI §§289-290]. The 'logic' of the post-1937 writings is not only a logic of secondary explicit rules (criteria) as has sometimes been claimed. On the contrary, Wittgenstein is outright rejecting the primacy of these secondary criteria. One must be able to use primary language-games before one can engage oneself in secondary ones. We can thus say that structuralization of our formal languages, exhibiting criteria, is only possible as structures amounting to secondary forms of life which rise out of the primary and unstructuralized ones [Supra V.1].

But here we encounter still one but, nevertheless, very common conceptual confusion. What about the claim by adherents of epistemological Realism concerning the metaphysical separability (taken for granted by the epistemological realists) between, for example, 'mind' (the Inner) and 'external nature' (the Outer), the 'observer' and 'the observed', which one sometimes encounters, for example, among 'philosophically minded' natural scientists, say, within astronomy and astrophysics, when dealing with galaxies and particles existing 'out there' in what we have grown accustomed to call the physical Universe? How can this metaphysical 'separation' be reconciled with the idea of us always existing in a 'form of life'?

Surprisingly enough, the answer is quite simple: provided we have understood Wittgenstein's point of the constant presence of the 'space of intention' we do not have to worry (in a an external and empirical sense) about any philosophical problems concerning some assumed external 'relation' between 'the mind' (the Inner) and the observed 'world' (the Outer) or 'universe' (as, e.g., is the case in certain epistemologically inspired interpretations of the 'measurement problem' in quantum physics). *All that we have to understand is that all existing 'furniture' of nature (for example, particles and fields) ultimately occur as intended facts.* That is, precisely as Wittgenstein already said in the second paragraph of the *Tractatus*, i.e., that '[t]he world is the totality of facts, not of things'[T §1.1]. Because of the common logical form (which only shows itself when reflecting on it) there are only facts; not 'metaphysical' objects (things-in-themselves) as such. In his post-1929 thought, Wittgenstein, like the phenomenologists, replaces the traditional metaphysical (Realistic) concept of 'reality' (objects) with the non-separable expression 'life'. Thus, in addition, also the concept of 'the world' (the Outer) in a metaphysical (Realistic) sense is rejected [Gefwert (1) 76].

One can only move from one form of life into another form of life (for example, we can transgress from one culture into another one) but one cannot (due to the fact that such an assumption is nonsensical) attempt to completely - in a 'metaphysical' ('observer' based) sense, as it were - step outside our forms of life altogether. To assume that this can be done is to crave for an illusion. One could, perhaps, say that a form of life exhibits something that I have (mistakenly) characterized as a 'transcendental anthropic principle' (in contrast to purely empirical ones).[25] We have an innumerable amount of such forms of life. Such anthropic forms of life are what we are grown into. It is what simply has to be accepted [PhI 226]. There is nothing 'external' relative to our form(s) of life. There is no metaphysical 'observer'. Note, that to even ask such a question is misleading (it amounts to 'prose') since it attempts to exhibit what can be characterized as a conceptual vacuum.

The upshot of this insight is, as we have already emphasized above (in connection with the private language argument(s) [Supra III.6]), that one could not, due to the fact that one in such a case would exist in a conceptual vacuum, be able to even understand one's own thoughts (i.e., expressions that are meaningless).

We can now understand that facts always occur as part of a certain context - a language-game (e.g., a mathematical calculation) - which, in turn, reflects a form of life. Thus one is always a 'participator' in a form of life. Borrowing an expression from the foundations discussion of quantum physics we can say that there need not necessarily be any conceptual problem concerning the 'detached observer': the old philosophical controversy between the doctrines of idealism and realism ultimately resolves into nothing by being the victim of the 'rules-as-theory' confusion [Infra V.3]. However, here we need a word of warning. This problem of the detached observer may, indeed, exist (and very much does so) as an empirical (causal) problem (say within quantum physics). We must, nevertheless, in order to be philosophically enlightened, be aware of the categorical distinction between a philosophical - in contrast to a scientific (empirical) - way of understanding and dealing with this problem (which is violated on numerous occasions in the foundational literature).[26]

From a philosophical point we can, analogously, say that just as the chessboard and not only the pieces applied (in the game) are part of the game we call chess so also is the 'foundation' (nature, universe) part of, for example, the scientific (secondary) language-games. They all belong to our forms of life where aspects of reality are provided by our linguistic observational apparatus (perception and 'seing-as'). As Wittgenstein said, '[t]he point here is not that our sense-impressions can lie, but that we understand their language. (And this language like any other is founded on convention)'[PhI §355]. The playground (form of life), in order to function in such a way, must provide contexts (language-games) which are invariant enough in order for *these* scientific moves to be made in *those* particular circumstances. To mention just a few examples, if people didn't usually have 'these expectations', 'meant thus' and 'calculated in a certain way' we could not describe a certain behaviour, say, within natural science or mathematics as 'expecting this', 'observing facts of nature' or as 'a mathematical calculation'. Without these invariant enough features of our language (and forms of life) the language-games would become meaningless and, as Wittgenstein says, '[i]f things were quite different from what they actually are - if there were for instance no characteristic expression of pain, of fear, of joy; if rule became exception and exception rule; or if both became phenomena of roughly equal frequency - this would make our normal language-games lose their point'[PhI §142].

The 'furniture of the universe' (chairs, tables, electrons, stars, planets, galaxies, elephants, etc.) when provided to us through our observations amount to 'players' ('participators'). But the 'furniture' (facts) amounting to 'reality' may of course also change. However, it does not matter if we talk, for example, about 'the moves of nature' or, alternatively, of 'the everchanging features of nature', as long as it exhibits enough invariance to make up a comprehensible 'playground'. The subject (thought, language) and nature (reality) are both exhibited as parts of language-games. What is important to understand is that despite different ways of talking (when, for example, speaking or writing in 'objective' or 'subjective' language, e.g., 'there are ... ' vs. 'I am of the opinion that ... ') all such discussions are constituted by language-games and are thus 'outside' what could be called the classic ego-centric predicament. The dichotomy between 'subject' and 'object' can only occur in everyday language: the provider of the innumerable common forms (language-games) of 'language' and 'nature' occurring in forms of life.

In our language there is only a sequential series of moves - the 'steps' that we make, say, in a dialogue - where the 'intentional' moves are determined by the internal rules (the philosophical grammar) regulating such practices. Wittgenstein characterized this extremely important point by saying that '[l]ike everything metaphysical the harmony between thought and reality is to be found in the grammar of the language'[PhG 162; Cf. Z §438]. But this was not a completely novel insight on his part. We find that Wittgenstein in his pre-1929 thought characterized a similar insight when he said that ' ... solipsism, when its implications are followed out strictly, coincides with pure realism. The self of solipsism shrinks to a point without extension, and there remains the reality co-ordinated with it'[T §5.64]. We can now realize that Wittgenstein's way of understanding a 'form of life' in his post-1937 thought has the merit that it enables one - as far as mathematics (and natural science) is concerned - to avoid the Scylla of the Realist inspired conceptual Platonism without steering into the Charybdis of the conceptualist idealism of Anti-Realism [Supra V.1].

IV.6 THE 'EARLIER' AND THE 'LATER' WITTGENSTEIN

We can now attempt do draw some conclusions concerning the connections between the 'early' (pre-1929), 'middle' (pre-1937) and the 'later' (post-1937) Wittgenstein. One notices that a characteristic feature of Wittgenstein's post-1929 production is that he, in a number of his texts, emphasizes the importance of what can, lacking a better word, be characterized as the 'transcendentality' of language. In his texts we find evidence for such a claim, for example, when Wittgenstein states that 'I cannot get out of language by means of language'[PhR 54]. I am prepared to characterize it as almost self-evident that this statement requires something reminiscent of a 'transcendental' reading. But, as I see it, there is even more evidence in support of such an interpretation. For example, in the *Big Typescript,* we find that Wittgenstein is writing that '[t]he aim of philosophy is to erect a wall at the point where language stops anyway'[BT 425]. He goes on to say that '[t]he results of philosophy are the uncovering of one or another piece of plain nonsense, and are the bumps that the understanding has got by running its head up against the limits //the end// of language. These bumps let us understand //recognize// the value of the discovery'[BT 425].

Wittgenstein was to repeat this point later. We find this same point (concerning 'limits of language'), interestingly enough, to be repeated almost *verbatim* in the most finished (and published) version of the *Philosophical Investigations,* where he writes that '[t]he results of philosophy are the uncovering of one or another piece of plain nonsense and of bumps that the understanding has got by running its head up against the limits of language'[PhI §119]. Thus it seems that we can conclusively establish that Wittgenstein, at least, from the beginning of the 1930's until the end of his life accepted an evolving version of this view. If we, taken the relevant literary sources into account, grant that we can establish that Wittgenstein in his post-1937 thought entertained something which can be characterized as a different kind of 'limit(s) of language' insight, then the next obvious question becomes: How is this view to be understood in his post-1937 thought?

To begin with we have to conclude that if we look at Wittgenstein's earlier texts - notably the *Tractatus* - we find it to have been a certain kind of non-empirical subject - what he called the 'metaphysical subject' (amounting to a certain kind of Kantian 'transcendental' subject) which provides the form of the World [T §5.641]. We have already dealt with the 'metaphysical subject' in his earlier texts [Gefwert (1) 78-87]. We shall, therefore, only shortly recapitulate Wittgensteins position. In a dogmatic way [cf. WVC 184-186], Wittgenstein states that Language and World are found together [cf. T §§5.621, 5.63]. By this he wants to convey the insight that when understood in the broadest possible sense Language and World are not the outcome of anything we learn. In fact they are not at all the outcome - the result - of our experience. Wittgenstein formulated this point by saying that '[t]he meanings of primitive signs (*die Bedeutungen von Urzeichen*) can be explained (*erklärt*) by means of elucidations (*Erläuterungen*). Elucidations are propositions that contain the primitive signs. So they can only be understood if the meanings of those signs are already known'[T §3.263]. Thus it seems that Wittgenstein at this time was of the opinion that we simply have to accept the insight that we, in the last instance, cannot explain how natural language comes into existence for somebody learning to speak. This enigma is connected with the - perhaps mysterious (but mistaken) - insight that in order to be able to learn a language one already has to understand **some** language. Indeed, this prompted Black to state that he finds this passage 'disturbing' in that '[i]t is impossible to explain a name's meaning explicitly: the only way to convey the meaning is to use the name in a proposition, thus presupposing that the meaning is already understood. On this view, the achievement of common reference by speaker and bearer becomes mysterious'.27

But what about the 'transcendental subject' in Wittgenstein's post-1929 writings? Can we still find traces of it here? Here I am inclined to say: Yes, partly, one can. But, in order to be able to appreciate this insight, we must undestand that one of the characteristic features one encounters in Wittgenstein's post-1937 texts is that he now takes a different approach to the problems concerning the 'metaphysical subject' which occurres in his pre- and post-1929 texts. Wittgenstein from now on wants to work entirely (e.g., in language-games of philosophical investigations) in our 'forms of life' and not emphasize the former limit(s) of language thesis anymore.28 For example, a philosophical investigation of a mathematical calculation in order to purify it from conceptual 'prose' amounts to a typical example of an investigation that takes place by language-games [Gefwert (1) 236-252].

Wittgenstein seems to emphasize that humans as a species are characterized by the fact that individuals learn to speak a language (a practice) but that they do not have any innate categories (the Inner) providing the form of language (as, for example, Fodor claims). This ability to learn language, in the last instance, can neither have nor does it require any kind of scientific explanation (justification) This is extremely difficult to understand for the person requiring factual (scientific/causal) knowledge in the sense of Cognitive Science - a scientific explanation - in order to grasp this point. Note, that such an answer is always (in science) formulated as a language-game and thus already reflects a form of life. Speech is a practice and by speaking a language human beings exhibit ' ... a way of living'[RFM VI §34]. The child learns to engage in rule-like activities by learning to do what others do, i.e., how to perform practices (which can be described as being rule-like, but not, however, in the 'rules-as-theory' sense)[Supra

V.3]. To 'follow a rule' amounts to a practice, i.e., one person cannot obey a rule only on one occasion [PhI §199]. Thus Wittgenstein again in his post-1937 philosophical texts seems to arrive at the same position as in his post-1929 writings when he stated that we just have to be content with the fact that ' ... any kind of explanation of a language [a scientific explanation] presupposes a language already'[PhR 54]. The result is - as he said later - that we, in the end, must accept the ultimate insight that '[l]anguage is just a phenomenon of human life'[RFM VI §47].

But Wittgenstein also takes a somewhat different attitude towards language learning in his post-1929 thought. A characteristic feature that one now encounters is that his views seem to have become more 'naturalized'. Thus he emphasizes the fact that the human child learns to speak within a linguistic community, i.e., '[t]he child learns this language from the grown-ups by being trained to its use'[BB 77]. But also here, in his 'later' texts, the second view inherited from the *Tractatus* remains: language is the vehicle of thought. He ends up in the position that what can be called the 'subject' of language is not the individual (empirical) subject but what he, in his post-1937 writings, came to call the 'form(s) of life' where the individual is being brought up [PhI §§19, 23]. According to the latter view it is - perhaps - correct to say that this non-Kantian 'metaphysical subject' (as a 'participator') is working when we **use** language. The expression 'form of life' (which seems to be assimilated from the book *Lebensformen* by Eduard Spranger[29]) piece by piece replaces the expression transcendental ('metaphysical') subject that we find in his 'observer' based pre-1929 texts.

The same can still, at least partially, be said in his later pre-1937 texts. But, by 1937, the situation has definitely changed. By now we find that empirical subjects are 'participators' when using language. Wittgenstein acknowledges also that there are innumerably many forms of life (in contrast to Husserl who only acknowledged one). The subject of language is not the empirical human being but the form of life into which the subject gets accustomed. The meaning of the words are not determined by the empirical 'I' but by the community (a 'we') to which we acknowledge the control of the rule-like practices which determine our thoughts and language.[30] This novel 'subject', like rules, exist only as public language (thoughts) of the individuals. It exists as a determining whole in relation to its parts. One could, perhaps, say that primary language-games amounts to an enormously complex 'fabric'. It is not possible to scientifically explain the structure (meaning) of the primary language-games as a whole by any term in a scientific sense, say, as a full-blooded 'theory of meaning', because this means going in a vicious circle [Infra V.1].

We have to understand, according to Wittgenstein, that '[y]ou can't get behind the rules, because there isn't any behind'[PhG 244]. This is to be understood so that provided any rule-like practices are to be followed at all, then some must be obeyed blindly. No explanation can be provided for them. All one can say here is: this is what we do. Thus we have to understand that scientific formulations (constituted by 'structuralized' theories of whatever kind), say, in Cognitive Linguistics, are what one could characterize as *a posteriori* in relation to the use of primary language-games [Infra V.3]. This means that there is **no** central core of meaning, not any definable quality of 'gameness' - no underlying universal concepts - that all games have in common when applying ordinary language. Thus, there cannot be any 'theory of meaning' for primary language-games in a metaphysical (Realist or Anti-Realist) sense [Infra V.1]. We can say that language-games, in Wittgenstein's terminology, exhibits 'family-resemblance' properties because it links all the different activities we call a game. A game (language-game) is a game just because we so use the word. Note, that the 'because' is obviously not an offer to establish a Realistic language-independent (empirical) reductionistic explanation.

We can then say, when we contemplate on the situation, that ordinary language-games amount to a labyrinth of paths which the encounter in a form of life which, for example, a child learning to speak, will 'find' ready (when we reflect on it). The wanderer on these paths, provided he is to be able to speak, will not hesitate if he is to walk on them or not. That is, one cannot *decide* what one learns when one is learning to speak in the first place (note: to decide something already presupposes the competence to speak). A form of life is not accepted because of the acceptance of a certain opinion [PhI §241]. On the contrary, the sharing of a form of life amounts initially to the sharing of the ways of engaging in rule-like practices which do **not** amount to some kind of interpretations but to 'blind obedience'[PhI §§201, 219]. The form(s) of life and primary language-games are found together and thus they become fused, i.e., we have to understand that ' ... to imagine a language means to imagine a form of life'[PhI §19].

It seems that in Wittgenstein's post-1929 thought the Kantian inspired theme is still inexorably connected to the shift in terminology from the transcendental 'I' of the pre-1929 period to the plural form 'we' ('forms of life') encountered in his post-1937 period [Gefwert (1) 78-81]. This shift in terminology does not necessarily seem to imply a complete and immediate break with the pure 'transcendental' pre-1929 view. Thus, for example, it has been claimed that ' ... the shift from 'I' to 'we' takes place within the transcendental ideas themselves'.[31] This amounts to a mistake as far as the post-1937 texts are concerned. The change in terminology from transcendental 'I' to participatory 'we' is clearly visible during this period when Wittgenstein, for example, insists that it is not the task of philosophical investigations to be engaged in empirical ones (e.g., doing science) or in mathematical calculations. Instead one is to exorcize 'prose' expressions in factual language-games by conceptual (philosophical) investigations [cf. WVC 186], say, in mathematical calculations [Gefwert (1) 195-201].[32]

Forms of life understood as 'participatory' language-games, as exhibited in the post-1937 writings, differs distinctively from the earlier ('observer' based) transcendental ('metaphysical') subject of language in Wittgenstein's pre-1929 writings. In these texts the 'observer' based bi-polarity between Language and the World are static and ahistorical. One can say that their 'structure' has to be provided as the result of a Kantian transcendental deduction.[33] We can therefore establish that the pre-1929 concept of the limit(s) of language is a genuine 'observer' based transcendental principle.

This has changed by 1937. Now we find that the form(s) of life is almost what could be characterized as an 'anthropological' unit. It seems that Wittgenstein is almost in an 'inductive way' trusting in the limits set by the human form(s) of life. But, we have to remember that both these versions of the limit(s) of language, nevertheless, have a certain analogous function; the first is 'observer' based whereas the second functions with 'participator' insight. Both are primary in relation to the empirical subject and reflect the differences that Wittgenstein's thinking had experienced during the evolution of his thought. We can now establish that whereas the earlier pre-1929 philosopher is a 'metaphysician' (a genuine transcendental philosopher) the post-1937 writings are provided by a philosopher who wants to perform conceptual analysis (in the widest possible sense) by being a 'participator' by everyday language-games.

Notes

[1] Stenius, Erik, *Wittgenstein's Tractatus: An Exposition of the Main Line of Thoughts*, sec.ed., Oxford University Press: Oxford (1964).

[2] Kant, Immanuel, *Critique of Pure Reason*, translated by Kemp-Smith, N., London (1929), op.cit., p. 96 (A 56/B 80).

[3] Spiegelberg, Herbert, 'The Puzzle of Ludwig Wittgenstein's Phänomenologie', in Shanker, S., (ed.), *Ludwig Wittgenstein: Critical Assessments*, London, Sydney, Dover, New Hampshire (1986), p. 234.

[4] Ibid., op.cit., p. 233.

[5] Soulez, Antonia, 'Wittgenstein and Phenomenology or: Two Languages for One Wittgenstein', in McGuinness, Brian and Haller, Rudolf (eds.), *Wittgenstein in Focus - Im Brennpunkt: Wittgenstein,* Rodopi: Amsterdam - Atlanta, Ga. (1989), pp. 157-183.

[6] Augustinus, Aurelius, *The Confessions of St. Augustine* (ca. 397), J.M. Dent & Sons Ltd: London (1907), p. 8.

[7] Much ink has been split over the question whether or not these (pre-1929) 'elucidations' [T §3.263] should be identified with (post-1929) 'ostensive definitions' which in fact applies to Schlick's conception of ultimate 'gestures' pointing toward facts outside language.

[8] For a certain way of reading such a position, cf. Hintikka, Merrill. B. and Jaakko, *Investigating Wittgenstein,* Basil Blackwell: Oxford (1986), pp. 176-187.

[9] One already finds the notion of a 'language-game' occurring in his lectures around 1930-1931 [L (1) 258]. We also find that it occures in the *Big Typescript,* written around 1930-1933 [cf. PhG 43, 171], in the lectures around 1933 [L (3) 11] and in the *Blue Book* from 1933-1934 [BB 17]. However, it is only in the *Brown Book,* dictated to Francis Skinner and Alice Ambrose around 1934-1935 [BB v], that one finds the notion of 'language-game' to be applied in Wittgenstein's texts for the first time in a full-blown way. However, it seems that he in this text still wants to emphasize that it can be understood as a theoretical (universal) language [cf. BB preface; 77-125]. He changed his position as far as primary language is concerned in his post-1937 texts.

[10] Cf. Hintikka, Merrill. B. and Jaakko, *Investigating Wittgenstein,* [cf.n.6], pp. 273-275.

[11] von Wright, Georg Henrik, 'The Origin and Composition of Wittgenstein's Investigations', in Luckhardt, C.G., (ed.), *Wittgenstein, Sources and Perspectives,* Hassocks (1979), p. 138.

[12] From an historical point of view it is interesting to note that it has been claimed that Wittgenstein did not have any predecessors in his philosophical thought. Thus, for example, von Wright writes that '[t]he later Wittgenstein, I should say, has no ancestors in the history of thought. His work signalizes a radical departure from previously existing paths of philosophy', von Wright, Georg Henrik, 'A Biographical Sketch', in Fann, K.T., (ed.), *Ludwig Wittgenstein: The Man and His Philosophy,* New Jersey and Sussex (1967), op. cit., p. 23. However, in view of the currently existing literature, one might nevertheless ask if such an interpretation is strictly correct. For example, an interesting conjecture concerning the development of Wittgenstein's notion of 'language-game' has been put forward by Weiler in his book *Mauthner's Critique of Language* where 'Mauthner explicates the concept of a situation which is presupposed by understanding by describing

simple situations of language-using which are remarkably reminiscent of Wittgenstein's language games'. Cf. Weiler, Gershon, *Mauthner's Critique of Language*, Cambridge University Press: Cambridge (1970), op.cit., p. 110. That Wittgenstein already in the *Tractatus* was aware of Fritz Mauthner (1849-1923) is evident from his comment that '[a]ll philosophy is a "critique of language" (though not in Mauthner's sense)'[T §4.0031]. But there are even more similarities between Mauthner and Wittgenstein. Thus Mauthner, in his *Beiträge zu einer Kritik der Sprache* (3 volumes, 1893-1902), expressed (1) the idea that rules of language are analogous to rules of games, (2) formulated an argument against 'private language', (3) emphasized ordinary language and (4) expressed the doctrine of 'meaning as use'. He also spoke of philosophy as 'grammar' and as 'therapy'. Weiler states that there are three cases of similarity from the first thirty pages of Mauthner's book that Wittgenstein might have derived, i.e., ' ... the ladder-image [occurring in the *Tractatus* §6.54] ... the comparison between the growth of language and the growth of a city [cf. PhI §18] and the very concept of *Spielregel* which is central to Mauthner and to Wittgenstein's *Investigations* [cf. PhI §21)]'. Ibid., op.cit., pp. 298-299.

[13] The idea of 'Language as the Universal Medium' in Hintikkas sense can be compared as a 'linguistic' (but, note, not a scientific) counterpart of certain Kantian doctrines.

[14] Beeson, Michael, J., *Foundations of Constructive Mathematics*, Berlin, Heidelberg, New York, Tokyo (1985), p. 97ff.

[15] Kannisto, Heikki, *Thoughts and Their Subject: A Study of Wittgenstein's 'Tractatus'*, Acta Philosophica Fennica, Vol. 40 (1986), op.cit., pp. 122-123.

[16] Cavell, Stanley, 'The Availability of Wittgenstein's Later Philosophy', in Cavell, S., *Must We Mean What We Say?*, Cambridge (1976), op.cit., p. 52.

[17] For example, Eccles writes that '[w]ithout making too dogmatic a claim, it could be stated that the goal of the neurosciences is to formulate a [causal] theory that can in principle provide a competent explanation of all behaviour of animals and man, including man's verbal behaviour', Popper, Karl R. and Eccles, John, C., *The Self and Its Brain*, Berlin, Heidelberg, London, New York (1977), op.cit., p. 358.

[18] It is not plainly wrong to interpret the post-1937 writings of Wittgenstein as a novel kind of Kantian philosophy. The reason why it is not wrong is because it is possible to read Wittgenstein in this ('observer' based) way

without making any specific and obvious mistake. However, the position we take in this work is that Wittgenstein in his post-1937 writings had already changed to a 'participator' insight concerning ordinary language.

[19] Monk, Ray, *Ludwig Wittgenstein: The Duty of Genius,* London (1990), op.cit., p. 288.

[20] Kenny, Anthony, *Wittgenstein,* Hammondsworth (1973), op.cit., p. 219.

[21] Harries, K., 'Two Conflicting Interpretations of Language in Wittgenstein's *Investigations*', *Kant-Studien,* Band **49** (1968), op.cit., p. 397.

[22] Shwayder, D.S., 'Wittgenstein on Mathematics', in Winch, P., (ed.), *Studies in the Philosophy of Wittgenstein,* London & New York (1969), op.cit., pp. 66, 74-75; Mandel, Ross, 'Heidegger and Wittgenstein: A Second Kantian Revolution', in Murray, M., (ed.), *Heidegger and Modern Philosophy,* New Haven (1978).

[23] Dreyfus, Hubert L., *Being-in-the-world,* A Commentary on Heidegger's 'Being and Time', Cambridge, Mass., (1991), p. 7.

[24] Wittgenstein accepts that we have language as universal medium, but not in the sense advocated by Hintikka, cf. Stenlund, Sören, *Language and Philosophical Problems,* Routledge: London (1990), pp. 9-14.

[25] Gefwert, Christoffer, *The Anthropic Principle and Intelligibility of Language,* in Linnaluoto, Seppo and Seppänen, Jouko (eds.), *SETI - Serach for Extraterrestrial Intelligence, An International Interdisciplinary Seminar,* 6-7 March, Heureka, Vantaa, Finland, Finnish Artificial Intelligence Society, pp. 195-207. For excellent different - but empirical - characterizations of this principle, cf. Barrow, J.D. and Tipler, F.J., *The Cosmological Anthropic Principle,* Oxford (1986).

[26] According to D'Espagnat we have to distinguish between two kinds of 'reality', namely 'empirical reality' and 'independent (metaphysical) reality' [cf. D'Espagnat, Bernard, *Reality and the Physicist,* Cambridge (1989), Part I and Part III.9]. As far as these terms are concerned D'Espagnat is forced to admit that the 'veiled (metaphysical) reality' (cf. Kant's *Ding-an-Sich*) remains forever hidden from human knowledge. However, we can in this case ask: If 'metaphysical reality' is 'veiled', then how do we ever really know that this assumed 'veiled reality' in fact exists? The answer is that such a question is senseless: we are meeting the limits of language [Supra I.7].

Any attempt to provide a factual (metaphysical) answer to such a question within 'philosophy of physics' exhibits 'prose' and is meaningless. Because Wittgenstein renounces such a 'metaphysical' interpretation and accepts that language, mathematics, formal logic and scientific practices exhibit forms of life (life-worlds) we can instead understand D'Espagnat's requirement as a requirement for structuralized secondary (mathematical, scientific) language-games as extensions within our unstructuralized (everyday) language-games. Note, that this does not mean that one gives up realism as such, only that one gives up metaphysical realism as a mistaken doctrine [PhG 210].

[27] Black, Max, *A Companion to Wittgenstein's Tractatus*, Cambridge (1964), op.cit., pp. 114-115. Cf. also the interesting comment by Kenny in 'The Ghost of the Tractatus', in Vesey, G., (ed.), *Understanding Wittgenstein*, London and Basingstoke (1974), p. 5. An interesting view has also been provided by Kannisto. Cf. Kannisto, Heikki, *Thoughts and Their Subject: A Study of Wittgenstein's Tractatus*, Acta Philosophica Fennica, Vol. **40**, Helsinki (1986), pp. 40-44.

[28] Wittgenstein now emphasizes, in contrast to what was the case in his pre-1929 writings (which is 'observer' based), that his primary aim is to stay within language. This means that he now wants to have a 'participator' based view. Alredy at this stage, in the post-1929 texts, we find this point reflected in his discussions with Waismann when he says that his aim is to ' ... remain entirely within grammar'[WVC 186] and, in addition, that everything he says from now on is ' ... to go on within grammar'[WVC 186]. This point is also expressed, for example, in a lecture during Easter Term, 1931, when he states that '[a]ll explanations [in mathematics and science] take place inside language'[L (2) 62].

[29] Spranger, Eduard, *Lebensformen: Geisteswissenschaftliche Psychologie und Ethik der Persönlichkeit*, M. Niemeyer: Halle (1922). Translated by Pigors, P.J. as *Types of Men*, M. Niemeyer: Halle; Hafner Publishing Co. (1928).

[30] As I have indicated in the conclusion to my earlier book (referring to an insight by prof. G.E.M. Anscombe) we find that due to the deeply roted grammatical illusion that we find in post-Cartesian philosophy in the claim of The First Person as standing for an identifiable object - the Inner - this position amounts to a grammatical illusion. Cf. Gefwert, C., *Wittgenstein on Mathematics, Minds and Mental Machines*, Ashgate Publishing Limited: Aldershot GB/Brookfield USA/Singapore/Sydney AUS (1998), p. 337.

[31] Williams, Bernard, 'Wittgenstein and Idealism', in Vesey, G., (ed.), *Understanding Wittgenstein,* Royal Institute of Philosophy Lectures, Vol. **VII** (1972-1973), London and Basingstoke (1974), op.cit., p. 79.

[32] We find this point to be echoed in a couple of quotations where Wittgenstein says that ' ... what belongs to grammar are ... the conditions necessary for the understanding of the sense [of propositions]'[PhG 88] and, some years later, in the post-1937 writings, when he writes that '[o]ur investigation ... is directed not towards phenomena, but, as one might say, towards the "possibilities" of phenomena. We remind ourselves, that is to say, of the kind of statement that we make about phenomena ... Our investigation is therefore a grammatical one'[PhI §90].

[33] Cf. Lear, Jonathan, 'Transcendental Philosophy', in Pettit, P. and McDowell, J., (eds.), *Subject, Thought and Context,* Oxford (1986), pp. 267-298.

V The Realist/Anti-Realist Illusion

V.1 INTRODUCTION

For as long as philosophy has been written one notices that the existing source material and literature may be viewed as a series of struggles between various kinds of realisms and anti-realisms.[1] There is a widespread conception that there is a genuine need to account for problems of meaning in mathematics, psychology and natural language and as a result of this there have emerged two rival accounts of the sense of propositions in natural language as well as mathematics. According to the terminology formulated by Michael Dummett (b. 1925) these are the Realist and the Anti-Realist conceptions of language and mathematics. From this definition it seems to follow that any disputed class must have as elements statements in relation to which both the Realist and the Anti-Realist are ready to admit that they do not possess criteria for decision. Today these decision criteria are usually characterized as expressing the conditions for an external 'theory of meaning' for both natural and mathematical language.

Despite the long tradition and historical background of the philosophical terms 'anti-realism' (for example, in the sense of William of Ockham's (about 1270-1349) Nominalism) and 'realism' (for example, in the sense of mathematical Platonism) I shall here restrict my use of the terms Realism and Anti-Realism to specifically refer to the two competitive research programmes concerned with meaning in mathematics (and natural language) in the sense required, originally, by Dummett. His aim is to be able to decide which 'theory of meaning', the Realist, or 'classical' (built on the Platonic concept of Truth accepting 'classical' truth-conditions) or the Anti-Realist, or 'intuitionistic' (built on the conception of Truth formulated on constructive assertion/truth-conditions), represents the correct and canonical conception of mathematics (and natural language).2

V.2 THE ANTI-REALIST RESEARCH PROGRAMME

In contrast to the scientific (empirical) and 'naturalistic theories' of language which we mentioned above [Supra II.2], those theories which are called 'theories of meaning', in the sense applied, for example, by Dummett (and Martin-Löf), are of a different kind. There is a crucial difference between the genuinely 'meaning theoretical' and the scientific and 'naturalistic' conceptions. Attempts to investigate language by formulating such a 'theory of meaning' in the Anti-Realist sense can therefore justifiably be characterized as being motivated by the request to formulate a semantical '*a priori* theory of meaning' in contrast to the 'naturalistic' (empirical) scientific theories of language that we discussed above in connection with the science of linguistics [Supra II.2]. Both views have a common goal in that they both attempt to structuralize a 'virtual' language (natural as well as mathematical). Despite the fact that these approaches have this goal in common they are nevertheless as 'theories' of a genuinely different kind.

    A 'theory of meaning' is characterized by the fact that the structure - the explicitly formulated rules - is *external*. That is, we are concerned with principles of rules of inferences as they are actually observed in the course of informal (or at least unformalized) reasoning in everyday life. But, in contrast to an ordinary empirical scientific theory such an '*a priori* theory of meaning' of, say, a fragment of natural language, is characterized by the fact that it cannot be falsified by some kind of an *experimentum crucis*. This is so due to the fact that a 'theory of meaning' is from the very beginning designed with the explicit intention to 'fit the facts' within a certain area of investigation. It is designed with the explicit intent of constructing 'classical' truth-conditions for the Realist interpretation or constructive assertion/truth-conditions for the Anti-Realist one. In either case the ultimate aim of such a 'theory of meaning' is to be self-justifying (analytic *a priori*) as far as its definitions and derivations are concerned. As an example of such an '*a priori* conceptual notation' one just has to think of Frege's *Grundgesetze*.

Because such conditions ('classical' truth-conditions (Realist) or constructive assertion/truth-conditions (Anti-Realist)) are related in an *a priori* way to the objects it attempts to capture ' ... it makes no sense to talk about objects of experience as though they were detached from our conceptual systems (as "bare objects" in Dummett's words)'.[3] Formulations of the 'meaning theoretical *a priori* conditions of language' in the Anti-Realist sense are characterized by their attempt to 'capture' the essential structure of the sentences (of 'a language with a specified structure') necessary in order to exhibit the conceptual content as intended. For example, this is the case, in the context of mathematics and computing science, by the conceptual notations created by Martin-Löf in his different versions of the Intuitionistic Theory of Types (Sets). At this point it is only fair and correct to emphasize the importance of the modern and highly successful versions of the Intuitionistic Theory of Types incorporating the 'propositions-as-types (sets) idea' by Curry and Howard [M-L (3) 6].

This structure has sometimes been characterized as an Anti-Realistic 'theory of meaning' of mathematics (for example, by Martin-Löf himself), in contrast, for example, to Davidson's empirical conception. It is specifically intended to be understood precisely as such an '*a priori* conceptual notation' of mathematical language.[4] According to Sundholm, we can say that Martin-Löf's theories ' ... represent a remarkable break [with the transformation of formal logic into mathematical logic in the sense of Tarski and Gödel] ... in that [they] return to the original Fregean paradigm: interpreted formal language with careful explanations of meaning'.[5] For an already powerful piece of mathematics Martin-Löf's theories show how, and to what extent, a 'theory of meaning' (actually it is rather a 'meaning theory' in the terminology of Anti-Realism) along the lines of Dummett's thinking is viable.

This is not, however, the first attempt to formulate such a 'theory of meaning'. We find such attempts also earlier in the history of logic.

As an example one can provide the attempt to formulate the conceptual notation for mathematical language one encounters in Frege's *Grundgesetze* despite the fact that it failed due to Russell's antinomy [GA Vol. ii, Appx. 253-265]. But when saying this one must be careful in that it may be correct to say that Frege's theory about sense and reference was an important source of inspiration for the later work in formal semantics (e.g. for Carnap and Church), but it is very misleading to describe this work as an explicit continuation and development of Frege's ideas and intentions. In the way the notion of 'theory' is used in formal semantics, what we call a 'semantic theory' or 'meaning theory' would be inconceivable for Frege (as well as for Husserl and the pre-1929 Wittgenstein), or rather, such a 'theory' would leave Frege's most fundamental problems unsolved. Indeed, according to Haaparanta, there is an affinity between Frege's logical investigations and the Kantian tradition, at least in so far as Frege recognized the difference between a conceptual component and an empirical component of thoughts and judgements.[6]

We have so far only talked about a 'conceptual notation' in general as standing for a 'theory of meaning'. But, in his William James Lectures in 1976, published 1991 as *The Logical Basis of Metaphysics*, we find that Dummett distinguishes between a 'theory of meaning' and a 'meaning theory'.[7] Despite the fact that there does not yet exist any established use of these terms they have created a lot of terminological confusion. The first published acknowledgement of this distinction goes back to Peacocke who in his article *The Theory of Meaning in Analytical Philosophy,* from 1981, writes that he is to ' ... follow the convention of calling such a theory for a particular language [which specifies the meaning of all the sentences of a particular language] a "meaning theory" (MT) for that language, and will reserve the phrase "theory of meaning" for a theory (together with the arguments for it) about the correct form for an MT'.[8] If we take this distinction seriously one notices that scholars sometimes use these terms interchangeably. In the relevant literature one sometimes finds that the term 'theory of meaning' is mistakenly applied when what is actually referred to is what more properly ought to be called a 'meaning theory'.

Dummett does not explicate on the distinction between a 'meaning theory' and a 'theory of meaning'. Instead one finds traces of both notions in what he characterizes as a (full-blooded) 'theory of meaning'. In his article *What is a Theory of Meaning?* we find that Dummett characterizes a 'theory of meaning' for an entire language, as ' ... a detailed specification of the meanings of all the words and sentence-forming operations of the language, yielding a specification of the meaning of every expression and sentence of the language'.[9] Now, from this latter characterization by Dummett we can clearly see the terminological confusion since what he calls a theory of meaning seems to be synonymous with what Peacocke calls a meaning theory.

Despite these terminological difficulties it seems that by a modest meaning theory is to be meant an *a priori* semantical theory, for, say, a fragment of natural language. It is not intended to convey the concepts expressible in it but to convey an understanding of that language to one who already has those concepts.[10] A full-blooded theory should also specify what it is for a speaker of the language to possess the concepts it expresses. As examples of attempts to formulate such modest meaning theories (Realist as well as Anti-Realist) one can provide different *a priori* semantical theories like, for example, model-theoretic semantics (Robinson et.al.), 'classical' truth-theoretic semantics (Davidson), game-theoretic semantics of two different kinds ('classical': Hintikka vs. constructive: Ranta), criterial and constructive semantics (Baker), conceptual role semantics and situation semantics (Barwise and Perry).

The general difference between a theory of meaning and different meaning theories can, according to Sundholm, be characterized by saying that different meaning theories for mathematical language make up the data for the correct theory of meaning.[11] It is still controversial if such a satisfactory 'super-theory', i.e., a theory of meaning, for the language of mathematics - in contrast to various meaning theories - can be formulated in the first place. Despite this, the very point of such a theory of meaning is to attempt to capture the criteria by which one theoretically (externally) understands what makes a certain meaning theory the correct and intended theory for an entire virtual language: it aims to explain the Anti-Realistic conception of Truth.

Dummett claims that unless and until the philosophy (methodology) of language reaches a point at which we know with reasonable certainty what form such a theory of meaning will take, the correctness of a piece of analysis carried out in another part of philosophy cannot be completely determined. Incidentally, it is at this point that we find a crucial difference between Dummett and Martin-Löf. Whereas Dummett approaches natural language as a whole (to be captured by an 'observer' based structuralized theory of meaning), we find that Martin-Löf (and Ranta), on the other hand, denies that such a formulation is possible and that one, consequently, formulates only a 'paricipatory' based fraction of a language (by a structuralized meaning theory). We can therefore say that Martin-Löf is an Anti-Realistic particularist. Since it is Dummett's notion (thought experiment) of a complete and full-blooded theory of meaning which we are here criticizing, from Wittgenstein's (philosophical) point of view, we will not explicitly deal anymore with Martin-Löf's structure. This has been done elsewhere [Gefwert (1) 102-112].

Now, according to Dummett, the ultimate task of the Anti-Realist research programme, as far as mathematics is concerned, is to provide a theory of meaning for natural and mathematical language. It is to provide a systematic account of how a natural and mathematical language functions, i.e., what makes a certain meaning theory (a structuralization) for natural and mathematical language into the intended theory for natural and mathematical practices. Thus one notices that the full-blooded Anti-Realist research programme concerning natural and mathematical language consist of two parts:

    (A)   The formulation of a meaning theory - the conceptual notation (structuralization) - for the practices of natural and mathematical language.

(B) The formulation of a theory of meaning making the formulated meaning theories the correct or intended ones.

Sundholm characterizes this important distinction between a theory of meaning and a meaning theory by saying that '[a] theory of meaning gives ... a general account, or view, of the very concept of meaning: what it is and how it functions. Such theories about meaning, however, do not hold undisputed rights to the apellation; in current philosophy of language one frequently encounters discussions of theories of meaning for particular languages. Their task is to specify the meaning of all the sentences of the language in question'.[12] Thus Sundholm's point is that there can be various meaning theories for the sentences of different formal languages, for example, we have the languages of mathematics (Constructive (Intuitionistic) Type-Theory, 'Classical' Meta-Mathematics and Model-Theory), formal logic, programming science, constructive game-theoretical semantics for a 'virtual' fragment of a natural language, etc., whereas a larger theory of meaning, according to Dummett, is assumed to determine what makes a certain meaning theory the correct or intended conceptual notation. But this is not enough. In addition, a successful theory of meaning, according to the Anti-Realist research programme, has the remarkable characteristic of becoming the long sought genuine 'philosopher's stone' in that the philosophical disputes over realism in mathematics boils down to the question concerning what form such a theory of meaning ought to take. I shall come back in more detail below to the prospects of such a theory of meaning to become such a remarkable 'philosopher's stone', from the point of Wittgenstein [Infra VI.1].

In order to begin to deal with the problem of a correct 'theory of meaning' we have to ask: In what sense do different 'meaning theories' stand in relation to each other? Within the context of mathematics the conflict between Realists and Anti-Realists, as characterized by Dummett, concerns the problem how to decide which logical system, i.e., 'classical' logic and set theory (including 'classical' model theory), as far as the Realist conception is concerned, or, intuitionistic logic and set theory (intuitionistic type-theory), as far as the Anti-Realist conception is concerned, amounts to the correct foundation (structuralization) of mathematics. As we have said, the aim of a theory of meaning for mathematical language, then, becomes in fact one of establishing between two rival formal systems, i.e., between two rivalling meaning theories (conceptual notations), which of them correctly codifies mathematical reasoning. In other words, which meaning theory can be shown to be self-justifiable: the 'classical' or the 'constructivist'. As Dummett states the problem, the question and ultimate task for a theory of meaning for mathematical language thus becomes to answer the question, '[w]hat plausible rationale can there be for repudiating, within mathematical reasoning, the canons of classical logic in favour of those of intuitionistic logic?'.13

Another proponent of this approach is Prawitz who, in terms resembling very much the one applied by Dummett, formulates the problem as follows:14

> A basic tenet of intuitionism is that classical logic contains some invalid forms of reasoning and consequently has to be rejected and, at least within mathematics, replaced by intuitionistic logic. In discussions of intuitionistic logic the question of the validity of this claim is often evaded, and instead intuitionistic logic is justified as being of interest from some special point of view which does not necessarily repudiate the canons of classical logic but allows the peaceful coexistence of the two systems.

The ultimate task in the foundations of mathematics, according to the Anti-Realist research programme, thus becomes the theoretical task to decide by appealing to a theory of meaning which of these conceptual notations amount to the correct codification - criteria - of mathematical practice.

But also in connection with the idea of a pure 'meaning theory' there seems to be a number of problems as well. If we look at the source material available we find that logicians and philosophers of the 19th and the early 20th century, due to their different interest, attempted to keep an *a priori* conceptual notation strictly separate from the idea of a scientific theory as it occurs in the empirical sciences. However, it is sometimes claimed that modern semantic 'meaning theories' (in the sense, for example, requested (1) by Davidson and (2) by Dummett), when they are scrutinized more closely, to a certain extent are characterized by the fact that they freely mix features which occur in naturalistic scientific theories with other features characteristic of the '*a priori* meaning theories'. If this is the case then one can, indeed, legitimately ask if there does exist such '*a priori* meaning theories' at all. Stenlund has drawn attention to this problem:[15]

> What we stand before here is *a complicated confusion of linguistic and logico-philosophical aims and interests with regard to language.* ... this confusion is unavoidable from a strictly naturalistic viewpoint, in which the philosophical, a priori investigation of meaning is something inconceivable, and is, therefore a mistaken enterprise. What remains then is only the study of language by the methods of science, but, according to Davidson and others, it is nevertheless somehow meant to be philosophy. This confusion seems to me to be the important common source of problems discussed in recent philosophy of language in several traditions. The attempts to assimilate philosophical and linguistic aims and notions seem to be a basic starting point for Davidson's and Dummett's discussion of theories of meaning and for the Chomsky tradition, the Montague tradition, situation semantics and in general for what is called 'formal semantics for natural languages'.

This problem seems to be reflected, for example, by **Dummett** when he says that 'I am maintaining that we have now reached a position where the search for such a theory of meaning can take on a genuinely scientific character; this means, in particular, that it can be carried on in such a way, not, indeed, that disputes do not arise, but that they can be resolved to the satisfaction of everyone, and, above all, that we may hope to bring the search within a finite time to a successful conclusion'.[16] What else can the 'scientific character' of such a theory of meaning possibly mean if not that it is in principle falsifiable? On the other hand, Dummett also writes that the characteristic feature of such a 'theory of meaning' is that it ' ... is concerned only with a single interpretation of a language, the correct or intended one: so its fundamental notion is that of truth simpliciter'.[17] Due to the possibility of encountering new counterevidence one cannot establish once and for all that the theory is true. The dilemma is that if a theory which is in principle falsifiable can establish that the claim made by it is correct only as far the evidence so far presented determines then it cannot be both empirical and *a priori*. These requirements categorically exclude each other. Nevertheless, Dummett requires such a theory of meaning to provide conclusive evidence that a meaning theory is 'true', i.e., that it is the correct or intended one. These two characteristic features of a theory of meaning seem to pull in opposite directions and have as of today not been solved by Dummett (or anyone else) in a satisfactory way.

We mentioned above that a theory of meaning also is intended to provide the correct account of a meaning theory and thus the intended meaning of mathematical language. But there is even more claims stated for such a theory of meaning. Another - and much more ambitious and demanding claim - is that such a theory of meaning is to provide the means to solve philosophical (epistemological, ontological, etc.) problems. If correct it would definitely establish philosophy as having the character of a theoretical enterprize and thus justify the claim of there existing a genuine ultimate 'theoretical philosophy'[Infra VI.2]. This point is reflected when Dummett presents the Realist/Anti-Realist distinction as an all-embracing framework, or 'philosopher's stone', which is to be applied in philosophical disputes occurring both in philosophy of language as well as in philosophy of mathematics. Indeed, Dummett generalizes this distinction to be crucial for philosophy as a subject and, according to him, a correct theory of meaning ' ... is the foundation of all philosophy'.[18] Thus it looks, on Dummett's account, as if philosophy as an activity (for different contexts) is to be subordinated to the correct theory of meaning of natural language (amounting to the genuine 'philosopher's stone'). In other words, philosophy, according to the Anti-Realist conception, is a theoretical (conventionalist) enterprize to its nature.

On this account philosophy as a discipline (like 'philosophy of mathematics', 'philosophy of psychology', 'philosophy of language', 'philosophy of physics', etc.) becomes regulated by a kind of super theory (theory of meaning) reminiscent of, say, a phenomenological investigation of mathematics in Husserl's sense. But this distinction also influences the way we are to understand the deductive practices of logic and mathematics and, consequently, also, on the Anti-Realist conception, what we are to understand by philosophy of mathematics: the theoretical task of establishing which of the adopted meaning theories of mathematical calculus is the correct one. For example, when Martin-Löf in his more 'philosophical' articles presents himself as exhibiting an outline of a ('philosophical' or 'phenomenological') theory of meaning [M-L (6) 3], one could, perhaps, understand these articles as exhibiting aspects of a forthcoming **internal** 'theory of meaning' (a 'phenomenology') for mathematical language contributing towards the establishment of the Intuitionistic Theory of Types as the **correct** meaning theory for mathematics [M-L (5)(6) & (7)]. However, from Wittgenstein's philosophical point of view, the external Anti-Realist requirement of Dummett (and Martin-Löf) concerning such a 'theory of meaning' as being a genuine philosophical doctrine is as mistaken as it can be since, in addition to a number of other things, it is not the philosopher's task to meddle in internal mathematical affairs [cf. PhI §124].

It is also a characteristic feature of certain Anti-Realistically inspired writers that they, when pursuing the Anti-Realist goal of a theory of meaning, sometimes incorporate certain important insights from Wittgenstein's philosophical writings [Infra V.2]. This is, of course, quite allright, but one had better be careful and keep in mind that these quotations might distort Wittgenstein's own intentions and thus be entirely misleading if seeking his explicit support for such claims. As an example one might take the well-known slogan 'meaning is use' as it is used in Anti-Realism.[19] Since the very point, according to Dummett, of the Anti-Realist research programme for mathematics is:

(1) To formulate an *a priori* conceptual notation (as has, indeed, been successfully done by Martin-Löf's Intuitionistic Theory of Types).

(2) To formulate the ultimate theory of meaning for mathematical language the aim of which is, once and for all, to supersede a Realist meaning theory (connected, for example, to 'classical' Model-Theory).

Therefore the slogan 'meaning is use' cannot within such a theoretical context be understood in its broadest possible sense (as Wittgenstein does). This would allow theories of meaning for both kinds of meaning theories ('classical' and constructive) to coexist and thus be used peacefully side by side which on this view amounts to an absurdity. According to the Anti-Realist view such a possibility is excluded since the genuine philosophical task, at least as far as mathematics is concerned, becomes precisely to decide by appealing to a theory of meaning which of the two rivalling meaning theories for mathematics ('classical' vs. constructivist) is the correct or intended one. It is thus assumed that the theory of meaning once and for all solves the assumed 'philosophical dispute' concerning which of the rivalling meaning theories correctly codifies (structuralizes) mathematical practice. From the Anti-Realist point of view the reason for the necessity of such a criterion of decidability is that, out of two candidates, there can be only one correct *'a priori* meaning theory' of mathematical practice, i.e., the constructive one, which is to be justified by a theory of meaning determining mathematical language.[20]

Thus one notices that, according to the Anti-Realist conception, the formulation and investigation of meaning theories (as well as the ultimate theory of meaning of Dummett) are to be regarded as belonging to the sphere of the special formal sciences, for example, like the computational core of the theory of linguistics, in the formulation of a constructive and computable Type-Theoretical Grammar whose syntax and semantics for 'virtual language' is to be captured by such a research programme. Here, as emphasized by Ranta, it is the case that '[t]his idea, to be called the sugaring point of view, later evolved into a kind of structuralist view of language as a family of systems, whose rules can be spelt out with precision, without the assumption that language as a whole is such a system. In this perspective, a type-theoretical grammar cannot be a total account of language, but a study of its type-theoretical aspects - of judgments, contexts, propositions, proofs, etc. This is almost everything there is in the language of mathematics, but it is more mixed up with other factors in everyday discourse'.[21]

What we then notice is that the 'philosophical' Realist/Anti-Realist dispute takes the explicit form of two competitive *research programmes* to use a term by Lakatos.[22] The ultimate goal of such a research programme is, according to Dummett, to establish by a theory of meaning which of the respective meaning theories (structuralizations), the Realist or the Anti-Realist, correctly captures the intended meaning of mathematical practice. We can then notice that a meaning theory as such is part of the formal sciences (mathematics, computing science, linguistics, etc.). As far as mathematics is concerned the upshot of the previous discussion seems to be that in the absence of such a satisfactory theory of meaning for mathematics only practical (utilitarian) criteria will determine the outcome, such as, which of the two meaning theories of mathematical language ('classical' Model Theory or the Intuitionistic Theory of Types) is *more useful* in actual practice concerning applied mathematical (programming, linguistic) computations. That is, what will in the end decide the outcome is not some kind of a theoretical decision (as Dummett, Prawitz, Martin-Löf and Sundholm requires) but instead a practical criterion: which meaning theory allows for more useful applications. Here I am, for example, thinking of the number of different areas of applications in the technology of computer programming such as automatic theorem proving and natural language processing, etc. [Gefwert (1) 126-130].

V.3 THE INTERPRETATION OF WITTGENSTEIN

Wittgenstein's writings are sometimes by the Anti-Realists interpreted, either (1) as having their historical origin in an explicit Anti-Realist research programme, or, (2) as providing frameworks (paradigms) which provide credibility to Anti-Realist texts. According to the Anti-Realists, the earlier Wittgenstein of the *Tractatus* is said to adhere to a Realist conception - mistakenly as far as mathematics is concerned [Gefwert (1) 88-93] - and the later Wittgenstein, in his post-1929 writings, is said to adhere to an Anti-Realist conception. The result is, as Shanker points out, that '[t]o a remarkable extent recent criticism of Wittgenstein's later philosophy has been overtaken by just such a critical model: the distinction between "Realism" and "Anti-Realism" propounded by Michael Dummett'.[23] This has led to the situation that we have two camps, the Realist and the Anti-Realist, one of which, the Anti-Realist, claims the post-1929 Wittgenstein as a partial adherent. Thus, for example, in his large book on Wittgenstein and mathematics, Wright states that 'I am not claiming ... that Wittgenstein's late philosophy was globally Anti-Realist ... I am claiming merely that it is a plausible interpretation'.[24] Within the Realist/Anti-Realist realm Wittgenstein plays a very important role, not the least because of his assumed 'transition' from Realism to Anti-Realism as a result of his encounter with Brouwer in 1928 [Gefwert (1) 159-164].

Nevertheless, despite its purely structural (and 'philosophical') aim of producing theories of meaning, the Realist/Anti-Realist framework has, as we said above, also to a certain extent been used in another direction, that is, in attempts to apply Anti-Realist arguments in order to interpret Wittgenstein's philosophical texts. This concerns his texts on mathematics as well as other topics, most prominently, his writings on language and psychology. According to this view Wittgenstein's later philosophy consists of the elaboration of a theory of meaning which belongs to the family of semantic theories which has been called 'constructivism'. As examples of articles and books concerning attempts to interpret Wittgenstein in an Anti-Realist fashion one can mention Dummett's article *Wittgenstein's Philosophy of Mathematics*, the first edition of Hacker's *Insight and Illusion* and Wright's *Wittgenstein on The Foundations of Mathematics*.[25]

A number of philosophers have acknowledged the importance of Anti-Realist interpretations of Wittgenstein's texts. Thus one can mention not only the 'earlier' Baker and Hacker as well as Wright, but also, for example, such writers as Rundle, Pollock, Richardson and Vision.[26] It is, however, an interesting fact that Dummett himself has never provided any explicit and systematic exegesis of Wittgenstein's philosophy of mathematics from an Anti-Realist point of view. Such an attempt would of course amount to the task of extracting and formulating some kind of theory of meaning from Wittgenstein's manuscripts and claim that it represents his genuine aim which he, for some reason, never succeeded (or wanted) to formulate. In fact there seems not to exist a single attempt (with one notable exception) in this direction notwithstanding the fact that Dummett, already in 1959, wrote an article on Wittgenstein's philosophy of mathematics, where he in accordance with the Anti-Realist conception, explicitly states that '[i]f ... one regards the different schools [Platonism and Constructivism] as rivals, there remains the philosophical problem of deciding which one of the various accounts is correct. Wittgenstein's book [RFM] is intended as a contribution to the latter task only'.[27]

However, the Anti-Realist interpretation of Wittgenstein's philosophy taking the explicit form of a criterial semantics, received its profoundest expression in the (Ph.D.) thesis, *The Logic of Vagueness*, submitted (to the University of Oxford) by Gordon Baker in 1970.[28] In his thesis Baker formulated an Anti-Realist interpretation of Wittgenstein based on the idea of what he - later - called Criterial Semantics.[29] He interpreted Wittgenstein's later texts as exhibiting a general critique of the assumed fundamental semantical principles of the *Tractatus*, and as the development of a radically different alternative semantic approach - or meaning theory - which he in his thesis called 'constructivism'. One can, perhaps, look at Baker's Criterial Semantics as being a preliminary attempt to formulate a constructive (external) structure. In accordance with the Anti-Realist research programme Baker also attempted to show that Wittgenstein's texts included - in addition to the rudimentary kernel of Criterial Semantics - an attempt to formulate a theory of meaning the aim of which was to show why Criterial Semantics was the correct meaning theory.

In addition Baker attempted to indicate the chronological pattern in which Wittgenstein's later philosophy developed. He characterizes this task by saying that 'Wittgenstein's rejection of most of the theses about sense that flow from pure classical semantics provides evidence that his later theory of meaning amounts to a thoroughgoing repudiation of the classical theory. [My purpose] ... is to develop a positive account of this later theory. I shall offer a rough sketch of a new semantic theory, to be called 'constructivism', and argue that Wittgenstein adhered to this theory, at least in respect of its fundamental contentions'.[30] Baker, who is today regarded as one of the best known scholars as far as analytical commentaries on Wittgenstein's *Nachlass* is concerned, now acknowledges that his attempt to formulate a criterial semantics was mistaken as far as its claim to capture the true intention of Wittgenstein's philosophical texts after 1929 is concerned.[31]

We need not bother here with the specific details of Baker's criterial semantics but instead ask: What can be said in favour of such an attempt to provide an Anti-Realist interpretation of Wittgenstein? What about the historical situation when Wittgenstein's assumed transition from Realism to Anti-Realism is claimed to have taken place? Within the Anti-Realist tradition it is not (or, actually, was not) uncommon to encounter the view that the transition from the *Tractatus* to the post-1929 writings exhibit Wittgenstein's transition from a Realist to an Anti-Realist position. Thus, for example, Hacker writes in the Anti-Realistically inspired first edition of *Insight and Illusion,* originally published in 1972, that ' ... whereas the verificationism of Carnap, Feigl, and Schlick, was quite self-consciously an application and development of the realist semantics of Frege, Russell, and Wittgenstein, the verificationism with which Wittgenstein briefly experimented from 1929-32 was a stepping-stone to a new kind of semantics ... [t]he convergence and affinities suggest that we view Wittgenstein's later philosophy as a generalized intuitionist theory, and that we view his transformation as being from realism in semantics to constructivism'.[32]

As we said above, as far as the philosophy of mathematics is concerned, this transition is often coupled with the meeting between Brouwer and Wittgenstein in 1928 [Gefwert (1) 159-164]. According to this interpretation, Wittgenstein in January, 1929, after his return to Cambridge, set out to formulate an entirely new account of mathematics - his assumed Anti-Realism - which, so the story goes, was a kind of constructivism (or finitism) closely modelled on Brouwer's Intuitionism, the result of which can be read in Wittgenstein's posthumously published texts. Common to all of these interpretations is the fact that they all regard Wittgenstein's constructivism (of whatever kind) as exhibiting a 'revisionist' attitude towards the method of mathematics, i.e., the position that either certain parts of mathematics (the non-finitary parts) simply do not exist or that they simply are to be left alone. A typical feature in the writings of members of the Anti-Realist camp is that they in their texts interpret and quotes Wittgenstein as if he actually was a member of one of the semantical 'tribes' of Realism (pre-1929) or Anti-Realism (post-1929) in his philosophical investigations.

Now, there have been a number of different interpretations attempting to clarify Wittgenstein's assumed transition in 1929 from a 'classical' to some kind of a 'constructivist' interpretation of mathematics. Common to all of these interpretations is that they regard Wittgenstein as having taken a certain methodological position as far as mathematics *simpliciter* is concerned. Thus, for example, Dummett writes that, ' ... Wittgenstein adopts a version of constructivism [which] is of a much more extreme kind than that of the intuitionists'.[33] And Bernays writes that Wittgenstein took ' ... a finitist and constructive attitude ... towards the problems of the foundations of mathematics [and] maintains everywhere a standpoint of strict finitism'.[34] Typical of these commentaries is that they accept the Procustruean method of denying the legitimacy of anything that does not fit the constructivist framework, i.e., they exclude 'classical' mathematics from mathematics proper.

A somewhat different interpretation, but, nevertheless one which still makes Wittgenstein essentially a mathematical finitist, has been provided by, respectively, Kreisel and Kielkopf. According to Kreisel ' ... Wittgenstein's views on mathematics are near those of strict finitism [but] perhaps one should say he concentrates on the strictly finitistic aspects of mathematics ... [because] all the mathematics which [he] considers clear fits comfortably within the framework of strict finitism'.35 Kielkopf, on his part, concludes that Wittgenstein is an ' ... open-ended strict finitist' who ' ... accepts strict finitism as an adequate philosophy of only as much mathematics as can be done by strict finitistic means. However, he resolves to understand the remainder of mathematics by deviating as little as possible from the strict finitistic philosophy'.36 According to this latter interpretation Wittgenstein is a 'liberal' finitist in that he primarily attempts to understand and re-formulate the non-finitist parts of mathematics but otherwise leaves the non-finitary parts of mathematics untouched. Nevertheless, this does not seem to be the correct reading of Wittgenstein's texts, since, as he is quoted as saying in his lectures on the philosophy of mathematics in 1939, he is definitely not interested in ' ... the absurdities ... of what the finitists say'[LFM 111].

Now, in order to fully understand the Anti-Realist - and revisionist - interpretation of Wittgenstein's texts on mathematics, we have, briefly, to present the general Anti-Realist philosophy of mathematics, which, in the context of mathematics, can also be characterized by the term 'Neo-Intuitionism' or 'Semantical Intuitionism'. According to Dummett, one can separate the real, or genuine, core of Intuitionism from the psychological view to which Brouwer gave such a prominent role [Gefwert (1) 146-151]. In this interpretation the core of Intuitionism consists of a certain account of the meaning of mathematical sentences based on the concept of proof-conditions (constructive assertion/truth-conditions) rather than that of 'classical' truth-conditions. Now, there are certain basic reasons why such an interpretation is tempting, namely, if one pursues such an interpretation one is led to exactly the same well-known features that one encounters in Brouwer's texts: the rejection of the completed infinite and the calling into question of the unrestricted validity of the law of excluded middle (= principle of bivalence). That this is the case, is shown, for example, in Dummett's claim that[37]

> The solution [to the problem of recognizing truth-conditions of a universal quantifier when platonistically understood] is to abandon the principle of bivalence, and suppose our statements to be true just in case we have established that they are, i.e., if mathematical statements are in question, when we have proved them, or when we at least have an effective method of obtaining a proof of them.

As far as Wittgenstein is concerned, this interpretation is tempting at least for the following three reasons: (1) it offers a way of making sense out of Wittgenstein's consistent claim that he accepted Brouwer's theses about mathematical proof and the rejection of the completed infinite in mathematics, while (2) simultaneously rejecting the thesis concerning the ontology of mathematics which Brouwer saw as providing their sole justification. According to the Anti-Realist interpretation, one needs only to understand that Wittgenstein already in the 1930's saw the same as Dummett has seen, namely, that the real and genuine core of Intuitionism consists of a certain theory of meaning which is completely detached from any psychological view concerning the ontology of mathematics. A further reason for this interpretation is that it provides us (3) with an elegant way of showing how Wittgenstein's verificationism also could have originated in the inspiration that the meeting with Brouwer initiated (to prove is to verify in mathematics), thus connecting the two, seemingly, unconnected parts of Wittgenstein's new insights [Gefwert (1) 165-174]. Thus, one can claim, according to the Anti-Realist interpretation, that the post-1929 Wittgenstein was a Neo-Intuitionist as far as mathematics is concerned.

But there is even the possibility of reading more into the Anti-Realist interpretation as far as Wittgenstein is concerned. This concerns his earlier position taken in the *Tractatus Logico-Philosophicus*. As we stated above, Wittgenstein was, according to the Anti-Realist interpretation, thought to have converted after his meeting with Brouwer in Vienna to an Anti-Realist (intuitionist/constructivist) position. Consequently, on this reading, Wittgenstein, at the time of writing the *Tractatus* adhered to a Realist, i.e., to a platonist interpretation of mathematics, where ' ... the general form of the sense of a statement consists in the stipulation of its ['classical'] truth-conditions'.[38] Thus Wittgenstein of the *Tractatus*, according to the Anti-Realist interpretation by Dummett (and others), was a Realist, whereas he, in his post-1929 philosophy, was an Anti-Realist. But, in view of what we have said elsewhere concerning operations in mathematics this seems to be a mistaken position [Gefwert (1) 94-101].

In the Anti-Realist conception of mathematics we can talk of knowledge of objects in mathematics. But, it is, on the other hand, in consideration of mathematics that the idea that all knowledge amounts to knowledge of objects is most obviously problematic. For example, that we could take the step of seeing a decision procedure [Gefwert (1) 210-219] as constructive depends on the possibility of not only having a grasp of a 'rule', in the sense of being able to act in accordance with it, i.e., having a certain practical ability to discriminate, but also in the sense of having an explicit structural conception of the 'rule' as a 'decision procedure' (being able to classify the action performed in accordance with the 'rule'). Now, we can ask if the grasp of a rule yield not only a practical ability (a practice) but, in addition, also theoretical understanding *(an a priori* theory of some kind)? If Wittgenstein, in the *Tractatus*, is accepting, as far as constructive *mathematics* is concerned, an external structure (in Martin-Löf's sense) as providing a framework showing that all mathematical practices (operations) can be performed according to constructive inference rules [Gefwert (1) 102-112] then he is forced to deny *a priori knowledge* in the context of mathematics and in doing so, because he recognises the constructive character of mathematical reasoning, is forced to deny the possibility of mathematical knowledge in the first place. Kant, on the other hand, distinguishes the rational agent as one who acts not merely in accordance with a moral rule, but because of the rule.

If there can be a conception of a rule, then there can also be theoretical knowledge of the structure governing the practice - like one sometimes sees, for example, in connection with a meaning theoretical reading of the Intuitionistic Theory of Types where the rules are implicitly (in Dummett's sense) being followed [Gefwert (1) 113-117]. Here we can say that knowledge of such a structure is not knowledge of objects or even of relations between actual objects, but of the possible relations of objects. If it is admitted that there can be theoretical knowledge of a practical ability (like calculating or chess), then any rule-governed practice in which rational agents engage is a potential source of such knowledge, including the practice of studying the theory of a practice (for example, like a calculation). But, any attempt to state the principle governing such activities immediately creates the possibility of constructing the rules of a new theory (a conceptual notation). The possibility of self-application requires that in this sense there can never be a 'complete' structure for the 'constructive use of reason' and hence no 'complete' formal framework for mathematical calculation (novel innovations are always possible as far as novel facilities provided are exact akin in rigour to that of calculating mathematical theorems). One can say that mathematics in this sense is inherently open-ended in an innovative sense.

We can now acknowledge that on the Anti-Realist view it looks evident that the *Tractatus* account of mathematics was Platonist according to the Realist terms that Dummett emphasizes. But, as we have seen above, this is not correct. It can very well be regarded as being Anti-Realistic [Gefwert (1) 88-93]. In fact the account of mathematics given in the *Tractatus* can be understood as being both transcendental as well as purely operationalistic [Gefwert (1) 94-101]. We have to understand that the claim by the Anti-Realist reading - that the *Tractatus* account of mathematics is Platonist in nature - is dictated by the necessity, when reading Wittgenstein, to interpret his pre-1929 position as exhibiting mathematical Platonism. Indeed, as Shanker says, '[w]e can quickly dispense with the suggestion that the *Tractatus* account of mathematics was platonist in the Realist terms that Dummett lays down'.39 We have to be aware that both these views (Realist and Anti-Realist) are mistaken as far as their interpretation of Wittgenstein's philosophical pre-1929 texts are concerned. Next I shall attempt to substantiate my thesis (that Wittgenstein neither adhered to a Realist nor an Anti-Realist view in his post-1929 writings) by tracing some of the steps which led up to the saying/showing doctrine [Gefwert (1) 56-69]. One thus sees an added point to the question - 'What is it to grasp or to follow a rule'? - which so preoccupied Wittgenstein in his later philosophy. To pursue this question, as we shall do below, is to explore the limits of rational thought.

V.4 THE 'RULES-AS-THEORY' CONFUSION

In order to understand Wittgenstein's conception of language and mathematics correctly it is first necessary to present his attitude to a problem concerning what can be characterized as 'rule-following scepticism' which has its origin in the problem concerning what is to be understood by a 'rule'. Now, according to Wittgenstein, a critical attitude and open mind concerning the fallibility of scientific theories is in principle a healthy attitude to adopt in science [Infra II.2]. However, such an attitude is not applicable in philosophy in that, here, according to Wittgenstein, we are not concerned with verifying scientific facts of any kind. To believe so would be a profound misunderstanding in that '[logic] takes it rise, not from an interest in the facts of nature, nor from a need to grasp causal connexions: but from an urge to understand this basis, or essence, of everything empirical'[PhI §89].

Now, we should, indeed, take a critical attitude in philosophy but ' ... we may not advance any kind of theory. There must not be anything hypothetical in our considerations'[PhI §109]. Especially, this concerns a radical extrapolation of the scientific attitude into a corresponding philosophical one amounting to a systematic doubt of what we claim to know, i.e., into the classical attitude called philosophical scepticism. A sceptic, in a philosophical sense, can be characterized as someone who doubts knowledge that is ordinarily taken for granted, i.e., the philosophical sceptic acts as a kind of a justificational 'addict'. When this is the case the sceptic may either (1) doubt that genuine knowledge is possible or (2) engage in a wild goose chase for further reasons, further justifications and further explanations because none seem sufficient and he/she believes more are needed. This position Wittgenstein regarded as confused.

Wittgenstein wrote, already in 1915, that '[s]cepticism is not irrefutable, but obvious nonsense if it tries to doubt where no question can be asked'[NB 44]. Later, in the *Tractatus,* he wrote that ' ... doubt can exist only where a question exists, a question only where an answer exists, and an answer only where something *can be said'*[T §6.51]. This insight Wittgenstein never had any reason to change. He never embraced any doctrine of generalized philosophical scepticism. In fact, one of his main interests in philosophy was, precisely, to exorcise this kind of scepticism from the philosophical realm. Therefore it is genuinely surprising to find out that one of the most influential interpretations in connection with Wittgenstein's conception of a philosophical investigation of mathematics has been turning this insight on its head: the interpretation of his comments concerning rule following as advocating a sceptical solution due to the philosopher and logician Saul Kripke (b. 19xx).[40]

There is today a widespread, important and powerful interpretation stating that Wittgenstein was engaged in a sceptical assault on the foundations of mathematics. This particular interpretation is, however, not a novel way of interpreting Wittgenstein's texts. It goes back to Waismann's *Lectures on the Philosophy of Mathematics,* delivered in Oxford in the 1950's and Dummett's article *'Wittgenstein's Philosophy of Mathematics'* of 1958.[41,42] The most prominent expression of this sceptical assault is, however, to be found in Kripke's *Wittgenstein: on Rules and Private Language* of 1982, which has its roots in the lectures Kripke gave at Princeton University during the academic year 1964-1965.[43] We can, following Davidson, call this the 'Kripkensteinian' reading which advocates semantic irrealism. According to this reading, Wittgenstein wanted to provide a sceptical interpretation of rule following. The main argument, according to Kripke, is that '[a] certain problem, or in Humean terminology, a 'sceptical paradox', is presented concerning the notion of a rule. Following this, what Hume would have called a 'sceptical solution' to the problem is presented'.[44]

This interpretation has been the source of many heated debates and has had numerous followers. Kripke himself describes the sceptical solution as 'insane and intolerable' but believes that it is none the less a conclusion we have to accept.[45] Thus we, for example, find Wright arguing that Wittgenstein repeatedly presented ' ... what would amount to a kind of Cartesian doubt about mathematical certainty'.[46] The original source in Wittgenstein's texts for the sceptically inspired interpretation is to be found in one of the crucial paragraphs of the *Philosophical Investigations* where we read that '[t]his was our paradox: no course of action could be determined by a rule, because every course of action can be made out to accord with the rule. The answer was: if everything can be made out to accord with the rule, then it can also be made out to conflict with it. And so there would be neither accord nor conflict here'[PhI §201].

How is this paragraph to be understood and what does the assumed 'paradox' look like? There are, basically, two ways of understanding §201, but, if the interpretation provided by Kripke is correct, then we have here a sceptical argument in the form of a 'paradox' concerning the possibility of correctly following a rule. On this interpretation any definition, formal, verbal or ostensive, any rule, sign, gesture or example *can* be taken in more than one way and so *can* be misunderstood (it is in principle decidable). On a sceptical reading the consequence of this interpretation is that '[t]here can be no such thing as meaning anything by any word. Each new application we make is a leap in the dark; any present intention could be interpreted so as to accord with anything we may choose to do. So there can be neither accord, nor conflict. This is what Wittgenstein said in §202'(actually §201).[47]

What Kripke wants us to believe is that no fact about one's mind or behaviour can constitute the meaning of a certain expression, let's call it 'E'. Nothing in the present use of the expression 'E' can constitute accord (or conflict) with the genuine intended meaning of 'E'. How can one then know if one is at present still using 'E' in a 'correct' way, i.e., with the same meaning (present intention) as one did, say, in yesterday's discussion (past intention)? On such a sceptical account one cannot. Nobody can. Not even an omnipotent deity were it able to look into one's mind. *There can be infinitely many interpretations* [Infra I.7]. The point is that a rule (or function) which can be made out to represent *anything* in fact represents nothing. The result is that there seems not to be any such thing as using a word in accordance with any rule, no such thing as meaning anything by any word and no such thing as meaningful language (despite the fact that we happily think, speak and write day in and day out without even for a second worrying about this apparent 'paradox'). From this position Kripke draws the radical conclusion that Wittgenstein either was unaware or he simply concealed the fact that he had stumbled on one of the most radical sceptical problems in the history of philosophy.[48]

According to the solution offered to Kripke's 'paradox', for example, by Kripke himself, a rule (and function) and its applications are essentially connected only through the mediation of a certain interpretation. Such an interpretation is provided by the mediation of a certain community, for example, in the case of mathematics and science the respective interpretations are provided by the communities of mathematicians and scientists. Kripke's interpretation tells us that only against the background of such a shared community practice is it possible to genuinely mean something by a certain expression: to 'follow a rule' is a social practice. There is no such thing as a solitary person (scientist) 'following a rule'. It is the community which provides the context for an 'objective' interpretation. Note, that 'community' is here understood as exhibiting a collective *decision* or *judgement* (the rules are collectively decidable). Thus Peacocke writes that '[w]hat it is for a person to be following a rule, even individually, cannot ultimately be explained without reference to some community'.[49] Not surprisingly, we find both Kripke and Wright advocating this 'community view' interpretation. Thus, for example, Kripke writes (concerning addition in arithmetical practice) that '[a]n individual who passes such tests is admitted into the community as an adder; an individual who passes such tests in enough other cases is admitted as a normal speaker of the language and member of the community'[50] and Wright tells us that '[n]one of us can make sense of the idea of correct employment of language save by reference to the authority of securable community assent on the matter'.[51]

Now, if we accept Kripke's 'community view' interpretation, then we are led to accept that Wittgenstein was formulating an argument based on 'rule-following scepticism', the aim of which, in order to establish the 'sceptical solution', is to dislodge us from the Realist truth-conditional interpretation of semantics and replace it with an Anti-Realist interpretation of semantics based on (communal) assertion-conditions. Kripke formulates this point by saying that[52]

> Wittgenstein proposes a picture of language based, not on *truth conditions,* but on *assertability conditions* or *justification conditions:* under what circumstances are we allowed to make a given assertion? Pictures, indeed, explicit theories, of this kind were hardly unknown before Wittgenstein and probably influenced him. The positivist verification theory of meaning is one of this kind. So, in a more special context, is the intuitionist account of mathematical statements. (The classical mathematician's emphasis on truth conditions is replaced by an emphasis on provability conditions).

Kripke then provides the following example how the 'community view' may come about. Consider a small child learning addition. It is obvious that his teacher will not accept just any response from the child. On the contrary, she must fulfil various conditions if the teacher is to ascribe to her mastery of the concept of addition. First, for small enough examples, the child must produce, almost all the time, the 'correct' answer. Now, '[i]f a child insists on the answer "7" to the query "2+3", and "3" to "2+2", and makes various other elementary mistakes, the teacher will say to him, "You are not adding ... you are as yet following no rule at all, but only giving whatever random answer enters your head"'.[53] The criterion for the teacher to acknowledge that the pupil has given the right answer is that the same answer is given that the teacher would give himself. From this it is possible to discern the rough assertability conditions for a sentence like 'Susan means addition by "plus"'. On the other hand, she is entitled, subject to correction by others, provisionally to say, 'I mean addition by "plus"' whenever she has the feeling of confidence, i.e., 'now I can go on!' and she can provide the 'correct' responses in novel cases. Thus we are, according to Kripke, led to realize that '[a]ny individual who claims to have mastered the concept of addition will be judged by the community to have done so if his particular responses agree with those of the community in enough cases ... '.54

This is the way that the argument concerning communal agreement comes into existence. Each person who claims to be following a 'rule' within a community, for example, as an 'adder', can be checked by others. But this requires that everyone involved in the practice of addition accepts the same *interpretation* of the rule of addition. It requires the competence to make an explicit decision concerning which rule is to count as the correct interpretation. The common interpretation, or disposition to follow the rule correctly, requires acceptance of the relevant assertability conditions. It is the disposition to interpret these theoretical assertion rules in the same way which in the 'community view' interpretation breathes life into a sign and what it signifies. According to Kripke's view we are thus led to believe that Wittgenstein sanctioned the insight that the expression 'meaning is use' both can and is to be understood as the result of a correct interpretation, i.e., where the rule (formulated as an assertion condition) is understood as constituting a 'theoretical entity' belonging to an *a priori* structure in the sense we see in the semantic meaning theories of mathematics which adhere either to the (Realist) 'classical' truth-conditional aspect or, alternatively, to the constructive (Anti-Realist) assertion/truth-conditional aspect of what such a theory (structuralization) ought to look [Gefwert (1) 88-93]. These are the basic outlines of the way Kripke (in addition to, for example, Dummett, Peacocke and Wright) wants us to understand Wittgenstein's position as far as 'rule scepticism' is concerned.55 Does this interpretation make sense? Does there exist any alternative view? We shall look at these questions in somewhat more detail below.

The validity of Kripke's interpretation has been disputed by a number of philosophers. For example, according to Baker and Hacker, it has currently ' ... become fashionable ... under the influence of Michael Dummett, to view Wittgenstein's development from the *Tractatus* to the *Philosophical Investigations* as a transformation of a realist into an anti-realist, a ['classical'] truth-conditional theory into an [constructivist] assertability-conditions theory ... Kripke, like others, falls victim to this distorted way of looking at Wittgenstein'.[56] In Anti-Realistic writings this claim is sometimes backed by referring to comments by Wittgenstein such as ' ... assertion is not something that gets added to the proposition, but an essential feature of the game we play with it ... [s]o we want to ask something like: under what circumstances do we assert a proposition? Or: how is the assertion of the proposition used in the language-game'[RFM Appx. III §§2,6]. Because an 'assertion' in Realist semantics is regarded as something being detached from it, i.e., following Frege, as standing for something 'psychological'[FA x], this statement is regarded by the Anti-Realist interpretation as incorporating 'assertion' as an essential feature of a constructivist meaning theory [cf. Gefwert (1) 102-112].

Statements like these, occurring in the *Remarks on the Foundations of Mathematics,* are sometimes referred to as providing evidence of Wittgenstein's Anti-Realist leanings. For example, according to Kripke 'Wittgenstein replaces the question "What must be the case for this sentence to be true?" by two others: first, "Under what conditions may this form of words be appropriately asserted (or denied)?"; second, given an answer to the first question, "What is the role, and the utility, in our lives of our practice of asserting (or denying) the form of words under these conditions?"'.[57] This interpretation does not seem to be correct, but it is, if one is to believe adherents of the Anti-Realist interpretation, the basic reason why one can talk of Wittgenstein's 'earlier' and 'later' philosophy in the first place. Indeed, as Baker and Hacker emphasize, thus[58]

> [f]orcing Wittgenstein into the invented position of
> constructivism, intuitionist semantics, assertion-conditions
> theories, is altogether misguided. It is a mistake stemming
> from a hankering after sweeping generalizations, global
> confrontations of semantic theories, and large-scale theory-
> building. But Wittgenstein builds no such theories. He does
> not contend that a language is a monolithic structure run
> through with truth-conditions or assertion-conditions which
> give meanings to sentences and words. It is not a calculus of
> rules, either in the form of classical logic or in the form of
> intuitionistic logic.

Despite many commentaries by adherents of the Anti-Realist school, advocating and supporting such a semantic view, these attempts seem, nevertheless, not to be the correct way to understand Wittgenstein. Why not? To begin with, as we pointed out above, Anti-Realism accepts rule-following scepticism as a legitimate attitude. *Wittgenstein, on the other hand, was intent on demonstrating that the principal problems arising from a sceptical assumption originate from conceptual confusion.* The alleged foundational problem does not exist simply because 'rules', as Wittgenstein understands them, are not theoretical entities formulated on a meta-level: they are not bits of an external *a priori* machinery or a linguistic (naturalistic) theory - a theory of rules - invented for hypothetical reasons as an answer to a misguided sceptical query. In the sense Wittgenstein understands rules (actually rule-like practices) there can be no alternative interpretation of them because then we would be dealing with different rules. As Wittgenstein says, '[a]nd hence also "obeying a rule" is a practice. And to *think* one is obeying a rule is not to obey a rule'[PhI §202]. That is, to genuinely obey a rule amounts to a practice and thus to act in a different way is to follow a different rule, that is, to engage in a different practice. As Winch points out,[59]

> [h]e [Kripke] does not notice for instance that the distinction
> Wittgenstein emphasizes is not so much that between
> "philosophical" and "common sense" *statements* about what

rule-following consists in, as that between our ordinary *practice* of rule-following and the philosophical *explanations* we are inclined to give of that practice. What Kripke calls "common sense philosophy" is an *interpretation* of our practice just as much as is, say, scepticism; and our practice is prior to any interpretation.

We have to realize that basically rules are not to be understood as being *extensional*, i.e., they are not to be regarded as 'theoretical entities' occurring on an assumed meta-level (in 'classical' terminology) external to the practice being investigated. According to Stenlund '[t]he extensional picture and the assumed meta-language *in which this picture exists,* are not just preconditions for *stating* the problem, they are preconditions for there *being* a sceptical problem'.[60] The point is to understand that rules are neither Platonic entities in some logical space nor mysterious mentalistic entities determining causally how we think. Thus, according to this second - anti-Kripkean interpretation - the crucial paragraph in the Anti-Realist interpretation, §201 of the *Investigations*, is to be read as a culmination of a sustained *reductio ad absurdum* which Kripke and the Anti-Realists, on the other hand, interpret as proven by the very premise that 'rules' are theoretical entities on a meta-level. If, instead, we understand the dilemma as a final proof of the *reductio* we find that the 'sceptical dilemma' disappears. By working backwards from the unsatisfactory sceptical conclusion through its way of reasoning I shall attempt to exhibit this subtle insight in somewhat more detail below.

V.5 CONCLUSION: UNDERSTANDING A 'RULE'

The problem concerning how to apply the rule in the same way forces us to consider the question: What does understanding a rule actually amount to? Is it the rule which guides me so that the practice of expanding the series somehow *follows* from it? As we said above: does the rule, somehow, in a mysterious way, contain its own application? No, according to Wittgenstein, it is a mistake to assume that a rule is somehow completely detached from a practice and thus mysteriously 'acts at a distance'[BB 14] in order to determine the practice to what it is. The meaning of an utterance does not consist in the meaning (as a mysterious object) somehow being 'transmitted' by the rule, analogously, for example, to what happens when electromagnetic waves transmit radio programmes. As Wittgenstein said, '[t]he mistake is to say that there is anything that meaning something consists in'[Z §16].

On the contrary. It is we by our practices who make the rules (which actually, then, are primary rule-like practices and not rules externally thought) what they are. It is not rules of their own accord (set somewhere in an eternal 'Platonic heaven' as theoretical entities) which determine the primary meanings, it is the way we apply the rules in our practice which makes them what they are. Indeed, primary rule-like activities (in Wittgenstein's sense) do not amount to theoretical entities (they are not part of any structuralization) and thus do not constitute an ' ... ultra-physics, the description of the "logical structure" of the world, which we perceive through a kind of ultra-experience ...'[RFM I §8].

It is precisely the competence to add that we attempt to establish with the numerous examples of arithmetic occurring in lectures of mathematics, which we provide in response to someone asking 'I don't understand how to calculate this task'. The point is that the rule shows itself in the arithmetical calculations and in order to establish such competence we do not teach someone arithmetic by formulating an arithmetical rule. As Wittgenstein said, '[f]or just where one says "But don't you see ... ?" the rule is no use, it is what is explained, not what does the explanation'[Z §302]. There is no such thing as understanding a rule correctly independently of being able to apply it correctly. Primary rules *show* themselves in our practices. A repeated activity (like always receiving the answer '4' when adding '2+2') is a rule-like activity: a practice. The criterion for something being a practice is that it is characterized by being a rule-like activity in contrast to a random activity. It is this which underlies, say, lectures and examinations in mathematics. The point is that it is not 'rules by themselves' which somehow magically breathe life into signs and expressions; it is our *practice* of using them which accomplishes this. Such a practice - shared activities - is the basis for emphasizing the need for a community, say, in connection with mathematical calculation. Indeed, as Malcolm says, '[a] rule can exist only in a human practice, or in what is analogous to it. And what a rule requires and what following it is, presupposes the background of a social setting in which there is quiet agreement as to what 'going on in the same way' is. This is agreement in acting, not in opinions'.[61]

This is where the interpretations of Wittgenstein as an adherent of 'rule-following scepticism', or Anti-Realism, go wrong, for example, in the case of their version of the community view interpretation. For an Anti-Realist, like Kripke, 'assertions' about meaning amount to 'a new approach' to how language has meaning and ' ... can be applied to give an account of assertions themselves, regarded as assertions within language'.[62] Such 'a new approach' amounts to the possibility of capturing linguistic meaning by formulating certain theoretical meaning-rules which can be applied by a certain language community in deciding what constitutes legitimate and correct assertion. But the discussion by Wittgenstein concerning what it is to follow rules was *not* meant to show that it only makes sense to talk of someone's linguistic behaviour as constituting an instance of following an explicitly formulated rule in the context of a community of rule followers in the Anti-Realist sense. Rather, his arguments were designed to show that it only makes sense to talk of following a rule primarily in the context of a *practice* - a rule-like regularity. There is a crucial difference between these two ways of reading Wittgenstein's texts.

This difference can be illuminated by the following example. To explain what 'one metre' means by pointing at a metre-rod and saying '[t]hat (length) is one metre' is perfectly correct. However, understanding and using this sentence as an explanation requires that one understands the *manner* in which measuring rods are used to measure the length of objects, for example, that they are applied by being laid alongside the objects and the length read off from the markings on the rod. The application of a rule in a practice is always manifest in the practice itself. *What is correct and incorrect when following a 'rule' in calculation is determined by an internal relation between the 'rule' and what counts as being in accord with it.* An internal relation is characterized by the condition that should the practice and the 'rule' somehow be separated, then we do not have the same practice any more. It is this internal relation which makes it into a normative practice. According to Wright this is what Wittgenstein means when he says [RFM III §41] that causality must play no part in a proof.63 Indeed, as Wittgenstein said, '[t]here is not any question at all here of some correspondence between what is said and reality; rather is logic *antecedent* to any such correspondence; in the same sense, that is, as that in which the establishment of a method of measurement is *antecedent* to the correctness or incorrectness of a statement of length'[RFM I §156]. The point is that, according to Wittgenstein, one cannot have any 'theoretical' opinion of whether an internal 'rule' is correctly applied or not. No 'philosophical debate' (in the sense of 'analytical philosophy') is possible. It amounts to a question of normativity, the result being that such an internal relation is not open to debate. No interpretation is possible in that one cannot provide any counterexample to an internal rule. To even ask such a question exhibits a grammatical confusion and any counterexample produced to an instance of an internal rule in fact amounts to a *novel* rule [Infra II.4].

We have to understand that a normative practice exhibiting an internal rule is not the outcome of a certain explicit decision, or convention (or 'collective interpretation'), having taken place in what could be characterized as a 'democratic conceptual marketplace' where the interpretation of rules are somehow decided by, for example, a suitable theory of meaning (i.e., where what most people would call 'the correct constructive assertion/truth-conditions' are being determined) as Kripke and the Anti-Realists assume. *The mistake is that the 'community view' applied by Kripke substitutes the internal relation between practice and 'rule' with the notion of community agreement which is not an internal property of the 'rule', the result being that the criterion of what 'is correct' becomes completely empty.* This has been emphasized, for example, by Baker and Hacker, who tells us that [64]

> [c]ommunity agreement shows that the members of the community are all playing the same game, as it were, but that they should agree in applying the rules of the game is not itself one of the rules of the game. It is a framework condition within which the community game is possible. But that acting thus-and-so *is* acting in accord with *this* rule is no more a matter of what people are disposed to do than that the fact that *p* is the fact that makes the proposition that *p* true is a matter of what people are disposed to believe.

It does not amount to a communal agreement, or consensus concerning a decision (i.e., an external relation), to notice that '102' follows '100' in the sequence of even integers in the practice of counting which would abrogate the internal relation. To continue a series of natural numbers correctly is not fixed, or determined, by communal agreement as far as arithmetical practice is concerned. As Hertzberg points out, [65]

> ... it is misleading to say that meaning is determined by community agreement ... It is one thing to say that the concept of meaning is *dependent* on, or *presupposes,* the existence of a community in which there is considerable agreement in the use of language. It is another thing to say that communal agreement *determines* what the meaning is, or that the correct use of an expression is *fixed* by the common way of acting displayed by the majority of those who have had the same training.

Thus we notice that what is still missing, for example, in an answer like the one provided by Malcolm, is an answer to the specific question *how* the existence of a language community makes linguistic meaning possible. Here the important thing to understand is that since one is actually dependent on the meaning of the relevant expressions applied there can be no language-independent method by which past actions can be projected on to future actions. This point is clearly stated by Rhees when he says that 66

> I am not saying, "People see that their reactions tally, and this makes communication possible". That would assume considerable understanding and language already. The agreement of which I am speaking is something without which it would not be possible for people to 'see' that their reactions tallied or that anything else tallied ... Neither does the agreement in reactions come first or anticipate language. It appears as the language does, it is a common way of taking the expressions of the language. They are common reactions within the course of language - not to anything there might have been before language or apart from it.

It is the factual dependence on language-games for a practice to establish itself that constitutes the conformity required for correctly following the (internal) rule of, for example, the natural numbers in arithmetic. *The conformity is set in language.* We are, to use an expression by Hertzberg, subject to ' ... the factual dependence of the language-game'.67 There is no linguistic agreement which is language-independent and thus there cannot exist any method (exhibiting assertion-conditions) by which it would be possible to decide what an expression means. It is in language that we exhibit how to follow a 'rule-like activity', for example, to calculate correctly. One has to understand that the 'rule' set in language and its application are two sides of the same coin: the practice. When performing a practice one does not decide if the 'rule' exhibits the distinction between sense and nonsense as far as the practice is concerned.

This point is shown in the following dialogue when Wittgenstein says that '"I have a particular concept of the rule. If in this sense one follows it, then from that number one can only arrive at this one". That is a spontaneous decision. But why do I say "I must", if it is my decision? Well, may it not be that I must decide? Doesn't its being a spontaneous decision merely mean: that's how I act; ask for no reason! You say you must; but cannot say what compels you'[RFM VI §24]. Thus we notice that it is not the linguistic community as such which determines if a rule has been correctly followed or not. We have to understand that '[t]he plurality ... does not provide a procedure for settling disagreements, rather it provides a space in which there can be disagreement (and hence agreement too), because there can be a confrontation of reactions'.[68]

It is the same mistake that occurs when one, for example, in constructive mathematics regards a (primary) rule as determining the totality of its applications. Just think of the different interpretations provided for the different forms of judgements occurring in Martin-Löf's Intuitionistic Theory of Types [M-L (3) 5-6]. In order to set matters right one must get rid of the theoretical picture which tends to distort our understanding. For example, calculation by algorithm is applied as a standard of rule-following (in, say, computer programming) because it is easily assumed to be free from error. Mathematical functions are thus seen as determining values for any of the indefinite number of arguments which they take. Likewise, rules are seen as determining the totality of their applications.

According to Wittgenstein, both views are mistaken: neither functions nor rules can when regarded as *a priori* (or hypothetical) 'theories of rules', and, as it were, in a metaphorical - and quasi-causal - way, mysteriously, ' ... act at a distance'[BB 14], determine their applications 'by themselves'. It is, rather, the other way around. It is the persons engaged in calculations who in their mathematical and linguistic practices exhibit and determine (fix) what constitutes to follow a rule and what does not. This is exhibited when Wittgenstein, in Lent Term, 1935, ended one of his lectures (Lecture XIII) concerning rules by saying that '[a] rule is best described as being like a garden path in which you are trained to walk, and which is convenient. You are taught arithmetic by a process of training, and this becomes one of the paths in which you walk. You are not compelled to do so, but you just do it'[L (3) 155].

Wittgenstein's insight is that to understand a rule (a rule-like activity) is to be able to perform a calculation (practice) correctly [PhI §190]. When calculating there is - contrary to Brouwer - no 'intuition' present [PhI §186; BB 143]. Justification of a practice comes to an end. An explanation terminates when we have to say that this and this is simply what I do because '[i]f I have exhausted the justifications I have reached bedrock, and my spade is turned. Then I am inclined to say: "This is simply what I do"'[PhI §217]. There are no justificational parts missing in such a normative explanation: no further justification is needed and no further rule can justify the application of the first rule. Such a demand by a 'rule-following scepticist' concerning additional justification only leads to a vicious infinite regress. It does not remove the difficulty which created the assumed need for it, it only ' ... pushes the question one step further back'[BB 86].

When performing a certain multiplication this very calculation - and nothing else - is the justification for this calculation. Nothing additional is needed. To understand a rule (a rule-like activity) is to be able to apply it, i.e., the point is that 'I cannot describe how (in general) to employ rules, except by *teaching* you, *training* you to employ rules'[RPP II §413]. *The philosophical insight is thus that one should not ask for explanations where no explanations can be given.* In this sense Wittgenstein aims at ' ... turning our whole examination around'[PhI §108]. There are no interpretations as far as rule-like activities (rules) are concerned [PhI §201]. This is, then, the second way of understanding §201. When understood in this way all the different points that Wittgenstein made about rule following can then be incorporated into a unified reading which the sceptical interpretation leaves unexplained.[69]

This has extremely important consequences for the way we are to understand Wittgenstein's comments on mathematics (as well as psychology). It is therefore crucial to understand, as Shanker emphasizes, that ' ... Wittgenstein was intent on demonstrating that, like all philosophical sceptical issues, the principal problems in the foundations dispute stem from conceptual confusion, and thus call for logical clarification as opposed to epistemological refutation. This is obviously a crucial - indeed, perhaps the single most important - issue in the interpretation of Wittgenstein's remarks on the philosophy of mathematics'.[70] How are we to understand this comment? To begin with, Wittgenstein was not intent on solving the foundations dispute by engaging in a mathematical research programme into the foundations of mathematics [Gefwert (1) 254-255]. Neither was he engaged in performing a refutation of some sort. As Black quite correctly points out, Wittgenstein ' ... was attempting something very different from "tentatively offering" another set of "foundations". A critic of the game is not another player'.[71] Wittgenstein seems to have perceived as his fundamental task in the philosophy of mathematics to remove the epistemological framework (e.g., Realist semantics and Anti-Realist semantics) altogether from *philosophical* considerations in the context of mathematics (and elsewhere) without which the foundations crisis in mathematics simply collapses of its own accord.

But what, precisely, was Wittgenstein up to then? It seems, if we use his own expressions, that he was solely concerned with a philosophical investigation, i.e., clarifying what he described as the grammar of those expressions which created philosophical problems. By the expression 'grammar' he did not mean ordinary grammar familiar from school nor any formal language. *By the notion of 'logical grammar', within the context of mathematics (and elsewhere), Wittgenstein seems to have meant the internal 'rules' regulating the linguistic expressions in the network of activities making up a calculation or language-game.* That is, the root of the philosophical problems lies in the transgression of the 'rules', however, not of ordinary school grammar, but rather, the internal 'rules' of a calculation, that is, its 'logical grammar'. This is correct as far as it goes.

Despite the interaction with Wittgenstein most of the commentaries in the 1930's by the philosophers of the Vienna Circle concerning the philosophy of science and mathematics seem to understand their foundational task as originating in the scientific tradition. Thus, it seems to have been this mistake which, for example, prompted Schlick, in 1930, in his paper entitled *Die Wende der Philosophie* (Turning-point in philosophy), to write that [72]

>...we are at present in the midst of an altogether final change in philosophy, and are just entitled to consider the fruitless conflict of systems at an end. The present age, I maintain, is

> already in possession of the means to make all such conflict essentially unnecessary; it is only a matter of resolutely using them. ... The methods proceed from logic. Their beginnings were obscurely perceived by Leibniz; in recent decades important stretches have been opened up by Gottlob Frege and Bertrand Russell; but the decisive turning-point was first reached by Ludwig Wittgenstein.

The aim of Wittgenstein's new philosophical method as far as mathematics is concerned was to force us to abandon the established epistemological and sceptical approach to the foundations dispute. The target of Wittgenstein's attack was the Cartesian tradition, emphasizing the importance of a doubtful attitude in *philosophy,* when attempting to achieve philosophical certainty by resolving these questions by applying epistemological arguments. Thus the key and background for being able to appreciate Wittgenstein's approach to philosophy of mathematics (and psychology), lies in his approach to epistemology (and scepticism) in general. His new method in philosophy is to make us understand that the very nature, e.g., of mathematical truth is such that it forces us to divorce altogether any epistemological and theoretical considerations from the philosophy of mathematics (as well as philosophy of psychology). This insight he carried over to his later texts. As he said in a lecture in 1932-3 '[t]he chain of reasons comes to an end, that is, one cannot always give a reason for a reason'[L (3) 5].

If this reading - contrary to Kripke's sceptical interpretation - is correct, then one can understand Wittgenstein's philosophical comments as attacks aimed at dissolving the conceptual problems occurring in the foundations dispute in mathematics, which its participants, not least within the meta-mathematical school, found problematic. Conceptual problems in the 'foundations' of mathematics often rest on the need to clarify the logical grammar of what constitute foundational beliefs, but this must in no way be confused with the misguided search for 'foundations' in order to secure our beliefs against sceptical doubts concerning the reliability of mathematics. Thus it seems evident that Wittgenstein in his philosophical writings did not set out from a sceptical attitude as far as the requirement of justifying mathematical certainty is concerned. The question of justifying, for example, the truth of mathematical propositions is, on Wittgenstein's account, seriously misconstrued, not because mathematics in ordinary practice is 'immune from doubt' since a mistake is always possible when performing, say, a mathematical proof, but, because it makes no sense to speak of a systematic 'epistemological ("philosophical") doubt' in the context of mathematical practice.

Notes

[1] Wiggins, David, 'Meaning and truth-conditions: from Frege's grand design to Davidson's'; Skorupski, John, 'Meaning, use, verification', both in Hale, B. and Wright, C., (eds.), *A Companion to the Philosophy of Language,* Basil Blackwell: Oxford (1997), pp. 3-28, 29-59.

[2] Dummett specifies this task in his article the 'Justification of Deduction' as being concerned with which rival types of semantics 'classical' or constructive] is the correct one. He seeks to appropriate to Frege a semantical account of his concept-script and seeks to appropriate him as father of much contemporary 'theory of meaning' where the formalism is surveyed as a whole, cf. Dummett, Michael, 'The Justification of Deduction', in Dummett, M., *Truth and other enigmas,* London (1978), op.cit. p. 314; In contrast to this version we also find an alternative view sparked by Jean van Heijenoort and Burton Dreben 'Introductory note to 1929, 1930 and 1930a', in *Kurt Gödel, Collected Papers, I,* (ed.) by Feferman, S., Dawson Jr, J.W., Kleene, S.C., Moore, G.H., Solovay, R.M and van Heijenoort, J., the Clarendon Press: New York and Oxford (1986), p. 44]. According to this view logic is a language and this language has to be learned like any other language. One has to bring the reader to 'catch on' in order to get into the language. According to Juliet Floyd these writers hold that the young Wittgenstein in the *Tractatus,* ' ... far from advocating a "theory of meaning" or a "semantical theory", insists on the nonsense of any attempt to theorize about the nature of logic, the nature of meaning, or the nature of language', Floyd, J., 'Frege and "Semantics"', Boston University (1996), Preprint, op.cit. p. 3.

[3] Stenlund, Sören, *Language and Philosophical Problems,* Routledge: London (1990), op.cit., p. 58.

[4]   Ibid., op.cit., p. 77.

[5]   Sundholm, Göran, 'Proof Theory and Meaning', in Gabbay, D. and Gunther, F., (eds.), *Handbook of Philosophical Logic,* Vol. III., Dordrecht (1986), p. 472.

[6]   Haaparanta, Leila, 'Analysis as the method of logical discovery: Some remarks on Frege and Husserl', *Synthése,* 77 (1988), pp. 73-97.

[7]   Dummet, Michael, *The Logical Basis of Metaphysics,* Cambridge, Mass., (1991), op.cit. p. 22.

[8]   Peacocke, C.A.B., 'The theory of meaning in analytical philosophy', in Flöistad, G., (ed.), *Contemporary Philosophy,* Vol.1., The Hague (1981), pp. 35-36.

[9]   Dummett, Michael, 'What is a Theory of Meaning?', in Guttenplan, S., (ed.), *Mind and Language,* Oxford University Press: Oxford (1975), p. 97; Cf also Dummett, Michael, 'What is a Theory of Meaning? II', (in Evans, G. and McDowell, J., (eds.), *Truth and Meaning: Essays in Semantics,* Oxford University Press: Oxford (1976), op.cit., p. 69-70; Cf. also p. 472.

[10] Dummett, Michael, *The Seas of Language,* Basil Blackwell: Oxford (1993), p. viii.

[11] Sundholm, Göran, 'Proof Theory and Meaning', in Gabbay, D. and Gunther, F., (eds.), *Handbook of Philosophical Logic,* Vol. III., Dordrecht (1986), op.cit., p. 472.

[12] Ibid., op.cit., p. 497.

[13] Dummett, Michael, 'The Philosophical Basis of Intuitionistic Logic', in Dummett, M., *Truth and Other Enigmas,* [cf.n.2], p. 215.

[14] Prawitz, Dag, 'Meaning and Proofs: on the conflict between classical and intuitionistic logic', *Theoria,* Volume XIII (1977), op. cit., p. 2.

[15] Dummett, Michael, 'Can Analytical Philosophy be Systematic, and Ought it to Be?', in Dummett, M., *Truth and Other Enigmas,* [cf.n.2] op.cit., p. 454.

[16] Dummett, Michael, 'Can Analytical Philosophy be Systematic, and Ought it to Be?', in Dummett, M., *Truth and Other Enigmas,* [cf.n.2] op.cit., p. 454.

[17] Dummet, Michael, *The Logical Basis of Metaphysics,* Cambridge, Mass., (1991), op.cit. p. 20.

[18] Dummett, Michael, *Frege: Philosophy of Language,* London (1973), op.cit. p. 669; In an interview conducted in 1995 we find that Dummett confirms this position as far as his conception of 'philosophy' is concerned. In this interview Dummett stresses that 'In particular, he [Wittgenstein] had the idea that you can't alter linguistic practice, and he got himself into the absurdity that philosophy couldn't alter linguistic practice even if that practice was shown to be inconsistent or led to a contradiction. You just have to accept contradictions as a fact. ... I don't think that there ever was any justification in his [Wittgenstein's] saying that philosophy can't interfere with anything. Our linguistic practice can be out of order just as our behaviour can be out of order or irrational. Philosophy has the right to point that out'[op.cit., p. 8]. Pataut, Fabrice, 'An Anti-Realist Perspective on Language, Thought, Logic and the History of Analytic Philosophy: An Interview with Michael Dummett', *Philosophical Investigations,* Vol. 19, No. 1, January 1996, pp. 1-33.

[19] The famous slogan 'meaning is use' has its origin in Wittgenstein's point that the signs themselves are dead and need 'use' to give them life as practice [PhG 132; BB 4; PhI §§430-433]. It is, however, important to understand that when we perform such basic rule-like practices (for example, when we speak) we follow the 'rules' in a 'blind' way. For example, they don't exist as a sub-linguistic 'mental language' as is assumed in Cognitive Science. We are not performing conventions (decisions) of any kind. These rule-like activities (Wittgenstein's 'logic' and 'rules') amount to ordinary linguistic practices. They gave substance to the expression 'language-game'. For example, an ordinary discussion (say, the language-game of a dialogue) exhibits this feature. Wittgenstein characterized such language-games by saying that they exhibit 'laws of thought'[RFM I §133]. Such 'laws of thought' can be characterized as exhibiting the 'necessary' conditions of thought. This shows us a couple of extremely important insights: (1) Our ways of thinking does not amount some kinds of conventions without which thought could be possible (like, for example, eating a meal without any - conventional - rules of regulating table manners) and (2) One cannot free oneself (in the sense, for example, in which an unprejudiced person might do, say, from the conventional rules of the current fashion) from the 'rules of thought'; any attempt to free oneself from these rules is an attempt to free

oneself from thinking (and speaking) altogether; it is not to move to a more liberal way of thought (speech) by some kind of a Carnapian 'principle of tolerance'.

[20] Dummett, Michael, 'The Philosophical Basis of Intuitionistic Logic', in Dummett, M., *Truth and Other Enigmas,* [cf.n.2] pp. 215-247; Cf. also the chapter called 'Concluding Philosophical Remarks' in Dummett, M., *Elements of Intuitionism,* Oxford University Press: Oxford (1977) pp. 360-389; Gefwert, Christoffer, 'Philosophy of Constructive Mathematics', in Gefwert, C., Orponen, P. and Seppänen, J., (eds.), *Logic, Mathematics and the Computer,* Finnish Artificial Intelligence Society, Helsinki (1996), pp. 44-61.

[21] Ranta, Aarne, *Type-Theoretical Grammar,* Oxford University Press: Oxford (1994), op.cit. p. v. The formulation of this 'language' (the type-theoretical grammar) amounts to a certain internal part of our informal 'natural language' (consisting of primary language-games). It can then be characterized as a secondary language-game in Wittgenstein's terminology. It is interesting to notice that a Type-Theorethical Grammar can in such a case be viewed as standing for a kind of idealistic language, a *characteristica universalis* in Leibnitz's terminology, in that it in principle can be extended to provide the possibility of translating a number of structuralized parts of different natural languages into each other by a computer. In this sense such a constructive grammar can be taken as a realization of Leibnitz's great plan of a universal language. For the original works, cf. Leibnitz, G.W., *Die philosophischen Schriften von Gottfried Wilhelm Leibnitz, Siebenter Band,* hrsg. von C.I. Gerhardt, Georg Olms, Hildesheim (1961), originally published in Paris 1890, pp. 184, 192; Leibnitz, G.W., *Opuscules et fragments inédits de Leibnitz,* Couturat, L., (eds.), Georg Olms, Hildesheim (1961), originally published in Paris 1903, pp. 29, 152, 283.

[22] Lakatos, Imre, 'A Reneaissance of Empiricism in the Recent Philosophy of Mathematics', *British Journal of the Philosophy of Science,* Vol **27**, Number 3, September (1976), pp. 201-223.

[23] Shanker, Stuart G., *Wittgenstein and the Turning-Point in the Philosophy of Mathematics,* London & Sydney (1987), p. 39.

[24] Wright, Crispin, *Wittgenstein on the Foundations of Mathematics,* London (1980), p. 29.

[25] Dummett, Michael, 'Wittgenstein's Philosopy of Mathematics', in Dummett, M., *Truth and Other Enigmas*, [cf.n.2] pp. 166-185; Hacker, P.M.S., *Insight and Illusion*, Oxford University Press: Oxford (1972); Wright, Crispin., *Wittgenstein on the Foundations of Mathematics*, London (1980).

[26] Cf. Baker, G. and Hacker, P.M.S., 'Critical Notice of Wittgenstein's Philosophical Grammar', *Mind*, April (1976); Baker, G., 'Meaning and Defeasibility', in Raz and Hacker, P.M.S., eds., *Law, Morality and Society*, Oxford University Press: Oxford (1977); Rundle, Bede, *Perception, Sensation, and Verification*, Oxford University Press: Oxford (1972); Pollock, J.L., 'Criteria and Our Knowledge of the Material World', *Philosophical Quarterly*, **17** (1967), pp. 63-69; Richardson, John, T. E., *The Grammar of Justification*, London (1976). As far as Baker and Hacker are concerned, they have long since abandoned the attempted Anti-Realist interpretation of Wittgenstein's post-1929 texts. A similar, Anti-Realist, interpretation of Wittgenstein has also been formulated by Crispin Wright in 'Truth-Conditions and Criteria', in *Proceedings of the Aristotelian Society*, Supp.Vol., L (1976) and 'Anti-Realist Semantics: The Role of Criteria', in Vesey, G., (ed.), *Idealism: Past and Present* , London (1982); For a commentary on Anti-Realism and Wittgenstein's notion of Language-Games cf., Vision, Gerald, *Modern Anti-Realism and Manufactured Truth*, London (1988), pp. 216-245.

[27] Dummett, Michael, 'Wittgenstein's Philosophy of Mathematics', in Dummett, M.A.E., *Truth and Other Enigmas*, [cf.n.9] pp. 166-185.

[28] Baker, Gordon, *The Logic of Vagueness*, PhD thesis, Oxford University (1970).

[29] Baker, G.P., 'Criteria: a new foundation for semantics', *Ratio*, (1974).

[30] Baker, Gordon, *The Logic of Vagueness*, PhD thesis, Oxford University (1970) op.cit., p. 200.

[31] In a letter to the author in July, 1980, Gordon Baker stated his reasons why he abandoned the Anti-Realist interpretation of Wittgenstein he had formulated in his PhD thesis: ' ... I now think that the supposition that language is at bottom systematic, that there is an integrated set of meaning rules to be discovered, is without any justification, indeed unjustifiable. The very idea of hidden meaning-rules governing the practice of speaking a

language is itself incoherent. Rules must have normative functions; they cannot, as it were, act at a distance'.

[32] Hacker, P.M.S., *Insight and Illusion*, Oxford University Press: Oxford (1972), op.cit., pp. 99, 104.

[33] Dummett, Michael, 'Wittgenstein's Philosophy of Mathematics', in Dummett, M.A.E., *Truth and Other Enigmas*, [cf.n.2] op.cit., pp. 169, 180.

[34] Bernays, P., 'Comments on Ludwig Wittgenstein's *Remarks on the Foundations of Mathematics*', in Benacerraf, P., and Putnam, H., (eds.), *Philosophy of Mathematics,* first edition (1964), op.cit. pp. 522, 519, 522.

[35] Kreisel, G., 'Wittgenstein's Remarks on the Foundations of Mathematics', *British Journal for the Philosophy of Science,* 9 (1958-9), op.cit., pp. 147-148.

[36] Kielkopf, C.F., *Strict Finitism: An Examination of Wittgenstein's 'Remarks on the Foundations of Mathematics'*, The Hague (1970), op.cit., pp. 186, 182.

[37] Dummett, Michael, *Elements of Intuitionism,* [cf.n.19], op.cit., p. 375.

[38] Dummett, Michael, 'Wittgenstein's Philosophy of Mathematics', in Dummett, M., *Truth and Other Enigmas*, [cf.n.2] op.cit., p. 176.

[39] Shanker, S.G., *Wittgenstein and the Turning-Point in the Philosophy of Mathematics,* [cf. n. 22], p. 48; Cf. also McGuinness, Brian, 'The So-Called Realism of the "Tractatus"', in Block, I., (ed.), *Perspectives on the Philosophy of Wittgenstein,* Oxford (1981), pp. 60-79.

[40] Hale, Bob, 'Rule-following, objectivity and meaning', in Hale, B. and Wright, C., (eds.), *A Companion to the Philosophy of Language,* Basil Blackwell: Oxford (1997), pp. 369-396.

[41] Kripke, Saul, *Wittgenstein: On Rules and Private Language*, Cambridge, Mass. (1980).

[42] Waismann, Friedrich, *Lectures on the Philosophy of Mathematics*, Grassl, W., (ed.), Amsterdam (1982).

[43] Dummett, Michael, 'Wittgenstein's Philosophy of Mathematics', in Dummett, M. *Truth and Other Enigmas*, [cf.n.9], pp. 166-185.

[44] Kripke, Saul, *Wittgenstein: On Rules and Private Language*, Cambridge, Mass. (1980), ibid., pp. 3-4.

[45] Ibid., p. 60.

[46] Ibid., p. 55.

[47] Wright, Crispin, *Wittgenstein on the Foundations of Mathematics*, [cf. n. 22], p. 312. According to Wright ' ... Kripke's ideas about these issues and mine seem to have developed in complete isolation from each other. Kripke's interpretation originated, as he recounts, in graduate seminars given in Princeton as early as the spring of 1965 and was subsequently developed through a series of conferences and colloquia from 1976 onwards. I first proposed such an interpretation of aspects of Wittgenstein's later thought on mathematics in ['Two-valuedness, Meaning and Intuitionism', unpublished Ph.D. thesis, University of Cambridge]; and the material that constitutes the first six chapters of Wittgenstein on the Foundations of Mathematics was first written up for graduate seminars given in All Souls College, Oxford in the summer of 1974. Kripke and I were, indeed, colleagues for several months at All Souls in the academic year 1977-8, when he held a Visiting Fellowship there. But we never discussed the interpretation of Wittgenstein', Wright, Crispin, 'Wittgenstein on Mathematical Proof', in Phillips Griffith, A., (ed.), *Wittgenstein Centenary Essays,* Cambridge (1991), op.cit., p. 86, n.3.

[48] Kripke, Saul, *Wittgenstein: On Rules and Private Language*, [cf.n.43], ibid., p. 60.

[49] Peacocke, Christopher, 'Rule-Following: The Nature of Wittgenstein's Arguments', in Holtzmann, S.H. and Leich, C.M., (eds.), *Wittgenstein: to Follow a Rule,* London (1981), op.cit., p. 73.

[50] Kripke, Saul, *Wittgenstein: On Rules and Private Language*, [cf. n. 42], op. cit., p. 91f.

[51] Wright, Crispin, *Wittgenstein on the Foundations of Mathematics*, [cf. n. 23], op.cit., p. 220.

[52] Kripke, Saul, *Wittgenstein: On Rules and Private Language*, [cf. n. 42], op. cit., pp.74-75.

[53] Ibid., op. cit., p.88.

[54] Ibid., op.cit., pp.91-92.

[55] Dummett, Michael, 'Truth' , in Dummett, M., *Truth and Other Enigmas*, [cf.n.2]; Kripke, Saul., *Wittgenstein: On Rules and Private Laguage* [cf. n. 42].

[56] Baker, G.P. and Hacker, P.M.S., 'On Misunderstanding Wittgenstein: Kripke's private language argument', in Baker, G.P. & Hacker, P.M.S., *Scepticism, Rules & Language,* Oxford University Press: Oxford (1984), op.cit., pp. 46-47.

[57] Kripke, Saul, *Wittgenstein: On Rules and Private Language*, [cf. n. 42], op.cit., p. 73; For other attempts to treat Wittgenstein's texts in an Anti-Realist fashion, cf. Richardson, John, T. E., *The Grammar of Justification*, London (1976), pp. 52-53 and Baker, Gordon, *The Logic of Vagueness*, [cf.n.29], pp. 209-210.

[58] Baker, G.P. and Hacker, P.M.S., 'On Misunderstanding Wittgenstein: Kripke's private language argument', in Baker, G.P. & Hacker, P.M.S., *Scepticism, Rules & Language,* [cf.n.55], op.cit., p. 49.

[59] Winch, Peter, 'Facts and Super-Facts', *The Philosophical Quarterly,* Vol. **33** No. 133, op.cit., p. 400.

[60] Malcolm, Norman, 'Wittgenstein on Language and Rules', *Philosophy* **64** (1989), op.cit., p.21; Cf also Malcolm, Norman., *Nothing is Hidden,* Basil Blackwell: Oxford (xxxx), chap. 9.

[61] Stenlund, Sören, *Language and Philosophical Problems,* Routledge: London (1990), op.cit., p. 117.

[62] Kripke, Saul, *Wittgenstein: On Rules and Private Language*, [cf. n. 42], op.cit., p. 77.

[63] Wright, Crispin, 'Wittgenstein on Mathematical Proof', in Phillips Griffith, A., (ed.), *Wittgenstein Centenary Essays,* [cf.n.45], op.cit., p. 96, n.12.

[64] Baker, G.P. and Hacker, P.M.S., 'On Misunderstanding Wittgenstein: Kripke's private language argument', in Baker, G.P. & Hacker, P.M.S., *Scepticism, Rules & Language*, op.cit., p. 75.

[65] Hertzberg Lars, 'Wittgenstein and the Sharing of Language', in Haller, R. - Brandl, J., (eds.), *Wittgenstein - Towards a Re-Evaluation*, Vienna (1990), op.cit., pp.47, 50.

[66] Rhees, Rush, 'Can there be a Private Language?', in Rhees, R., *Discussions of Wittgenstein*, Routledge: London (1970), op.cit., pp. 56-57.

[67] Hertzberg, Lars, 'On the Factual Dependence of the Language-Game', in Hintikka, J., (ed.), *Essays on Wittgenstein in Honour of G.H. von Wright*, Acta Philosophical Fennica, Vol. **28**, Nos. 1-3, Amsterdam (1976), p. 126.

[68] Hertzberg, Lars, 'Wittgenstein and the Sharing of Language', [cf. n. 64], op.cit., p. 52.

[69] Cf. Baker, G.P., and Hacker, P.M.S., *Wittgenstein, Rules, Grammar and Necessity. Vol. 2 of an Analytical Commentary on the Philosophical Investigations*, Oxford University Press: Oxford (1985).

[70] Shanker, Stuart G., *Wittgenstein and the Turning-Point in the Philosophy of Mathematics*, [cf. n. 22], p. 2.

[71] Black, Max, 'Verificationism and Wittgenstein's Reflection on Mathematics', in Shanker, S. (ed.), *Ludwig Wittgenstein: Critical Assessments*, Vol. III., From the *Tractatus* to *Remarks on the Foundations of Mathematics*, Wittgenstein on the Philosophy of Mathematics, London (1986), op.cit., p. 69.

[72] Schlick, Moritz, 'The Turning-Point in Philosophy', in Schlick, M., *Philosophical Papers*, **Vol. II** (1925-36), (eds.), by Mulder, H., and van de Velde-Schlick, B., Dordrecht (1979).

VI Conceptual Investigations

VI.1 INTRODUCTION

We have, so far, established that Wittgenstein's conception of philosophy does not require one to formulate any kind of (foundational) theories. As theoretical enterprizes in philosophy such attempts fail. That is, when one engages in philosophical investigations one is not to formulate any kind of (1) scientific theories (empirical hypotheses) [Supra II.2], or (2) a priori semantical Realistic (Platonistic) or Anti-Realistic (Intuitionistic) 'theories of meaning'[Supra V.2]. To assume this theoretical view amounts to a mistake. A central theme throughout Wittgenstein's work is the view that everyday language is all right as it stands, provided we could just avoid being misled by linguistic forms when we philosophize and theorize. We are not as philosophers to engage ourselves in any theory-construction because philosophical investigations amount to conceptual investigations [Z §458]. Such investigations are not theoretical as this term is usually understood. We have also been given reason for this position which amounts to Stenlund's insight concerning non technical-scientific language as the universal medium of our primary language-games [Supra I.1].

But, we are still left with a problem: What about the philosophical (conceptual) investigations themselves [Z §458; RPP I §949]? What kind of language-games are they? According to Wittgenstein they amount to secondary language-games. But note, that this is not to say that conceptual analyses (philosophical investigations) are taking place on any kind of metatheoretical level (they are not second-order). As he said [PhI §121; MS 116]:

> ... if philosophy speaks of the use of the word 'philosophy' there must be a second-order philosophy. But it is not so: it is, rather, like the case of orthography, which deals with the word 'orthography' among others without then being second-order.

How is conceptual analysis, or what he characterized as the new subject of 'modern philosophy', then to be understood? We are now in the position that we can make an attempt to provide an answer to this question.

To begin with, according to von Wright, it is impossible to characterize Wittgenstein's position in philosophy by current classifications:[1]

> [t]hat this characterization is profoundly untrue of Wittgenstein's *Denkart* is obvious to every serious student of his philosophy. Yet it is even today quite common to label Wittgenstein, if not a 'logical positivist' so at least an 'analytical philosopher'. There are deeper reasons for this misunderstanding than just the difficulties of getting rid of a label once attached. If Wittgenstein is not an analytical philosopher, what kind of philosopher is he then? This question certainly cannot be answered in terms of current classifications. He is not a phenomenologist or hermeneuticist, nor an existentialist or hegelian, least of all is he a marxist.

But, how are we to look at his position in philosophy? To begin with, what we are to do is to look at Wittgenstein's conception of philosophy under the general term of nominalism. Note, however, that this does not mean that we regard Wittgenstein as being equivalent to a 'classical' nominalist. This is easily seen, for example, when he says that '[w]e are not analysing a phenomenon (e.g. thought) but a concept (e.g. that of thinking), and therefore the use of a word. So it may look as if what we were doing were Nominalism'[PhI §385]. The reason that they do it is because '[n]ominalists make the mistake of interpreting all words as names, and so of not really describing their use, but only, so to speak, giving a paper draft on such a description'[PhI §385].

According to the classical nominalists the world was constituted of singular objects ('particulars') which were named when so required. It therefore emphasizes philosophical separability. In addition, what we call a 'universal' is born when numerous objects ('particulars') are called by one and the same general name. But as we have seen, this referential ('metaphysical') view of language is in Wittgenstein's texts replaced by a view which emphasizes the use of primary language-games as the universal medium. This apparent small change leads to conclusive differences in the way one looks at things. When the objects of the classical nominalist where determined in what we could call 'a pre-linguistic sense' it is the case that for Wittgenstein the way one uses a word 'A' determines what belongs to A. Thus we cannot, according to Wittgenstein, speak of the world as spreading into objects - reminiscent of Kant's 'things-in-themselves' - in any sense 'prior to language'. That is, there isn't any 'metaphysics', as the term is generally understood in a Realistic sense, because the essential thing about metaphysics is that ' ... it obliterates the distinction between factual and conceptual investigations'[Z §458].

Any question concerning the correctness, in a categorial sense, of the conceptual spread is senseless. In this sense our 'grammar' (in Wittgenstein's sense) is indeed 'arbitrary'. We cannot 'ground' our 'grammar' because any such possible 'grounding' ought to be a picture of the world from another language (for example, a 'meta-language'). But, the problem is that such a language is different in kind and has a different 'grammar'. Consequently, we do not have such an 'independent' (or mental) language at our disposal and we cannot do anything else except being satisfied with our own language (and grammar) without any 'foundations' (remember that a languageless 'reference to reality' is not such a 'ground'). However, if we, on the other hand, would allow such 'another language' to exist then we are to understand that the same problem would reappear also in connection with it, etc. *ad. inf.* [cf. L (1) 277-278].

But, now one can ask: Does such practices of interpretation deal with our primary language-games? The answer is negative. As Wittgenstein said, '[w]hat we have rather to do is to accept the everyday language, and to note the false accounts of the matter as false. The primitive language-game which children are taught needs no justification; attempts at justification need to be rejected'[PhI 200]. We can then understand that the way we use language is without justification in the sense that '[t]he rules of grammar may be called "arbitrary", if that is to mean that the *aim* of the grammar is nothing but that of the language'[PhI §496]. But, then we can ask: What about the different practices we call conceptual investigations in Wittgenstein's 'modern philosophy'? How does such practices function? Are these practices 'arbitrary' or 'systematic'? We shall look at these important problems next.

VI.2 IS PHILOSOPHY THEORETICAL?

Wittgenstein began his first lecture, in January, 1930, by characterizing the task of his novel conception of philosophy. Here he said that '[p]hilosophy is the attempt to be rid of a particular kind of puzzlement. This "philosophic" puzzlement is one of the intellect and not of instinct. Philosophic puzzles are irrelevant to our every-day life. They are puzzles of language'[L (1) 1]. He went on, later, during Michaelmas Term, 1930, to contrast his 'method' of philosophy with the method of science by saying that '[i]n science you can compare what you are doing with, say, building a house. You must first lay a firm foundation; once it is laid it must not again be touched or moved. In philosophy we are not laying foundations but tidying up a room, in the process of which we have to touch everything a dozen of times'[L (1) 24; cf. PhI §118].

It thus seems evident that Wittgenstein wanted his novel 'method' of philosophy to be a radical break with the tradition setting out from the systematic epistemological doubt which has been assumed to be the correct 'method' in philosophy (requiring a 'theory of knowledge') - as well as in natural science - ever since the days of René Descartes (1596-1650). This view seems to be reflected in Wittgenstein's statement from 1930 (written in a notebook) where he says that '[i]t is all one to me whether or not the typical Western scientist understands or appreciates my work, since he will not in any case understand the spirit in which I write'[CV 7]. According to Wittgenstein the distinction between the (empirical) method applied in science (as well as the 'analytic *a priori*' way, say, in mathematics) in contrast to the way philosophy is to be properly done is extremely important. For example, one of the crucial points making philosophy completely distinct, say, from the activity of formulating scientific theories is that in science you can exhibit certain theses, or theories (the essence of which is that they can always, in principle, be disputed by experiments), whereas this is not the case in philosophy where, provided they are carefully performed, ' ... it would never be possible to debate them [the philosophical theses], because [when they have been thoroughly elaborated] everyone would agree to them'[PhI §128].

But this is not all there is to note as far as this novel 'method' of philosophy is concerned. Whereas traditional 'philosophy' (epistemology), in the spirit of Descartes, maintains that the source of our beliefs must be identified or their grounds be justified in order to eliminate doubt, Wittgenstein, on the other hand, in his post-1929 thought insisted that the proper concern of philosophical investigations is to remove the 'logical' ('grammatical') confusions that are exemplified, for example, by the entertainment of sceptical theses in situations where doubt is excluded. And this is not achieved by formulating ever more ingenious theoretical and formal - 'philosophical' - constructions as required by, say, the schools of logical empiricism or analytical philosophy (whether it is Realist or Anti-Realist in kind).[2]

Wittgenstein sometimes contrasts earlier achievements and compares these achievements with his novel 'method'. Thus he says, for example, that

> [o]ne keeps hearing the remark that philosophy really makes no progress, that the same philosophical problems that had occupied the Greeks are still occupying us. But those who say that don't understand the reason it is //must be// so. The reason is that our language has remained the same and seduces us into asking the same questions over and over. As long as there is a verb "to be" which seems to function like "to eat" and "to drink", as long as there are adjectives like "identical", "true", "false", "possible", as long as one talks about a flow of time and an expanse of space, etc., etc., humans will continue to bump up against the same mysterious difficulties, and stare at

something that no explanation seems able to remove ... I read, " ... philosophers are no nearer to the meaning of 'Reality' than Plato got, ... ". What a strange state of affairs. How strange in that case that Plato could get that far at all? Or, that we were not able to get farther! Was it because Plato was so smart?[BT 424; CV 15].

The fact that one is not constructing theories of any kind (for example, empirical linguistic theories) when performing a philosophical investigation is reflected in one of Wittgenstein's lectures (Lecture X), in 1934, where he said that '[o]n all questions [concerning natural history of language] we discuss I have no opinion; and if I had, and it disagreed with one of your opinions, I would at once give it up for the sake of argument because it would be of no importance for our discussion'[L (3) 97]. One is not formulating any theory of language (empirical nor analytical) when performing a philosophical investigation. He indicates this when he says that the '[d]ifficulty of philosophy [is] not the intellectual difficulty of the sciences, but the difficulty of a change of attitude'[BT 406]. We clearly notice that Wittgenstein in this quotation emphasizes the difference between philosophy and methods of (natural) science. The essential difference between them is that in empirical science one formulates different theories (scientific hypotheses) which one attempts to falsify by experiments. In the mathematical context one attempts to formulate 'theories' (structures) which are 'analytical a priori'. But, this is not the case in philosophy where the '[r]esistances of the will [to do just this] must be overcome'[BT 406].

According to Wittgenstein the difference between methods of (natural) science and the 'method' of philosophy concerns also conceptual investigations of formal (mathematical) languages (calculations). In the practice which ordinarily is called 'philosophy of mathematics' we are not to formulate any conceptual notations. What we are to do is to formulate (indirect and direct) mathematical structures because we want to justify some position. This amounts to the task of mathematicians (like Martin-Löf) to perform [Gefwert (1) 103ff]. By requiring such mathematical (and logical) investigations in 'philosophy' (like Logical Empiricism requires when it comes to 'philosophy/foundations of mathematics') we find, according to Wittgenstein, that '"[m]athematical logic" has completely deformed the thinking of mathematicians and of philosophers, by setting up a superficial interpretation of the forms of our everyday language as an analysis of the structure of facts. Of course in this it has only continued to build on the Aristotelian logic'[RFM V §48].

This point is clearly reflected when Wittgenstein emphasizes that conceptual (philosophical) investigations of mathematical calculations are completely different than mathematical calculations themselves. The latter ones amount to the practice of formulating mathematical conjectures and proving theorems. A mathematician should, of course, have hypotheses and attempt to calculate (prove) them within mathematics: that is what makes her into a mathematician in the first place. But one need not - *when acting as a philosopher* - necessarily have any purely mathematical opinions concerning the correctness (truth) of proofs exhibited by different mathematical calculations (for example, concerning the question whether Fermat's theorem is proved or not or, say, whether a certain theorem of 'classical' model-theory is correct)[LFM 103]. When acting as a philosopher one does not engage in disputes concerning purely mathematical tasks (for example, like questions concerning the correctness (truth) of theorems proved as well as the correctness of the method applied). Such jobs are the explicit tasks of mathematicians and is of no concern to the philosopher. *The task of a philosopher is to perform what we call conceptual investigations.* The general difference is, then, that the task of, e.g., a mathematician is to formulate and prove (judge) mathematical propositions to be correct (by a suitable mathematical method) whereas the task of a philosopher (who could be the mathematician when engaged in conceptual analysis) amounts (in retrospect) to 'purify' the calculations (proofs) from redundant expressions, which we can call for 'word-language' or 'mathematical prose', by different conceptual investigations.

As we pointed out above it was the arguments occurring within 'rule scepticism', having their origin in the way we usually tend to think that rules are to be understood, i.e., similarly to the way theoretical entities in hypothetical scientific theories, as well as in *a priori* conceptual notations, are assumed to work, which led to the 'sceptical paradox' set by Kripke [Supra V.3]. The answer provided by some of the Anti-Realists, including Kripke (and Dummett), in order to escape this dilemma, was a version of the 'community view' solution [Supra V.3]. But we noticed that this also leads us to require an additional method - the semantical meaning theoretical way [Supra V.2] - of looking at the problem. According to this view, language (exhibiting its 'surface grammar' in ordinary discourse) is, essentially, in good logical order as it is but has an underlying 'depth grammar' which is *au fond* a certain kind of function-theoretical logical calculus which can be 'unearthed' (by logical analysis) and put to empirical tests (falsification) like any other scientific theory. Note that this is not how Wittgenstein applies the terms 'surface grammar' and 'depth grammar' in his writings [cf. PhI §664].

To apply the 'scientific' model of 'rules-as-theory' in philosophy, which we are accustomed to from mathematics, computing science and linguistics (for example, as semantical meaning theories (structures) occurring in the 'foundations' literature) is, according to Wittgenstein, completely mistaken. Note, that this concerns also empirical theories of science. The reason why it is mistaken is that '[p]hilosophers constantly see the method of science before their eyes, and are irresistibly tempted to ask and answer questions in the way science does'[BB 18]. According to Wittgenstein '[t]his tendency is the real source of metaphysics, and leads the philosopher into complete darkness'[BB 18; cf. PhI §109].

It was this kind of, basically, theoretical view of language (for example, as 'analytical *a priori*' semantical 'theories') that Wittgenstein wanted to overthrow when it came to the possibility to deal with *philosophical* problems of language (including formal languages). According to Wittgenstein's view it is a characteristic and categorical feature of philosophical - conceptual - problems that they cannot be properly dealt with by a theory, be it of whatever kind. Consequently, one (1) never formulates a theory (of meaning) in a philosophical investigation and (2) the outcome of a genuine philosophical investigation never amounts to a question if a scientific (empirical) theory is correct. Thus, as Wittgenstein is reported to have remarked at a meeting at the Moral Sciences Club in Cambridge,[3]

> I used at one time to say that, in order to get clear how a sentence is used, it was a good idea to ask oneself the question: "How would one try to verify such an assertion?" But that's just one way among others of getting clear about the use of a word or sentence. For example, another question which it is often very useful to ask oneself is: "How is this word learned?", "How would one set about teaching a child to use this word?" But some people have turned this suggestion about asking for the verification into a dogma - as if I'd been advancing a theory about meaning.

VI.3 WHAT IS A PHILOSOPHICAL INVESTIGATION?

It is often said that one of his early ideas which Wittgenstein never gave up is his conception of philosophy. According to von Wright, this is, basically, correct. However, it is not a truth without modifications because [4]

> [i]t holds for his conception of philosophy as an activity and not a doctrine *(Lehre)*, and of philosophy as critique of language. But it does not hold for his specific view that philosophical problems are due to linguistic confusions, to what he later called "bewitchment" *(Verhexung)* of our thinking by the means of language. There is no statement to this effect in the early writngs. There he speaks of the philosophic problems resting on a misunderstanding of the ("true") logic of our language, on a confusion of the *grammatical* with the *logical* form of thought.

In order to correctly understand Wittgenstein's post-1929 view of philosophy we are to realize that there are two important 'points' in his (partly) novel conception concerning how philosophical investigations ought to be performed. We find both of them outlined already in his earlier texts [cf. T §§4.003, 4.0031, 4.111].

The first 'point' is the rejection of any semantic paradigm, be it (1) the Realist 'atomistic' paradigm in semantics based on 'classical' truth-conditions underlying, for example, the meta-mathematical programme (including 'classical' model-theory) or, (2) the Anti-Realist 'molecular' paradigm in semantics being based on assertion-conditions (i.e., constructive truth-conditions). Indeed, any semantical 'meaning theoretical' doctrine must be rejected as being of any importance in philosophy at all based as they must be on the interpretation of rules as theoretical entities [Supra V.3]. *Thus any interpretation of Wittgenstein's philosophy if based on the semantical doctrines of either Realism or Anti-Realism is absolutely mistaken* [Supra V.4]. Any interpretation attempting to establish his writings as belonging to some semantical paradigm or stressing the importance of formal methods for his way of doing philosophy exhibits a profound misunderstanding of his philosophical thought. Indeed, one can take a comment by Hintikka (in another context), as providing, from Wittgenstein's point of view, one of the clearest examples of such a misunderstanding (concerning the relation between philosophy and mathematics) when he states that ' ... it is not likely that any substantial progress can be made in the genuinely philosophical study of mathematics without using the concepts and results of [symbolic logic and foundational studies] to a much greater extent than has happened so far'.[5]

Now, the second 'pillar' is Wittgenstein's rejection of any interpretation of rules (like the one embraced by Kripke based on the idea of 'rule-following scepticism') from the realm of philosophy altogether [Supra V.3]. The attitude towards philosophy following from the acceptance of the doctrine of 'rule-following scepticism' is the common denominator for the misconceptions concerning how to cope with 'philosophical problems' (reminiscent of 'pseudo-scientific' tasks) in language and mathematics. This is the way that, for example, analytical (positive) 'philosophy' works. According to Wittgenstein this was a completely mistaken view. He sometimes compares philosophy to a kind of therapy [PhI §133], to a method of healing, the aim of which is to ' ... show the misleading analogies in the use of language'[BT 408], analogous to what one is accustomed to in Freudian psychoanalysis, where in a number of therapeutic sessions one attempts to dissolve mental repressions by a proper dialogue.

So far we have only outlined the general features of Wittgenstein's novel (and negative) 'method' of philosophy. Now we face the more pertinent question: What are the characteristic features of a philosophical investigation according to Wittgenstein's novel 'method'? In order to even begin to answer this question we have to correctly understand it. To begin with, the philosophical investigation is, on Wittgenstein's conception, characterized by being a purely *descriptive* activity [PhI §109]. A philosophical investigation is a certain descriptive practice carried out by ordinary language: secondary language-games [Supra IV.3]. But we have to be clear that there is no unique method (as is the case, for example, with a conceptual notation) to be applied here. In philosophy there are numerous different kinds of dialogues depending on the conceptual problem to be investigated. Thus a sufficient condition seems to be that a philosophical investigation can be performed verbally (of course, it can also be performed in writing). This is, partially, what is meant by philosophy as therapy. This point is echoed when we find Wittgenstein writing that '[p]hilosophy isn't anything except philosophical problems, the particular individual worries that we call "philosophical problems". Their common element extends as far as the common element in different regions of our language'[PhG 193].

There does not exist a single 'philosophical method' (a 'universal method' like the 'principle of verification' for the logical empiricists) but different 'methods' for different contexts. We find that Wittgenstein, later, emphasizes this same point when he says that '[t]here is not a philosophical method, though there are indeed methods, like different therapies'[PhI §133]. As we find already in the *Tractatus*, philosophy amounts to critique of ordinary language (and thus includes also conceptual problems in formal languages) but is itself a necessary part of ordinary language. One can say that ordinary language due to its openness gives birth to philosophical problems and thus the requirement of philosophical therapy. But, we must be aware that '[i]n philosophizing we may not terminate a disease of thought. It must run its natural course, and slow cure is all important. (That is why mathematicians are such bad philosophers.)'[Z §382].

One consequence of this is that there may occur philosophical problems whenever one encounters speaking and writing human beings. In our primary language there are no single things which are common to everything (i.e., there are no 'universals') which are being investigated by philosophical investigations (there is no second-order object/meta-language distinction at the primary language stage). Here we find that novel conceptual problems, or conceptual 'bumps' *(Beulen)*, as Wittgenstein said, may occur any time. By this he wants to draw our attention to the insight that '[p]roblems are solved (difficulties eliminated), not a *single* problem ... "But then we will never come to the end of our job!" Of course not, because it has no end'[MS 213].

The expression 'philosophy' (like many other words, e.g., 'number') exhibits family resemblance properties. There is, in principle, no single method to be found in philosophy. To even ask if there is one shows that one has misunderstood the nature of the topic. The characteristic feature of a philosophical description (session) is that it is always made with a certain purpose in mind, i.e., the dissolution of conceptual (philosophical) problems, in order to exorcise what Wittgenstein called 'prose' from the practice being investigated by uncovering ' ... one or another piece of plain nonsense and of bumps that the understanding has got by running its head up against the limits of language'[PhI §119]. The topics to be investigated may also be conceptual problems occurring within different mathematical calculations [Gefwert (1) 236-252]. Wittgenstein formulates this general point when he said that '[t]he work of the philosopher consists in assembling reminders for a certain purpose'[PhI §127]. This is to be understood so that these reminders occur in what can be characterized as a kind of Socratic dialogue the purpose of which is to dissolve conceptual puzzles. Indeed, we find that Schlick compared

Wittgenstein to Socrates, the reason being that both emphasize the importance of philosophical dialogues when dealing with conceptual problems.6

According to Wittgenstein the task of philosophy is to conceptually heal persons (philosophers, mathematicians, scientists and ordinary persons) who are conceptually 'sick'. That is, they want in a certain situation to say too much (they exhibit 'prose'). Parallel to Freudian psychoanalysis such a philosophical therapy can be called conceptual analysis. Such a therapeutical activity takes place by a philosophical (secondary) language-game the aim of which is to exhibit what Wittgenstein characterized as ' ... the transparency of arguments'[BT 414]. The aim of such a language-game can be compared ' ... to locks on safes, which can be opened by dialing a certain word or number, so that no force can open the door until just this word has been hit upon, and once it is hit upon any child can open it. // ... and if it is hit upon, no effort at all is necessary to open the door//it//'[BT 417]. It is an interesting fact that a characteristic point of Wittgenstein's texts is that they on numerous occasions are written in precisely such a dialog form between two persons the aim of which is to dissolve conceptual illusions (of course, one can have such dialogues also with oneself).

But, who needs such conceptual therapy? To begin with, we can say that a conceptually 'healthy' person living in ordinary everyday circumstances, 'taking care of business as usual' (say, like a blacksmith or farmer), ordinarily has no need of a philosophical discourse - that is, no need of conceptual analysis. When performing ordinary different tasks in our everyday life we might, but usually we do not, encounter conceptual problems. We have to understand that if such anomalies occured enough frequently in our daily life then communication would simply break down. As Witigenstein says, '[w]e don't encounter philosophical problems at all in practical life ... We encounter them only when we are guided not by practical purpose in forming our sentences, but by certain analogies within our language'[BT 427].

We can thus establish that the therapeutic task of philosophy is not to create concepts but, on the contrary, to destroy conceptual 'castles in the air'[Cf. PhI §118]. It aims to purge a practice of unnecessary concepts. That is, a philosophical discourse is needed when we encounter conceptually 'pathological' situations ('prose'). This point is echoed when Wittgenstein writes that '[a]ll that philosophy can do is to destroy idols. And that means not making any new ones - say out of "the absense of idols"'[BT 413]. One way of characterizing the aim of philosophy is to say that the aim of philosophical discourse is to turn *latent* nonsense into *patent* nonsense [PhI §464]. When sufferring from philosophical problems we have a bit of hidden conceptual nonsense in our mind and the only way to cure it is to bring it into the open: to dissolve the assumed 'problem'. We can say that the aim is to exhibit something which is a *repressed* bit of nonsense into *explicit* nonsense. In a philosophical investigation one gives expression to certain repressed bits of conceptual nonsense, just as in a Freudian treatment one makes explicit certain repressed emotions. Being able to do precisely this - in the philosophical conceptual analysis as well as in the psychoanalytical analysis - is part of being cured of the bad problems which troubles one in the conceptual (philosophical) confusion analogously to what is the case in the psychotic repression.

VI.4 THE PSYCHOANALYTICAL ANALOGUE

There is also another way in which the philosophical 'method' of Wittgenstein is reminiscent of psychoanalysis, namely in that the requirement of the 'patient's' acceptance of the result of an analysis plays an extraordinarily important role. A necessary condition in order to succeed is that the 'patient' must be sane enough to be able to reason rationally. When this precondition is met (as it always is in a conceptual analysis in contrast to what sometimes is the case in the psychoanalytical case) the task becomes to dissolve a conceptual pseudo-problem by means of a Socratic dialogue between the philosopher (therapist) and a 'patient' (which can, according to Wittgenstein, in addition to an ordinary person, be, for example, another misguided philosopher). In this case the 'patient' on which conceptual analysis is performed is the person who is suffering from conceptual (philosophical) illusions.

When undergoing conceptual analysis (in contrast, for example, to mathematical analysis, i.e., to prove) the conceptual puzzlement - the philosophical problem - must be precisely described or diagnosticized. This is necessary in order for the person who is under the influence of the conceptual (philosophical) illusion to be able to acknowledge and identify *this* as precisely *that* problem. For example, if I am troubled by questions like 'What is Thought?', 'What is Language?', 'What is Justice?', 'What is a Number?' or 'What is Time?', the cure might become (depending on the context) the task of showing - through a carefully performed proper conceptual analysis - why such questions cannot be answered in a reductionist way (for example, like ... is ...). It amounts to the task of showing that language, indeed, allows these questions (and similar ones) to be asked [BB 1] but that these questions themselves (when disconnected from any explicit application/context) are of such a peculiar kind that they transgress the limit(s) of language: they are redundant and meaningless [Supra IV.6].

Let us take a quick view of how such a 'session' of conceptual analysis might happen. The session itself takes place between, say, two persons (say, a philosopher and an ordinary person) engaged in something which can be characterized as a kind of philosophical (Socratic) dialogue. It is in this sense that the problems of 'patients' requiring conceptual analysis seems to be analogous to patients requiring psychoanalysis. In both cases the cure starts by getting a clear view of the state that troubles the person. We identify the conceptual problem, that is, we make the diagnosis. The conceptual (philosophical) 'disease' is the concept that is applied. Two absolute requirements in order to perform the conceptual analysis are that the 'patient' thinks (1) that the answer can be put into words and (2) that it lies within the world of experience. The 'patient' is cured when she understands the limits of what can and what cannot be said by gradually working outwards through what can be said (within the context). One of the crucial features is that the person then actually experiences the saying-showing distinction (what can be said in contrast to what can only be shown).

The task of the conceptual 'therapist' (philosopher) is, like a Socratic mid-wife, to act carefully as an aid and guide to the patient by emphasizing relevant interpretations and pointing out grammatical confusions. But it is the patient who in the end must somehow exhibit this experience. It is a characteristic feature of conceptual therapy (analysis) that the 'patient' can - in the end - only judge any success relative to herself. The therapy (analysis) amounts to a struggle against a resistance within oneself concerning the mistaken use of language: a resistance of will. One is unwilling to give up certain ways of thinking (which is either silent or loud thinking but which is always public). It is this unwillingness which has to be fought and which is the barrier between conceptual illusion and genuine philosophical enlightment. As Wittgenstein says, we can, indeed, ' ... only convict someone else of a mistake if he acknowledges that this really is the expression of his feeling. // ... if he (really) acknowledges this expression as the corrrect expression of his feeling.// For only if he acknowledges it as such, *is* it the correct expression (Psychoanalysis)'[MS 213; 410].

The result is that Wittgenstein came to see the philosophical task of dissolving the problems as one of human understanding. To perform conceptual investigations (philosophy), a man must be able not only to see questions where those not given to conceptual problems see none, but also to look on these questions in a particular way. A man can obey the Socratic injunction - know thyself - only if he can understand the scope and limit(s) of his own understanding. This means, first and foremost, the ability to recognize the precise scope and limit(s) of language-games: the prime instrument of human understanding.

In view of what we have said above it does not become too farfetched to compare (but not to identify) Wittgenstein's philosophical method - as he himself actually did - with the psychoanalytical method of Sigmund Freud (1856-1939).[7] His readings of Freud seemed concerned chiefly with the works published before the First World War. We can mention *The Psychopathology of Everyday Life* and, in particular, *The Interpretation of Dreams* as the books of Freud that he cites most frequently. We also find that Wittgenstein was indeed personally acquainted with the practice of psychoanalysis in that he had (at least) on one occasion, in 1926, been subjected to it [cf. Gefwert (1) 26]. As far as additional work related to Freud is concerned it seems that he was probably familiar with it simply through osmosis. For example, Breuer and Freud's *Studies in Hysteria* figured in the Wittgenstein family library. His own position on the question of Freud's relation to Breuer is, for example, indicated in a passage, dated 1939-1940, where he says that

> I believe that my originality (if that is the right word) is an originality belonging to the soil rather than to the seed. (Perhaps I have no seed of my own.) Sow a seed in my soil and it will grow differently than it would in any other soil. Freud's originality too was like this, I think. I have always believed - without knowing why - that the real germ of psychoanalysis came from Breuer, not Freud. Of course Breuer's seed-grain can only have been quite tiny [CV 369].

This and similar comments in his *Nachlass* are by no means to be understood as indicating that he was altogether uncritical of Freud's method of psychoanalysis. On the contrary. We notice that Freud's work explicitly challenges Wittgenstein's account by suggesting (1) that the nature of the Inner is an empirical and not a substantive issue, and (2) by suggesting that scientific (empirical) discoveries may overturn our psychological concepts. But psychoanalysis does not provide the whole truth about the Inner, nor does it show that all our psychological concepts are based on a mistaken empirical premise. Thus we have to be aware that this comparison is not a too farfetched one. Nevertheless, it seems that Wittgenstein thought that his style of philosophizing and Freudian psychoanalysis required a similar gift. One could, perhaps, say that the relation between Wittgenstein and Freud, despite their similarity, can be treated as the confrontation between two types of rationality. The crucial difference seems to be that while Freud defends a kind of classical scientific rationalism we find that Wittgenstein clearly belongs to quite another order of thought.

One could, perhaps, say that Wittgenstein was interested in a particular aspect of psychoanalysis. More precisely, it seems that he was interested in the view of psychoanalysis as an interpretative art in comparison with philosophical investigations. But also here, within this limited area, he expressed certain reservations about this analogy in that he thought that there were problems which needed to be conceptually excavated. Nevertheless, as McGuinness says, the important point is that [8]

> [t]he advance that he thought possible was to be made by the individual, and here Wittgenstein himself drew the analogy with psychoanalysis: the individual was to be the judge of success, that is, relative to himself. The philosopher is plagued by a problem. Some expression disturbs him, seems to demand to be used in a certain way which he cannot quite allow. ... He has to find a context in which the disturbing question is at home. When its full context is shown, it is no longer problematic. This is where a lesson learnt from Freud that we have already mentioned comes in: the idea that the meaning is not there all at once but is something that appears in the course of discussion, so that understanding is a process extended in time.

Wittgenstein emphasizes on numerous places in his texts that philosophy can be compared to a method of healing. Thus he says, for example, that '[t]he philosopher's treatment of a question is like the treatment of an illness'[PhI §255]. He also characterizes a typical philosophical problem as having the form 'I don't know my way about'[PhI §123]. This point is exemplified by the metaphor of the fly (standing for the person experiencing conceptual (philosophical) puzzles) in the fly-bottle (standing for a conceptual (philosophical) puzzle): 'What is your aim in philosophy? - To shew the fly the way out of the fly-bottle'[PhI §301]. This metaphor Wittgenstein seems to have regarded as being extraordinarily important in that he also emphasized the importance of it (or something reminiscent of it) on a number of occasions in his discussions with his friends and disciples.

For example, according to Malcolm, we find that Wittgenstein in his discussions used to compare philosophy to a man who wants to leave a room but doesn't know how. The window is too high up on the wall and the chimney is too narrow. However, if the man would only turn around he would immediatedly see that the door has been open all the time.[9] Nevertheless, it seems that examples like these were not enough to convey the essence of Wittgenstein's novel 'therapeutical methods' (sic!) of philosophy to the big public because we find there to have occured all kinds of mistaken versions and interpretations of them. This misunderstanding seemed, not least because of Wittgenstein's assumed connection to the Logical Empiricists and the Vienna Circle and, in particular, through their mistaken verificationist interpretation of the *Tractatus*, to have been widely spread as one can notice from comments by persons who were not too closely connected to him.

As is well attested, the influence of Wittgenstein's *Tractatus* concerning philosophy on the Vienna Circle was profound. It had a decisive influence on the school called Logical Empiricism. The authors - Carnap, Hahn and Neurath - of the manifesto concerning the positions of logical empiricism as far as logic, mathematics and science is concerned, called *Wissenschaftliche Weltauffassung*, hailed Wittgenstein, together with Einstein and Russell, as the leading representatives of a 'scientific view of the world'.[10] Analytic philosophy was the 'philosophy' characteristic of a culture dominated by scientific rationality. Thus, it was not too difficult by certain members of the Vienna Circle to reinterpret Wittgenstein's thinking so as to fit the analytic mould. For example, he said that '[p]hilosophy is not one of the natural sciences'[T §4.111]. But we must note that the logical positivists would not have claimed that to be the case. He also said that philosophy is 'something which stands above or below, but not beside the natural sciences'[T §4.111]. How does this differ, for example, from Carnap's view that philosophy is the logical syntax of the language of science?[11] Is not the logic of science exactly something which stands 'above' or 'below' but not 'beside' the sciences themselves? Wittgenstein said many more things about what philosophy is and what it is not which can without much ado be reconciled with the opinions both of earlier and later so-called analytical philosophers. But, as von Wright emphasizes, we also find profound differences.[12]

Once Wittgenstein, due to the Logical Empiricists, had mistakenly been labelled a positivist, people found it hard to see him in any other light. So when, from 1929 on, he returned to philosophy and gradually moved into his later position this new style of philosophizing was not to be regarded as a *rejection* of positivism. Rather, it was seen as a reconstruction of Wittgenstein's assumed earlier positivistic position in the *Tractatus* on new and deeper foundations. Carnap, for one, regarded it as such in the beginning of the 1930's when he adopted the Language-as-Calculus view of 'language' as being equal to formal language (which seems later to have been adopted by certain cognitive scientists) due to his discussions with Gödel.

This mistaken view seems to have continued through the 1930's and 1940's. For example, in the late 1940's, we find that Wittgenstein's 'novel position' is being characterized as a kind of 'therapeutic positivism'.[13] Such a characterization made him utterly furious and he acted angrily against it. According to Monk, '[w]hen, for example, A. J. Ayer drew the comparison [between 'therapeutic positivism' and analytical philosophy] in an article in the *Listener*, he received from Wittgenstein a strongly worded letter of rebuke'.[14] Nothing could be further from his intention than such an interpretation if by 'therapeutic positivism' is meant (like the Ayer seems to have intended) that we in philosophy are to formulate foundational 'theories' by formal language of some kind (note the similarity with scientific theories) the aim of which are to solve 'philosophical' problems. We therefore note that Wittgenstein renounced logical positivism (as well as 'therapeutic positivism') in philosophy. He emphasized non-formal everyday language-games (in contrast to Logical Positivism) as being crucial when performing philosophical (secondary) language-games. On the other hand, it is a fact that Wittgenstein was inclined to see some sort of connection between his works and Freud's. For example, he once described himself to Rhees as a 'disciple of Freud', and at various times, as we have seen, summed up the achievement of both himself and Freud in strikingly similar manner.

VI.5 CALCULATION AND PHILOSOPHY

A few years after his return to Cambridge in 1929, in the academic year 1932-33, Wittgenstein gave a series of lectures called 'Philosophy for Mathematicians'[L (3) 205-25]. They seem to have been a great success in that between thirty and forty people (many of whom were mathematicians) attended them (including his favourite students Francis Skinner, H.M.S. Coxeter, Margaret Masterman and Alice Ambrose).[15] In these lectures Wittgenstein used pages 7-19 [L (3) 215, n.] of the book *Pure Mathematics* by G.H. Hardy[16] as context for his comments (the 'dialogue') concerning the necessity to purge pure mathematical calculus from distorting and unnecessary 'prose'. As Ambrose says, '[t]his, or an excerpt of comparable detail, was read out in the lecture'[L (3) 215, n.]. This series of lectures was primarily directed to mathematicians.

In these lectures (as well as in the lectures given in the intervening years until 1939) one can get a glimpse of Wittgenstein's method at work [cf. Gefwert (1) 210-236]. Indeed, as Wittgenstein put it at the end of these lectures,

> [t]he talk of mathematicians becomes absurd when they leave mathematics, for example, Hardy's description of mathematics as not being a creation of our minds. He conceived philosophy as a decoration, an atmosphere, around the hard realities of mathematics and science. These disciplines, on the one hand, and philosophy on the other, are thought of as being like the necessities and decorations of a room. Hardy is thinking of philosophical opinions. I conceive of philosophy as an activity of clearing up thought [L (3) 225].

Furthermore, as Wittgenstein explicitly stated,

> [w]hen one talks of the foundations of mathematics there are two different things one might mean. One might mean the kind of thing meant by saying that algebra is the foundation of calculus. In order to learn calculus one learns algebra. Mathematics in this sense is like a building, and in this sense calculus such as *Principia Mathematica* is a bit of mathematics. The bottom layer is the one you begin with. One might also mean by foundations a means of shoring up something that is problematic. If there were something problematic about mathematics as such, then no foundation is less problematic, and giving one does not help. This is not to say that a calculus has no philosophical importance. The drudgery, the calculation, are unimportant, but the calculus may be useful philosophically in showing various things [L (3) 121-122].

What does Wittgenstein mean by such statements? According to Martin Heidegger (1889-1976), the famous German philosopher, the crucial philosophical insight is to grasp that one cannot have a theory of what makes a theory possible.[17] Wittgenstein would have accepted this claim as such. As we stated above, philosophy does not amount to any kind of theory construction [Supra V.4]. But, what does, then, the 'philosophy of mathematics' (as well as the 'philosophy of psychology'), in the sense in which Wittgenstein understands the term, consist of? The general answer is that what we could call for 'philosophy of mathematics' is a precise conceptual analysis (description) of the rule-like practices of mathematical calculations (the proofs) - the conceptual analysis of mathematical 'phenomena'. In philosophy '[w]e must do away with all explanation, and description alone must take its place. And this description gets its light, that is to say its purpose, from the philosophical problems'[PhI §109]. That is, we can say that '[p]hilosophy is a tool which is useful only against philosophers and against the philosopher in us'[MS 219, 11].

Here I would especially like to draw the attention to Wittgenstein's comment that philosophy is to be useful against *the philosopher in us*. What he meant by this claim is that we are all in varying degrees trapped in philosophical (conceptual) problems which occur when we use language. This is so because using a language (when we do 'philosophy' in the ordinary sense) makes it possible to formulate all kinds of illusions and we have to understand that '[p]hilosophy is embedded not in propositions, but in a language [and] in our language there is an entire mythology embodied'[MS 213, 423, 434].

The philosophical task concerning, for example, mathematical proofs is to describe the rule-like practice of calculations (proofs) as carefully as possible in order to dissolve the malignant outgrowths (the 'prose') occurring in connection with them and which obscures our thinking [Gefwert (1) 236-252]. Since philosophical problems seems to arise when we get lost in these rule-like mathematical practices it is '[t]his entanglement in our rules [that] we want to understand'[PhI §125]. But here we have to remember: This does not mean that it is the task of the philosopher to explicitly engage in justifying mathematical proofs as such. This belongs to the sphere of the mathematician. There is a crucial difference between what, respectively, a mathematician and what a philosopher is doing. Wittgenstein formulated the general point by saying that "[p]hilosophy ... leaves mathematics as it is, and no mathematical discovery can advance it"[PhI §124]. That is, in philosophy (and thus, as is sometimes assumed in what we are according to Realism or Anti-Realism accustomed to call 'philosophy of mathematics') one does not have to justify that a mathematical proof is a genuine proof as, for example, Hilbert assumed when setting out on his meta-mathematical research programme [Gefwert (1) 255-262]. In fact such a justification is neither possible nor desirable when we perform philosophical investigations. The only language presupposed in order to be able to carefully describe and thereby be able to conceptually 'purify' the different calculi exhibiting 'prose' in mathematical practice is our natural (and mathematical) language as it is given to us [Supra IV.4].

The result is, as Wittgenstein puts it, that '[t]he picture we have of the language of the grown-up is that of a nebulous mass of language, his mother tongue, surrounded by discrete and more or less clear-cut language games, the technical languages'[BB 81]. This fact, as such, is no cause for us to get worried (except for the 'philosopher' inspired by natural science and foundational studies), since ' ... the language is itself the vehicle of thought'[PhI §329]. Indeed, according to Wittgenstein, we are always expressing our thoughts by language, since '[understanding] a sentence means understanding a language'[BB 5]. For example, as we have seen elsewhere, talk about 'object-languages' and 'meta-languages' in the meta-mathematical programme exhibit, on Wittgenstein's account, an illusion (Language-as-Calculus) which gets its nourishment by the 'prose' provided by language [Gefwert (1) 255-261].

Once this insight becomes clear and, consequently, on Wittgenstein's account, the need for any mathematical 'foundations' is rejected, the first hurdle on the road to philosophical insight is passed. Thus the task of Wittgenstein's novel philosophy of mathematics is to make our understanding of mathematical practice conceptually clear. Another way of putting it is to say that the aim of a philosophical investigation of mathematics is to silence our urge to ask traditional 'philosophical' (metaphysical) questions, for example, beginning with

What is ... ?

which one also sometimes, in addition to 'metaphysical' questions, encounters within science (e.g., when dealing with a factual question like 'What is an atom?' requiring a reductionist answer in order to be properly dealt with in physics). Such scientifically and mathematically inspired questions have previously passed for 'philosophical' questions, for example, when one asks 'What is a natural number?', 'What is a set?' or 'What is a class?'[cf. BB 1]. It is these kinds of mistakes that we are not allowed to make because they lead us astray. In fact, such questions are completely redundant as far as mathematical practice is concerned. So, as Kenny says, ' ... one thing that philosophical therapy involves for mathematicians, is giving expression to repressed doubts, repressed puzzlements, things that one was told not to take any notice of - "Learn mathematics, and then you won't worry any more about these doubts"'.[18]

Philosophical problems arise when we allow our language to take us on journeys because of mistaken analogies. Wittgenstein characterized this point by saying that ' ... philosophical problems arise *when language goes on holiday'*[PhI §38]. Our language, when 'going on holiday', permits us to formulate such quasi-philosophical questions (like 'What is a natural number?' or 'What is a rule?'), but, such questions, when set in a mistaken 'philosophical' (and metaphysical) context, are both misleading as well as redundant. Note, that in ordinary circumstances somebody, say, an ordinary child, when doing arithmetic would not ask such questions, on the contrary, he/she would concentrate on calculating. It is only a philosopher or a mathematician (an adult) who is familiar with philosophical terminology and jargon in 'analytical philosophy' that would ask such questions. Once this becomes evident through philosophical 'therapy' (the dialogue one performs in a philosophical investigation) one aspect of the philosophical task is already achieved: the urge to ask such 'metaphysical' questions has simply evaporated as far as the case under scrutiny is concerned. But to achieve this 'therapeutic' result is no easy task and thus the difficult thing to achieve is that '[t]he philosopher must twist and turn about so as to pass by the mathematical problems, and not run up against one, - which would have to be solved before he could go further. His labour in philosophy is as it were an idleness in mathematics'[RFM V §52].

From this one ought to understand, as Wittgenstein emphasized, that one of the basic philosophical insights becomes that one ' ... *cannot gain a fundamental understanding of mathematics by waiting for the result of a theory'*[WVC 129]. By the expression 'a theory' within the context of mathematics he is, of course, referring to what is called an '*a priori* mathematical theory' (like, for example, Hilbert's Meta-Mathematical Theory or the Intuitionistic Theory of Types by Martin-Löf). For example, Wittgenstein said, concerning 'classical' set theory, that '[i]n set theory what is calculus must be separated off from what attempts to be (and of course cannot be) *theory*. The rules of the game have to be separated off from the inessential statements about the chessmen'[PhG 468]. Here Wittgenstein again wants to draw our attention to the mistake of applying the empirical model familiar from science (despite the fact that we here deal with *a priori* theories): we construct hypothetical theories which we try to falsify by experiments [Supra II.4].

In mathematicas he does not accept that we have any general *a priori* theory providing the structure externally, precisely as he had already said in his earlier thought [Gefwert (1) 56-69]. However, we have a method (internal structure) constituting a calculation. As he said, '[t]here is no meaning to saying you can describe beforehand what a solution will be like in mathematics *except in the cases where there is a known method of solution*'[L (3) 7; my italics]. One can then say that an object with a certain property, or the solution of the problem (the task) of whether a certain object has a certain property, can be found out only when the solution (the object) can be looked for in the (analyzed) calculation. We have to realize that '[y]ou can only *search* within a system: And so there is necessarily something you *can't* search for'[PhR §150], that is, '[i]n mathematics, we cannot talk of systems in general, but only within systems'[PhR §152].

The ability to provide a meaningful description of what one is looking for is founded on a crucial condition: that what one is looking for can be described in general terms. But this Wittgenstein denies, in that the meaning of the generic description of the object given *before* it is 'directly perceived', or the meaning that the expression 'in the same way' has *before* the discovery, is not able to normatively condition the adoption of the grammatical rule which makes a certain sign produce what was looked for. According to Wittgenstein, it is quite the other way around: it is *the free decision* of counting, by definition, a certain operational procedure as the procedure identified, though in general terms, by the description provided before the 'discovery' which establishes *ex novo* how the description - or the expression 'in the same way' - have to be understood after the discovery. The result is, as he said in a somewhat different context, that '[c]onfusions in these matters are entirely the result of treating mathematics as a kind of natural science. And this is connected with the fact that mathematics has detached itself from natural science; for, as long as it is done in immediate connection with physics, it is clear that *it* isn't natural science'[PhG 375].

Now, the predominant picture today is that the reason why Hilbert's Programme was regarded as important by certain foundationally inclined mathematicians is because Hilbert - apparently - succeeded in making mathematical proof an object of mathematical study in the form of what today is called 'proof theory' *(Beweistheorie)*. However, originally, the 'proof-theory' also created the illusion that one could by external ('observer' based) meta-mathematical methods solve problems regarding the absolute consistency of mathematical proofs. According to Wittgenstein, these problems are actually philosophical problems and, therefore, not mathematical in nature [Gefwert (1) 267]. They cannot (in an absolute sense) be solved by means of any mathematical (and meta-mathematical) proof whatsoever. The assumed problem regarding universal consistency of mathematics cannot be solved by any mathematical 'theory' of any kind.

This is, precisely, the reason why Wittgenstein repudiated the meta-mathematical ('observer' based) approach. Indeed, since the problem of absolute consistency in mathematics is philosophical and not mathematical by nature it is not necessary to apply any mathematical methods in order to deal with the assumed 'problem'. It is against this background that one is to understand Wittgenstein's comment that there ' ... can't in any fundamental sense be such a thing as meta-mathematics'[PhR 153]. Wittgenstein is not engaged in investigating mathematical calculations (proofs) by providing any kind of consistency proofs (by some kind of 'proof-theory') as the 'observer' based meta-mathematical research programme requires according to the language-as-calculus paradigm. We find that this point is emphasized when Wittgenstein later said that ' ... the *mathematical* problems of what is called foundations are no more the foundations of mathematics than a painted rock is the support of a painted tower'[RFM VII §16].

What we should do in the philosophy of mathematics, according to Wittgenstein (in his post-1937 philosophy), is to investigate conceptual problems of mathematical calculations. For example, in a philosophical investigation of mathematics the category of concepts being investigated is assumed to be mathematical. The task becomes to exhibit certain illusions brought about in ordinary mathematical practice by conceptual problems. We must clarify and dissolve such conceptual problems occurring in connection with mathematical calculations (phenomena). Thus we ought to clearly distinguish between Wittgenstein's points of 'clarifying the logical syntax of proof' and Hilbert's idea that we ought to 'prove that a proof is a proof' or that a 'calculus is a calculus'[WVC 175].

To clarify the logical syntax of proof, in Wittgenstein's sense, is to engage in a philosophical (conceptual) investigation of the proof (calculation) whereas to 'prove that a proof is a proof' or that 'calculus is a calculus' amounts to a purely meta-mathematical task of providing consistency proofs by applying the formalist (Carnap's) notion of logical syntax [Gefwert (1) 255-262]. This distinction is crucial. The rejection of the notion of 'mathematical theories' in connection with foundational research programmes of mathematics was by no means, as Russell assumed, a rejection of serious thinking on the part of Wittgenstein.[19] On the contrary, it amounted to the adoption of an exceedingly deep and penetrating - but completely different - notion (reminiscent of Heidegger) of what it amounts to understand and deal with conceptual problems occurring in mathematical calculations when being a 'participator' in form(s) of life.

We therefore note that in order to clarify what is meant by Wittgenstein's 'new method' of philosophy in connection with different mathematical calculations ('phenomena') as we find formulated in his manuscripts and lectures around 1929-1933 and later, we have to elucidate certain topics which are relevant in order to correctly see what this philosophical conception amounts to when applied to mathematical calculations. As Wittgenstein, according to G.E. Moore, emphasized in one of his lectures, ' ... philosophy [has] now been "reduced to a matter of skill", yet this skill, like other skills, is very difficult to acquire'[L (1) 322]. It is certain aspects of this novel conceptual 'skill' in connection with calculations which we have investigated elsewhere [Gefwert (1) 195ff]. We have done it in order to be able to clarify some of the startling consequences it has for our understanding of mathematical proofs in accordance with Wittgenstein's point that '[p]hilosophy solves, or rather gets rid of, only philosophical problems; it does not set our thinking on a more solid basis'[MS 219].

In his lectures on the 'foundations of mathematics' in 1939 Wittgenstein said (lecture XII) that [LFM 111],

> [m]athematical propositions are first of all English sentences; not only English sentences, but each mathematical proposition has a resemblance to certain non-mathematical propositions. - Mathematicians, when they begin to philosophize, always make the mistake of overlooking the difference in function between mathematical propositions and non-mathematical propositions.

This statement alludes to the importance of being clear about the distinction concerning the use of ordinary English statements (primary language-games) in contrast to genuine mathematical statements (secondary language-games) in the practice of mathematics. For example, if we take a simple and traditional existential statement like

$$\exists x P(x)$$

we translate it by saying, for example, that 'for some x, P(x)' or 'there exists an x such that P(x)', etc. Whatever formulation (translation) one uses here in order to read the formula a natural prerequisite is that one has to be able to speak a natural language (and, in addition, to perform ordinary unstructuralized mathematical proofs) before attempting to explain and apply the structuralized formalism in genuine calculations (as, for example, adherents of Martin-Löf's conception does [Gefwert (1) 102-113]).

When this is the case the translations are, indeed, redundant. Thus the primary skill required is to be able to speak a natural language (primary language-games). But this primary skill of being able to speak a natural language (say, English) is not itself to be understood as an explanation of the structuralization of the calculations. We require the competence of natural language (say, English) in order to be able to explain, in this case, the use of the existential quantifier. But, once we speak a natural language and attempt to explain the expressions used in calculations then it is totally irrelevant whether they are expressed in mathematical notation (reflected in the natural language) or in some natural language, for example, in English, German, French, Spanish or Italian. When we explain Martin-Löf's structure of mathematics (secondary language-games) it is simply very convenient to express the statements of the structure, say, in English. This requirement concerns all parts of constructive mathematical language. But, this insight (distinction) is not always understood properly in the relevant philosophical discussion concerning aspects of mathematical language [Gefwert (1) 253-255].

Wittgenstein said that ' ...what a mathematician is inclined to say about the objectivity and reality of mathematical facts, is not a philosophy of mathematics, but something for philosophical treatment'[PhI §254]. Thus the need for a philosophical investigation in mathematics arises, interestingly enough, on Wittgenstein's account, primarily (although not necessarily so), within the community of conceptually bewildered mathematicians and not, primarily, as one might suspect, within the academic philosophical community interested in the 'philosophy of mathematics' detached as they are from mathematical practice. According to Ambrose, '[i]t is ... obvious that Wittgenstein's comments are directed to pronouncements which the mathematician as a philosopher makes. These pronouncements, and their opposites as well, he held to be the oucome of tempting ways of describing what the mathematician does when he attempts to prove some mathematical proposition he thinks to be true'.[20] Nevertheless, it seems that Wittgenstein was very disillusioned concerning the prospects of his views on philosophy of mathematical calculations of having any impact whatsoever on professional mathematicians or scientists. One can notice this when he writes, for example, that '[n]othing seems to me less likely than that a scientist or mathematician who reads me should be seriously influenced in the way he works'[CV 62].

We thus come to the conclusion that, as far as mathematics is concerned, it is the activity of clearing up conceptual problems, that is, to delete expressions exhibiting 'prose' occurring in connection with different mathematical calculations (and scientific investigations), that Wittgenstein understood by philosophical investigations within these contexts. In his lectures Wittgenstein performed philosophical dialogues, both with himself and with his pupils and colleagues, as can be seen in his lectures for mathematicians in 1932-33 as well as in his lectures on the 'foundations of mathematics' in 1939 (notably the long dialogues with Alan Turing) [L (3) 205-25; LFM; Gefwert (1) 295-299]. The result of such philosophical investigations ought to be a purified conceptual understanding of different calculations in mathematics. In general, one can, as Wittgenstein formulated the point in one of his lectures (lecture XII), in 1934-35, say that the philosophical activity consists ' ... of three activities: to see the commonsense answer, to get yourself so deeply into the problem that the commonsense answer is unbearable, and to get from that situation back to the commonsense answer'[L (3) 109].

This conception is completely opposite to the way we ordinarily understand the 'classical' foundational doctrines occurring in connection with mathematics and science. Within these research programmes the task is to build novel and (as it seems) ever more sophisticated foundational theories in order to cope with 'philosophical' problems. Wittgenstein's philosophical method emphasizes the opposite. Here the task is to correctly understand what is being said. This is why he sometimes compares it with the position taken, for example, in phenomenology. As he put it in *The Big Typescript*, the problem with philosophy is ' ... nicht die intellektuelle Schwierigkeit der Wissenschaften, sondern die Schwierigkeit einer Umstellung'[BT 406].

We are not to mix a philosophical investigation of a calculation with the performance of the mathematical calculation itself. This is a mistake that we usually make in 'analytical philosophy' (in the foundational programmes). One has to understand that philosophy and mathematics (as well as the sciences) are essentially different in nature. This has been pointed out by Stenlund who emphasizes that the aim of the philosopher of mathematics ' ... is to get clear about existing notions and results that have given rise to philosophical puzzles and not to contribute to the construction of new mathematical notions and methods. In this respect the philosophical and the mathematical interests and efforts are essentially different. It is not just a difference in subject matter or in degree of rigour or generality, but a difference in kind'.[21]

What we have said so far has dramatic consequences when we attempt to understand the correctness of mathematical calculations. But, it also has the interesting consequence that much of what has been written about Wittgenstein's texts concerning mathematics (at least) does not seem to be genuine philosophical investigations of mathematical calculations. Up to this date commentaries are for the most part concerned with different attempts to correctly interpret the way Wittgenstein is assumed to understand philosophical investigations within mathematics to look like. Almost all commentaries are concerned with investigating certain exegetical aspects of Wittgenstein's texts on philosophy and mathematics (as, indeed, this text also is). This point has not gone unnoticed. As Kenny says, it seems to be a fact that while ' ... we may say that Wittgensteinian scholarship has blossomed' it is still the case that 'Wittgensteinian philosophy, as opposed to Wittgensteinian scholarship, has not made progress, and some of the gains we owe to Wittgenstein seem in danger of being lost'.[22] We can therefore conclude that what is still lacking are novel and genuine (philosophical/conceptual) investigations, even modest ones, applying Wittgenstein's 'method' (the Socratean 'dialogue technique') to questions of, say, mathematical calculations, scientific 'theories' of language or Cognitive Science.[23]

We have the same situation as far as published articles and books commenting on Wittgenstein's philosophical texts on mathematics are concerned. There are a number of publications which concern themselves with exegetical problems concerning the correct interpretation of his texts. But one almost never encounters any genuine philosophical investigation faithful to Wittgenstein's philosophical 'method' of conceptual investigations as far as, for example, mathematical calculations are concerned. This is especially the case if we look for applications of Wittgenstein's conceptual investigations in higher mathematics. It is an almost paradoxical situation when taking into account Wittgenstein's own characterization of philosophy of mathematics [PhG 367]. Nearly all commentaries on Wittgenstein's texts are devoted to contrasting them with contemporary philosophical 'schools' in order to make sense of his texts. Similarly, almost all commentaries on Wittgenstein's philosophy of mathematics amount to the same: exegetical commentaries on his philosophical texts and their relation to current philosophical doctrines concerned with mathematics. With the notable exceptions of Shanker's and Stenlund's investigations (as examples) we do not seem to encounter genuine philosophical investigations of mathematics in accordance with Wittgenstein's conceptual 'method'.[24] Why? After all, the main task that Wittgenstein set for himself in his post-1929 investigations was to rewrite what was to be understood by philosophy and how this novel view of conceptual investigations was to be applied, for example, in mathematical calculations.

In his own (philosophical) texts Wittgenstein discusses what genuine philosophical investigations of mathematical calculations ought to look like and, as Stenlund points out, '[i]t was one of Wittgenstein's achievements to show that the employment of word-language in mathematics is a main source of conceptual confusion in the philosophy of mathematics'.[25] However, the conceptual problems in mathematics do not occur simply as additional formulations accompanying genuine mathematical calculations. No, surprisingly enough, they occur in the midst of these mathematical calculations because '[t]here is an almost irresistible temptation to give certain informal modes of expression, which accompany technical-mathematical notions and results, a conceptual role for which there is no justification in the actual mathematics. And this fact has been most devastating in mathematical logic, meta-mathematics and set-theory'.26

This is a fact that very few logicians, mathematicians, programmers, psychologists (and analytic philosophers in general) seems to be aware of. Thus, as Wittgenstein points out, '[i]f a philosopher draws the attention of a mathematician to a distinction, or a misleading mode of expression, the mathematician always says "Sure, we know all that, it isn't really very interesting". He does not realize that when he is troubled by philosophical questions it is because of those very unclarities that he passed over earlier with a shrug of the shoulders'[MS 219,10]. Comments like these are important because they clearly exhibit what Wittgenstein's new 'method' of philosophy attempts to achieve but, unfortunately, they seldom seem to be taken seriously, for example, by mathematicians, psychologists and analytic philosophers. This establishes the fact, as we already have emphasized above, that almost nowhere are such investigations performed, that is, there are no attempts to systematically perform, for example, ' ... an exact scrutiny of mathematical proofs'[PhG 367] in order to reveal conceptual muddles occurring in connection with different mathematical calculations (proofs) in accordance with Wittgenstein's philosophical insights.

There are, however, some genuine investigations of arithmetic and 'classical' set theory to be found in Wittgenstein's own texts (for example, concerning Skolem's Proof and Cantor's Proof). We have looked at them elsewhere [Gefwert (1) 236-253]. These investigations, however, have nothing to do with the mistaken conception of providing a secure 'foundation' for arithmetic as the 'classical' logicians, intuitionists and meta-mathematicians like, e.g., Frege, Russell, Whitehead, Carnap, Brouwer, Hilbert, Gödel, Church and Turing assumed to be the case when they formulated their respective foundational views on mathematics. This is due to the fact that mathematics is in no need of any 'foundation' in the first place. Such formulations are indeed redundant and amount to 'prose' (or 'gas').27

We find this insight to be clearly stated when Wittgenstein, already in 1929, says that '[o]ne always has an aversion to giving arithmetic a foundation by saying something about its application. It appears firmly enough grounded in itself. And that of course derives from the fact that arithmetic is its own application. Arithmetic doesn't talk about numbers, it works with numbers. The calculus presupposes the calculus'[PhR 130]. As he said a few years later, '[t]he application of the calculation must take care of itself'[RFM III §4]. Indeed, conceptually one finds that calculations presuppose only themselves (they cannot be reduced to some 'universal method' of 'logical syntax', e.g., in Carnap's sense). Therefore they have in the end to be treated in philosophy as independent 'family-resemblance' calculations - as conceptually independent 'islands' - regardless of whatever redundant view (foundational doctrine) one applies when performing conceptual investigations.

Notes

[1] von Wright, Georg Henrik, 'Wittgenstein and the Twentieth Century', in Egidi, R., (ed.), *Wittgenstein: Mind and Language,* Synthese Library, Vol. 50, Kluwer Academic Publishers: Dordrecht/Boston/London (1995), p. 3.

[2] Gefwert, Christoffer, 'Wittgenstein: Is Philosophy Systematic?', in Pihlström, S., Kuokkanen, M. ja Sandu, G., (eds.), *Filosofisia Tienviittoja: Heikki Kanniston 50-vuotispäivän kunniaksi,* Reports from the Department of Philosophy, University of Helsinki, No. 3 (1995), pp. 129-134.

[3] Gasking, D.A.T., and Jackson, A.C., 'Wittgenstein as a Teacher', in Fann, K.T., (ed.), *Ludwig Wittgenstein: The Man and His Philosophy,* Sussex (1967), op.cit., p. 54.

[4] von Wright, G.H., 'Wittgenstein in the Twentieth Century', [cf.n.1], p.12.

[5] Hintikka, Jaakko, *The Philosophy of Mathematics,* Basil Blackwell: Oxford (1986), op.cit., p. 1.

[6]   Schlick, Moritz, 'The Future of Philosophy', in Mulder, H. and van de Velde-Schlick, Barbara F.B. (eds.), Schlick, M., *Philosphical Papers*, Dordrecht (1979), pp. 213-217.

[7]   For a good exposition of Wittgenstein's relation to the psychoanalytic thought of Freud, cf. Bouveresse, Jacques, *Wittgenstein reads Freud: The Myth of the Unconscious*, Princeton, New Jersey (1995).

[8]   McGuinness, Brian, 'Freud and Wittgenstein', in Kenny, A., McGuinness, B., Nyíri, J.C., Rhees, Rush and von Wright, G.H., (eds.), *Wittgenstein and his Times*, Basil Blackwell: Oxford (1982), op.cit., p. 40.

[9]   Malcolm, Norman, *Ludwig Wittgenstein: A Memoir*, Oxford (1967), p. 51.

[10] Hahn, H., 'Einstein, Russell und Wittgenstein seien hier als diejenigen unter den führenden Denkern der Gegenwart genannt, die die wissenschaftlivche Weltauffassung am wirkungsvollsten in die Öffentlichkeit vertreten und auch stärksten Einfluß auf den Wiener Kreis ausüben', *Wissenschaftliche Weltauffassung, Der Wiener Kreis*, hrsg. vom Verein Ernst Mach, (1929) Arthur Wolf Verlag: Wien, p. 54.

[11] Carnap, Rudolf, 'Philosophie wird durch Wissenschaftslogik ersetzt; Wissenschaftslogik ist nichts anderes als logische Syntax der Wissenschaftslehre', *Der logische Aufbau der Welt*, Weltkreis Verlag: Berlin-Schlachtensee (1934), pp. iii-iv.

[12] According to von Wright, 'Wittgenstein's early sketches for a Preface [to the 'Big Typescript'] should be read in juxtaposition to Carnap's Preface to *Aufbau*. They afford an impressive and nice illustration to the contrast between the protagonists and the critics of the spirit of Modernity. Although we have no documentary evidence for it, the thought is close at hand that Wittgenstein wrote his words in reply to Carnap's. The way the two prefaces match seems to me too good to be a result of sheer coincidence', von Wright, Georg Henrik, 'Wittgenstein and the Twentieth Century' [cf.n.1], pp. 4-5.

[13] Farrell, Brian., 'An Appraisal to Therapeutic Positivism', *Mind*, Vol. 55 (1948); Cf. also Lazerowitz, Morris, 'Wittgenstein and the Nature of Philosophy', in Fann, K.T., (ed.), *Ludwig Wittgenstein: The Man and his Philosophy*, New Jersey (1967), pp. 131-147.

[14] Monk, Ray, *Ludwig Wittgenstein, The Duty of Genius*, London (1990), p. 336.

[15] Cf. Ambrose, Alice (ed.), *Wittgenstein's Lectures: Cambridge 1932-1935, From the notes of Alice Ambrose and Margaret Macdonald*, Basil Blackwell: Oxford (1979), pp. ix-xi.

[16] Hardy, G.H., *Pure Mathematics*, 5th ed., Cambridge (1928),

[17] Dreyfus, Hubert L., *Being-in-the-world*, Cambridge, Mass. and London, England (1991), pp. 202-208.

[18] Kenny, Anthony, 'Wittgenstein on the Nature of Philosophy', in McGuinness, Brian., (ed.), *Wittgenstein and his Times*, Basil Blackwell: Oxford (1982), op.cit., p. 3.

[19] Ambrose, Alice, 'Mathematical Generality', in Ambrose, A., and Lazerowitz, M., (eds.), *Ludwig Wittgenstein, Philosophy and Language*, London (1972), sec. impr. (1973), op.cit., p. 3.

[20] Kenny, Anthony, *The Legacy of Wittgenstein*, Oxford (1984), op.cit., p. vii.

[21] A notable exception to this is, for example, the partly historical investigation of Wittgenstein's writings on mathematics by Pascuale Frascolla. Cf. Frascolla, P., *Wittgenstein's philosophy of mathematics*, London (1994); Another important book is the one by Segerdahl, Pär, *Language Use, A Philosophical Investigation into the Basic Notions of Pragmatics*, Department of Philosophy, Uppsala University (1993).

[22] Stenlund, Sören, *Language and Philosophical Problems*, Routledge: London (1990), op.cit., p. 133.

[23] As an example of philosophical investigations concerning 'language, mind and machines', 'notions of language and theories of meaning' and 'form and content in mathematics', cf. Stenlund, Sören, *Language and Philosophical Problems*, Routledge: London (1990).

[24] Shanker, Stuart, *Wittgenstein and the Turning-Point in the Philosophy of Mathematics*, London (1987), Chapter I; When Stenlund wrote his book, he said that his ' ... most important source of inspiration has been the work of Ludwig Wittgenstein. It is perhaps correct to say that most of what I have written consists of applications or elaborations of thoughts that can be found, in one form or another, in Wittgenstein. But I am making no exegetical

claims', Stenlund, Sören, *Language and Philosophical Problems,* [cf.n.23], pp. vii-viii.

[25] Stenlund, Sören, *Language and Philosophical Problems,* [cf.n.23], op.cit., p. 131.

[26] Ibid., op.cit., p. 131.

[27] To explicitly show that the different 'philosophical' doctrines of Logicism (Russell and Whitehead), Intuitionism (Brouwer) and Formalism (Hilbert) amount to redundant interpretational doctrines when dealing with mathematical calculations is an important task to be performed in conceptual investigations when dealing with philosophy of mathematics [cf. Gefwert (1) 255-262]. Of course this way of understanding philosophy as 'purifying' mathematical calculations from redundant interpretations can be extended to other contexts as well. Remember that Wittgenstein wanted his Socratic way of performing conceptual (philosophical) investigations to be applied in every kind of conceptual (philosophical) problem that we may encounter in our everyday life (and not only in mathematical or psychological contexts [PhI 232]).

Conclusion

We can now understand why Wittgenstein did not adhere to any of the philosophical 'schools' of Realism (Platonism), Idealism (Nominalism) nor Rationalism during his entire philosophical career. The adherents of these views are characterized by the fact that [PhR 86]

> ... they indicate that ... they can say something specific about the essence of the world.

The reason for such a claim is that these views amount to 'observer' based **interpretations** (they belong to the paradigm of language-as-calculus). But in a primary sense this is an impossible position [cf. BB 57ff.]. The reason is simply: One cannot **begin** by assuming that learning to communicate amounts to such a transformative interpretation. According to Wittgenstein, it is important to understand that such interpretations amount to **metaphors** which currently tyrannizes us because while we are in the language of the metaphors we are usually unable to move outside of them [PhR 82]. For example, when discussing concepts Wittgenstein would not have adhered to a Realistic sounding statement which tells us that '[c]oncepts organize the world for us, but the reality is more complex than any definitions'.[1] In this (scientific) statement one has adopted an assumed metaphysical ('observational') separability between World and Reality where the first term belongs to the second (but not the other way around). But, according to Wittgenstein, such a separation cannot be accepted because [PhR 84]

> [w]hat belongs to the essence of the world cannot be expressed by language.

If we set this statement against the vocabulary of modern 'philosophical' texts (external semantical interpretations), then we can say that there is no problem of separability which is present between our World and Reality in such a case.[2] In fact, such an assumed 'separation' is not a genuine problem at all: it is redundant and amounts to a pseudo-problem (to be dismantled by a grammatical investigation). The reason is that there simply is nothing like an ontological and metaphysical - Realistic - solution (the Outer) to this illusionary 'problem'. We don't have any 'things-in-themselves' ('pure objects') as one says in a Kantian formulation. But, note, that we do not have any Idealistic 'thoughts-in-themselves' ('pure thoughts') - solipsistic or intuitionistic (in the sense of the Significs Circle and Brouwer) - solution either, as it is usually understood, if we put emphasis on the other side of the same picture (the Inner)[Gefwert (1) 161-162].

In fact, we have to understand that these positions, the Outer and the Inner, amount to the opposite sides of the **same** picture. It is important to note that whatever side we put the emphasis on the picture remains essentially the same. Note, that it does not make any difference even if the picture is formulated as a 'collective' of individuals. It is still remains essentially as the same picture. It is still an interpretation (for example, when we assume the Inner somehow to be constituted by 'neurological processes' on a sub-linguistic level). We have also shown that this is a problem when we face the question concerning the possibility to formulate semantical (meaning) theories which adheres to linguistic separability in the sense of the 'observer' based paradigm of language-as-calculus.

Wittgenstein's investigations in general and his account of the Inner in particular might therefore be said to have a Kantian value. Not because of any detailed similarities to Kant, but because it sets limits (in Stenlunds sense) on the speculative enterprise of resolving all issues from reason alone. In contrast with Kant, however, it is important to note that Wittgenstein's emphasis on resolving conceptual confusions means that his grammatical 'method' contains no substantive doctrine at all. Such an investigation is not an application of a philosophical 'full-blooded theory of meaning' in the first place (nor is it a structure of any kind in the sense of Chomsky's innate linguistic capacity or Fodor's 'mentalese'). A grammatical (philosophical) investigation in Wittgenstein's sense is conceptual (therapeutical) in nature. By such investigations he wants us to achieve conceptual clarity in our practices [BB 69]. Clarity, however, should not be seen as a negligible or irrelevant virtue; indeed, if we contrast Wittgenstein's approach with that of the metaphysician's arrogant claim to absolute truth, it is the latter that comes to seem faintly ridiculous.

This suggests that the key difference between Wittgenstein and his great predecessors (with certain exceptions) is the abandonment of metaphysics.[3] Wittgenstein held that the attempt to reach profound truths (facts) on the basis of purely conceptual investigations was futile - according to him, grammar is autonomous and conceptual analysis can teach us nothing about 'reality' nor resolve the puzzle of how we should understand the 'world' and how we should live. The ordinary philosopher is like the thumb-catcher who believes that speed and dexterity will enable her to overcome the impossibility of her own task [L (3) 166]. In its own terms, therefore, Wittgenstein believed that metaphysics was doomed to failure. But paradoxically, he did not reject the work of previous philosophers as empty nonsense - on the contrary, he once told a friend that he considered it among the noblest products of the human mind.[4]

So where does this leave philosophy after Wittgenstein? What is there left for a philosopher to do? Here the first point to understand is that Wittgenstein's grammatical investigations partly amounts to investigations of 'philosophical' practices (for example, in the practice of 'analytical philosophy') and that he saw them as an enduring necessity. It is the nature of the (conceptual) problems in different practices (e.g., in 'analytical philosophy') that makes one call Wittgenstein's investigations for philosophical investigations. But our primary practices do cover a much wider area than the purely 'philosophical' ones. We have innumerable amounts of them occurring as our everyday language-games. But note: Mastery of our concepts do **not** presuppose a grammatical understanding of how they function and, since that functioning is often more complicated and less orderly than we imagine, language will always lay traps for us, creating puzzles and confusions we need to dissolve (by performing grammatical investigations). This is particularly true when we engage in any theoretical discipline, for there the danger of getting tangled up in our concepts is then even greater [CV 64].

This concerns, for example, our attempts to understand the Inner. The importance of a proper understanding of the Inner could be illustrated across a range of disciplines from psychoanalysis to scientific investigations of the brain (e.g., neurophysiology) and from aesthetics to artificial intelligence. It is language-games which are primary and not perception. We have to understand that when we accept this we always function as a 'participator' by our natural language-games which amounts to the 'universal medium'. We are never an 'observer' in a metaphysical sense (as we are according to the language-as-calculus view). This calls for a general rethinking of our approach to psychological concepts. We can then say, as far as the Inner is concerned, that it will always remain as mysterious as life itself. What a Wittgensteinian investigation does, however, is to strip away the conceptual confusions from the real uncertainties we face when we attempt to understand it.

Wittgenstein's novel way of understanding grammar (including philosophy) as being therapeutic is diametrically opposed to the view we find, for example, in analytical philosophy (Logical Empiricism or semantical Realism/Anti-Realism) which regards philosophy as a kind of positive super-science [Supra V.2]. In contrast to Wittgenstein's conception of philosophy the aim in 'analytical philosophy' is to build ever more ingenious 'theories of meaning' of different kinds. Then the earlier, superseded, theories (in the sense of Popper's fallibilism) become an expanding museum of exhibits in the history of philosophy - reminiscent of Madame Tussaud's wax-cabinet - where new figures are constantly being added but from which no 'outdated' figures are ever removed.

This is not the case for a mature Wittgensteinian view of what grammatical activities amount to. On the contrary, he want's a grammatical investigation to be performed in accordance with his 'new method' which aims to dissolve conceptual problems, what he called 'gas' (or 'prose'), by an often painful and careful Socratian **dialogue**. Note, that his post-1937 manuscripts are written in such a dialogue form. The aim of such investigations are to clear our thought - dissolve certain conceptual problems - that occurres within the practice being investigated. In general terms one can say that the reason for this is that '[i]n philosophy, all that isn't gas is grammar'[LC 112]. The problems we encounter when performing such conceptual analyses are genuinely conceptual ones (in contrast, for example, to psychoanalytical ones) and such problems do not require written theoretical formulations as is, for example, required in order to solve those factual problems we encounter in science and mathematics.

For example, by conceptual (grammatical) problems, say, in connection with mathematical calculations, we can provide the following examples. Within different mathematical calculi there exist certain preconditions - due to the adoption of the paradigm of language-as-calculus - like, say, the application of mathematical induction in Skolem's proof of the associative law of arithmetic in order to inductively justify a universal statement or the notion of infinity occurring in Cantor's proof of the actual infinity of the transfinite cardinals. Both have their roots (preconditions) in the way one understands mathematical infinity within this 'observer' based paradigm [Gefwert (1) 243-248]. These proofs exhibit conceptual attitudes concerning, respectively, mathematical induction (of universal statements) and mathematical infinity. They have thus had direct influence on the way these calculi have been performed (by, respectively, Skolem and Cantor) and, consequently, on the way they have been understood and their interpretations established.

According to Wittgenstein such interpretational conceptions exhibits 'gas' or 'prose' (in this case concerning the unrestricted use of 'mathematical induction' to justify universal statements as well as the application of the 'actual infinity' in mathematics). When they are uncritically taken for granted they give rise to mistaken conceptions in the sense of language-as-calculus. (I have explained the concept of 'prose' in mathematical calculations elsewhere [Gefwert (1) 236ff]).

Thus the task in grammatical investigations of mathematical calculations (proofs) amounts to exorcize misguided conceptions from mathematical calculations which occur as redundant 'prose' within calculations and which are dissolved when the mathematician realizes that he does not want to say what he, in fact, has said.

One can highlight the difference between Wittgenstein's way of doing conceptual investigations in contrast to other (theoretical) characterizations of 'philosophy' (for example, in 'analytic' philosophy) by emphasizing that, according to Wittgenstein, when one practices investigations of mathematical concepts there is no external theoretical foundation that we can use (e.g., there is no applied analytical *a priori* structure like meta-mathematics). Grammatical (conceptual) investigations do not enjoy the priviledge of having been formulated in an external meta-language. They are expressed by ordinary (grammatical) language-games and are therefore subject to the same limitations as our language-games of ordinary language is.

A grammatical (conceptual) investigation is performed by an independent conceptual analysis concerning, for example, a proof (calculation) [RFM V §52]. Note, that this point, as far as Wittgenstein is concerned, is completely opposite to Brouwer's (as well as Dummett's) intuitionistic thought, which explicitly states that 'philosophy of mathematics' is **part** of mathematical practice (it belongs to the calculation, say, like Martin-Löf's structure) and where the explicitly 'philosophical' part consists in the task of **justifying** (Brouwer: by mentalistic introspection; Dummett: by an explicit 'meaning theory') that constructive (finitary and synthetic) proofs are the only legitimate ones which are possible in mathematics [Gefwert (1) 14-15].

But this is not all we have to understand. What we have to understand is that, in addition to this, we have to make an ordinary **proof** (a synthetic judgment) into a **canonical calculation** (an analytical judgment). When we have done it successfuly we can say of a synthetic judgment that it suppresses a certain part of an underlying analytical judgment so '[t]hat every synthetic judgment is grounded on an analytic judgment, and ... (it) is obtained by so to speak suppressing a certain part of the analytical judgment, or the analytical connection'[M-L (8) 4]. What we, however, have to understand is that this insight belongs to mathematical practice. That is, it does not belong to a grammatical (conceptual) investigation in the first place. Mathematical (methodological) investigations and grammatical (conceptual) investigations are completely distinct although the latter determines our understanding of the first.

In contrast to the purely mathematical view we find that Wittgenstein called attention to the importance of conceptual clarity in calculations (proofs). For example, mathematicians sometimes use formulations in calculations which are conceptually (grammatically) confusing. As a result of this they sometimes make conceptual mistakes in their publications, for example, when they unknowingly allow interpretations which does not belong to the calculations to occure in them. We therefore need to check the calculations (proofs) and purge them from these illegitimate conceptual interpretations. But note: We have to understand that the aim of grammatical (conceptual) investigations are not mathematical as such. Such investigations can conceptually go deeply into the roots of mathematical practice in order to dissolve the interpretations without infecting the calculation as such. We are now in a position to understand that a grammatical investigation never *justifies* anything (to be a correct, or true, calculation). To justify (in this 'factual' sense) does not belong to the task of a grammatical investigation. The factual justification is already performed by the mathematical proofs (calculations) whereas a grammatical (conceptual) investigation aims to purge calculations from unnecessary 'prose' [Gefwert (1) 200-201].

It is important to understand that, relative to a (synthetical or analytical) mathematical proof, a grammatical investigation is performed *a posteriori* (in Kantian terminology). Another way of formlating this is to say that a grammatical investigation amounts to a secondary ('higher order') language-game. What it does is to make a practice conceptually evident, for example, in contrast to what is the case in the practice of pure (constructive) calculations where we mathematically analyse a synthetic form to become an analytic form of calculation by applying the structure [Gefwert (1) 118-126]. As long as one can perform ordinary synthetical calculations (proofs) in constructive mathematics (e.g., by computer) there is no need to mathematically analyze them by exhibiting the analytical connection. But, when we encounter conceptual problems, say, with 'classical' proofs, we must engage ourselves in grammatical (conceptual) investigations in order to make the practices conceptually evident. What we have to understand is that grammatical (conceptual) investigations relative to mathematical ones constitute categorically different language-games (practices).

But such a grammatical kind of practice might seem very odd, say, to mathematicians, philosophers and scientists who are not accustomed to perform such investigations. The result, according to Wittgenstein, is that

> [a] mathematician is bound to be horrified by my mathematical comments, since he has always been trained to avoid indulging in thoughts and doubts of the kind I develop. He has learned to regard them as something contemptible and, to use an analogy from psycho-analysis (this paragraph is reminiscent of Freud), he has acquired a revulsion from them as infantile. That is to say, I trot out all the problems that a child learning arithmetic, etc., finds difficult, the problems that education represses without solving. I say to those repressed doubts: you are quite correct, go on asking, demand clarification [PhG 381-382].

The whole 'metaphysical' (and 'foundationally' inclined) Realistic/Anti-Realistic debate concerning what is to be counted, for example, as the 'correct foundation' or the 'correct theory of meaning' rests on an illusion [Supra V.5]. For example, there is no correct 'full-blooded theory of meaning' which takes the place of conceptual (grammatical) investigations (like, say, external meta-mathematics in the Realistic research programme is assumed to do). But, we also have other examples. One can, for example, mention the distinction between *langue* and *parole* within structuralism or *competence* and *performance* in Chomskian linguistics as exhibiting this feature. These conceptions have all been called by a common term for the **code theoretical** appoach.5 It is characteristic for this code conception of language, which has dominated linguistics and philosophy of language throughout this century, that one distiguishes between language itself, or the linguistic system that constitutes the code (and, which, as a rule, has taken the form of a calculus, a formal system), and the linguistic practices, the uses of language, in which the code is employed.

In opposition to this code theoretical view Wittgenstein was trying to convince us, for example, that 'philosophy ... leaves mathematics as it is, and no mathematical discovery can advance it'[PhI §124]. It is similar with scientific practices (as well as with other everyday practices).6 He constantly emphasized that it is the intention of philosophy to get rid of unnecessary 'prose' (or 'gas') which occure, for example, in different mathematical calculations (proofs) [Gefwert (1) 236-253]. When we engage in a grammatical (conceptual) investigation with the intention of purging a proof from 'prose' (redundant concepts) this is what actually takes place. When this is done successfully we change the way a certain practice is to be understood as a result of a grammatical (conceptual) investigation. This may sound strange to people who are accustomed to apply, for example, external 'classical' predicate logic and set theory (as well as 'classical' model-theory) in the 'foundational' ('philosophical') investigations in accordance with the 'observer' based language-as-calculus paradigm. Nevertheless, it need not be. But, what is a novel feature in this kind of approach is that the direction of this relationship is the very opposite to that which is usually taken by foundationally inclined 'philosophers' adhering to academic philosophy in the analytical sense. This is the case, for example, in philosophy of mathematics as well as philosophy of psychology. *But, we have to understand that on Wittgenstein's account it is not philosophy that should be influenced, for example, by mathematics and psychology; on the contrary, it is mathematics and psychology that should be vitally influenced by philosophy.*

Wittgenstein's philosophical investigations aims to offer the means to make one aware of the grave mistake in demanding foundational research programmes (say, in mathematics) in order to deal with some assumed reductive 'philosophical' problems. There are no interpretations present. We have, for example, looked at such problems - in connection with mathematics - in more detail elsewhere [Gefwert (1) 195-201]. Taking into account what we have said so far, Wittgenstein would certainly have rejected (as far as 'observer' based 'philosophy' is concerned), for example, a claim in a well-known book on the foundations of constructive mathematics in which it is stated that '[i]t is possible to distinguish at least five different philosophies of constructive mathematics, plus at least one "semi-constructive" philosophy that we find in a modern book on the foundations of constructive mathematics'.7

We have to understand that there can only be one philosophical - conceptual - investigation for each conceptual problem at a time. We aim to change a concept (and 'dissolve' a conceptual problem) each time we perform an investigation (as a dialogue between one another or with oneself). Note, that such an investigation does not result in a **universal** (as it does in foundational theories). But it is not a simple task to perform such an investigation because [BT 423]

> [h]uman beings are deeply embedded in philosophical, i.e. grammatical confusions. Freeing them from these presupposes tearing them away from the enormous number of connecting links that hold them fast. A sort of rearrangement of the whole of their language is needed. (Man muss sozusagen ihre ganze Sprache umgruppieren.) - But of course that language has developed the way it has because some human beings felt - and still feel - inclined to think that way. So the tearing away will succeed only with those in whose life there already is an instinctive revolt against the language in question and not with those whose instinct is for the very herd which created that language as its proper expression.

Thus genuine conceptual (philosophical) problems - when compared to foundational ones - can be characterized as being categorically distinct from each other. The result of a conceptual (philosophical) investigation (in contrast, for example, to the result of a pure mathematical investigation, when we have reached an analytic form of a calculation), is that '[w]e never arrive at fundamental propositions in the course of our investigation; we get to the boundary of language which stops us from asking further questions. We don't get to the bottom of things, but reach a point where we can go no further, where we cannot ask further questions'[L (3) 34].

We have the same problem when it comes to questions concerning our mental life. There is ample evidence, for example, provided by the failure of structuralism, behaviourism and the limitations of rational Cognitive Science that the Kantian conception of mind - that is, of individual 'mental processes' and their behavioural manifestations - has led the study of mental life up the same blind alley again and again. The individual psychological 'processes' they purport to study by this strategy are mere stipulations. Thus, they do not amount to genuine objects of study. For example, the formal models employed by cognitive scientists adhering to a code theoretical approach fail to account for important aspects of mental life since *they are mistaken about the very thing they try to model.*

We have to understand that the problems which arise through a 'observational' bewitchment of our thought are not questions in search of a factual answer (as in mathematics or science), but, as Wittgenstein put it, to ' ... bumps that the understanding has got by running its head up against the limits of language'[PhI §119]. Note, that by the 'limits of language' here is not meant a metaphysical code theoretical approach. Instead we mean the possibility of expressing meaningful language-games (we have here adopted a 'participator' insight of language-games instead of an 'observer' based view). But note: We are always free to transgress the language-games. That is, by the freedom to transgress the limits of language-games we simply mean the freedom to express nonsense. Recall, that a main reason why these 'bumps' occur is that we do not command a clear view of the (meaningful) use of our words

[PhI §122]. We miss the 'perspicuous presentation' which will expose to us the undistorted and meaningful use of language and bring words back from what Wittgenstein call's ' ... their metaphysical to their everyday use'[PhI §116]. The clarity which the perspicuous presentation provides us is thus an absolute. When it is successfully applied it makes the philosophical (conceptual) problems that we encounter to disappear completely [PhI §133].

The follower of Wittgenstein's method and technique of unravelling conceptual knots is therefore confronted with one strain of conceptual investigations (philosophy) which has a future, both as a training for individuals (in everyday life) and as an essential part of the system of academic disciplines (for example, in mathematics, psychology, linguistics, etc.) when facing conceptual problems.[8] What we have attempted to show in this book is what philosophical investigations - conceptual investigations - amounts to when we accept, say, the impossibility of a private language to occure (which is contrary to the positions taken in 'observer' based code theoretical disciplines like formal logic, mathematics, psychology and Cognitive Science when understood according to language-as-calculus). The result of such investigations makes it clear that the received ways of subdividing the subject matter of 'philosophy' often conceal the common roots of many problems.[9]

As a result of this book we should be able to note that Wittgenstein's philosophy appears far less original and unique than it does when seen in the light of the standard internal philosophical historiography, at least when it comes to the kind of problem that he takes up. Some of his ideas would no longer seem as if they simply came unbidden from a solitary, spontaneous act of creation on the part of a dedicated genius. As a result of this the disquietude is gone and the philosopher can attain his aim which amounts to 'Friede in den Gedanken'[CV 43].

Notes

[1] Saariluoma, Pertti, *Foundational Analysis: Presuppositions in experimental psychology*, Routledge: London and New York (1997), op.cit. p. 58.

[2] In an interview conducted by Joachim Schulte in 1987 we find Dummett saying that he finds it extremely difficult to accept ' ... Wittgenstein's utter separation of mathematics from philosophy ... I presume that Wittgenstein thought that a mathematician who changed his procedures for philosophical reasons, as Brouwer did, would be committing an error: he ought to keep that part of his thinking completely separate from the purely mathematical affair. I have never been able to sympathise with that idea. I do not see why our thought should be partitioned into these various compartments between which no communication is possible', Dummett, M., *Origins of Analytical Philosophy*, London (1993), op.cit., pp. 174-175; Cf. Gefwert, C., *Wittgenstein on Mathematics, Minds and Mental Machines*, Ashgate Publishing Limited: Aldershot, Brookfield USA, Singapore, Sydney (1998), pp. 15-18.

[3] Against the background of what one can learn from Wittgenstein, it is clear that the feeling of linguistic immanence amounts to a metaphysical experience. The 'observer' based philosophical thesis that human beings are trapped in a language is as much nonsense as the opposing thesis that we can transcend language. The borders of language are not borders in the sense that they constrain our will. It is not as if we could only imagine or surmise something beyond the boundaries of language, but not get there, even in thought. A 'border' or 'boundary' in this sense has simply become a misleading metaphor.

[4] von Wright, G.H., 'Wittgenstein and The Twentieth Century', in Egidi, R., ed., *Wittgenstein: Mind and Language*, Kluwer Academic Publishers: Dordrecht (1995), pp.14-16.

[5] According to this view a language is seen as a code; the words and sentences codify a content or a meaning such that it can be deciphered by a grammatical or semantical analysis. Since a language is the same code for all users of a language within a linguistic community, the social nature and communicative potential of language are ensured: speakers of the same language use the same code, and can mean the same thing by the same words. Cf. Taylor, Talbot, *Mutual Misunderstanding: Scepticism and the*

Theorizing of Language and Interpretation, Duke University Press: Durham and London (1992).

[6] Cf. Stenlund, Sören, *Language and Philosophical Problems,* Routledge: London and New York (1990), pp. 1-3.

[7] Beeson, Michael, *Foundations of Constructive Mathematics,* Springer Verlag: Berlin, Heidelberg, New York, Tokyo., (1985), op.cit., p. 47.

[8] Reminscent of Freud's psychoanalysis it seems to me that Wittgenstein's conception of philosophy (conceptual therapy) easily allows itself to be applied, for example, in a 'philosophical clinique' where a philosopher who is trained in conceptual therapy meets persons (the 'patients') who need to discuss problems they encounter in life which conceptually takes them astray. Note, that the persons that are to be treated by philosophical dialogues are **not** suffering from pathological problems (although it might seem like that). The pathological cases should be treated by adequately trained medical personell, e.g., psychiatrists. There is a clear distinction between these two cases and it is imperative that they need to be separated (analogously to the distinction between psychology and psychiatry). The problems which are being discussed when performing conceptual therapy (of both kinds) amount to problems that persons have difficulties to come to grips with due to different reasons. But one thing we have to remember: The problems that are being discussed in this kind of therapeutical sessions always amount to conceptual problems.

[9] It is interesting to note that there are a number of philosophers and scientists who partly, and from different angles, emphasize similar points as Wittgenstein does during his philosophical career (for example, the private language argument even if he gives this idea a new and radical content). As examples I can mention certain ideas by Descartes, Locke, Condillac, Kant, Herder, Turgot, de Tracy, Humboldt, Wordsworth, Goethe, Frege and de Saussure. What their specific connection to Wittgenstein's thought amounts to remains however to be seen by future investigations in the history of philosophy. Such investigations would distinguish themselves from standard surveys in the history of philosophy with respect to which names would be included as having made the most significant contributions. We therefore need an entirely novel history of philosophy that takes philosophical thinking on the nature of language during different epochs as its unifying perspective.